Ruby on Rails for Agile Web Development

A Hands-on Guide to Building Dynamic and Efficient Web Applications

Sajjad Umar

www.orangeava.com

First Published: August 2024

Published By: Orange Education Pvt Ltd, AVA™

Address: 9, Daryaganj, Delhi, 110002, India

275 New North Road Islington Suite 1314 London,

N1 7AA, United Kingdom

ISBN (PBK): 978-81-97396-59-5

ISBN (E-BOOK): 978-81-97396-50-2

Scan the QR code to explore our entire catalogue

www.orangeava.com

Dedicated To

To my loving wife and my supportive parents,

Thank you for your endless love, encouragement, and inspiration

About the Author

Sajjad Umar is a seasoned Ruby on Rails backend engineer with a wealth of experience in developing a diverse range of web applications. With a strong background in Ruby on Rails, he has successfully delivered projects spanning from complex IoT systems to robust e-commerce solutions. Having collaborated with numerous companies and clients worldwide, Sajjad has gained valuable insights into industry best practices and a deep understanding of web development.

In addition to his technical expertise, Sajjad is actively involved in fostering the Ruby on Rails community. Sajjad's passion for knowledge-sharing extends beyond local communities, as he regularly contributes to the field through blogging, writing articles, and creating content on his popular YouTube channel, Desi Developer. Moreover, he is dedicated to keeping the community informed through his role as the curator of the Ruby on Rails Monthly newsletter.

Sajjad's commitment to the Ruby on Rails ecosystem is further demonstrated by his presence as a keynote speaker at various conferences. By sharing his experiences and expertise, he inspires and educates fellow developers, helping them enhance their skills and stay up-to-date with the latest trends and advancements in web development.

With his extensive technical knowledge, community involvement, and dedication to sharing insights, Sajjad Umar brings a unique perspective and valuable expertise to his book, *Ruby on Rails for Agile Web Development*. Readers can trust his guidance and benefit from his wealth of experience in mastering Agile web development using Ruby on Rails.

About the Technical Reviewer

Phil Smy is a seasoned software development leader with over 30 years of experience in creating innovative software solutions. His expertise spans full-stack development, AI integration, and product management, making significant impacts in various industries, including e-commerce and entertainment. For over 20 years, he has been developing using the Ruby on Rails framework.

Phil lives in Japan with his wife, dog, and lots of guitars. He spends his days working on his farm, making YouTube videos about entrepreneurship and software, and contributing to open-source projects.

Acknowledgements

Writing this book has been a journey filled with learning, challenges, and growth, and I could not have done it without the support and encouragement of many individuals.

First and foremost, I would like to express my deepest gratitude to my wife. Your unwavering support, patience, and love have been my greatest source of strength and motivation. Thank you for always believing in me and for understanding the countless hours I dedicated to this project.

To my parents, thank you for instilling in me the values of hard work and perseverance. Your endless encouragement and belief in my abilities have been instrumental in my achievements. I am forever grateful for your guidance and support throughout my life.

I would also like to thank my editor, whose keen eye and insightful feedback have greatly improved the quality of this book. Your expertise and dedication have been invaluable.

A heartfelt thank you to my technical reviewer. Your thorough review and insightful suggestions have significantly enhanced the accuracy and clarity of the technical content. Your expertise has ensured that this book is a reliable and practical guide for readers.

A special thanks to my colleagues and friends in the software development community. Your shared knowledge and experiences have greatly contributed to the depth and breadth of this book. I am grateful for the discussions, collaborations, and shared passion for coding and development.

Lastly, I would like to acknowledge my readers. Thank you for your interest in this book. I hope it serves as a valuable resource in your journey to mastering Ruby on Rails and Agile web development. Your support and feedback are what make writing worthwhile.

Thank you all for being a part of this journey with me.

Preface

Welcome to *Ruby on Rails for Agile Web Development*. This book is the culmination of countless hours of research, coding, and collaboration. It has been crafted to guide you on a comprehensive journey through the world of Agile web development using Ruby on Rails.

The aim of this book is to make the learning process both accessible and enjoyable for everyone, whether you are just starting out or are an experienced developer seeking to expand your skills.

Throughout this book, you will embark on a step-by-step learning journey. Starting with the basics of the Ruby language, we will gradually explore the architecture of Rails and delve into the principles of agile development. You will learn how to implement CRUD operations, manage databases, and build RESTful APIs. We will also cover essential topics such as authentication, authorization, and security best practices. Additionally, this book introduces advanced concepts to help you build dynamic and scalable applications, and you will learn how to deploy your applications seamlessly.

To reinforce your learning experience, each chapter concludes with a short quiz section. These quizzes allow you to test your knowledge and understanding of the material covered, serving as a valuable tool for self-assessment. They help you gauge your progress, identify areas for improvement, and ensure that you are comprehensively grasping the concepts discussed.

Structure of the Book

This book is organized into twelve chapters, each focusing on essential aspects of Agile web development with Ruby on Rails:

Chapter 1: Introduction

- **Overview of Ruby**: Understanding the fundamentals of Ruby, its history, and its key features.
- **Ruby Syntax and Structure**: Introduction to the basic syntax and structure of Ruby code.

- **Object-Oriented Programming**: Concepts of object-oriented programming in Ruby.
- **Ruby on Rails Architecture**: An introduction to the Rails framework, understanding MVC architecture, and exploring the components of Rails applications.

Chapter 2: Agile Development Fundamentals

- **Introduction to Agile Development**: Understanding the limitations of traditional approaches and the need for agile in web development.
- **Agile Manifesto and Principles**: Origins, four values, and twelve principles of Agile Software Development.
- **Agile Methodologies**: Overview of Scrum, Kanban, Lean Software Development, and Extreme Programming (XP).
- **Benefits and Challenges**: Advantages and limitations of using agile methodologies in web development.

Chapter 3: Getting Started with Ruby on Rails

- **Overview of Ruby on Rails Framework**: Guiding principles and benefits of using Rails.
- **Installation and Setup**: Steps to install Ruby, Rails, and setting up a new Rails project.
- **Creating Your First Rails Application**: Understanding the Rails directory structure, creating the first page, and starting the Rails server.

Chapter 4: CRUD Operations and Database Management

- **Introduction to CRUD Operations**: Understanding CRUD and its significance in web applications.
- **Creating Models, Views, and Controllers**: Extending MVC architecture for CRUD integration.
- **Implementing CRUD Functionality**: Adding, reading, updating, and deleting contacts.
- **Working with Associations and Relationships**: Understanding data relationships and incorporating associations.

- **Database Management in Rails**: Managing database schema, migrations, and seed data.

Chapter 5: Basics of Styling and Front-end Development

- **Overview of CSS and Stylesheets**: Core concepts of CSS, including selectors, properties, box model, and layout.
- **Introduction to CSS Frameworks**: Reasons to use CSS frameworks and choosing the right one.
- **Styling Layouts, Views, and Templates**: Installing TailwindCSS and adding styles to views and elements.
- **Responsive Design Techniques**: Techniques for creating responsive web designs.

Chapter 6: Authentication and Authorization

- **Introduction to User Authentication**: Understanding the importance of authentication and common methods.
- **Implementing User Registration and Login**: Creating a brand new Rails app and implementing the authentication flow.
- **Role-Based Authorization**: Key components and implementing role-based authorization.
- **Enhancing UI**: Adding Flowbite Component Library and basic styling.

Chapter 7: Testing and Test-Driven Development

- **Importance of Testing in Agile Development**: Benefits of testing in Agile methodologies.
- **Types of Testing in Web Development**: Overview of unit, integration, and acceptance testing.
- **Introduction to Testing Frameworks in Rails**: Overview of popular testing frameworks.
- **Writing Unit Tests for Models and Controllers**: Importance and implementation of unit tests.
- **Integration and Acceptance Testing**: Strategies for writing effective integration and acceptance tests.

- **Test-Driven Development (TDD) Approach**: Overview and a step-by-step guide to practicing TDD in Rails.

Chapter 8: RESTful APIs and Web Services

- **Understanding RESTful Architecture**: Introduction to REST and its principles.
- **Building API Endpoints in Rails**: Setting up Rails for API development and creating RESTful routes.
- **Consuming APIs in Rails Applications**: Making HTTP requests and handling API responses.
- **Authentication and Authorization for APIs**: Implementing token-based authentication and securing API endpoints.

Chapter 9: Deployment and Scaling

- **Understanding Deployment Basics**: Strategies for deploying Rails applications.
- **Continuous Integration and Deployment (CI/CD)**: Implementing CI/CD pipelines.
- **Scaling Rails Applications**: Tips for effective scaling and performance optimization.
- **Monitoring and Performance Optimization**: Importance of monitoring and strategies for optimization.

Chapter 10: Building A Real-World Rails Application

- **Establishing MVP Requirements**: Setting up the foundation for a minimal viable product.
- **Database Expansion**: Expanding the database to meet MVP requirements.
- **Development of User Interface**: Creating a simple yet functional user interface.
- **Implementation of Access Management**: Managing user access and core feature integration.

Chapter 11: Advanced Topics in Ruby on Rails

- **Background Jobs and Asynchronous Processing**: Introduction to background jobs and Active Job in Rails.
- **Caching and Performance Optimization Techniques**: Overview of caching and performance optimization strategies.
- **Sending Emails and Internationalization**: Introduction to email sending, internationalization, and localization.
- **Introduction to JavaScript Frameworks**: Integrating JavaScript frameworks with Rails.
- **Securing Rails Applications and File Uploads**: Best practices for security and handling file uploads.

Chapter 12: Conclusion

- **Recap of Key Learnings**: Summary of what has been covered.
- **Next Steps**: Resources and references for further learning and development.
- **Quiz Answers**: Answers to all short quizzes provided in the book.

Let's begin this exciting journey together and unlock the full potential of Agile web development with Ruby on Rails.

Happy coding!

Sajjad Umar

Get a Free eBook

We hope you are enjoying your recently purchased book! Your feedback is incredibly valuable to us, and to all other readers looking for great books.

If you found this book helpful or enjoyable, we would truly appreciate it, if you could take a moment to leave a short review with a 5 star rating on Amazon. It helps us grow, and lets other readers discover our books.

As a thank you, we would love to send you a free digital copy of this book, and a **30%** discount code on your next cart value on our official websites:

www.orangeava.com

www.orangeava.in (For Indian Subcontinent)

☑ **Here's how:**

Leave a review for the book on Amazon.

Take a screenshot of your review, and send an email to **info@orangeava.com** (it can be just the confirmation screen).

Once, we receive your screenshot, we will send you the digital file, within 24 hours.

Thank you so much for your support – it means a lot to us!

Downloading the code bundles and colored images

Please follow the links or scan the QR codes to download the ***Code Bundles and Images*** of the book:

https://github.com/ava-orange-education/Ruby-on-Rails-for-Agile-Web-Development

The code bundles and images of the book are also hosted on ***https://rebrand.ly/b5b4b8***

In case there's an update to the code, it will be updated on the existing GitHub repository.

Errata

We take immense pride in our work at **Orange Education Pvt Ltd,** and follow best practices to ensure the accuracy of our content to provide an indulging reading experience to our subscribers. Our readers are our mirrors, and we use their inputs to reflect and improve upon human errors, if any, that may have occurred during the publishing processes involved. To let us maintain the quality and help us reach out to any readers who might be having difficulties due to any unforeseen errors, please write to us at :

errata@orangeava.com

Your support, suggestions, and feedback are highly appreciated.

DID YOU KNOW

Did you know that Orange Education Pvt Ltd offers eBook versions of every book published, with PDF and ePub files available? You can upgrade to the eBook version at **www.orangeava.com** and as a print book customer, you are entitled to a discount on the eBook copy. Get in touch with us at: **info@orangeava.com** for more details.

At **www.orangeava.com**, you can also read a collection of free technical articles, sign up for a range of free newsletters, and receive exclusive discounts and offers on AVA™ Books and eBooks.

PIRACY

If you come across any illegal copies of our works in any form on the internet, we would be grateful if you would provide us with the location address or website name. Please contact us at **info@orangeava.com** with a link to the material.

ARE YOU INTERESTED IN AUTHORING WITH US?

If there is a topic that you have expertise in, and you are interested in either writing or contributing to a book, please write to us at **business@orangeava.com**. We are on a journey to help developers and tech professionals to gain insights on the present technological advancements and innovations happening across the globe and build a community that believes Knowledge is best acquired by sharing and learning with others. Please reach out to us to learn what our audience demands and how you can be part of this educational reform. We also welcome ideas from tech experts and help them build learning and development content for their domains.

REVIEWS

Please leave a review. Once you have read and used this book, why not leave a review on the site that you purchased it from? Potential readers can then see and use your unbiased opinion to make purchase decisions. We at Orange Education would love to know what you think about our products, and our authors can learn from your feedback. Thank you!

For more information about Orange Education, please visit **www.orangeava.com**.

Table of Contents

1. Introduction **1**

Introduction 1

Structure 1

Overview of Ruby 2

History and Origin of Ruby 3

Key Features and Characteristics of Ruby 4

Syntax and the Basic Structure of Ruby Code 6

Comments 6

Variables 6

Data Types 7

Control Structures 7

Methods 8

Introduction to OOP Concepts in Ruby 9

Classes and Objects 9

Encapsulation 11

Inheritance 12

Polymorphism 12

Ruby on Rails Architecture 14

Introduction to the Rails Framework 14

Understanding the Model-View-Controller (MVC) Architectural Pattern 15

Components of Rails 16

Models 16

Views 16

Controllers 17

Understanding the Flow of Data and Requests in a Rails Application 17

Conclusion 21

Short Quiz 21

2. Agile Development Fundamentals **24**
Introduction 24
Structure 25
Introduction to Agile Development 25
Understanding the Limitations of Traditional Approaches 26
The Need for Agile in Web Development 27
Agile Manifesto and Principles 28
Origins of the Agile Manifesto 28
The Four Values of the Agile Manifesto 28
Individuals and Interactions over Processes and Tools 29
Working Software over Comprehensive Documentation 29
Customer Collaboration over Contract Negotiation 29
Responding to Change over Following a Plan 29
Twelve Principles of Agile Software Development 30
Agile Methodologies 32
Scrum: Embracing Flexibility and Collaboration 32
Kanban: Visualizing Work and Continuous Flow 34
Lean Software Development: Eliminating Waste and Adding Value 36
Extreme Programming (XP): Emphasizing Quality and Adaptability 38
Benefits of Agile in Web Development 40
Challenges and Limitations of Agile in Web Development 41
Conclusion 43
Short Quiz 44
3. Getting Started with Ruby on Rails **46**
Introduction 46
Structure 47
Overview of Ruby on Rails Framework 47
Guiding Principles of Rails 47
Benefits of Using Ruby on Rails 48
Installing Ruby and Rails 48

Installing Ruby 49
Ruby Managers 49
Version Managers 49
Installing Ruby Version Manager (RVM) 50
Installing Ruby Via RVM 51
Verifying the Installation 51
Installing Rails 52
Verifying the Installation 52
Setting Up a New Rails Project 53
Understanding the Rails Directory Structure 54
The "`app`" Directory 56
The "`config`" Directory 57
The "`db`" Directory 59
The "`public`" Directory 59
The "`test`" Directory 60
The "`vendor`" Directory 60
Creating the First Page of Your App 61
Generating Your First Controller 62
Creating Your First View 64
Defining the Route 64
Starting the Rails Server 65
Accessing Your Page in the Browser 66
Conclusion 67
Short Quiz 67
4. CRUD Operations and Database Management 70
Introduction 70
Structure 71
Introduction to CRUD Operations 72
Mapping CRUD to User Actions 72
Creating Models, Views, and Controllers 73
Extending the MVC Architecture for CRUD Integration 73
Generating Models, Views, and Controllers for Contacts 73

Setting Up the Foundation for CRUD Operations 80

Implementing Create Functionality 84

Enabling Read Functionality 94

Upgrading with Update Functionality 99

Managing Deletions with Delete Functionality 101

Working with Associations and Relationships in Ruby on Rails 103

Understanding Data Relationships 104

Database Management in Ruby on Rails: Evolving Schema, Seed Data, and Data Integrity 104

Evolving Database Schema Using Migrations 105

Populating the Database with Seed Data 105

Ensuring Data Integrity and Efficiency 106

Conclusion 107

Short Quiz 108

5. Basics of Styling and Front-End Development 111

Introduction 111

Structure 112

Overview of CSS and Stylesheets 112

CSS Essentials: The Core Concepts You Need 112

Selectors and Properties: Mastering CSS Rules 113

Box Model and Layout: Understanding Spacing and Arrangement 113

Fonts and Colors: Crafting Text Styles 113

Backgrounds and Borders: Enhancing Visuals 114

Positioning and Layout: Arranging Elements Efficiently 114

Introduction to CSS Frameworks 115

Reason to Use CSS Frameworks 116

Popular CSS Frameworks 116

Choosing the Right Framework 117

The Framework of Choice for our Contacts App 117

Styling Layouts, Views, and Templates 118

Installing TailwindCSS 118

Global Styles: Setting the Application's Tone 119
Adding Styles to Views and Elements 123
Templates and Partials: Reusable Modular Design 129
Responsive Design Techniques 132
Conclusion 134
Short Quiz 134
6. Authentication and Authorization 137
Introduction 137
Structure 137
Understanding the Importance of User Authentication 138
Exploring Common Authentication Methods 138
Understanding the Authentication Process in Web Development 139
Implementing User Registration and Login 140
The Approach 140
The Product 141
The Tech Stack 141
Benefits of Using PostgreSQL in Rails 141
Creating a Brand-New Rails App (WagePro) 142
Creating a Simple Home Page 144
Sign Up a New User 152
Role-Based Authorization in Rails 154
Key Components of Role-Based Authorization 155
Implementing Role-Based Authentication 155
Making It Look Good 164
Do It Yourself 172
Conclusion 172
Short Quiz 173
7. Testing and Test-Driven Development 176
Introduction 176
Structure 176
Importance of Testing in Agile Development 177

Benefits of Testing in Agile Methodologies 177
Ensuring Software Quality and Reliability through Testing 178
Types of Testing in Web Development 178
Introduction to Testing Frameworks in Rails 180
Popular Testing Frameworks and Their Key Features 180
RSpec 180
Minitest 181
Capybara 181
Choosing the Right Testing Framework 181
Writing Unit Tests for Models and Controllers 182
Writing Unit Tests for Models 182
Minitest Unit Test 183
RSpec Unit Test 184
Writing Unit Tests for Controllers 185
Minitest Unit Test 186
RSpec Unit Test 188
Integration Testing and Acceptance Testing 189
Integration Test Using RSpec 190
Acceptance Tests Using Capybara with RSpec 192
Acceptance/System Test Using Minitest 194
Test-Driven Development (TDD) Approach 196
Principles of TDD 196
Advantages of TDD 196
The Red-Green-Refactor Cycle 196
Implementing Test-Driven Approach in WagePro 197
Conclusion 204
Short Quiz 205
8. RESTful APIs and Web Services 207
Introduction 207
Structure 208
Understanding RESTful Architecture 208
Key Components of RESTful Architecture 208

Benefits of RESTful Architecture 209
Building API Endpoints in Rails 210
RESTful APIs Implementation 211
Consuming APIs in Rails Applications 216
Authentication and Authorization for APIs 219
Token-Based Authentication.....219
API Key-Based Authentication.....221
OAuth-Based Authentication..... 222
Implementing API Key-Based Authentication 224
Conclusion.....232
Short Quiz.....233
9. Deployment and Scaling..... 235
Introduction.....235
Structure.....236
Understanding Deployment Basics.....236
Key Concepts.....236
Deployment Strategies..... 237
Continuous Deployment..... 237
Blue-Green Deployment..... 237
Canary Releases 238
Deployment.....238
Deploying Your Rails App on Render.....238
Automatic Deployment Using render.yaml.....241
Continuous Integration and Deployment (CI/CD)..... 247
Scaling Rails Applications 258
Understanding the Need for Scaling 258
Tips for Effective Scaling 259
Monitoring and Performance Optimization 261
The Importance of Monitoring.....261
Strategies for Performance Optimization 261
Conclusion.....263
Short Quiz.....263

Further Reading 265
10. Building A Real-World Rails Application 266
Introduction 266
Structure 267
Establishing MVP Requirements 267
Database Expansion 267
Pagination 269
Employee Search 270
Roles Management and Authorization 270
Organization Management 271
Adding Required Routes 274
Salary Slip Management 282
Associations 283
PDF Creation 283
SalarySlipsController 285
Conclusion 290
Short Quiz 290
11. Advanced Topics in Ruby on Rails 293
Introduction 293
Structure 294
Background Jobs and Asynchronous Processing 294
Active Job in Rails 294
Queuing Systems and Workers 295
Caching and Performance Optimization Techniques 300
Page Caching 300
Action Caching 300
Fragment Caching 301
Low-Level Caching 301
Performance Optimization Strategies 302
Sending Emails 303
Introduction to Internationalization and Localization 305
Rails Internationalization (I18n) API 306

Key Components of Internationalization and Localization ...306
Benefits of Internationalization and Localization ...307
Introduction to JavaScript Frameworks with Rails ...307
Evolution of JavaScript Frameworks ... 308
Integrating JavaScript Frameworks with Rails ... 308
Benefits of Using JavaScript Frameworks with Rails ... 308
Drawbacks of Using JavaScript Frameworks with Rails ...309
Hotwire ... 310
Securing Rails Application ... 310
File Uploads ...312
Configuring Storage Services ...313
Attaching Files to a Model ...313
Creating the File Upload Form ...313
Handling File Upload in the Controller ...313
Displaying Uploaded Profile Images ...314
Conclusion ...314
Short Quiz ...315
Further Reading ...317
12. Conclusion ...318
Introduction ... 318
Structure ... 318
A Short Recap ... 318
Next Steps in Your Ruby on Rails Journey ... 319
Advance Topics to Explore ...320
Some Useful Resources ...321
Ruby and Rails Communities and Conferences ...321
Newsletters ...321
YouTube Channels ...322
Answers to Short Quizzes ...322
Index ...328

CHAPTER 1
Introduction

Introduction

A long time ago, they say, two Homo Sapiens on the planet Earth engaged in a discussion to determine the name of their groundbreaking invention that would one day change the world. On 24th February 1993, the conversation started as follows, "*Let us decide the codename now, tentative one*". The person on the other end replied, "OK". The first person again asked, "What is your best up to now?" He said, "*I'm content with coral*". The first person responded, "*I thought ruby is cool as a codename, isn't it?*".

Well, that is how **Ruby** (the programming language) was named. This conversation took place between Yukihiro Matsumoto (the creator of Ruby Language), also known as Matz, and one of his colleagues, Keiju Ishitsuka.

Fast forward a few years, Ruby became so popular that a new server-side web application framework emerged. It was named Ruby on Rails and was completely written in the Ruby programming language. Rails (short form of Ruby on Rails) was created by David Heinemeier Hansson in 2004.

This chapter will provide an overview of the Ruby Language along with the architecture of the Rails framework. So, if you are a beginner, this chapter will help you level the ground with everyone else reading the book. If you are an experienced developer, this chapter will help you recall the basics of Ruby and Rails, so that you have a solid foundation to easily grasp the knowledge shared in the upcoming chapters of the book.

Structure

In this chapter, we will discuss the following topics:

- Overview of Ruby
    - History and Origin of Ruby
    - Key Features and Characteristics of Ruby
    - Syntax and the Basic Structure of Ruby Code
    - Introduction to OOP Concepts in Ruby

- Ruby on Rails Architecture
    - Introduction to the Rails framework
    - Understanding the Model-View-Controller (MVC) Architectural Pattern
    - Exploring the Components of Rails Applications: Models, Views, and Controllers
    - Understanding the Flow of Data and Requests in a Rails Application

Overview of Ruby

As defined on the official website (ruby-lang.org), "*Ruby is a dynamic (and object-oriented), open-source programming language with a focus on simplicity and productivity. It has an elegant syntax that is natural to read and easy to write*".

Let's expand on the key points in the definition:

- **Dynamic Language**

  Ruby is a Dynamic Language, which means it performs most of its operations while the code is running, rather than during the initial compilation. This approach offers some advantages, such as shorter compilation time and the ability to write shorter and easier-to-understand code.

  Although dynamic languages may be slower in terms of performance and sometimes encounter issues with converting data types, they are generally preferred for most programming tasks, except for a few specific cases. Dynamic languages excel in situations where you want to focus on quickly solving problems and writing straightforward code.

  It's important to note that there are some cases where other languages with stricter rules about data types may be more suitable, mainly when performance is crucial or when you need to ensure the highest level of reliability and safety. However, for most general programming needs, dynamic languages strike a good balance between productivity and flexibility, making them a popular choice for many developers.

- **Open Source**

  Ruby is an open-source programming language with a strong and active community of developers. This community has created many helpful resources, such as libraries and frameworks, and tools that make Ruby even more powerful and useful. These resources can help you build strong and scalable applications in a faster and easier way. By using Ruby, you can tap into this supportive community and take advantage of the tools and resources they have created to make your coding journey smoother.

- **Simple and Productive**

  One of the defining characteristics of Ruby is its focus on simplicity. The language emphasizes clean and concise code, allowing developers to express their ideas naturally and intuitively. Ruby's syntax is designed to be readable, resembling natural language, which makes it easier for developers to understand and maintain their codebase.

  See how easy it is to write your very first method in Ruby, which says, "**Hello to the Ruby World**":

  ```
  def say_hello
    "Hello to the Ruby World."
  end


  puts say_hello
  # Hello to the Ruby World.
  ```

  In the preceding code, the "**def**`" keyword is being used to define a method named "**say_hello**". The "**say_hello**" method simply returns a string, "**Hello to the Ruby World**", and the method body ends with an "**end**" keyword.

  The "**puts**" keyword is responsible for printing the value returned by the "**say_hello**" method on the screen.

  The line starting with the "**#**" symbol is how you can add comments in Ruby code.

  We will practice more Ruby syntax in the upcoming sections of this chapter called "**Syntax and the Basic Structure of Ruby Code**".

- **Object-Oriented**

  Lastly, we added object-oriented to the Ruby definition to emphasize that it is an Object-Oriented language where everything you write in Ruby is an object.

  We will dive deep into object-oriented concepts with Ruby in the upcoming section of this chapter called **"Introduction to Object-Oriented Programming Concepts in Ruby"**.

History and Origin of Ruby

Ruby, a dynamic and object-oriented programming language, has an intriguing history that traces its origins back to the mid-1990s. Developed by Yukihiro Matsumoto, known as "*Matz*" among the Ruby community, the language was born out of a desire to create a programming language that balanced functionality with human-friendly syntax.

Matsumoto began his work on Ruby in February 1993, drawing inspiration from several programming languages, including Perl, Smalltalk, Eiffel, Ada, and Lisp. He envisioned a language that would prioritize simplicity and productivity, allowing programmers to express their ideas naturally and intuitively.

The name "*Ruby*" was chosen by Matsumoto to convey the beauty and elegance he aspired to bring to the programming world. He believed that programming should be a joyful and creative experience, and the name "*Ruby*" captured this essence perfectly.

The first public release of Ruby, version 0.95, occurred on 21 December 1995. It gained popularity gradually, primarily in Japan, where Matsumoto hailed from. As more developers started using Ruby, its community began to grow and the language started gaining international recognition.

In 2000, the release of Ruby 1.6 brought significant improvements, including better support for Unicode and enhanced performance. This version marked a turning point for Ruby's global expansion, attracting developers from around the world who recognized its unique features and advantages.

The breakthrough moment for Ruby's international adoption came with the publication of "*Programming Ruby: The Pragmatic Programmer's Guide*" in 2001, written by Dave Thomas and Andrew Hunt. This influential book introduced Ruby to a wider audience and solidified its position as a powerful and versatile programming language.

Since then, Ruby has continued to evolve and thrive. In 2005, Ruby on Rails, a web application framework written in Ruby, was released by David Heinemeier Hansson, revolutionizing web development with its elegant and efficient approach. Ruby on Rails further propelled Ruby's popularity and solidified its position as a go-to language for web development.

Today, Ruby enjoys a strong and vibrant community of developers worldwide. Its simplicity, expressiveness, and focus on developer happiness have made it a favorite choice for building web applications, scripting, and automation tasks. Ruby's ecosystem boasts numerous libraries, frameworks, and tools that empower developers to create robust and scalable solutions efficiently.

As we delve into the world of Ruby programming in this book, it is essential to appreciate the language's history and the vision of its creator. Understanding the origins of Ruby provides valuable insights into its design philosophy and sets the stage for exploring its capabilities and potential in agile web development.

Key Features and Characteristics of Ruby

Ruby offers a range of powerful features and characteristics that make it a popular choice among developers. Its elegant syntax, focus on simplicity, and a strong emphasis on developer happiness contribute to its unique appeal. In this section, we will explore the key features and characteristics of Ruby that set it apart from other programming languages.

- **Simplicity and Readability**

  Ruby is designed with a focus on simplicity, aiming to provide a language that is easy to understand and write. Its clean and intuitive syntax resembles natural language, allowing developers to express their ideas in a concise and readable manner. This simplicity not only enhances developer productivity but also makes Ruby code more maintainable and accessible to beginners.

- **Dynamic Typing**

  Ruby is dynamically typed, meaning that variable types are determined at runtime rather than during compilation. This flexibility allows for more expressive code and enables developers to write programs quickly. With dynamic typing, developers can easily modify and manipulate objects, resulting in more fluid and adaptable code.

- **Object-Oriented Programming (OOP)**

  Ruby is a fully object-oriented programming language, where everything is an object. This means that data and behavior are encapsulated within objects, promoting modularity, reusability, and code organization. Ruby's seamless integration of OOP principles enables developers to build complex systems and promotes good software design practices.

- **Metaprogramming**

  Metaprogramming is a powerful feature of Ruby that allows developers to modify or extend the behavior of the language itself. With metaprogramming, developers can define new methods, modify existing ones, and dynamically generate code at runtime. This flexibility opens up possibilities for creating expressive and concise code, implementing domain-specific languages, and enhancing productivity.

- **Blocks and Closures**

  Ruby incorporates the concept of blocks and closures, which are powerful constructs for defining reusable code snippets. Blocks enable developers to encapsulate a set of instructions and pass them as arguments to methods, enhancing code modularity and readability. Closures, on the other hand, capture the surrounding context and allow for the persistence of local variables, enabling functional programming patterns.

- **Garbage Collection**

  Ruby has a built-in garbage collector that automatically manages memory allocation and deallocation. This feature relieves developers from manual memory management, reducing the risk of memory leaks and making Ruby programs more robust and stable.

- **Rich Standard Library and Gems**

  Ruby boasts a comprehensive standard library that provides a wide range of built-in classes and modules, offering functionality for common programming tasks. Additionally, Ruby's package manager, RubyGems, allows developers to easily install and manage third-party libraries, known as gems. The extensive ecosystem of gems enhances Ruby's capabilities, providing developers with a vast selection of tools and frameworks to accelerate development.

- **Strong Community Support**

  Ruby benefits from a passionate and supportive community of developers worldwide. The Ruby community actively contributes to the language's growth, creating libraries, frameworks, and documentation to assist developers in their projects. The community's collaborative nature and willingness to share knowledge make Ruby a welcoming language for beginners and seasoned developers alike.

Syntax and the Basic Structure of Ruby Code

Ruby is known for its elegant and readable syntax, which makes it a joy to write and read. Understanding the basic structure of Ruby code is essential for building robust and efficient applications. In this section, we will explore the key elements of Ruby syntax and how they come together to form a well-structured Ruby program.

Comments

Comments are used to annotate and document code, providing additional context and explanations. In Ruby, single-line comments start with the # symbol, and multi-line comments are enclosed between **`=begin`** and **`=end`** delimiters. Comments are ignored by the Ruby interpreter and do not affect the program's execution.

```
# This is how you write a single line comment in Ruby.


=begin
This is how you write
a multi-line comment in Ruby.
=end
```

Variables

Variables are used to store and manipulate data in Ruby. They can hold various types of values, such as numbers, strings, or objects. Ruby uses dynamic typing, meaning you don't need to declare a variable's type explicitly. Variables are created by assigning a value to them using the assignment operator (=).

```
# Assigning a string value to the variable 'book_name'
book_name = "Ruby on Rails for Agile Web Development"

# Assigning a string value to the variable 'author_name'
author_name = "Sajjad Umar"

# Assigning a numeric value to the variable 'num_of_chapters'
num_of_chapters = 12
```

Data Types

Ruby supports a wide range of data types, including strings, numbers, booleans, arrays, hashes, and more. Here are some examples:

```
# String
message = "Welcome to: Ruby on Rails for Agile Web Development."

# Number
count = 12
pi = 3.14159

# Boolean
is_active = true
is_hungry = false

# Array
fruits = ["apple", "banana", "orange"]

# Hash
author = { name: "Sajjad Umar", age: 25 }
```

Control Structures

Ruby provides various control structures to control the flow of execution in a program.

Some commonly used control structures include conditionals (**if**, **else**, and **elsif**), loops (**while**, **for**, and **each**), and iterators.

```
# Conditional
age = 25
if age >= 18
  puts "You are an adult."
else
  puts "You are a minor."
end

# Loop
count = 12
while count > 0
  puts count
  count -= 1
end

# Iterator
fruits = ["apple", "banana", "orange"]
fruits.each do |fruit|
  puts fruit
end
```

Methods

Methods allow you to define reusable blocks of code. They take input parameters, perform specific actions, and may return a value. Method definitions start with the **def** keyword, followed by the method **name** and **parameters**.

```
# Method definition
def greet(name)
  puts "Hello, #{name}!"
end
# Method invocation
greet("Sumar")   # Output: Hello, Sumar!
```

These are the fundamental elements of Ruby syntax and the basic structure of Ruby code. Understanding these concepts will lay a solid foundation for writing clear, concise, and efficient Ruby programs. In the following sections of this chapter, we will explore these concepts further and delve into more advanced topics to enhance your Ruby programming skills.

Remember, practice is key to mastering Ruby syntax. Experiment with code examples, explore Ruby's extensive documentation, and gradually build your understanding of the language's nuances.

Introduction to OOP Concepts in Ruby

Object-oriented programming (OOP) is a powerful paradigm that allows developers to organize code into reusable and modular structures called objects. Ruby is a fully object-oriented language, and understanding its object-oriented concepts is crucial for writing clean, maintainable, and scalable code. In this section, we will explore the key concepts of OOP in Ruby and provide code examples to illustrate their usage.

Note: *Comments are added in the code examples to provide explanations for different aspects of the code. However, it's important to note that Ruby code is designed to be self-explanatory and readable. In general, heavily commenting Ruby code is not necessary as the code itself is expressive and can convey its purpose. Comments should only be added where they add value or clarify complex logic for the reader.*

Classes and Objects

In Ruby, everything is an object, and objects are instances of classes. A class serves as a blueprint for creating objects with similar characteristics and behaviors. It defines the properties and methods that objects of that class can possess. Here's an example of a basic class definition in Ruby:

```
# The Person class represents a person with a name and age.


class Person

  attr_accessor :name, :age


  # The initialize method is called when a new instance of the Person class is created.

  # It takes two parameters: name and age, and assigns them to the corresponding instance variables.

  def initialize(name, age)

    @name = name
```

```
    @age = age
  end

  # The greet method prints a greeting message that includes the
person's name and age.
  def greet
    puts "Hello, my name is #{@name} and I am #{@age} years old."
  end
end

# Creating objects (instances) of the Person class
person_one = Person.new("Sajjad Umar", 25)
person_two = Person.new("Sumar", 30)

# Accessing object properties and invoking methods

# The name property of person_one is accessed using the name method
provided by the attr_accessor.
puts person_one.name   # Output: Sajjad Umar

# The age property of person_two is accessed using the age method
provided by the attr_accessor.
puts person_two.age    # Output: 30

# The greet method of person_one is invoked, which prints the greeting
message.
person_one.greet      # Output: Hello, my name is Sajjad Umar and I am
25 years old.

# The greet method of person_two is invoked, which prints the greeting
message.
person_two.greet      # Output: Hello, my name is Sumar and I am 30
years old.
```

Encapsulation

Encapsulation is the practice of bundling data and methods together within a class, hiding the internal details and providing controlled access to the object's properties and behaviors. This helps in maintaining data integrity and ensuring that the object's state is consistent. In Ruby, instance variables (prefixed with `@`) are used to encapsulate data within objects. They are accessible only from within the object's methods. For example:

```
# The BankAccount class represents a bank account with a balance.


class BankAccount
  def initialize(balance)
    @balance = balance
  end


  # The deposit method increases the account balance by the specified
amount.
  def deposit(amount)
    @balance += amount
  end


  # The withdraw method decreases the account balance by the specified
amount,
  # if the amount is less than or equal to the current balance.
Otherwise, it displays an insufficient funds message.
  def withdraw(amount)
    if amount <= @balance
      @balance -= amount
    else
      puts "Insufficient funds!"
    end
  end


  # The display_balance method prints the current balance of the
account.
  def display_balance
    puts "Current balance: #{@balance}"
  end
```

```
end

# Creating an instance of the BankAccount class with an initial balance
of 1000.
account = BankAccount.new(1000)

# Depositing 500 into the account.
account.deposit(500)

# Withdrawing 200 from the account.
account.withdraw(200)

# Displaying the current balance of the account.
account.display_balance    # Output: Current balance: 1300
```

Inheritance

Inheritance is a fundamental concept in OOP that allows classes to inherit properties and behaviors from other classes. It promotes code reuse and allows for the creation of specialized classes based on existing ones. In Ruby, a class can inherit from another class using the < symbol. The subclass (derived class) inherits all the methods and attributes of the superclass (base class).

Polymorphism

Polymorphism allows objects of different classes to be treated as if they are objects of a common superclass. It enables the use of a single interface to represent multiple types, providing flexibility and extensibility in code. In Ruby, polymorphism is achieved through method overriding.

An example of Inheritance and Polymorphism:

```
# The Vehicle class represents a generic vehicle.


class Vehicle
  # The drive method defines the action of driving.
  def drive
    puts "The vehicle is driving."
  end
end
```

```ruby
# The Car class inherits from the Vehicle class and represents a specific
type of vehicle, a car.

class Car < Vehicle
  # The drive method overrides the drive method in the Vehicle class
  # to define the specific driving behavior of a car.
  def drive
    puts "The car is zooming down the road."
  end
end

# The Motorcycle class inherits from the Vehicle class and represents a
specific type of vehicle, a motorcycle.

class Motorcycle < Vehicle
  # The drive method overrides the drive method in the Vehicle class
  # to define the specific driving behavior of a motorcycle.
  def drive
    puts "The motorcycle is racing on the highway."
  end
end

# Creating instances of different vehicle classes.
vehicle = Vehicle.new
car = Car.new
motorcycle = Motorcycle.new

# Calling the drive method on each instance.
vehicle.drive       # Output: The vehicle is driving.
car.drive           # Output: The car is zooming down the road.
motorcycle.drive    # Output: The motorcycle is racing on the highway.
```

In this example, inheritance is demonstrated by the Car and Motorcycle classes inheriting from the Vehicle class. They inherit the drive method from the Vehicle class and can override it to define their specific driving behavior. Polymorphism is showcased by the ability of different objects (instances of the Vehicle, Car, and Motorcycle classes) to respond to the same method name drive in different ways. Each subclass overrides the drive method inherited from the Vehicle class to define its specific driving behavior, demonstrating polymorphic behavior.

Ruby on Rails Architecture

The Rails framework, also known as Ruby on Rails, is a robust and popular web application framework written in Ruby. It follows the principles of convention over configuration, which means that Rails makes assumptions about how things should be done, allowing developers to focus on building the application's unique features rather than dealing with tedious configurations.

In this section, we will explore the fundamental concepts of the Rails framework. We will delve into its history, discussing its origins and the motivations behind its creation. We will also highlight the key features and advantages that make Rails a preferred choice for web development projects.

Introduction to the Rails Framework

Ruby on Rails, often referred to as Rails, is a web application framework that was created by David Heinemeier Hansson. Its development began in 2003 while Hansson was working on the project management tool Basecamp at 37signals (now known as **Basecamp**). Hansson needed a framework that would allow him to rapidly develop web applications with a focus on simplicity and productivity.

Inspired by the principles of Agile software development, Hansson wanted to create a framework that would enable developers to build web applications quickly, following best practices and conventions. He aimed to eliminate the repetitive and time-consuming tasks associated with web development, allowing developers to focus on solving business problems and delivering high-quality software.

The motivation behind Rails was to provide a framework that embraced simplicity, convention over configuration, and the *Don't Repeat Yourself* (DRY) principle. Rails was designed to encourage developers to write clean, concise, and maintainable code by following established patterns and conventions. By reducing the need for manual configuration and minimizing code repetition, Rails aimed to increase developer productivity and the overall efficiency of the development process.

Rails gained widespread attention and adoption due to its innovative features and the success of applications built with the framework, such as Basecamp, GitHub, Airbnb, and Shopify. Its popularity was also fueled by the active and supportive Ruby and Rails community, which contributed to the development of additional gems and plugins, expanding the capabilities of Rails and making it even more powerful.

The combination of Ruby's expressive syntax, Rails' convention-based approach, and the supportive community contributed to the rapid growth of Rails as a leading web application framework. Today, Ruby on Rails remains a popular choice for web developers seeking a productive and efficient platform for building robust and scalable web applications.

Understanding the Model-View-Controller (MVC) Architectural Pattern

The Model-View-Controller (MVC) is an architectural pattern that provides a structured way of organizing and designing software applications. Rails, as a web application framework, follows the MVC architecture to separate different concerns and facilitate the development of maintainable and scalable applications.

At its core, the MVC architecture divides the application into three main interconnected components: the Model, the View, and the Controller. Each component has a specific role and responsibility, ensuring a clear separation of concerns and promoting code reusability.

Figure 1.1 illustrates how MVC architecture divides the entire application into three components that interact with each other:

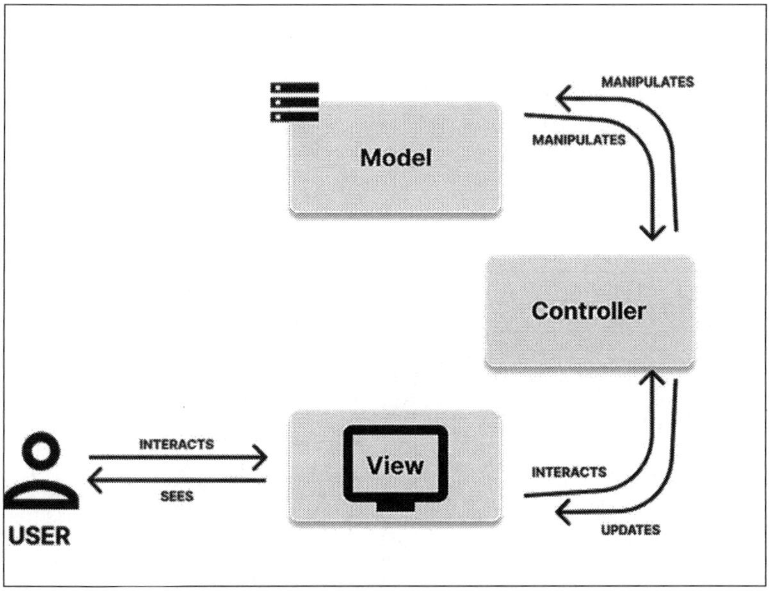

Figure 1.1: *MVC Interaction Diagram*

Figure 1.1 demonstrates the flow of interactions within the MVC architecture. The user interacts with the **`View`**, which represents the presentation layer of the application. The **`View`** displays the user interface and handles user input. When the user interacts with the **`View`**, it communicates with the **`Controller`**.

The **`Controller`** acts as the intermediary between the **`View`** and the **`Model`**, which represents the data layer. The **`Controller`** receives input from the **`View`** and processes it accordingly. It may manipulate the **`Model`**, depending on the requirements of the user's action. Once the **`Controller`** has processed the input, it responds to the View.

Upon receiving a response from the **`Controller`**, the **`View`** updates the user interface based on the changes. It may retrieve data from the **`Model`** or display appropriate messages to the user. The updated user interface is then presented to the user, completing the interaction cycle.

Components of Rails

In Ruby on Rails, the MVC architectural pattern divides the application's functionality into three distinct components: Models, Views, and Controllers. These components work together harmoniously to create robust and maintainable web applications. In this section, we will explore each component in detail, understanding their roles, responsibilities, and interactions within a Rails application.

Models

Models in Rails are responsible for managing the application's data and business logic. They represent the underlying structure and behavior of the application's data, typically interacting with the database. Models encapsulate data validation, retrieval, manipulation, and persistence. They provide an interface to interact with the database tables, enabling developers to perform tasks like creating, reading, updating, and deleting records.

Rails follow the principle of "*Convention over Configuration*", which means that the framework makes assumptions based on naming conventions. By naming a model "*User*", Rails will automatically map it to a database table called "*users*". This convention simplifies the development process and reduces the need for explicit configuration.

Models also define associations between different entities, such as one-to-one, one-to-many, or many-to-many relationships. These associations allow developers to establish connections between models and efficiently retrieve related data.

Views

Views in Rails are responsible for presenting information to users and handling user interfaces. They represent the visual and interactive elements of the application, allowing users to view and interact with the data. Views are typically HTML templates with embedded Ruby code (ERB), which allows dynamic content generation.

Views are designed to be lightweight, focusing on rendering data received from the Controller or directly from the Model. They should avoid containing complex logic and calculations, instead relying on the Controllers and Models to provide the necessary data and perform computations. By separating the presentation logic from the business logic, Views ensure a clear separation of concerns and enhance maintainability.

Rails provide a rich set of view helpers and partials to facilitate view rendering and reusability. View helpers offer convenient methods for generating HTML tags, handling form submissions, and managing other common view-related tasks. Partials allow developers to encapsulate reusable view components, reducing code duplication and improving code organization.

Controllers

Controllers in Rails serve as the intermediaries between Models and Views. They handle user requests, retrieve data from Models, and orchestrate the interaction between Models and Views. Controllers process user input, perform any necessary data manipulations, and determine which View to render.

Controllers receive the user input, validate it if required, and interact with the relevant Models to retrieve or update data. They then pass the necessary data to the appropriate View for rendering.

Controllers also handle the overall flow of the application, managing redirections, authentication, and authorization. They ensure that the user's requests are processed correctly and respond with the appropriate HTTP status codes and error messages when necessary.

Rails encourages developers to keep Controllers lean by following the "*Skinny Controller, Fat Model*" principle. This means that most of the business logic and data manipulation tasks should reside in the Models, while the Controllers focus on coordinating the interactions between Models and Views.

Each component has a specific purpose and contributes to the overall functionality and structure of the application. By leveraging the strengths of each component and adhering to the conventions and best practices of Rails, developers can build scalable, maintainable, and user-friendly web applications.

Understanding the Flow of Data and Requests in a Rails Application

Understanding the flow of data and requests is essential for building efficient and responsive web applications. Rails follow a convention-based approach to handle incoming requests and route them to the appropriate controllers, where the necessary data processing and response generation take place. Let's explore the flow of data and requests in a Rails application in detail.

When a user interacts with a Ruby on Rails application, the following steps occur to process their request and display the requested information:

1. **Web Browser**

   The user uses a web browser (for example, Chrome, Firefox, or Safari) to access the Rails application by entering a URL or clicking on a link.

2. **Web Server**

   The web server (for example, Apache or Nginx) receives the request from the web browser and forwards it to the Rails application for processing.

3. **Router**

   The router in the Rails application examines the request's URL and determines which controller and action should handle it. The router acts like a traffic cop, directing the request to the appropriate destination.

   Here is an example of a **`config/routes.rb`** file in the Rails application:

```
# Example routes.rb file
Rails.application.routes.draw do
  # Define routes for the 'orders' resource
  resources :orders do
    # Define an additional route 'active_orders' that operates on
the collection of orders
    get :active_orders, on: :collection
  end

  # Define routes for the 'products' resource
  resources :products
  # ...
end
```

4. **Controller**

   Once the router identifies the controller and action, the corresponding controller is invoked. Controllers are responsible for handling user requests, processing data, and preparing a response.

Here is an example of a Controller file in the Rails application:

```
class ProductsController < ApplicationController
  # Define a controller class named 'ProductsController' that inherits from 'ApplicationController'

  # Action to display a list of all products
  def index
    # Retrieve all products from the database and assign them to the '@products' instance variable
    @products = Product.all
  end

  # Action to create a new product
  def create
    # Create a new 'Product' object with parameters obtained from the request
    @product = Product.new(product_params)

    # Attempt to save the product to the database
    if @product.save
      # If the product is successfully saved, redirect to the 'index' action
      redirect_to products_path
    else
      # If there are validation errors and the product cannot be saved, render the 'new' view
      render :new
    end
  end

  # ...
end
```

5. **Model**

   If the controller needs data from the database, it interacts with the model.

Models represent the application's data layer and handle tasks such as retrieving, updating, and deleting data. Models encapsulate the business logic and data validation rules.

Here is an example of a Model file in the Rails application:

```
class Product < ApplicationRecord

  # Define a model class named 'Product' that inherits from
'ApplicationRecord'


  # Validation: ensure that the 'name' attribute is present
(not empty)

  validates :name, presence: true


  # Validation: ensure that the 'price' attribute is a number
greater than 0

  validates :price, numericality: { greater_than: 0 }

end
```

6. **View**

Once the controller has processed the data, it passes it to the view. Views are responsible for presenting data to the user in a visually appealing and user-friendly manner.

Here is an example of a View file in the Rails application:

```
<!-- This is how you add a single-line comment in a view html.erb
file -->


<!-- products/index.html.erb -->

<!-- This is the view file for displaying a list of products -->


<h1>Product Listing</h1>

<!-- Display a heading for the product listing -->


<ul>

  <% @products.each do |product| %>

    <!-- Loop through each product in the @products instance
variable -->
```

```
    <li><%= product.name %> - <%= number_to_currency(product.
price) %></li>
    <!-- Display each product's name and price -->
  <% end %>
</ul>
<!-- End of product listing -->
```

7. **Web Server (Response)**

   After the view has generated the HTML, the web server receives the response from the Rails application. The response includes the HTML markup, CSS stylesheets, JavaScript files, and other assets needed to display the web page.

8. **Web Browser (Rendering)**

   Finally, the web server sends the response back to the user's web browser. The browser interprets the received HTML, applies styles, executes JavaScript code, and renders the web page on the user's screen.

Conclusion

In this chapter, we had a comprehensive introduction to the world of Ruby and Ruby on Rails. We explored the origins of Ruby, its key features, syntax, and object-oriented programming concepts. Additionally, we delved into the architecture of Rails, understanding the Model-View-Controller (MVC) pattern, and exploring the components of Rails applications.

In the next chapter, we will embark on a journey into Agile Development Fundamentals. We will delve into the principles and practices of Agile development, examining how it revolutionized the web development landscape. We will explore the core concepts of Agile methodologies and their application to web development projects. So, fasten your seatbelts as we dive into the next chapter and unlock the power of Agile Development Fundamentals!

Short Quiz

1. **What is Ruby?**

   a. A programming language

   b. A web framework

   c. A database management system

   d. A hardware device

2. **Who created Ruby?**
    a. Yukihiro Matsumoto
    b. Guido van Rossum
    c. Larry Page
    d. Linus Torvalds
3. **What are some key features of Ruby?**
    a. Simplicity and productivity
    b. Performance and scalability
    c. Security and encryption
    d. Cross-platform compatibility
4. **What is the basic structure of Ruby code?**
    a. Class, method, variable
    b. Loop, condition, function
    c. Module, attribute, constant
    d. File, folder, package
5. **What is the MVC pattern used for in web development?**
    a. Managing databases
    b. Handling user authentication
    c. Separating application logic and user interface
    d. Generating dynamic web pages
6. **What is the role of a controller in a Rails application?**
    a. Handling user input and interacting with models
    b. Displaying data to the user
    c. Storing and retrieving data from the database
    d. Defining the visual appearance of the web page
7. **Which component of a Rails application is responsible for managing the data layer?**
    a. Model
    b. View

   c. Controller

   d. Router

8. **How does data flow in a Rails application?**

   a. User interacts with the view, which communicates with the model

   b. User interacts with the model, which updates the view

   c. User interacts with the controller via view, which manipulates the model and updates the view

   d. User interacts with the view, which directly updates the database

9. **What is the purpose of a view in Rails?**

   a. Handling user input and performing calculations

   b. Defining the structure and layout of the web page

   c. Retrieving data from the database

   d. Storing data in the model

10. **What is the role of a web server in a Rails application?**

    a. Parsing and executing Ruby code

    b. Managing the database

    c. Handling incoming requests and serving responses

    d. Rendering the view templates

CHAPTER 2
Agile Development Fundamentals

Introduction

Once upon a time, long before the Internet took over our lives, software engineers had a different way of developing software. They didn't have the fancy tools we have today, so they borrowed ideas from the construction and manufacturing industries. They believed that creating software was similar to building physical structures or making products. This led them to adopt a method called the waterfall model, which was introduced by an American computer scientist named Winston W. Royce in 1970.

In the early days, the waterfall method worked well. It followed a strict step-by-step process, where each phase of development had to be completed before moving on to the next. Engineers believed that by thoroughly understanding the requirements, planning meticulously, and designing everything up front, they could ensure quality and minimize risks. It was like following a blueprint for building a house.

However, as software projects became more complex, the limitations of the waterfall model started to show. Engineers realized that trying to define and document all the requirements upfront was difficult. It often resulted in incomplete or inaccurate specifications, just like trying to plan every detail of a project without room for adjustments.

The waterfall approach also had another problem. Once a phase was completed, it was challenging to make changes or incorporate new ideas. Imagine building a house and realizing halfway through that you need an extra room or want to change the layout. It would be costly and time-consuming to go back and make those changes.

The software world was changing rapidly, and customer needs were evolving. Businesses wanted software that could adapt to their changing requirements and stay competitive in the market. That's when Agile methodologies emerged. Agile methodologies embraced a more flexible and iterative approach. They focused on collaboration, adapting to changes, and delivering incremental value. It was like building a house in small steps, where you could make adjustments along the way and respond to the homeowner's changing preferences.

Agile methodologies revolutionized software development, allowing engineers to work closely with customers, learn from their feedback, and continuously improve the software. It became a more customer-centric and adaptable way of creating software, reflecting the dynamic nature of the modern world.

So, while the waterfall model served its purpose in the past, the ever-changing landscape of software development required a more agile and flexible approach. In this chapter, we will dive deeper into the principles and practices of agile development and see how it has transformed the way we build software.

Structure

In this chapter, we will discuss the following topics:

- Introduction to Agile Development
  - Understanding the Limitations of Traditional Approaches
  - The Need for Agile in Web Development
- Agile Manifesto and Principles
  - Origins of the Agile Manifesto
  - The Four Values of the Agile Manifesto
  - Twelve Principles of Agile Software Development
- Agile Methodologies
  - Scrum: Embracing Flexibility and Collaboration
  - Kanban: Visualizing Work and Continuous Flow
  - Lean Software Development: Eliminating Waste and Adding Value
  - Extreme Programming (XP): Emphasizing Quality and Adaptability
- Benefits of Agile in Web Development
- Challenges and Limitations of Agile in Web Development

Introduction to Agile Development

Agile Software Development is an iterative and flexible approach to software development that prioritizes adaptability, collaboration, and customer satisfaction. Unlike traditional methods, Agile embraces change as an opportunity and encourages regular feedback and collaboration among cross-functional teams. By breaking the project into short iterations, known as sprints, Agile allows for continuous improvement, delivering working software incrementally, and incorporating changes based on customer feedback. Agile empowers teams to embrace complexity, foster collaboration, and deliver high-quality software that meets the evolving needs of customers in a dynamic and fast-paced environment.

Understanding the Limitations of Traditional Approaches

Traditional software development methodologies, such as the Waterfall model, have long been the foundation of software development projects. These methodologies follow a linear and sequential approach, where each phase of development is completed before moving on to the next. While they were once effective in specific contexts, it is crucial to recognize their limitations in today's rapidly evolving software landscape.

One of the primary limitations of traditional approaches is their inherent inflexibility. These methodologies rely on extensive planning and documentation up front, with a fixed set of requirements. Once the project is underway, any changes or new insights that emerge may disrupt the entire development process, causing delays and additional costs. This rigidity makes it difficult to respond to evolving customer needs or market demands, hindering the ability to deliver value in a timely manner.

Another limitation of traditional approaches is the limited customer involvement and feedback throughout the development process. Customers typically provide requirements at the beginning of the project, and their involvement may be minimal until the final product is delivered. This lack of ongoing collaboration and feedback can result in a disconnect between the software being developed and the actual needs and expectations of the customer. It increases the risk of building a product that may not meet customer requirements, leading to dissatisfaction and potential rework.

Moreover, traditional methodologies often emphasize adherence to predefined plans and documentation, sometimes at the expense of delivering working software. The focus is primarily on following a predetermined path rather than embracing the flexibility to adapt and refine based on evolving insights and changing circumstances. This approach can lead to delays in delivering value to the customer and hinder the ability to respond quickly to market opportunities.

Additionally, traditional methodologies prioritize process and hierarchy over individuals and interactions. These approaches may hinder effective collaboration and communication within development teams, limiting their ability to share knowledge, address challenges, and make collective decisions. The lack of empowerment and engagement can stifle creativity and innovation within the team, impacting the quality and efficiency of the development process.

The inflexibility, limited customer involvement, focus on plans over working software, and lack of emphasis on collaboration can hinder the ability to deliver value efficiently and effectively. To overcome these limitations, organizations have turned to Agile methodologies that prioritize adaptability, customer collaboration, and iterative development.

The Need for Agile in Web Development

Web development is a dynamic and rapidly evolving field that requires adaptability, responsiveness, and continuous improvement. Traditional software development approaches often struggle to keep up with the unique demands of web development projects. This is where Agile methodologies come into play, offering a compelling solution to address the specific needs of web development.

In the world of web development, timelines are often tight, requirements change frequently, and client expectations are high. Agile methodologies, such as Scrum and Kanban, provide a framework that embraces these challenges and enables teams to deliver high-quality web applications effectively.

One of the primary reasons for the need for Agile in web development is the ever-changing nature of web technologies and user expectations. Websites and web applications need to be constantly updated, refined, and enhanced to remain competitive and deliver an optimal user experience. Agile methodologies allow development teams to iterate quickly, incorporate feedback, and respond promptly to changing requirements, ensuring that the final product meets the evolving needs of the users and the market.

Furthermore, web development projects often involve cross-functional teams, including designers, developers, and stakeholders, who need to collaborate seamlessly throughout the development process. Agile methodologies foster collaboration and communication through practices like daily stand-up meetings, sprint planning, and regular reviews. This collaborative approach improves transparency, minimizes miscommunication, and promotes shared ownership of the project's success.

Another critical aspect of web development is the need for rapid deployment and frequent releases. Websites and web applications are often updated frequently to introduce new features, fix bugs, and address security concerns. Agile methodologies, with their emphasis on incremental development and iterative delivery, enable web development teams to release smaller and focused updates more frequently. This allows for faster time-to-market and the ability to gather user feedback early on, facilitating continuous improvement and enhancing the overall quality of the web application.

So, the need for Agile in web development arises from the unique challenges and requirements of this fast-paced and ever-changing domain. Agile methodologies empower development teams to be flexible, responsive, and collaborative, enabling them to deliver successful web applications that meet user expectations, adapt to evolving technologies, and drive business value in today's digital landscape.

Agile Manifesto and Principles

The Agile Manifesto and its principles serve as a foundational framework for Agile software development, enabling teams to deliver software in a collaborative, flexible, and customer-centric manner. Developed in response to the limitations of traditional methodologies, the Agile Manifesto represents a paradigm shift in how software is approached. This section explores the origins of the Agile Manifesto, examines its four core values, and delves into the 12 principles that guide Agile software development practices. Understanding the Agile Manifesto and its principles is crucial for embracing the Agile mindset and successfully implementing Agile methodologies.

Origins of the Agile Manifesto

Imagine this scenario: It's a chilly February in 2001, and a group of 17 software development experts gathers in a cozy lodge in Snowbird, Utah. These folks have all experienced the frustrations of traditional development approaches and are determined to find a better way of working. They want software development to be more effective, efficient, and aligned with customer needs.

During their meeting, they shared their stories, vented their frustrations, and exchanged ideas. And you know what? Something amazing happened. They came up with a groundbreaking document called the Agile Manifesto.

The Agile Manifesto is a set of values and principles that revolutionized the way software is developed. It emphasizes collaboration, adaptability, and customer focus. Instead of rigid processes and heaps of documentation, it champions individuals working together, creating working software, collaborating with customers, and embracing change.

This manifesto became the backbone of Agile methodologies, guiding teams to work in an iterative and customer-centric way. It sparked a transformation in the software development world, empowering organizations to be more flexible, responsive, and innovative.

The Four Values of the Agile Manifesto

Let's start by quoting the official website: https://agilemanifesto.org.

We are uncovering better ways of developing software by doing it and helping others do it. Through this work, we have come to value:

- **Individuals and interactions** over processes and tools.
- **Working software over comprehensive** documentation.
- **Customer collaboration** over contract negotiation.

- **Responding to change** over following a plan.

That is, while there is value in the items on the right, we value the items on the left more.

The Agile Manifesto outlines four fundamental values that underpin the agile approach to software development. These values serve as guiding principles, shaping the mindset and actions of agile teams. Let's try to understand these values one by one.

Individuals and Interactions over Processes and Tools

Agile recognizes the importance of people and their interactions in driving successful software development. It prioritizes effective collaboration, open communication, and teamwork among team members. Agile teams value building strong relationships, fostering trust, and creating an environment that encourages collaboration. By focusing on individuals and their interactions, rather than overly relying on rigid processes and tools, agile teams can maximize their potential for success.

Working Software over Comprehensive Documentation

Agile places emphasis on delivering working software as a primary objective. While documentation is necessary, agile teams prioritize building functional software that is continuously tested, refined, and delivered. By delivering tangible results, they can gather valuable feedback, respond to changing needs, and ensure the software remains relevant and valuable. This iterative approach enables teams to adapt and make improvements based on user feedback, delivering software that provides real value to customers.

Customer Collaboration over Contract Negotiation

Agile emphasizes the importance of collaboration with customers throughout the development process. It values actively involving customers as partners and engaging them in decision-making. Agile teams seek to understand customer needs, gather feedback, and incorporate it into their work. By fostering close collaboration with customers, agile teams can align their efforts with customer expectations, ensuring that the software they develop meets their needs effectively.

Responding to Change over Following a Plan

Agile embraces the reality that change is constant in software development. It encourages teams to be flexible and responsive to changes in requirements, technology, and market conditions. Agile teams value the ability to adapt quickly, adjust their course, and make necessary changes based on new insights. By being responsive to change, they can deliver software that remains relevant and valuable, even in dynamic and evolving environments.

These four values form the foundation of agile development, shaping the way teams approach their work. By embracing these values, agile teams can foster a collaborative and adaptive environment that promotes innovation, embraces change, and ultimately delivers high-quality software that meets the needs of customers and stakeholders. In the next section, we will explore the 12 principles of agile software development, which further expand upon these core values and provide actionable guidance for agile teams to follow.

Twelve Principles of Agile Software Development

Building upon the four core values of the Agile Manifesto, the agile software development approach is further defined by 12 principles that guide the mindset and practices of agile teams. These principles provide a framework for effective collaboration, continuous improvement, and customer satisfaction. Let's explore each of these principles in more detail:

1. **Customer Satisfaction through Early and Continuous Delivery:** Agile teams strive to deliver valuable software to customers as early and frequently as possible. By prioritizing early and continuous delivery, teams can gather feedback and ensure that customer needs are met throughout the development process.

2. **Welcome Changing Requirements, Even Late in Development:** Agile teams embrace change as a natural and valuable part of software development. They are open to accommodating changing requirements, even if they arise later in the development process. Agile teams understand that responding to change leads to better outcomes and increased customer satisfaction.

3. **Deliver Working Software Frequently:** Agile teams aim to deliver working software in short iterations, typically in weeks rather than months. This iterative approach allows for regular feedback, early bug detection, and continuous improvement, resulting in higher-quality software.

4. **Collaborate Daily with Customers and Stakeholders:** Agile teams prioritize close collaboration with customers and stakeholders. Regular and active involvement of customers in the development process ensures that the software aligns with their needs, improves transparency, and builds trust.

5. **Build Projects around Motivated Individuals:** Agile teams recognize the value of motivated and empowered individuals. They create an environment

that supports and encourages team members, allowing them to unleash their creativity, problem-solving skills, and passion for their work.

6. **Face-to-Face Communication as the Most Effective Method:** Agile teams value face-to-face communication as the most efficient and effective way to exchange information. Direct and frequent interactions enhance understanding, foster collaboration, and reduce miscommunication.

7. **Working Software as the Primary Measure of Progress:** Agile teams measure progress by the amount of working software delivered. This tangible output provides a clear indication of project advancement and allows for valuable feedback from customers and stakeholders.

8. **Sustainable Development and Continuous Pace:** Agile teams maintain a sustainable pace of work, avoiding burnout and ensuring the long-term productivity and well-being of team members. They prioritize a healthy work-life balance and strive for a consistent and sustainable development rhythm.

9. **Continuous Attention to Technical Excellence and Good Design:** Agile teams focus on maintaining technical excellence and high-quality software through continuous attention to good design, refactoring, and adherence to best practices. They prioritize sustainable coding practices, automated testing, and regular integration to ensure the software's maintainability and adaptability.

10. **Simplicity – Maximizing the Amount of Work Not Done:** Agile teams value simplicity in both software development and the overall process. They strive to maximize the amount of work not done by eliminating unnecessary tasks, features, and complexity. By keeping things simple, teams reduce waste and increase efficiency.

11. **Self-Organizing Teams:** Agile teams are self-organizing, empowered to make decisions and determine the best way to accomplish their work. They encourage collaboration, shared ownership, and trust among team members, fostering a sense of ownership and accountability.

12. **Regular Reflection and Continuous Improvement:** Agile teams regularly reflect on their performance and seek opportunities for continuous improvement. They adapt their processes, practices, and tools based on feedback, lessons learned, and evolving customer needs. Continuous improvement is a key aspect of the agile mindset.

These 12 principles guide agile teams in their quest to deliver high-quality software that meets customer needs, embraces change, and fosters a collaborative and adaptive work environment. By embracing these principles, teams can unlock the full potential of agile development and drive successful software projects.

Agile Methodologies

In the world of software development, different teams and organizations adopt various approaches to implement agile principles and practices. These approaches, known as Agile methodologies, provide structured frameworks and guidelines for executing agile projects. Agile methodologies offer flexibility, adaptability, and a focus on customer value, allowing teams to deliver software in an iterative and incremental manner. Let us explore some of the most widely used Agile methodologies and how they contribute to the success of software development projects.

Scrum: Embracing Flexibility and Collaboration

Imagine you are a part of a team developing a new mobile application. You have a vision for the app, but you know that customer demands and technology trends can change rapidly. How do you ensure that your development process is flexible enough to adapt to these changes while still delivering a high-quality product? This is where Scrum comes in.

Scrum is like a well-oiled machine that keeps your team organized and focused. Just as a machine operates smoothly and efficiently when all its parts are properly maintained and synchronized, Scrum keeps your team organized and focused. Each team member plays a specific role, contributing to the overall productivity and success of the project. Just as a machine requires regular maintenance and adjustments to keep it running optimally, Scrum relies on regular meetings, reviews, and adaptations to ensure that the project stays on track and delivers value to the stakeholders. Let's dive into how it works using our mobile app development as an example. In Scrum, you have three key roles: the Product Owner, the Scrum Master, and the Development Team.

The Product Owner acts as the voice of the customer. They gather requirements, prioritize features, and manage the product backlog, which is a dynamic list of all the desired functionalities of the app. Think of the Product Owner as the captain steering the ship and ensuring that the team is building what customers truly need.

The Scrum Master is like the team's coach. They facilitate the Scrum process, remove any obstacles that may hinder progress, and ensure that the team is following Scrum practices. They also protect the team from distractions and help them stay focused on their goals.

The Development Team consists of members with various skills, such as designers, developers, and testers. Together, they work collaboratively to turn the items from the product backlog into increments of working software. They break down the tasks, estimate their effort, and commit to delivering them within a short time frame called a *sprint*.

Imagine each sprint as a mini-project within the overall development process. It's like a race against time to complete a set of tasks. A sprint typically lasts between one to four weeks. At the start of the sprint, the team selects a set of backlog items to work on based on their priority. They create a sprint backlog, which outlines the specific tasks they will tackle during the sprint.

To keep everyone on the same page, the team holds daily scrum meetings, also known as stand-ups. These are short, focused gatherings where each team member shares what they accomplished the previous day, what they plan to do next, and any challenges they are facing. It's a great opportunity for collaboration, as team members can offer help or provide insights.

At the end of the sprint, the team showcases their completed work during a sprint review. Stakeholders, such as product managers or clients, are invited to see the progress and provide feedback. This feedback loop is invaluable as it helps the team validate their assumptions and make necessary adjustments.

Following the sprint review, the team holds a sprint retrospective. This is a moment of reflection where they discuss what went well, what could be improved, and how they can enhance their performance in the next sprint. It's a continuous learning process that fosters a culture of improvement and innovation.

By working in sprints, the team can deliver working software incrementally. This means that even after just a few sprints, you have a functional app that can be tested and used by real users. This early value delivery is a game-changer, as it allows you to gather feedback and make adjustments early in the development process.

Scrum provides the flexibility and adaptability needed in today's fast-paced world. It empowers teams to respond to changing customer needs and market dynamics quickly. With regular feedback loops, collaboration, and iterative development, Scrum helps you stay ahead of the curve and deliver a product that truly delights your customers.

So, with Scrum, you are not only building an app; you are building a dynamic and collaborative team that can navigate the ever-changing landscape of software development.

Figure 2.1 shows all the elements involved in a scrum process:

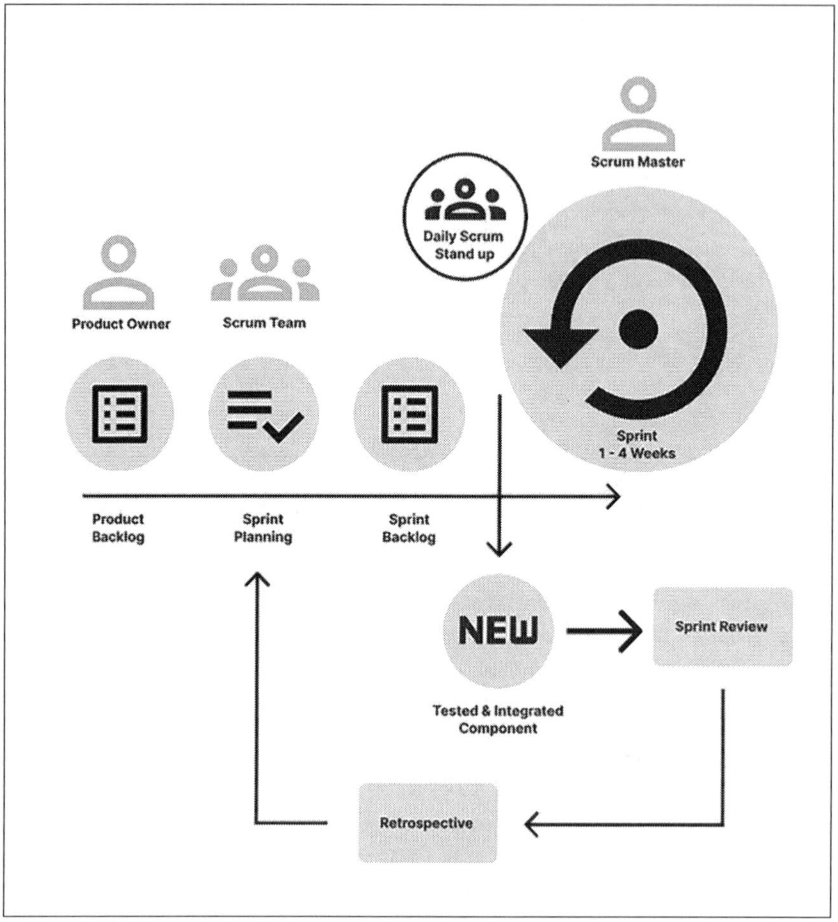

Figure 2.1: *Scrum Process*

Kanban: Visualizing Work and Continuous Flow

Imagine a team working on a complex web development project. They have a multitude of tasks, from designing user interfaces to writing code and conducting tests. How do they keep track of all the work and ensure a smooth, continuous flow? This is where Kanban comes into play.

Kanban, a popular Agile methodology, takes inspiration from manufacturing processes. It originated from the Toyota Production System and focuses on visualizing work and optimizing workflow efficiency. The core idea behind Kanban is to have a visual board that represents the workflow, allowing the team to see and manage their tasks effectively.

Visualize the workflow as a series of columns on a board. Each column represents a specific stage in the development process. For example, you might have columns like "`To Do`," "`In Progress`," "`Testing`," and "`Done`." Tasks or user stories are represented by cards or sticky notes, which move across the board as they progress through the workflow.

Let's delve deeper into how Kanban works. Imagine you are part of a web development team working on an e-commerce website. You start with a set of user stories in the "`To Do`" column. These user stories describe specific functionalities or features that need to be implemented.

As the team begins working on a user story, they move it to the "`In Progress`" column. This signifies that the work has started. Each team member can take ownership of a user story and move it across the board as they complete their part of the task. This visual representation allows the team to have a shared understanding of the work in progress.

One of the key principles of Kanban is to limit work in progress (WIP). This means that the team should focus on completing the tasks at hand before taking on new ones. By setting WIP limits for each column, the team ensures that they don't overload themselves and maintain a smooth workflow. For instance, if the "`In Progress`" column has a WIP limit of three, the team will not start new tasks until one of the ongoing tasks is completed or moved to the next column.

Kanban promotes a continuous flow of work. As a task in the "`In Progress`" column is completed, it moves to the next column, such as "`Testing`" or "`Review`." This flow continues until the task reaches the final column, "`Done`." The team strives to keep the flow steady, avoiding bottlenecks and minimizing idle time.

Another important aspect of Kanban is to embrace incremental improvement. As the team works through the tasks, they continuously analyze their workflow, identify areas for improvement, and make adjustments. This could involve optimizing the process, eliminating waste, or reassigning resources to ensure a smoother and more efficient flow.

Kanban provides a visual and transparent way to manage work, enabling the team to see the big picture and identify potential bottlenecks or delays. It promotes a collaborative environment where team members can communicate and coordinate their efforts effectively. With clear visibility into the workflow, stakeholders and clients can also gain insights into the progress and make well-informed decisions.

By embracing Kanban, web development teams can optimize their workflow, improve productivity, and deliver value more consistently. It encourages a continuous flow of work, reduces waste, and empowers teams to deliver high-quality products efficiently. Kanban is a powerful tool that empowers teams to visualize, manage, and optimize their work processes, ensuring a seamless and efficient development journey.

Figure 2.2 shows a simple Kanban Board and all its elements:

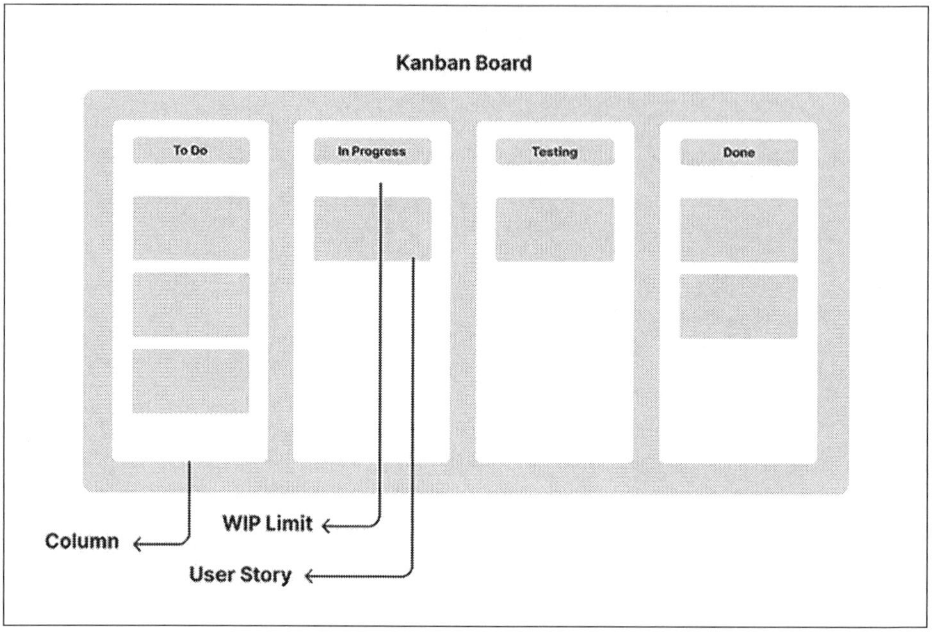

Figure 2.2: *Kanban Board*

Lean Software Development: Eliminating Waste and Adding Value

In the world of web development, efficiency and value are paramount. Lean Software Development, another Agile methodology, focuses on eliminating waste and maximizing value delivery throughout the development process. Inspired by lean manufacturing principles, this approach aims to streamline workflows, reduce unnecessary activities, and ensure that every effort adds value to the final product.

Imagine a web development team working on an e-learning platform. They want to create a platform that provides a seamless learning experience for users. With Lean Software Development, they strive to achieve this by identifying and eliminating anything that does not directly contribute to the user's learning journey.

One of the key concepts of Lean Software Development is the identification and elimination of waste. Waste refers to any activity or process that consumes resources but does not add value to the end product. The team analyzes their workflow and identifies areas where waste occurs, such as redundant documentation, unnecessary handovers, or waiting time between tasks.

To eliminate waste, the team focuses on a few core principles. One principle is to create cross-functional teams where individuals possess a diverse range of skills. This allows for greater collaboration and reduces the need for excessive handovers or dependencies on specific team members. By having a multidisciplinary team, the project can progress smoothly, with team members able to contribute to different aspects of the development process.

Another principle of Lean Software Development is to embrace continuous improvement. The team actively seeks feedback from users, stakeholders, and team members throughout the development cycle. This feedback loop helps identify areas where improvements can be made, ensuring that the final product meets the users' needs and expectations. Continuous improvement also involves regularly reflecting on the development process itself and identifying ways to optimize and refine it.

Lean Software Development also emphasizes the importance of delivering value early and often. Rather than working on long, monolithic development cycles, the team breaks down the project into smaller, manageable iterations or increments. Each increment focuses on delivering a usable and valuable subset of features. By doing so, the team can gather feedback from users and stakeholders early on, incorporate it into the subsequent iterations, and ensure that the final product aligns with their needs.

The concept of lean thinking also applies to the management of resources. Lean Software Development encourages teams to optimize resource utilization and avoid overproduction. This means allocating resources based on current needs and avoiding excessive work on features or functionalities that are not essential or add limited value. By doing so, the team can conserve resources, reduce costs, and maintain a lean and efficient development process.

In Lean Software Development, the focus is on adding value to the end product at every stage of the development journey. By eliminating waste, embracing continuous improvement, and delivering value early and often, web development teams can optimize their processes and create products that meet user expectations and provide a high level of satisfaction.

By adopting Lean Software Development principles, web development teams can achieve greater efficiency, reduce unnecessary activities, and deliver value-driven products. Lean thinking encourages teams to question traditional practices, identify waste, and strive for continuous improvement. It empowers teams to focus on what truly matters, eliminate non-value-adding activities, and deliver exceptional products that meet user needs effectively. Lean Software Development is a powerful approach that drives efficiency, maximizes value, and ensures the delivery of high-quality web applications.

Figure 2.3 shows the lean development process:

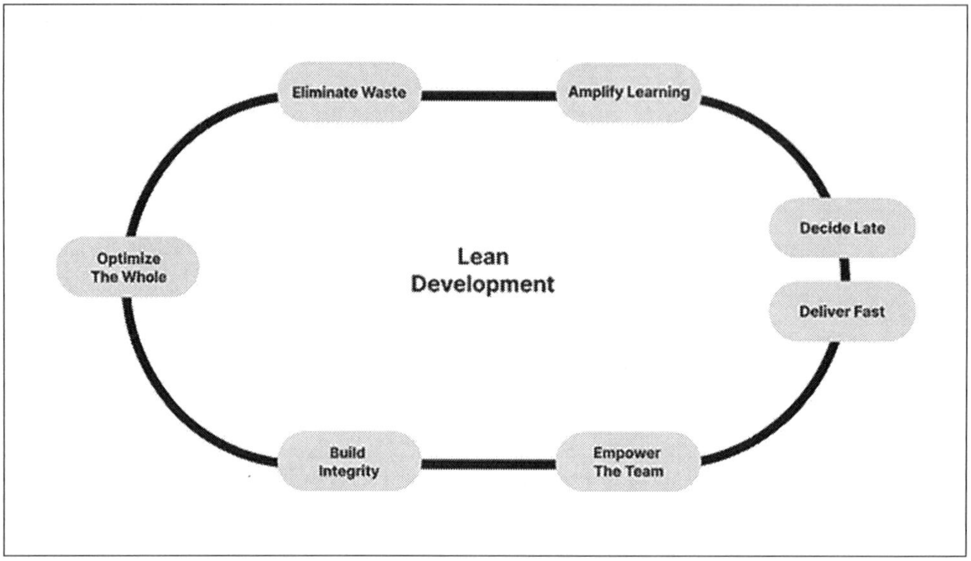

***Figure 2.3**: Lean Development Process*

Extreme Programming (XP): Emphasizing Quality and Adaptability

In the realm of Agile methodologies, Extreme Programming (XP) stands out as an approach that places a strong emphasis on quality and adaptability. XP was developed in the late 1990s by Kent Beck, Ron Jeffries, and other software engineers who sought to address the challenges of rapidly changing requirements and the need for continuous improvement.

Imagine a web development team building a social networking application using Extreme Programming. They understand that the success of their application depends on both the quality of the code and the ability to adapt to evolving user needs. With XP, they aim to strike a balance between these two critical aspects.

One of the core principles of Extreme Programming is continuous testing and feedback. The team writes automated tests for their code and runs them frequently to catch any potential issues early on. This rigorous testing ensures that the application functions as intended and helps maintain a high level of quality. By continuously seeking feedback from users, stakeholders, and team members, the team can refine and improve the application iteratively, ensuring that it remains aligned with changing requirements.

XP also promotes the concept of pair programming, where two developers work together on the same piece of code. This collaborative approach allows for constant knowledge sharing, code review, and the generation of innovative ideas. By working in pairs, the team can catch errors more effectively, enhance the overall code quality, and improve the collective understanding of the codebase.

To enable adaptability, XP employs short development cycles called iterations or sprints. The team breaks down the project into small, manageable increments, each typically lasting one to two weeks. At the end of each iteration, they deliver a working piece of the application, which can be tested and evaluated by stakeholders. This iterative approach enables the team to incorporate feedback, make necessary adjustments, and respond quickly to changes in requirements or user preferences.

Another key practice in Extreme Programming is frequent refactoring. Refactoring involves restructuring the code to improve its design and maintainability without altering its functionality. By regularly refactoring the code, the team ensures that it remains flexible and adaptable to future changes. This practice reduces the accumulation of technical debt and helps prevent the codebase from becoming complex and difficult to maintain over time.

Extreme Programming also promotes a customer-centric approach. The team works closely with the project's stakeholders and end-users, involving them in the development process. This collaboration ensures that the final product meets the users' needs and expectations. By incorporating user feedback early and often, the team can make well-informed decisions and prioritize features based on their value to the end users.

The philosophy of Extreme Programming revolves around embracing change. Instead of resisting change or considering it a burden, XP encourages teams to view change as an opportunity for improvement and innovation. By welcoming change, the team can quickly adapt to evolving requirements, market trends, or user feedback, ensuring that the final product remains relevant and valuable.

Extreme Programming emphasizes the importance of simplicity in both the code and the development process. It advocates for the use of simple and straightforward solutions, avoiding unnecessary complexity. This approach reduces the chances of errors, enhances code maintainability, and promotes a clearer understanding of the application's functionality.

By adopting Extreme Programming, web development teams can achieve a strong focus on quality, adaptability, and collaboration. Through continuous testing, pair programming, short development cycles, and a customer-centric approach, XP enables teams to deliver high-quality software that meets changing requirements effectively. This methodology promotes a culture of constant improvement and embraces change as an opportunity for growth. Extreme Programming is a valuable approach for web development teams aiming to deliver exceptional applications while maintaining flexibility and adaptability.

Figure 2.4 shows the XP methodology:

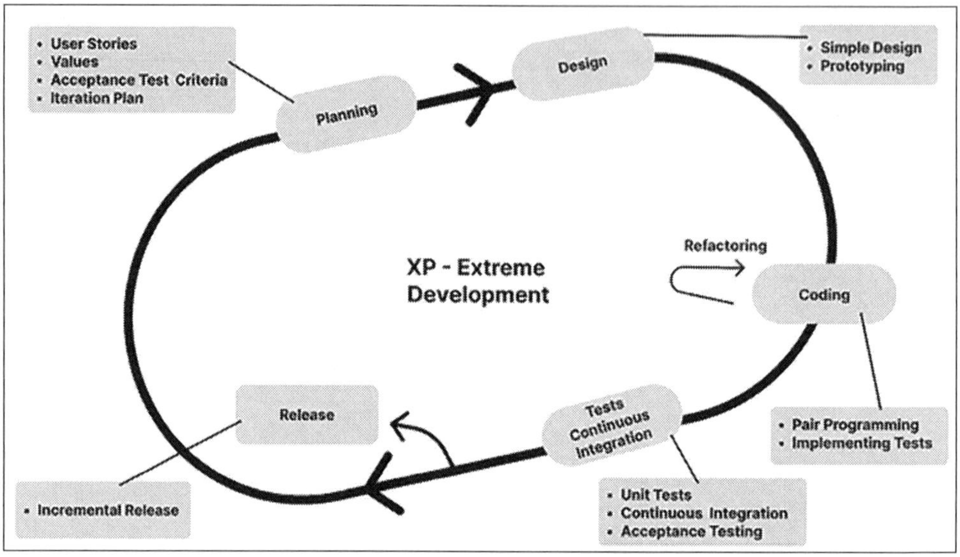

Figure 2.4: *Extreme Programming (XP)*

Benefits of Agile in Web Development

Agile development offers a plethora of advantages that contribute to the success of web development projects. In this section, we will have a look at some of the remarkable benefits that come with adopting an agile approach.

- **Flexibility and Adaptability**

  Agile development is inherently flexible, allowing teams to adapt to changing requirements, market shifts, and customer feedback. This enables developers to respond quickly to new opportunities and challenges, ensuring the final product aligns with the evolving needs of users.

- **Faster Time-to-Market**

  Agile methodologies emphasize incremental progress and regular iterations. This leads to quicker releases of functional components or features, enabling faster delivery of value to users and stakeholders.

- **User-Centric Approach**

  With Agile, user feedback is incorporated early and frequently in the development process. This ensures that the final product meets the actual needs of users, resulting in higher customer satisfaction and engagement.

- **Continuous Improvement**

  Agile development promotes a culture of continuous improvement. Regular retrospectives and feedback loops allow teams to reflect on their processes and outcomes, leading to ongoing enhancements and optimization.

- **Risk Mitigation**

  Agile practices reduce the risk of project failure by breaking down work into manageable iterations. If challenges arise, they are identified and addressed early, minimizing their impact on the overall project.

- **Enhanced Communication**

  Agile methodologies emphasize clear and frequent communication among team members, stakeholders, and customers. This open dialogue leads to better understanding, fewer misunderstandings, and ultimately, more successful outcomes.

- **Collaboration and Team Morale**

  Agile frameworks encourage collaboration and cross-functional teamwork. This fosters a sense of ownership, shared responsibility, and higher levels of job satisfaction among team members.

- **Higher Quality**

  Agile development emphasizes continuous testing and integration. By addressing issues early and consistently, teams produce higher-quality code and reduce the chances of introducing critical defects.

- **Transparency and Visibility**

  Agile methodologies provide transparency in the development process. Stakeholders gain visibility into progress, making it easier to track milestones, monitor budgets, and manage expectations.

- **Adaptable Scope**

  Agile development allows for changes to be made to the project scope without derailing the entire project. This is particularly useful when new opportunities or requirements emerge.

By embracing Agile development, web development teams can harness these benefits to create more successful, user-centric, and adaptable applications. The principles and practices of Agile empower developers to navigate the complexities of modern web development while maintaining focus on delivering value and meeting the dynamic needs of the market.

Challenges and Limitations of Agile in Web Development

While Agile methodologies offer numerous benefits, they also come with their own set of disadvantages and challenges in the context of web development:

- **Uncertainty and Instability**

  Agile development relies on adapting to change, which can sometimes lead to uncertainty and instability, especially in projects with rapidly changing requirements. This constant flux can make it challenging for teams to establish clear project timelines and deliverables.

- **Scope Creep**

  Agile's iterative approach can sometimes result in scope creep, where additional features or requirements are continuously added to the project scope without proper evaluation of their impact on timelines and resources. This can lead to project delays and increased costs.

- **Resource Allocation Issues**

  Agile teams often work on multiple tasks simultaneously, which can lead to resource allocation issues. Without proper prioritization and resource management, teams may struggle to allocate sufficient time and resources to critical tasks, leading to inefficiencies and delays.

- **Dependency Management**

  Agile development often involves cross-functional teams working on different components of a project simultaneously. Managing dependencies between these components can be challenging, especially when changes are made to one component that impacts others.

- **Client Involvement and Feedback**

  While Agile promotes client involvement and feedback throughout the development process, managing client expectations and ensuring timely feedback can be challenging. Delays in client feedback can disrupt project timelines and lead to misunderstandings.

- **Documentation**

  Agile places less emphasis on extensive documentation and upfront planning, which can sometimes lead to a lack of documentation and inadequate project documentation. This can pose challenges for new team members joining the project or for maintaining the project in the long term.

- **Technical Debt**

  Agile's focus on delivering working software quickly can sometimes result in the accumulation of technical debt – shortcuts or compromises made during development that may need to be addressed later. If technical debt is not managed effectively, it can slow down development and lead to quality issues in the long term.

- **Team Collaboration and Communication**

  While Agile promotes collaboration and communication among team members, managing communication effectively can be challenging, especially in distributed or remote teams. Without clear communication channels and processes, misunderstandings and misalignment can occur.

- **Overemphasis on Speed**

  Agile's focus on delivering working software quickly can sometimes lead to an overemphasis on speed at the expense of quality. Rushing through iterations or skipping essential testing processes can result in the release of buggy or incomplete features.

- **Resistance to Change**

  Implementing Agile methodologies often requires a cultural shift within organizations, and some team members may resist or struggle to adapt to the Agile mindset and practices. Resistance to change can hinder the successful implementation of Agile and impact project outcomes.

Overall, while Agile methodologies offer many benefits for web development, it's essential for teams to be aware of and address these disadvantages effectively to ensure successful project delivery.

Conclusion

In this chapter, we embarked on an exploration of Agile Development, a paradigm that revolutionized software development methodologies. We delved into the history and origins of Agile, tracing its roots to the challenges posed by traditional approaches. Recognizing the limitations of these conventional methods, we understood why Agile emerged as a solution for the evolving needs of the dynamic tech landscape.

We dived deep into the essence of the Agile Manifesto and its guiding principles. We learned how a group of forward-thinking software developers came together to address the shortcomings of rigid methodologies and prioritized collaboration, flexibility, and customer satisfaction.

The chapter also unveiled various Agile methodologies, each offering a unique approach to software development. We uncovered Scrum's iterative framework, Kanban's visual workflow management, Lean's focus on value optimization, and Extreme Programming's emphasis on quality and adaptability.

As we conclude this chapter, it's essential to remember that Agile isn't just a set of practices; it's a mindset that encourages adaptability, responsiveness, and continuous improvement. Our journey through Agile's history, principles, and methodologies has laid a foundation for understanding the modern approach to software development.

In the upcoming chapter, we will embark on a hands-on journey into the world of Ruby on Rails. We will guide you through the process of setting up a Rails project, exploring its directory structure, and creating your first application. Get ready to dive into practical coding and unleash the power of this renowned web framework. Stay engaged, as our quest for knowledge and mastery of web development continues.

Short Quiz

1. **What is the primary goal of Agile development?**
   a. To deliver a project within strict deadlines
   b. To ensure comprehensive documentation
   c. To adapt to changing requirements and deliver value early
   d. To strictly follow a sequential development process
2. **Which of the following is a limitation of traditional development approaches?**
   a. Lack of project management tools
   b. Inability to meet project deadlines
   c. Difficulty in managing project scope
   d. Difficulty in adapting to changing requirements
3. **What was the main motivation behind the creation of the Agile Manifesto?**
   a. To promote strict adherence to development processes
   b. To address the limitations of traditional approaches
   c. To enforce hierarchical control over development teams
   d. To eliminate the need for collaboration in development
4. **What are the four values of the Agile Manifesto?**
   a. Plan, Design, Code, Test
   b. People, Processes, Tools, Documentation
   c. Individuals and interactions, Working software, Customer collaboration, Responding to change
   d. Scope, Schedule, Budget, Quality
5. **Which Agile methodology focuses on iterative development and continuous improvement?**
   a. Scrum
   b. Kanban

c. Lean Software Development

d. Extreme Programming (XP)

6. **What is the purpose of visualizing work and implementing continuous flow in Kanban?**

a. To ensure that each team member has an equal workload

b. To monitor project progress and identify bottlenecks

c. To strictly enforce a predetermined schedule for each task

d. To eliminate the need for collaboration in development

7. **Which Agile methodology emphasizes the elimination of waste and adding value?**

a. Scrum

b. Kanban

c. Lean Software Development

d. Extreme Programming (XP)

8. **Which Agile methodology emphasizes quality and adaptability through practices like pair programming and short development cycles?**

a. Scrum

b. Kanban

c. Lean Software Development

d. Extreme Programming (XP)

9. **What is the purpose of the 12 Principles of Agile Software Development?**

a. To enforce strict rules and regulations in development teams

b. To provide guidelines for effective project management

c. To guide teams in implementing Agile practices and principles

d. To define a standardized development process for all projects

10. **What is one of the key advantages of Agile development in web development?**

a. Strict adherence to project schedules

b. Comprehensive documentation at each stage

c. Early delivery of value and frequent customer feedback

d. Limited need for collaboration and teamwork

CHAPTER 3
Getting Started with Ruby on Rails

Introduction

Once upon a time in the world of web development, there was a need for a framework that could bring simplicity and joy to the coding process. Developers longed for a tool that would allow them to focus on building brilliant web applications without being bogged down by complexities. And in the bustling world of programming languages, a language named Ruby stepped into the limelight.

Ruby, with its elegant and natural syntax, quickly won the hearts of developers. It was a dynamic, open-source language that promised to make programming a delightful experience. However, Ruby alone couldn't weave the magic of web development without a framework that would harness its potential.

In the midst of this quest for the perfect web framework, Ruby on Rails made its grand entrance. Also known simply as Rails, this web framework was the brainchild of David Heinemeier Hansson. Inspired by his work on the Basecamp project, David introduced Rails to the world in 2004.

Rails embraced the essence of Ruby's simplicity and productivity, offering developers a seamless and efficient way to create web applications. Its philosophy revolved around the "*convention over configuration*" principle, allowing developers to focus on writing the code that mattered, while the framework took care of the rest.

With Ruby on Rails, developers found themselves entering a world of possibilities. It was like embarking on an adventure, with Rails guiding them through the maze of web development. They were free to unleash their creativity, shaping their applications with ease and confidence.

In this chapter, we will dive deep into the realm of Ruby on Rails. We will start by installing Ruby and Rails on your system, just as pioneers set out to explore new territories. As we progress, you will learn how to set up your first Rails project, discovering the essence of Rails' directory structure and elements that will become your trusty companions on this web development expedition.

As we venture deeper, you will witness the magic of Rails unfold. Together, we will create a basic Rails application, and with each line of code, you will see the power of simplicity in action. With routes, controllers, and views at your disposal, you will feel the thrill of building your own web application from scratch.

By the end of this chapter, you will not only have mastered the art of getting started with Ruby on Rails but also gained insight into the history and origin of this remarkable framework. So, tighten your seatbelt, and let's embark on this thrilling journey together!

Structure

In this chapter, we will discuss the following topics:

- Overview of Ruby on Rails Framework
  - Guiding Principles of Rails
  - Benefits of Using Ruby on Rails
- Installing Ruby and Rails
  - Installing Ruby
  - Installing Rails
- Setting Up a New Rails Project
- Understanding the Rails Directory Structure
- Creating the First Page of Your App
  - Generating Your First Controller
  - Creating Your First View
  - Defining the Route
- Starting the Rails Server
  - Accessing Your Page in the Browser

Overview of Ruby on Rails Framework

Ruby on Rails, affectionately known as Rails, is a creation of brilliance born in 2004. The ingenious mind behind its inception, David Heinemeier Hansson, brought to life a web development framework that would redefine the way developers approach building applications. Rails is built on the solid foundation of the Ruby programming language, inheriting its clean and expressive syntax.

Guiding Principles of Rails

Rails embraces a set of guiding principles that make it stand out in the crowded landscape of web development frameworks. Imagine this: as you step into the world of Rails, you are greeted with open arms by the philosophy of "*Convention over Configuration.*" This powerful principle means that Rails has already made some key decisions for you, such as organizing your files and naming conventions. This thoughtful convention-driven approach means less time fiddling with configurations and more time focusing on the art of coding.

Another captivating facet of Rails is its fondness for "*Don't Repeat Yourself*" (DRY) coding. It's like Rails is telling you, "*Hey, no need to repeat yourself, I've got your back!*" This emphasis on writing concise and reusable code allows you to create robust and maintainable applications without unnecessary duplication.

Benefits of Using Ruby on Rails

Now, let's talk about the delightful perks of hopping on the Rails bandwagon! First and foremost, Rails is all about developer productivity. With its clean syntax and intuitive design, writing code feels like composing a beautiful symphony of logic. Rails empower you to build web applications with elegance and joy, making the development journey an exhilarating experience.

Imagine having a magical treasure trove of gems at your fingertips. No, not the sparkling gemstones you'd find in a fantasy novel, but rather a collection of ready-made libraries that simplify your life as a developer. Rails boast a treasure trove of gems that provide ingenious solutions for common tasks, saving you time and effort while building exceptional applications.

In the realm of software development, quality reigns supreme. Rails, being the wise mentor it is, encourages test-driven development and automated testing. With tools like RSpec and Capybara, you can write tests to ensure the stability and correctness of your applications, ensuring a top-notch user experience.

The elegance of Rails' Model-View-Controller (MVC) architecture is a sight to behold. It's like witnessing a well-choreographed dance, where each element knows its role to create a mesmerizing performance. Rails' MVC structure encourages clear separation of concerns, making your codebase more modular and maintainable. This separation fosters collaboration within development teams, leading to harmonious co-creation.

So, fasten your seatbelts, dear readers, as we journey further into the enchanting world of Ruby on Rails - the world is your canvas, and Rails is your paintbrush. Let's paint masterpieces together. But before we do that, let's set up the development environment.

Installing Ruby and Rails

Before we start installing Ruby and Rails in your system, let's clear up a few things.

The installation process is not always the same for different operating systems, and things might change frequently. Follow this checklist guide as a reference, and if you get stuck anywhere, simply make a quick search on the internet by pasting the error you get in your terminal.

With that being said, let's install Ruby.

Installing Ruby

In this section, we will walk through the process of installing Ruby on macOS running on MacBook Pro (M1) step by step. If you are using a different operating system, you can refer to the official Ruby installation guide for detailed instructions tailored to your specific system. For your convenience, here is the link to the official Ruby installation guide: https://www.ruby-lang.org/en/documentation/installation. Let's get started.

Ruby Managers

When it comes to installing Ruby, you have a few options:

- **Package managers:** If you are using a UNIX-like operating system, your system's package manager is the easiest way to go. Just be aware that the installed version may not always be the latest.
- **Installers:** You can use installers to get a specific version of Ruby or even install multiple versions. Windows users have their own installer too.
- **Version managers:** These tools help you switch between different Ruby versions on your system, making it easy to work with multiple projects.
- **Building from source:** For the curious and adventurous, you can build Ruby from its source code, giving you a deeper understanding of how it works.

You have the freedom to choose the installation method that best fits your preferences. Detailed instructions for all these methods are available at the link provided above. In this guide, we will demonstrate using Package Managers, a commonly preferred method.

Version Managers

Ruby managers are widely utilized by Ruby developers to handle multiple Ruby versions seamlessly. These tools offer the convenience of effortless or even automatic switching between different Ruby versions, depending on the specific project's requirements. While it's important to note that Ruby managers are not officially supported by the Ruby core team, you can find ample support within their respective communities. Embracing a Ruby manager can greatly enhance your development experience, allowing you to work efficiently on various projects with different Ruby versions without any hassle.

When it comes to managing Ruby versions, the options are plentiful, each offering its unique set of features and advantages. Some popular choices include **rbenv**, **rvm**, **asdf-vm**, **chruby**, **uru**, and many more. Among these, **rbenv** and **rvm** stand out as the most widely used version managers in the Ruby community. RVM is our go-to choice for its ease of use and effectiveness. Therefore, in this book, we will utilize RVM for the demonstrations.

Installing Ruby Version Manager (RVM)

RVM is a command-line tool that allows you to easily install, manage, and work with multiple ruby environments from interpreters to sets of gems. You can find the official installation guide at https://rvm.io/rvm/install

RVM works on various operating systems, including UNIX-like systems and Windows (with Cygwin or Bash on Ubuntu on Windows). To get started, you will need some basic requirements like **bash**, **curl**, and **gpg2**, as well as the GNU version of tools. The good news is that RVM does its best to automatically detect and install anything that is needed, making the setup process smooth and hassle-free. So, whether you are on a Mac, Linux, or Windows system, RVM has got you covered and will ensure you have everything you need to manage your Ruby versions effectively.

The first step is to install GNU Privacy Guard (GPG) keys by running the following command on your terminal:

```
gpg --keyserver keyserver.ubuntu.com --recv-keys 409B6B-
1796C275462A1703113804BB82D39DC0E3 7D2BAF1CF37B13E2069D6956105B-
D0E739499BDB
```

Refer to the preceding official link if you run into any issues.

The next step is to install RVM by running the following command:

```
\curl -sSL https://get.rvm.io | bash -s stable
```

Note: *If you are on Ubuntu, please follow the Ubuntu-specific guide provided in the preceding link.*

The next and final step is to load and verify the installation. To load RVM, close out your current shell or terminal session, and open a new one. Alternatively, you can load RVM with the following command:

```
source ~/.rvm/scripts/rvm
```

Now, you can verify your installation by running the following command:

```
type rvm | head -n 1

# rvm is a function
```

After executing the preceding command, you will see a confirmation message such as "*rvm is a function*," indicating that the installation was successful! Now you are all set to make the most of RVM and manage your Ruby versions seamlessly.

Installing Ruby Via RVM

Installing Ruby with RVM is as simple as 1, 2, and 3. Just open the terminal and run:

```
rvm install 3.2.2
```

This should take care of installing Ruby; in this case, Ruby version 3.2.2. At the time of writing this book, 3.2.2 is the latest stable version of Ruby.

Figure 3.1 shows the process of installing Ruby with the **`rvm install`** command:

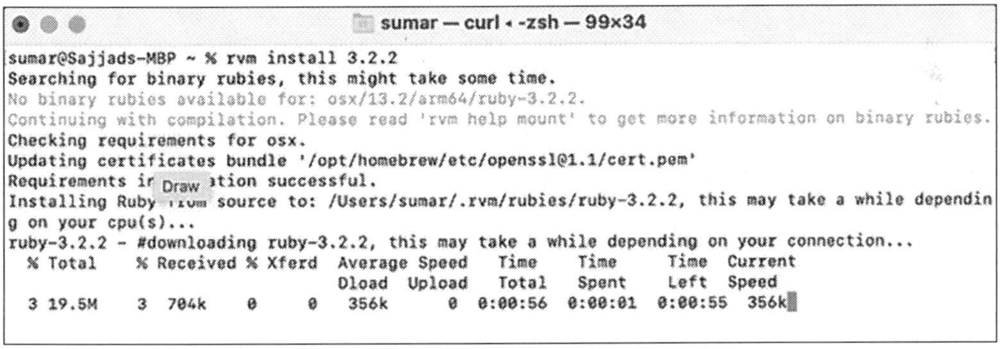

Figure 3.1: *Installing Ruby with RVM*

At the end of the installation process, you should see a message similar to this on your terminal screen: "`Install of ruby-3.2.2 - #complete`".

You can read the documentation of Ruby Version Manager to learn more helpful commands by visiting the preceding official installation guide link.

Verifying the Installation

To use the newly installed Ruby, run the following command:

```
rvm use 3.2.2
```

Note: *Replace `3.2.2` with the version of Ruby you just installed.*

Now to verify if that worked correctly, run the following command:

```
ruby -v
# ruby 3.2.2 (2023-03-30 revision e51014f9c0) [arm64-darwin22]
```

This command should output the current ruby version on your terminal, as shown earlier (starting with # sign).

Optionally, you can set a version of Ruby to use as the default for new shells by running the following command:

```
rvm use 3.2.2 --default
```

If you find yourself stuck in following any of the preceding steps - the internet is your friend, make use of it.

Installing Rails

With Ruby installed, you should now have **RubyGems** (package manager for Ruby) installed in your system. You can verify by running the following command:

```
gem -v
```

```
# 3.4.10
```

We will use the `gem install` command from RubyGems to install rails. Before proceeding, we need to check if we have all the prerequisites installed. These include:

- Ruby (we just installed ✓)
- SQLite3 Database (need to verify if already installed)

Many popular UNIX-like operating systems ship with an acceptable version of SQLite3. For others, the installation guide can be found at https://www.sqlite.org/index.html

You can verify the installation of the SQLite3 database by running the following command on your terminal:

```
sqlite3 --version
# 3.39.5
```

This should output the currently installed version of the SQLite3 database (✓). We will use more powerful databases like PostgreSQL in the upcoming chapters, but for the sake of simplicity, we will stick with SQLite3 in this chapter.

Now, we are ready to install Rails. In your terminal, run the following command:

```
gem install rails
```

This will start the installation of Rails; this process can take some time depending on your hardware and internet speed.

Verifying the Installation

Once installed, you can verify the installation by running the following command:

```
rails --version
OR the short version
rails -v

# Rails 7.0.6
```

This should output the version of Rails you just installed. If that is the case, congratulations - you now have a working Ruby on Rails setup on your machine.

If you encounter any roadblocks during the installation or while using RVM, don't worry! A helpful approach is to search for the specific error message you see in your terminal on the internet. You will likely find plenty of resources and community support to guide you through any issues you may face. So, keep exploring, and with a little help, you will overcome any obstacles in your installation process!

Setting Up a New Rails Project

With Ruby on Rails installed, we are ready to create our very first Rails application.

For this section, we will create a simple contacts app named "**`Contacts`**" to understand the ins and outs of a Rails application. Later on, we will expand this app to add some cool features.

Open up the terminal and navigate to the preferred directory/folder (or not). For example, we are inside the "**`book`**" directory. Then, run the following command:

```
rails new contacts
```

Where "**`rails new`**" is the rails command used to create a new application, and "**`contacts`**" is the name of the application. The name can be anything, but it is recommended to stick with "**`contacts`**" so that you can easily follow along.

After running the "**`rails new`**" command, you should see something like this on your terminal screen:

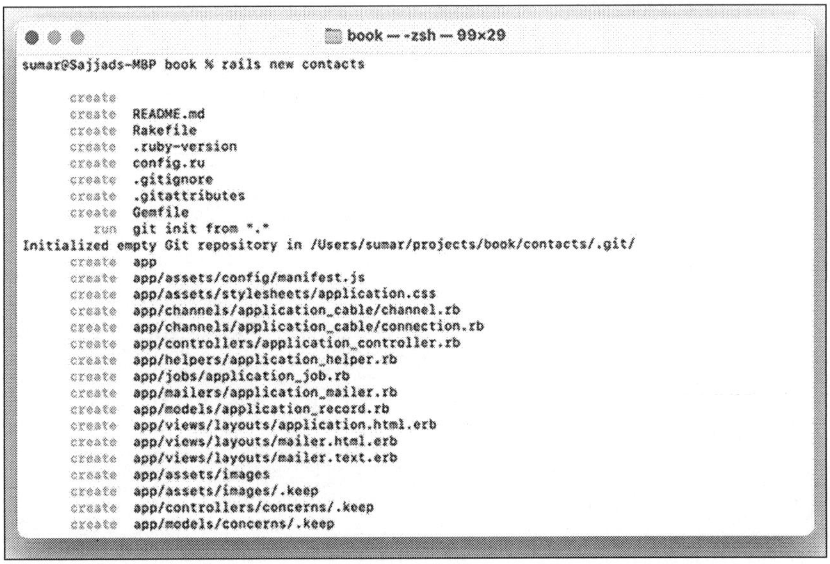

Figure 3.2: *Creating a New Rails App with the "rails new" Command*

Figure 3.2 shows that Rails is doing its magic to create a new application for you.

Once done, move to the app directory by running the `` `cd` `` (change directory) command:

```
cd contacts
```

Inside the "`contacts`" (our application) directory, run the "`ls -a`" command to list down all the contents inside the directory. *Figure* 3.3 shows the content of our contacts application:

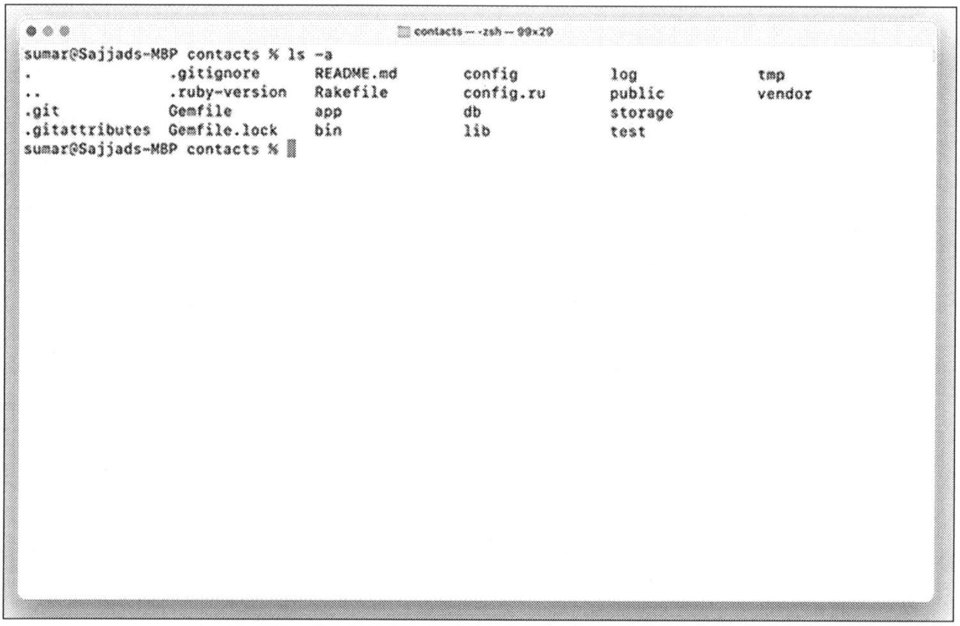

***Figure 3.3**: Contents of our Rails Application*

Now, it's time to understand how our Rails app is structured and what are the most important files and folders inside of our app. Let's jump right in!

Understanding the Rails Directory Structure

To explore the directory structure of our first Rails application, let's open it in an Integrated Development Environment (IDE). You have the flexibility to choose the IDE that suits you best, and two popular options for Ruby on Rails development are Visual Studio Code and RubyMine. Visual Studio Code is a free IDE, while RubyMine comes with a paid license. Both IDEs offer robust features to enhance your Rails development experience, so pick the one that aligns with your preferences.

Figure 3.4 shows our app opened in Visual Studio Code:

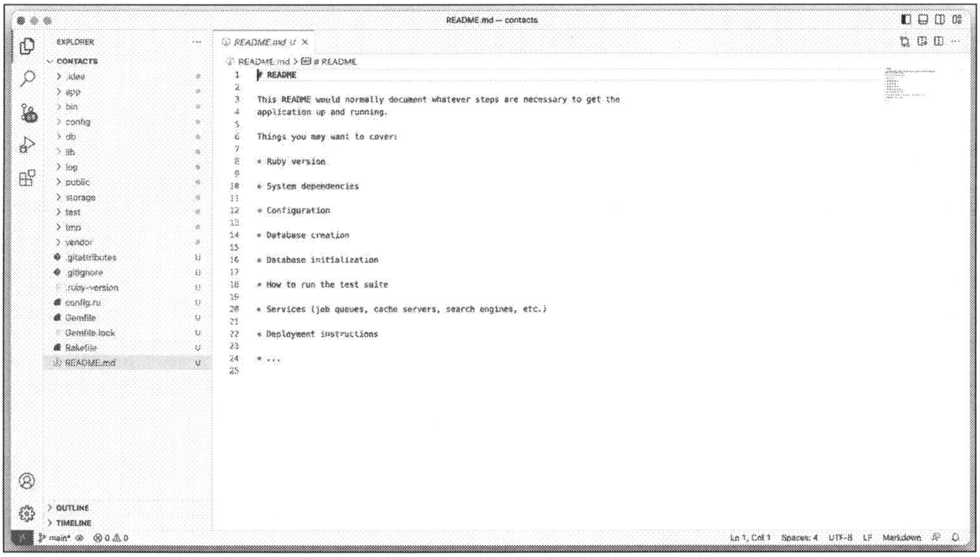

Figure 3.4: *Contacts App in Visual Studio Code IDE*

On the other hand, *Figure* 3.5 shows our app opened in RubyMine:

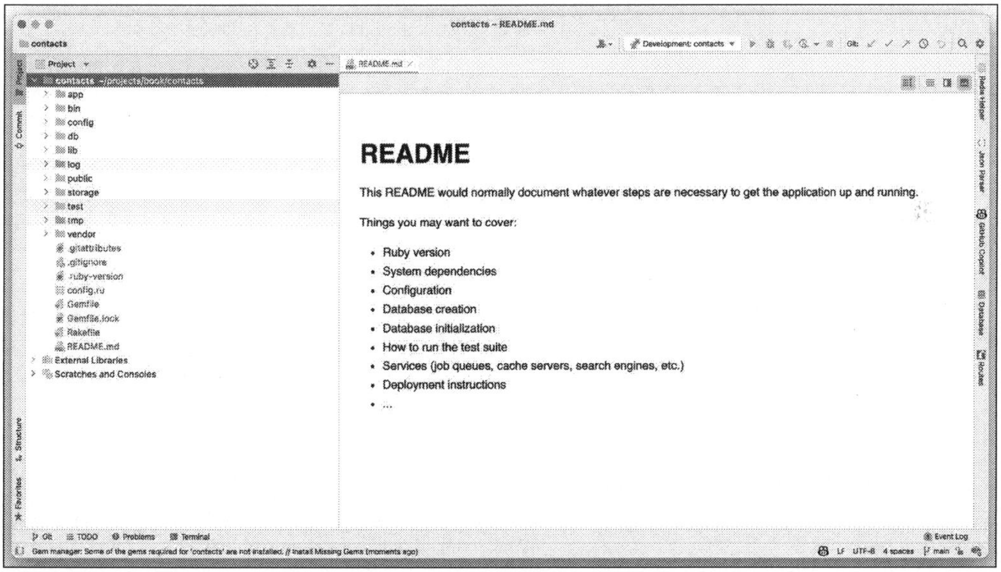

Figure 3.5: *Contacts App in RubyMine IDE*

As RubyMine is used, so the following topics will be explained using screenshots of RubyMine IDE.

Pro Tip: *You can try RubyMine for a month OR if you are a student, you can get a one-year renewable license of RubyMine for free. Find all the details on the RubyMine website.*

In a Ruby on Rails application, one of the core principles that guide its design is "*Convention over Configuration.*" This principle suggests that the framework makes assumptions about how things should be structured and behave, allowing developers to focus more on building the application's unique features rather than spending time on configuration.

Please note that this section will provide an introduction to the most essential directories in our Rails application. Each directory and file serves a unique purpose, and as we progress through the book, we will delve into more of them individually, exploring their functionalities in greater detail. So, let's begin by familiarizing ourselves with the key directories that play a vital role in building robust and efficient Rails applications.

The "app" Directory

This is where the magic happens, following the Rails convention. The framework assumes that the main application code, including **`controllers`**, **`models`**, and **`views`**, will be placed here. The convention helps Rails automatically link the components together, reducing the need for explicit configurations.

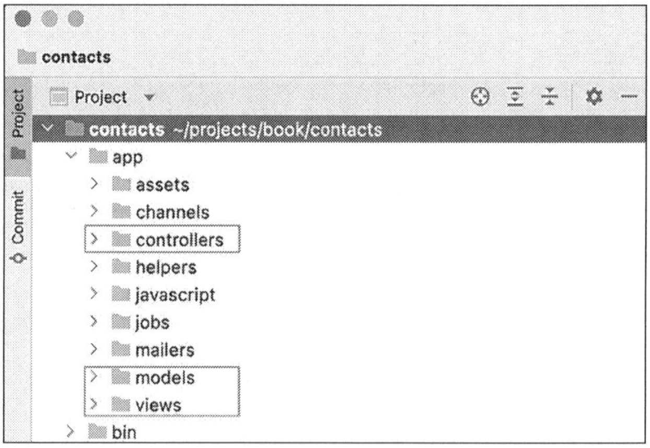

Figure 3.6*: Exploring Contents of the app Directory*

In addition to the main components mentioned earlier, the "**`app`**" directory in a Ruby on Rails application houses several other essential folders that contribute to the app's functionality:

- **`assets`**: This directory holds the assets used in your application, such as images and stylesheets. Additionally, it includes configuration files to manage asset compilation and preprocessing, ensuring optimal performance.
- **`channels`**: In this folder, you will find channels that establish connections with ActionCable, a feature in Rails that seamlessly integrates WebSockets with the rest of your application. This enables real-time communication between the client and server, facilitating features like live chat or notifications.

- **`helpers`**: The "**`helpers`**" folder contains application helpers, which are utility modules that provide reusable methods for your views. These helpers simplify view logic and can be shared across different parts of your application.
- **`javascript`**: This directory houses JavaScript files that are specific to your application. You can organize and manage client-side functionality here, making your application interactive and responsive.
- **`jobs`**: The "**`jobs`**" folder contains app jobs, which are classes responsible for handling background tasks. Jobs allow you to execute time-consuming processes outside of the main request-response cycle, improving application responsiveness.
- **`mailers`**: In the "**`mailers`**" folder, you will find app mailers, which are responsible for sending emails from your application. Mailers allow you to compose and send customized emails, such as welcome emails or password reset instructions.

Organizing these folders within the "**`app`**" directory makes it easier for developers to work on projects collaboratively and efficiently. Each folder serves a specific purpose, contributing to the seamless development of web applications using Rails.

The "config" Directory

Here, Rails houses the important configuration files, following its conventions for setup. For instance, the "**`routes.rb`**" file provides the rules for mapping URLs to controllers, while "**`database.yml`**" holds the configuration for the database connection.

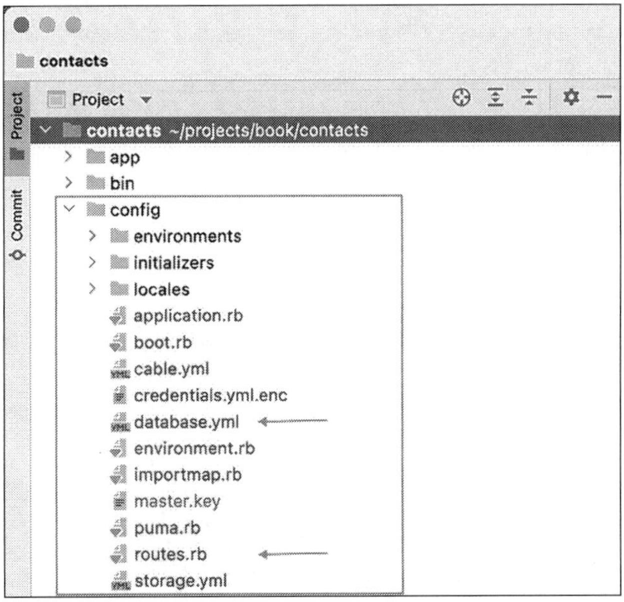

***Figure 3.7**: Exploring Contents of the config Directory*

Besides **routs.rb** and **database.yml**, - inside the "**config**" directory, you will find several important files and folders that play a crucial role in configuring and customizing your application. Let's dive into each of them:

- **environments:** This folder contains configuration files specific to different environments, such as development, test, and production. Each environment file defines settings and variables that tailor the behavior of your application to the respective environment.
- **initializers:** The "**initializers**" folder holds Ruby scripts that run during the application's boot process. These scripts allow you to perform application-wide configurations or set up third-party libraries before the application starts.
- **locales:** In the "**locales**" folder, you can find internationalization (i18n) files that store translations for different languages. These files allow your application to be displayed in multiple languages, enhancing its accessibility and global reach.
- **application.rb:** This file is the heart of Rails' configuration. It contains application-specific settings and configurations that apply across all environments. You can use this file to define middleware, autoload paths, and various other application-level settings.
- **cable.rb:** The "**cable.rb**" file is responsible for configuring **ActionCable**. Here, you can set up options related to **ActionCable**, such as the connection adapter and allowed request origins.
- **environment.rb:** This file is loaded during the application's initialization process and sets up the runtime environment. It sets the default Rails version and loads the respective environment-specific configuration files.
- **importmap.rb:** The "**importmap.rb**" file is part of Rails' JavaScript **importmap** feature. It allows you to specify how JavaScript modules should be loaded and mapped within your application.
- **credentials.yml.enc and master.key:** These files store encrypted credentials for your application, such as API keys and passwords. The "**credentials.yml.enc**" file contains the encrypted data, while the "**master.key**" file is used to decrypt the credentials.
- **puma.rb:** The "**puma.rb**" file configures the Puma web server, which is the default server used by Rails applications. Here, you can specify the number of worker processes, threads, and other server-related settings.
- **storage.yml:** The "**storage.yml**" file defines configuration options for Active Storage, Rails' built-in file and image attachment library. It allows you to specify storage services and their associated settings.
- **boot.rb:** This file is responsible for loading Rails and its dependencies. It sets up the load paths and initializes the Rails environment.

The "**config**" directory in a Rails application contains essential configuration files and folders that govern how your application behaves, handles internationalization, manages credentials, and sets up server options, among other important functionalities. These files are crucial in tailoring your application to specific environments and customizing its behavior according to your needs.

The "db" Directory

This directory contains files and folders to manage the database. The "**migrate**" folder (you might not have it yet!) contains version-controlled scripts that define the changes to the database schema, allowing developers to evolve the database structure with ease.

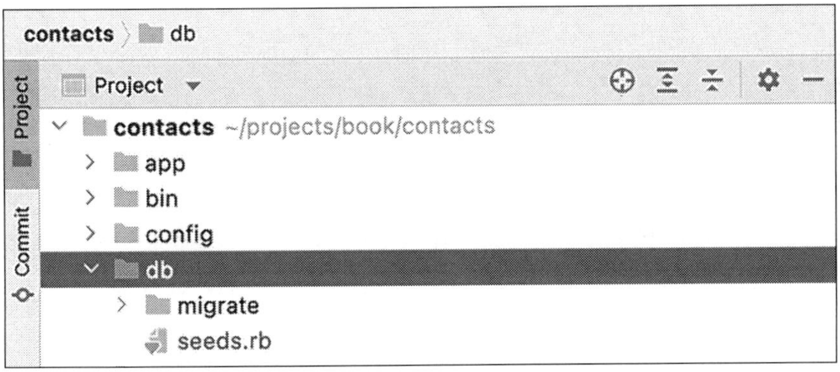

Figure 3.8*: Exploring Contents of the "db" Directory*

Besides the "**migrate**" folder, there are **seeds.rb**. The "**seeds.rb**" file is a Ruby script that allows developers to define data that should be inserted into the database when the application is first set up or whenever the database needs to be reset. This is particularly useful when you need to create test data for your application or set up some initial data for users, settings, or configuration.

As we progress through this book, you will encounter more database-related files and folders within this directory. These files play a crucial role in structuring and maintaining your application's database, ensuring smooth data management and interaction with your application.

The "public" Directory

Rails adhere to conventions for storing static files that should be directly accessible to users. Images, stylesheets, JavaScript files, Text files, HTML files, and other public assets are placed here.

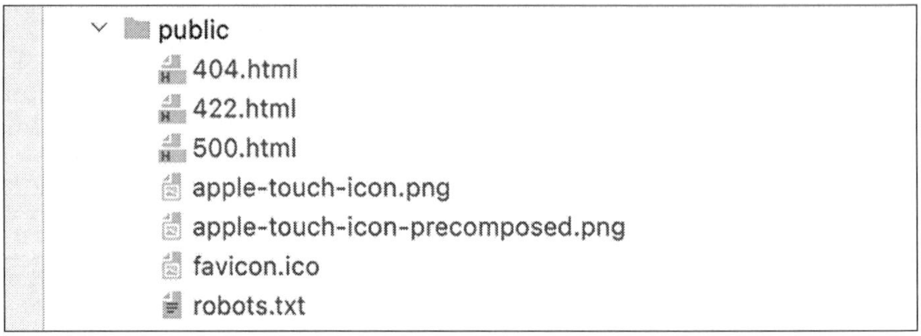

***Figure 3.9**: Exploring Contents of the "public" Directory*

The "`test`" Directory

The test directory is reserved for test files written using testing frameworks like RSpec, Minitest, or Capybara. It allows running tests effortlessly and encourages developers to maintain test coverage.

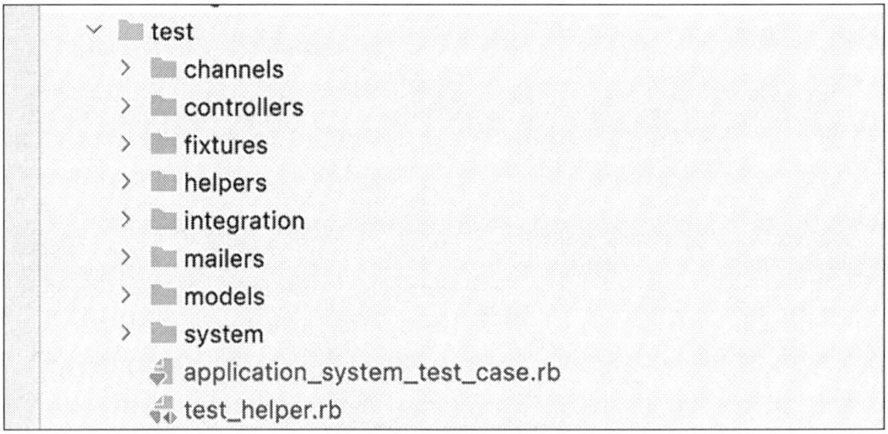

***Figure 3.10**: Exploring Contents of the "test" Directory*

The "vendor" Directory

In this directory, developers can include third-party code or libraries, adhering to Rails conventions to manage external dependencies.

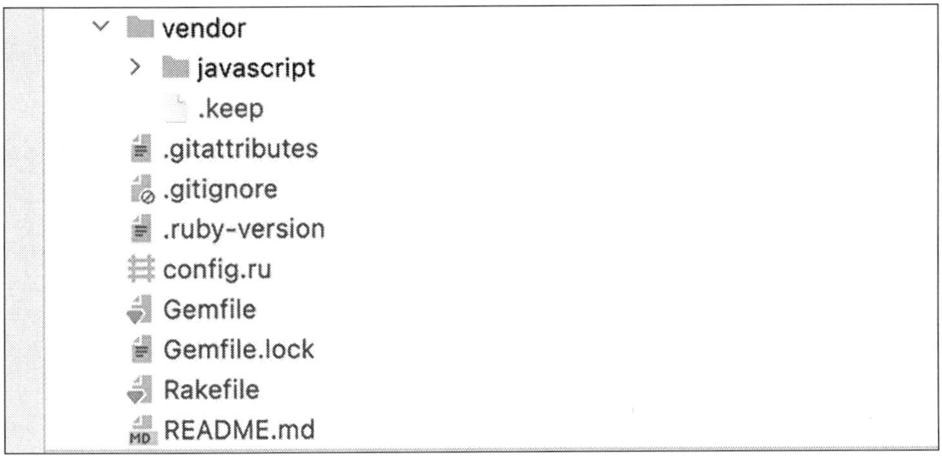

***Figure 3.11**: Exploring the "vendor" Directory and Other Files*

Besides all the folders we have mentioned so far, there are a few other files in the root of the application that are worth mentioning:

- **`Gemfile`**: The "**`Gemfile`**" is a plain text file where you specify the gems your application depends on, along with their versions.
- **`Gemfile.lock`**: The "**`Gemfile.lock`**" is a generated file that keeps track of the exact versions of the gems installed in your application. When you run the "**`bundle`**" command (we will run this command soon!), it not only installs the gems specified in the **`Gemfile`** but also creates or updates the **`Gemfile.lock`**. This ensures that your application uses the same gem versions across different environments and when collaborating with other developers. It helps maintain consistency and avoids potential conflicts caused by different gem versions.

By embracing "**`Convention over Configuration`**," Ruby on Rails empowers developers to be more productive, as they can quickly grasp the project structure and get things done without excessive configuration. This approach streamlines development, fostering a consistent and efficient workflow for building web applications. It is this principle that makes Rails a joy to work with and continues to attract developers to the framework.

Now that we are familiar with the content of our application, let's build the very first page of our Contacts application.

Creating the First Page of Your App

The very first page we will be creating is the "**`Home`**" page; it will be a very simple page with our Application Title and some text.

Before we do that, let's make sure all the dependencies that our app depends on are installed properly (all dependencies are enlisted in the Gemfile) by running the following bundle command on your terminal while you are inside the root directory of your application ("**contacts**" directory):

```
bundle install
```

Running the command "**bundle install**" ensures that all the dependencies (gems) specified in your **Gemfile** are properly installed and up-to-date. This command also updates the **Gemfile.lock** file, which serves as a record of the exact versions of each gem that are currently installed in your project.

Figure 3.12 shows the **bundle** command in action:

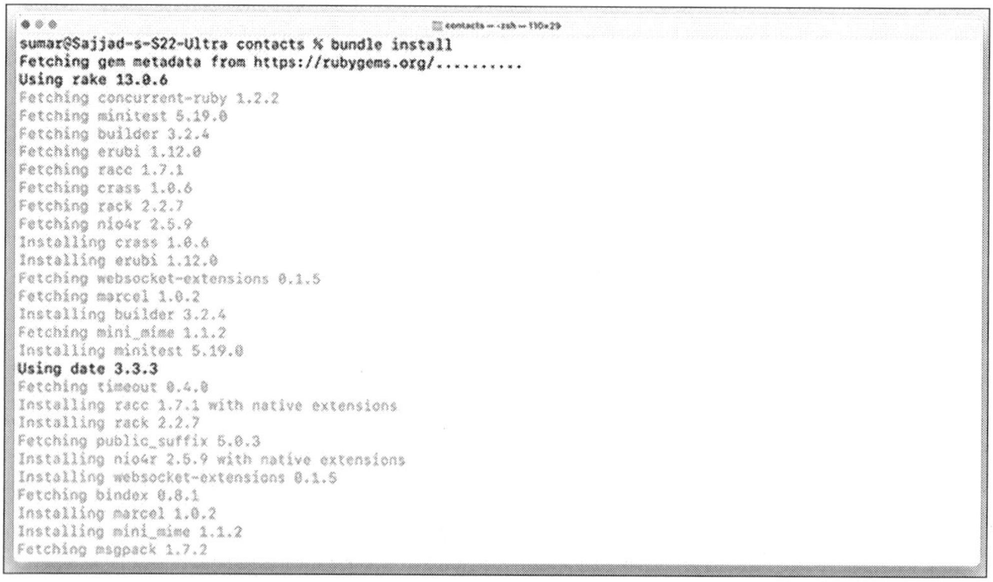

Figure 3.12: *Bundle Install Command*

To create the "**Home**" page, we need two of the three components from the MVC architecture:

1. Controller
2. View

We don't need a Model because we are not touching the database just yet.

Generating Your First Controller

For all the commands we will be executing throughout this chapter, it's important to ensure that we are inside our application's root directory, which, in this case, is named "**contacts**." This means that unless specified otherwise, we should navigate to the "**contacts**" directory in our terminal before running any commands. Staying within the application's root directory ensures that the commands are executed in the right context and avoid any unintended consequences. So, let's keep that in mind as we proceed with building our Rails application.

Now to generate the controller, run the following command in your terminal:

```
rails generate controller home
```

This command will create our "**`home_controller.rb`**" file inside the "**`app/controllers`**" folder along with a few other files, as shown in *Figure 3.13*:

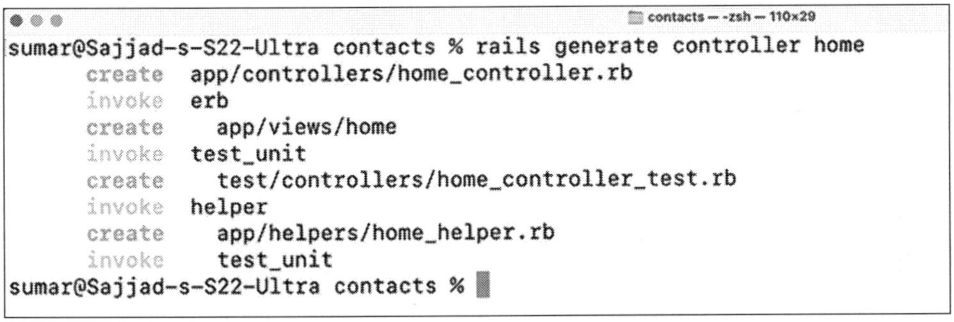

***Figure 3.13**: Rails Generate Controller Command*

For now, we only care about `` `app/controller/home_controller.rb` ``. Let's navigate to this file in our IDE and add the following "**`dashboard`**" method inside it. You can name the method whatever you want, but we suggest using "**`dashboard`**" so that you can easily follow along:

```
def dashboard
  # Nothing inside this method
end
```

The line starting with the **#** sign is a Ruby comment. The entire file will look something like this:

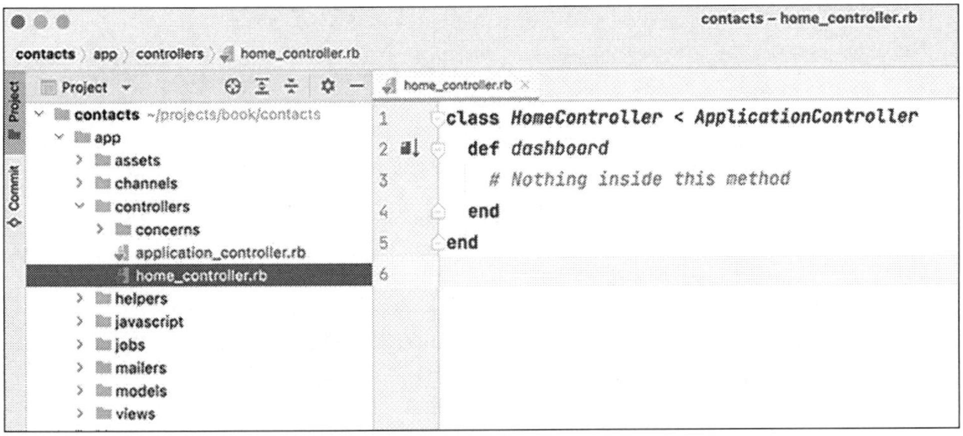

***Figure 3.14**: Home Controller*

We are done with our home controller, now it's time to create our first View.

Creating Your First View

Figure 3.13 shows the rails generate controller command. In addition to creating the "**HomeController**," it also created a new folder inside the "**app/views**" directory of our application called "**home**". This is where Rails expects us to create a view for our "**HomeController**." One thing we need to make sure of is to name our view in the following format:

```
<action_name>.html.erb
```

Following this convention will help rails automatically link views to their respective controller actions.

In our case, the action name in the controller is "**dashboard**." So, the view name should be "**dashboard.html.erb**." Now create a new file named "**dashboard.html.erb**" inside the "**app/views/home**" directory and add the following content:

```
<h1>Dashboard</h1>

<p>My Very First Rails App</p>
```

The entire file should look something like this:

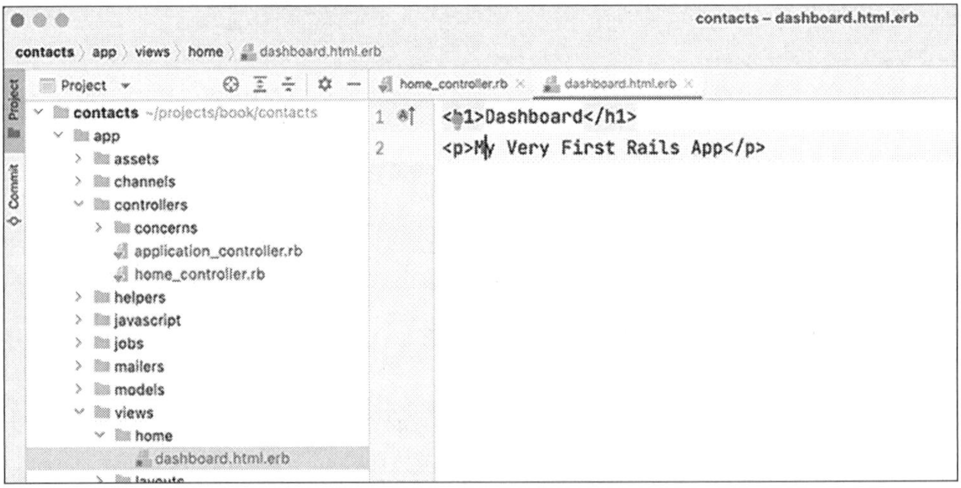

***Figure 3.15**: dashboard.html.erb*

Defining the Route

The very last thing we need to do is to add a URL mapping so that we can access this page in a browser. For that, we need to edit our "**config/routes.rb**" file and add the following line:

```
get '/dashboard', to: 'home#dashboard'
```

The entire file should look something like this:

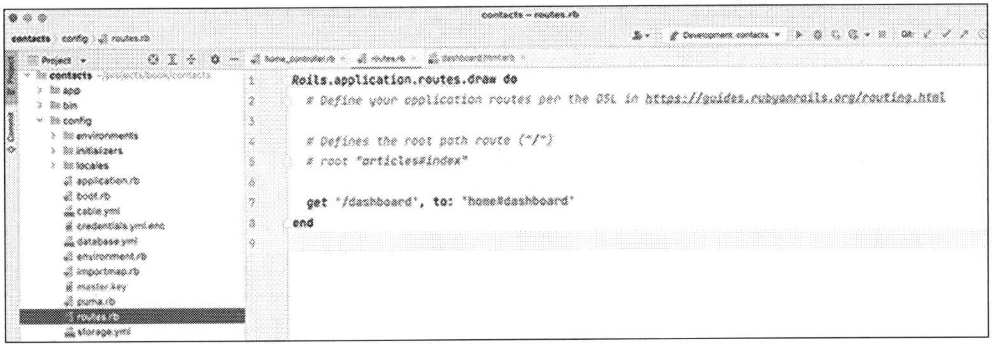

***Figure 3.16**: routes.rb*

That is it!

In total, we did three things: Created a controller with dashboard action, created a dashboard.html.erb view, and added a GET route for "**`dashboard`**" that points to our **`home`** controller **`dashboard`** action.

Now, it is time to run the development server and visit our App in the browser for the very first time!

Starting the Rails Server

To start the development server, all we need to do is run the following command:

```
rails server
```

This command will spin up our Rails server and start listening on http://127.0.0.1:3000, as follows:

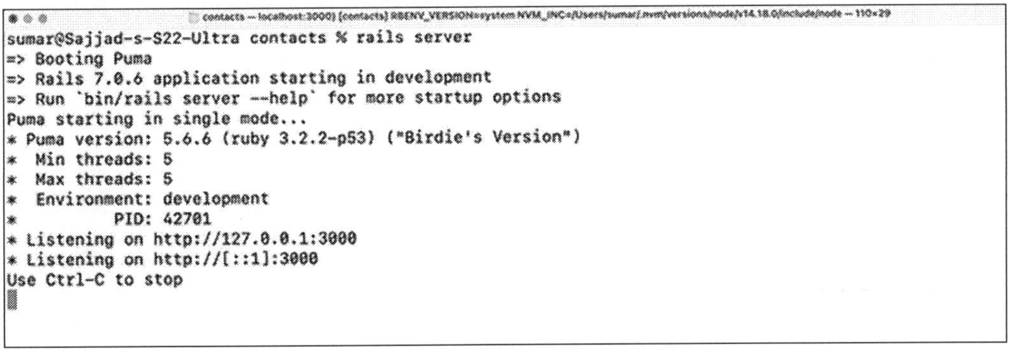

***Figure 3.17**: Starting Rails Server*

Now, you can copy the link in your terminal and paste it into the browser of your choice, and you should see the Rails welcome page:

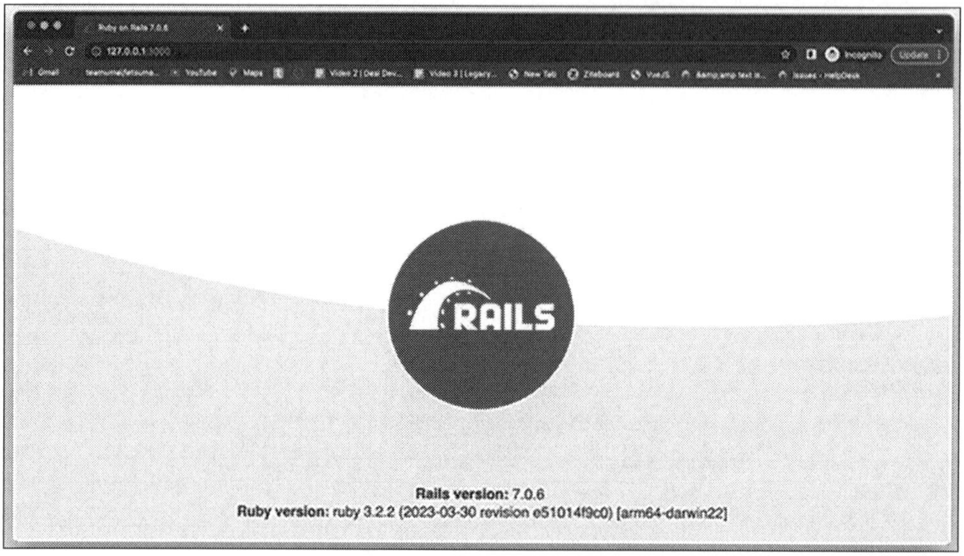

Figure 3.18: *Rails Welcome Page*

This means our server is up and running!

Accessing Your Page in the Browser

Now it's time that we visit our "**`dashboard`**" page in the browser. To do that, simply add "**`/dashboard`**" to the end of your base URL. The preceding URL will become "http://127.0.0.1:3000/dashboard".

Figure 3.19 shows our very first Ruby on Rails page that we just created:

Figure 3.19: *Dashboard Page*

Simple but beautiful - isn't it?

Take a moment to celebrate your very first Rails page! It is a milestone for sure.

Conclusion

In the journey of this chapter, we embarked on the exhilarating realm of Ruby on Rails, where we got a bird's-eye view of its structure, principles, and installation process. We uncovered the guiding principles that drive the Rails framework, understanding how it embraces Convention over Configuration to simplify our development endeavors. We explored the benefits that come with using Ruby on Rails, recognizing its potency in creating efficient and maintainable web applications.

We ventured into the practical domain, meticulously installing Ruby and Rails on our system. We navigated through the intricacies of setting up a new Rails project, deciphering its directory structure, and eventually crafting our very first web page. With each step, we uncovered essential aspects like generating controllers, creating views, defining routes, and initiating the Rails server.

As we close this chapter, remember that we have merely scratched the surface of the immense capabilities of Ruby on Rails. In the upcoming chapter, aptly titled "CRUD *Operations and Database Management*," we will take our knowledge to the next level. Brace yourself to dive deep into the world of Create, Read, Update, and Delete (CRUD) operations. We will not only expand our Contacts app but also master the art of managing databases in the context of web applications. Exciting times lie ahead as we unlock the potential of database-driven functionalities. Stay tuned for an enriching learning experience!

Short Quiz

1. **What is the primary goal of Agile development?**

    a. It holds the configuration files

    b. It contains third-party libraries

    c. It is where the main application code, including models, views, and controllers, is placed

    d. It stores assets like images and stylesheets

2. **Which directory in a Rails application contains version-controlled scripts defining changes to the database schema?**

    a. `app`

    b. `db`

   c. `config`

   d. `public`

3. **What is the purpose of the "`config`" directory in a Rails application?**

   a. It contains JavaScript files

   b. It houses the main application code

   c. It holds database-related files

   d. It stores important configuration files

4. **In which directory would you typically find test cases in a Rails application?**

   a. `app`

   b. `db`

   c. `public`

   d. `test`

5. **Which principle guides the design of a Rails application and makes assumptions about how things should be structured and behave?**

   a. Convention over Configuration

   b. Don't Repeat Yourself (DRY)

   c. Separation of Concerns (SoC)

   d. Model-View-Controller (MVC)

6. **What is the role of the "`Gemfile.lock`" in a Rails application?**

   a. It holds the configuration for the database connection

   b. It contains version-controlled scripts defining changes to the database schema

   c. It lists all the third-party gems and libraries required for the application

   d. It is where the main application code is placed

7. **What is the role of the "`Gemfile.lock`" in a Rails application?**

   a. It contains the secret credentials for the application

   b. It stores the version information of all installed gems, ensuring consistency across different environments

   c. It is where the main application code is placed

   d. It holds the configuration for the database connection

8. **In which directory can you find the "`seeds.rb`" file in a Rails application?**

   e. `app`

   f. `db`

   g. `config`

   h. `public`

9. **Where should all the commands be run when working on a Rails application?**

   i. Inside the "`app`" directory

   j. Inside the "`db`" directory

   k. Inside the `root` directory of the application

   l. Inside the "`config`" directory

10. **Which tool helps manage multiple Ruby installations on your system and allows easy switching between different Ruby versions?**

    m. Gemfile

    n. Gemfile.lock

    o. Rake

    p. Version Manager (for example, rbenv or RVM)

Chapter 4
CRUD Operations and Database Management

Introduction

In this chapter, we are about to supercharge our Contacts app with some serious firepower. As we embark on this chapter's journey, you will discover how Agile development principles can breathe life into your Contacts app. Just like the iterative and adaptive nature of Agile, we are going to iteratively enhance our app's functionalities step by step.

Imagine having the ability to Create, Read, Update, and Delete contacts seamlessly, responding to user needs like a well-choreographed dance. This is where CRUD operations come into play. We will guide you through each step, breaking down the complex into easily digestible concepts. By the time we are done, CRUD will become second nature to you.

But wait, there's more! Agile development isn't just about one thing; it's about fostering connections and fluidity. As we journey through this chapter, you will not only master CRUD but also learn the art of handling data relationships and associations. Your app will become a web of interconnected features, harmoniously working together.

Of course, we can't overlook the heart of your app – the database. Agile development means being agile with your data too. We will demystify database management, from migrations that evolve your schema gracefully to seeding data for a smooth start. By the end, you will be orchestrating your database like a maestro.

So get ready to Agile-ize your Contacts app! By the end of this chapter, it won't just be CRUD operations; it'll be a symphony of Agile-inspired functionalities. Say goodbye to rigid structures and hello to a dynamic, responsive app that evolves with your users' needs. Let's dive in and infuse Agile magic into every line of code!

Structure

In this chapter, we will discuss the following topics:

- Introduction to CRUD Operations
  - Understanding CRUD and Its Significance in Web Applications
  - Mapping CRUD to User Actions
- Creating Models, Views, and Controllers
  - Extending the MVC Architecture for CRUD Integration
  - Generating Models, Views, and Controllers for Contacts
  - Setting Up the Foundation for CRUD Operations
- Implementing Create Functionality
  - Adding a "`New Contact`" Form
  - Capturing User Input and Saving It in the Database
- Enabling Read Functionality
  - Creating a List View to Display All Contacts
  - Implementing a "`View Contact`" Feature for Individual Details
- Upgrading with Update Functionality
  - Integrating an "`Edit Contact`" Option
  - Pre-filling Form with Existing Data for Modification
  - Updating the Database with New Information
- Managing Deletions with Delete Functionality
  - Adding a "`Delete Contact`" Feature
  - Confirming User Intent and Removing Contacts
- Working with Associations and Relationships
  - Understanding Data Relationships Between Contacts and Other Entities
  - Incorporating Associations for Connected Data Models
- Database Management in Rails
  - Evolving Database Schema Using Migrations
  - Populating the Database with Seed Data
  - Ensuring Data Integrity and Efficiency Through Effective Management

Introduction to CRUD Operations

Unveiling the Power of CRUD

In the realm of web development, CRUD operations are the building blocks that empower interactive and dynamic web applications. CRUD, which stands for Create, Read, Update, and Delete, forms the core functionality of countless digital experiences we encounter daily. It's like having a versatile toolkit at your disposal, allowing you to shape, manage, and interact with data seamlessly.

Significance of CRUD in Web Applications

CRUD operations might sound technical, but their significance is profound. These operations enable users to perform essential tasks within web applications, turning static content into dynamic experiences. Think of your favorite e-commerce website: when you add an item to your cart (Create), view product details (Read), update your shipping address (Update), or remove an item from your order (Delete), you are essentially engaging in CRUD operations.

Mapping CRUD to User Actions

Understanding CRUD operations is like deciphering the language of user interaction with a web application:

- **Create (C):** This action corresponds to the ability to add new data records or entries to your application. In a contacts app, this would mean adding a new contact to your address book.
- **Read (R):** Reading is all about retrieving and displaying data. In our contacts app, it's akin to viewing your list of contacts or accessing an individual contact's details.
- **Update (U):** Updating involves modifying existing data records. In the context of our app, it means editing a contact's information, like changing a phone number or email address.
- **Delete (D):** Deletion lets users remove data records they no longer need. Within our contacts app, it equates to removing a contact entry from your address book.

To bring these concepts to life, we will take our trusty `Contacts` app and enhance it with CRUD functionality. We will show you, step by step, how to transform this basic app into a dynamic powerhouse that allows users to create, read, update, and delete their contacts. Along the way, you will gain valuable insights into how CRUD operations are implemented in the context of Ruby on Rails, one of the most powerful web development frameworks available.

Creating Models, Views, and Controllers

This section explores how to create Models, Views, and Controllers using Rail commands.

Extending the MVC Architecture for CRUD Integration

In the previous chapters, we introduced you to the Model-View-Controller (MVC) architectural pattern, which is the cornerstone of Ruby on Rails (Rails) development. It's an elegant way to separate an application into distinct components, each with a specific role. In MVC, models represent the data and business logic, views handle the presentation and user interface, and controllers manage the flow of data between models and views.

Now, as we are going to implement CRUD operations in our **`Contacts`** app, we will extend this MVC architecture to accommodate these fundamental actions. The beauty of Rails is that it streamlines this process, making it intuitive and efficient.

Generating Models, Views, and Controllers for Contacts

The Model: Representing Your Data

In our Contacts app, the model plays a pivotal role. It's responsible for defining the structure of the data we are dealing with – in this case, contact information. We will create a Contact model to define the attributes of a contact, such as their name, email address, and phone number.

To create a model, we have a rails command that we need to run on the terminal. The command format is as follows:

```
rails generate model <Model Name> <attribute_name>:<data_type> …
```

Here's an example of generating the Contact model and its attributes:

```
rails generate model Contact first_name:string last_name:string
email:string phone:string
```

Note: *"string" is the default datatype for attributes, so you can omit the datatype and shorten the command as follows:*

```
rails generate model Contact first_name last_name email phone
```

According to one of the core principles of Rails, that is, "*Convention of Configuration*", the model name should be singular.

Figure 4.1 shows the execution of the model generation command in the terminal of our **`contacts`** app:

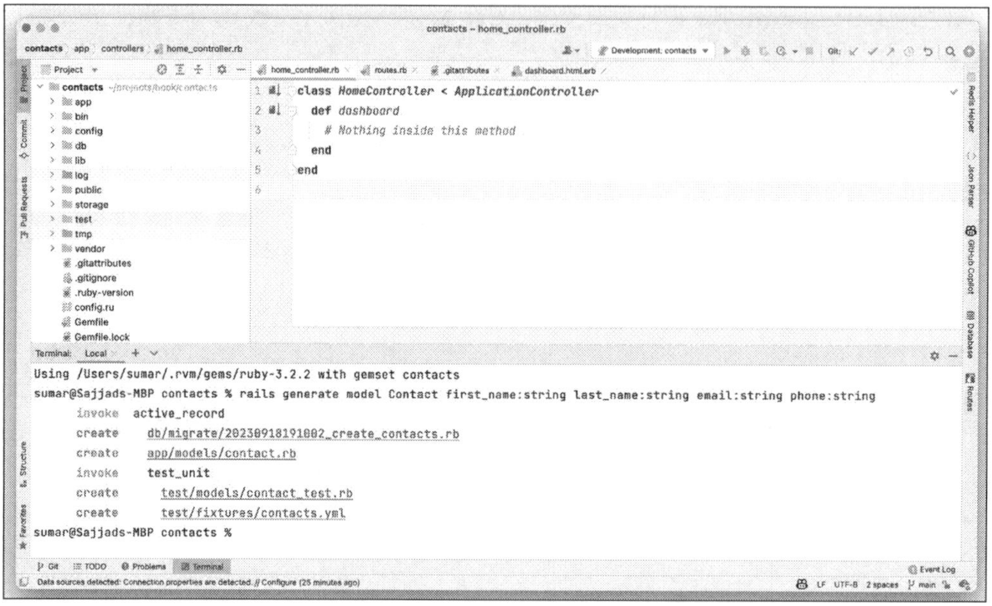

***Figure 4.1**: Running Rails Model Generation Command*

The model generation command has created quite a few files for us, let's have a look at some of these files one by one.

The Migration File

In Ruby on Rails, a migration file is a Ruby script that defines changes to the database schema. It's an essential part of Rails' database management system, allowing you to version control and manage the structure of your application's database.

Here are the key aspects of a migration file:

- **Database Schema Changes:** Migration files define operations for creating, modifying, or deleting database tables, columns, indexes, and other schema-related changes.
- **Timestamps:** Each migration file has a timestamp in its filename, indicating when the migration was created. This helps Rails maintain a chronological order for applying migrations. In *Figure* 4.1, the long number in the migration file name `` `20230918191002_create_contacts.rb` `` is the time stamp, that is, **`'20230918191002'`**.
- **Ruby Script:** A migration file is essentially a Ruby script. It includes a class that inherits from **`ActiveRecord::Migration`**, and this class defines methods for making changes to the database schema.

- **Up and Down OR Change Methods:** Traditional migration files contain **`up`** and **`down`** methods. The **`up`** method specifies the changes to apply to the database, while the **`down`** method defines how to revert those changes. In more recent versions of Rails, migration files often use the `change` method instead of separate **`up`** and **`down`** methods. This approach provides a more concise and expressive way to define both the migration and its reversal.
- **Idempotent:** Migration files are designed to be idempotent, meaning that applying the same migration multiple times should have the same result as applying it once. This property is crucial for managing database schema changes safely.

Figure 4.2 shows the content of the migration file generated by the model generation command:

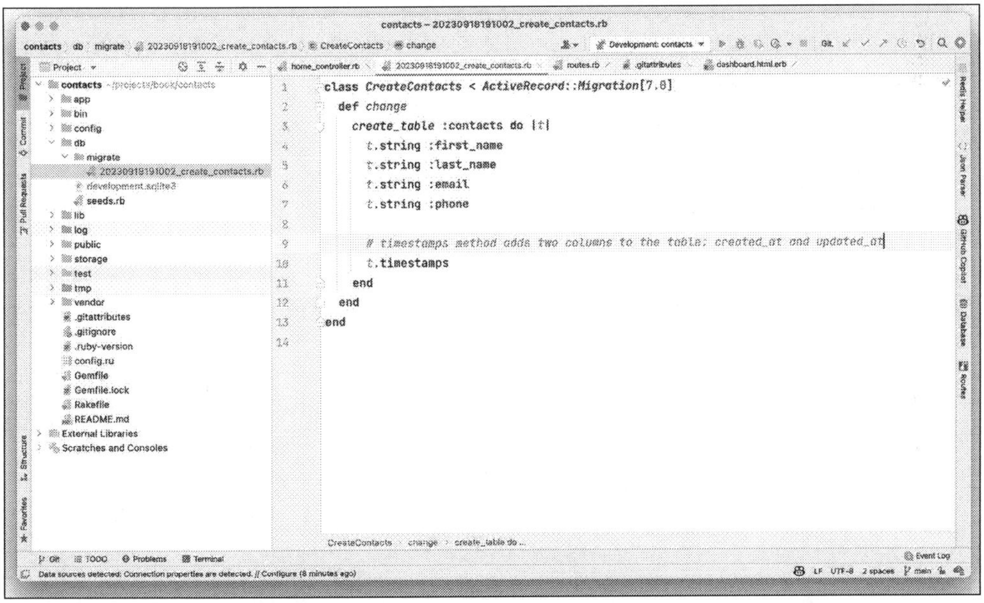

***Figure 4.2**: Contents of the Migration File*

All the attributes we added in the model generation command have been added to the migration script along with their datatypes.

Pro Tip: *At this point, you can manually edit the migration file and add more attributes if needed.*

The Model File

A model file is a Ruby class that represents a specific database table. *Figure* 4.3 shows that the model class inherits the **`ApplicationRecord`** class.

`ApplicationRecord` is a special base class in Rails that is used as a parent class for all model classes in a Rails application. It's an abstract representation of a database table and is designed to provide common functionality and configuration options that can be shared across multiple models.

By inheriting from **`ApplicationRecord`**, Rails models gain access to various features provided by ActiveRecord (Object-Relational Mapping (ORM) library in Rails), including database table associations, data validation, and querying capabilities. This class allows developers to define the structure and behavior of their application's data models while benefiting from Rails' built-in database management functionality.

Here's a breakdown of all the components of a model file:

1. **Database Representation:** A model file defines how data should be structured in a particular database table. Each model typically corresponds to a single table in the database.
2. **Data Validation:** Models include validations to ensure that the data stored in the database meets specific criteria. For example, you can specify that a user's email address must be unique or that a contact must have a first name and last name.
3. **Business Logic:** Besides defining data structure, models can also include business logic related to the data they represent. This can involve calculations, data transformations, and more.
4. **Associations:** Models can define associations between different tables. For example, in our contacts application, you might have a "**`Contact`**" model associated with many "**`Addresses`**" or "**`Emergency Contacts`**" tables.
5. **Database Operations:** Models provide methods for creating, reading, updating, and deleting records in the associated database table.
6. **Callbacks:** Models can define callbacks that trigger certain actions before or after specific events, such as before saving a record or after destroying a record.

Figure 4.3 shows the content of the model file generated by the model generation command:

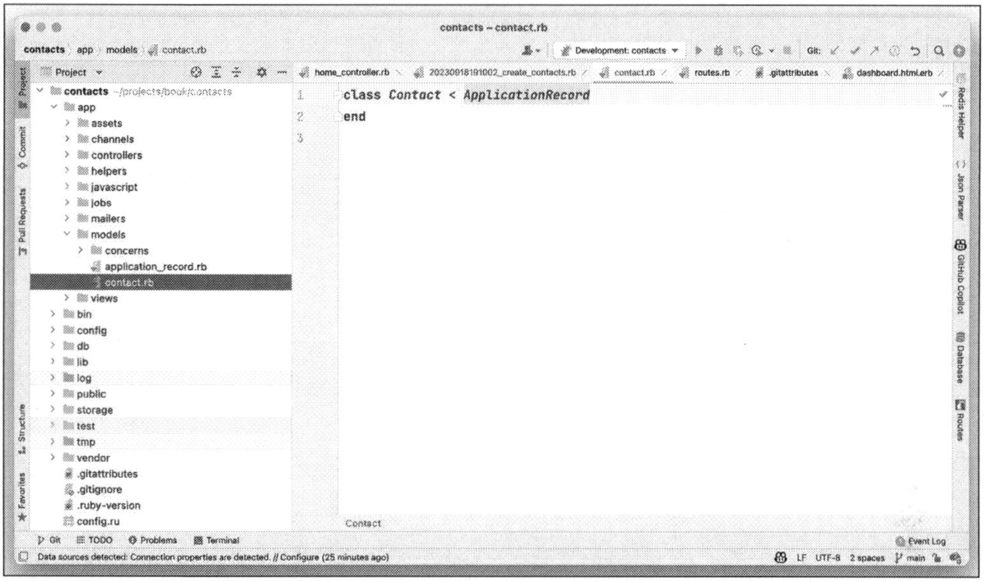

Figure 4.3: *Contents of the Model File*

There is nothing inside the model class yet, but as we progress with this chapter, we will be adding some of the components mentioned earlier.

The rest of the files created by the model generation command (**`test/fixtures/contacts.yml`** and **`test/models/contact_test.rb`**) are related to writing automated tests for our application. We will delve into these files extensively in *Chapter 7, Testing and Test-Driven Development*.

Once we have the migration file ready with all the required attributes, it is time to run the migration to create the corresponding database table:

```
rails db:migrate
```

Figure 4.4 shows the **`rails db:migrate`** command in action and generated **`schema.rb`** file:

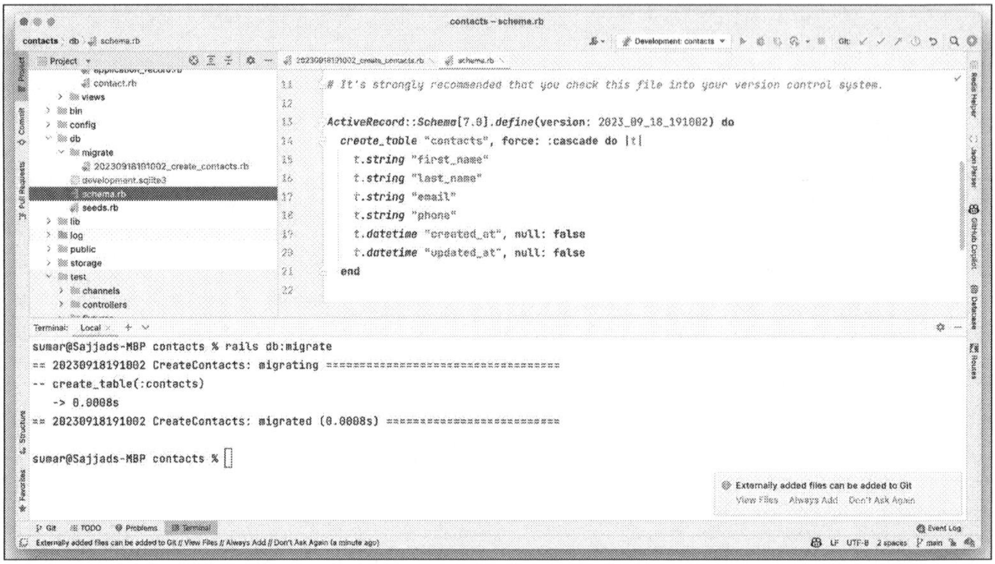

Figure 4.4: *rails db:migrate command in action*

The '**`schema.rb`**' file is an automatically generated file that represents the current schema or structure of the database associated with the Rails application. It provides a snapshot of the database's tables, columns, indexes, and their relationships in a format that Rails can use to recreate the database schema when needed. This file is crucial for database version control, schema migrations, and ensuring that multiple developers working on the same project have a consistent database structure.

The next step is to create the "**`View`**". However, since views usually correspond to the "**`Controller`**" actions, let's create both the **`View`** and the **`Controller`** in one go with the following command:

```
rails generate controller Contacts index
```

In the preceding command, the "**`rails generate controller <Controller Name>`**" part is responsible for creating the controller, while the \`**`index`**\` keyword is telling the rails generator to create an "**`index`**" action "**`inside`**" the controller, an "**`index.html.erb`**" view file, and adds an index route in the **`routes.rb`** file. According to one of the core principles of Rails, that is, "**`Convention of Configuration`**," the controller name should be plural.

Figure 4.5 shows the "**`rails generate controller`**" command in action:

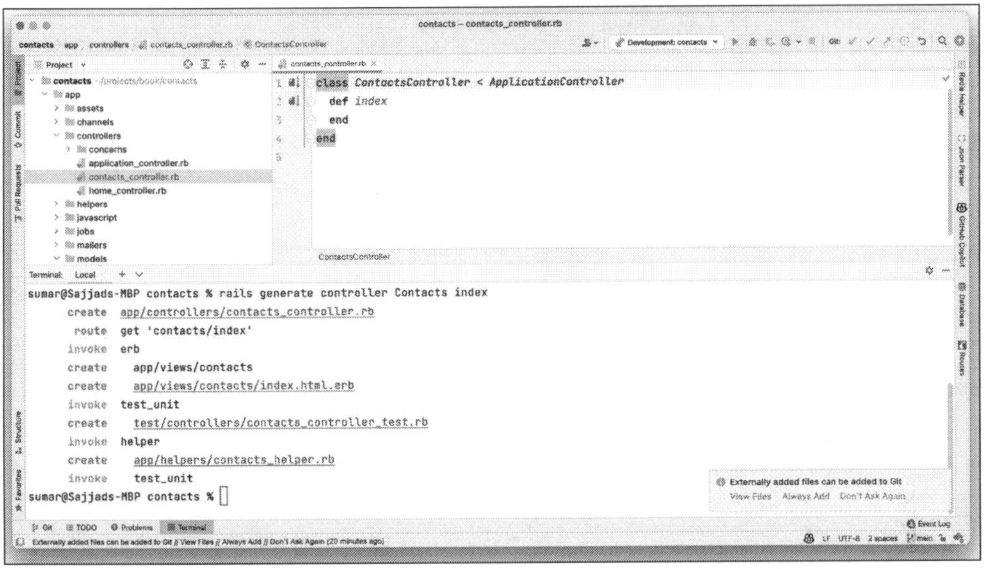

***Figure 4.5**: Rails generate controller command in action*

The controller generation command has generated the following files for us:

1. `app/controllers/contacts_controller.rb`
2. `app/views/contacts/index.html.erb`
3. `test/controllers/contacts_controller_test.rb`
4. `app/helpers/contacts_helper.rb`

Along with all these files, it also added the `get 'contacts/index'` route in the **`routes.rb`** file.

If you look closely at the contents of the **`contacts_controller.rb`** file (see *Figure* 4.5), it has the empty index action method added by the rails generate controller command.

Note: *If you only want to create the controller, helper, and test file, use the following command instead:*

```
rails generate controller <Controller Name>
```

The Controller: Managing Interactions

Controllers act as intermediaries between models and views, directing traffic in your application. In our **`Contacts`** app, we have created a controller specifically designed to handle CRUD operations for contacts. This controller will receive requests from the user, interact with the model to perform CRUD actions, and then render the appropriate view to show the result. It's the glue that binds models and views together seamlessly.

The View: Crafting the User Interface

The view layer of MVC is where the user interacts with your application. In our context, views will dictate how contact information is presented to users. We have already generated the view to display a list of contacts, and we will generate more views to see individual contact details and provide forms for creating and editing contacts. Rails excels at rendering views based on data from models, simplifying the development of user-friendly interfaces.

Helper and Test Files

In addition to the controller and view files, we have test and helper files. Let's dig into those, one by one:

- **Helper Files**: Helper files are part of the MVC (Model-View-Controller) architecture, where they belong to the "`View`" component. These files contain methods and functions that can be used to assist and simplify the creation of views or templates. Helpers are especially useful for adding reusable logic or HTML elements to views. For example, you might have a helper method that formats a date, and you can call this method within your views to display dates consistently. Helper files are typically named after the corresponding controller and are located in the `app/helpers` directory.
- **Test Files:** Test files, on the other hand, are used for writing automated tests to ensure that your Rails application functions correctly. Rails provides a testing framework that includes tools for unit testing, integration testing, and more. Test files are typically located in the test directory of your Rails application and are organized based on the type of tests they contain. For instance, unit tests for models are placed in the `test/models` directory, while integration tests for controllers can be found in the `test/controllers` directory. Testing is an essential part of Rails development to validate that your application behaves as expected and to catch and fix issues early in the development process. We will have a deep look at testing in *Chapter 7, Testing and Test-Driven Development*, of this book.

Setting Up the Foundation for CRUD Operations

Now, it's time to set up the foundation of CRUD operations. We will see how all these operations map to the controller actions.

To implement CRUD, we need to have the following action methods in our controller:

1. `new`: Responsible for presenting the form to create new contacts.
2. `create`: Responsible for creating the contact record in the database.

3. **show**: Responsible for showing details about a specific contact.
4. **edit**: Responsible for presenting the form to edit a contact.
5. **update**: Responsible for updating a contact.
6. **destroy**: Responsible for deleting a contact from the database.

Now, let's add all the action methods inside our **contacts** controller:

```
class ContactsController < ApplicationController
  # GET request to /contacts/new
  def new
  end

  # GET request to /contacts/:id
  def show
  end

  # POST request to /contacts
  def create
  end

  # GET request to /contacts/:id/edit
  def edit
  end

  # PATCH/PUT request to /contacts/:id
  def update
  end

  # DELETE request to /contacts/:id
  def destroy
  end
end
```

Once we add these methods to the controller, it will look something like *Figure* 4.6:

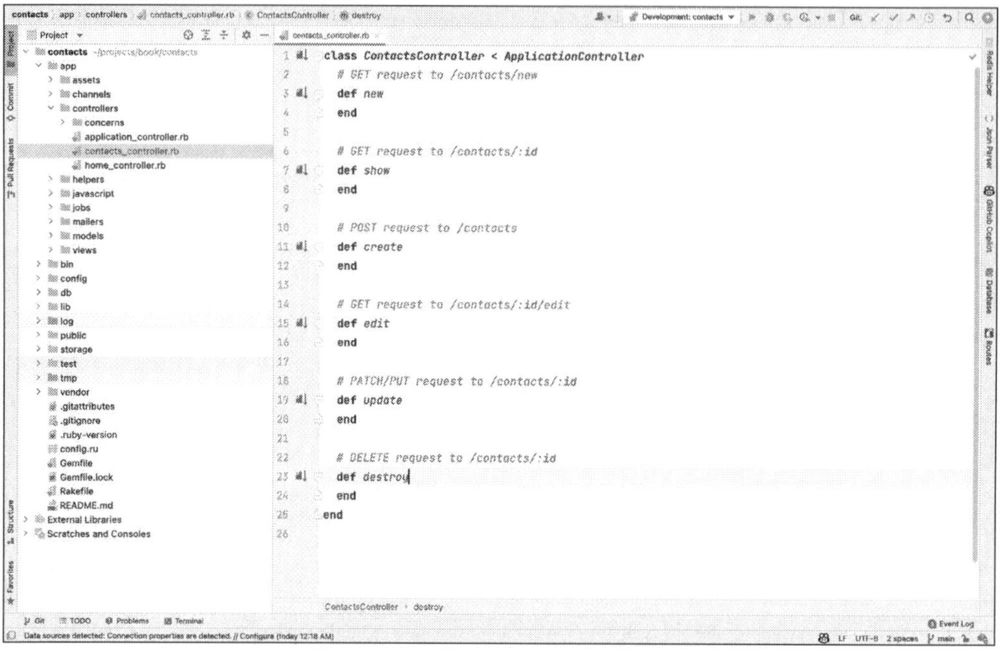

Figure 4.6: *Contacts controller with all CRUD actions*

Comments above each method show the appropriate route for each action. Next, we will add all these routes to our **routes.rb** file:

```
get 'contacts/new'
get 'contacts', to: 'contacts#index'
get 'contacts/:id/edit', to: 'contacts#edit', as: 'edit_contact'
get 'contacts/:id', to: 'contacts#show', as: 'contact'
post 'contacts', to: 'contacts#create'
patch 'contacts/:id', to: 'contacts#update'
delete 'contacts/:id', to: 'contacts#destroy'
```

Once you add the preceding code to the **routes.rb** file, it should look something like *Figure 4.7*:

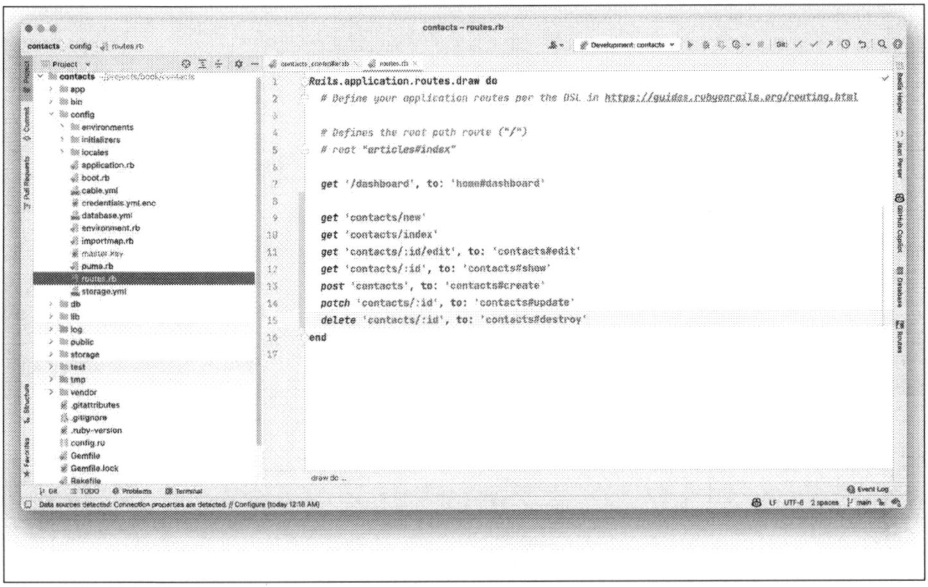

Figure 4.7: *routes.rb file*

At any point during the development, you can run the following command in the terminal to view all the routes defined by your app:

```
rails routes
```

This command will output all the routes defined by your app in the following manner:

```
                         Prefix Verb   URI Pattern
Controller#Action
                               dashboard GET    /dashboard(.:format)
home#dashboard
                            contacts_new GET    /contacts/new(.:format)
contacts#new
                          contacts_in-
dex GET    /contacts/index(.:format)
contacts#index
                              edit_con-
tact GET    /contacts/:id/edit(.:format)
contacts#edit
                                        con-
tact GET    /contacts/:id(.:format)
contacts#show
                                contacts POST   /contacts(.:format)
contacts#create
...
...
```

With all the routes in place, we are now ready to implement the CRUD actions.

Implementing Create Functionality

There are two parts to implementing the create functionality for a web application:

1. Presenting a form for users to fill in the contact information, that is, name, phone number, and more.

2. Saving the information provided by the user to the database.

To present the form where the user can input contact information, we use the '`new`' method, whereas to save it in the database, we use the '`create`' method.

To understand where we are at the moment, let's run the local server using the following command:

```
rails server
```

Now, in your browser, navigate to the following URL: http://localhost:3000/contacts/new.

You should see an error page indicating that the requested page is missing the HTML template.

Figure 4.8 shows the template missing error page for our `contacts/new` page:

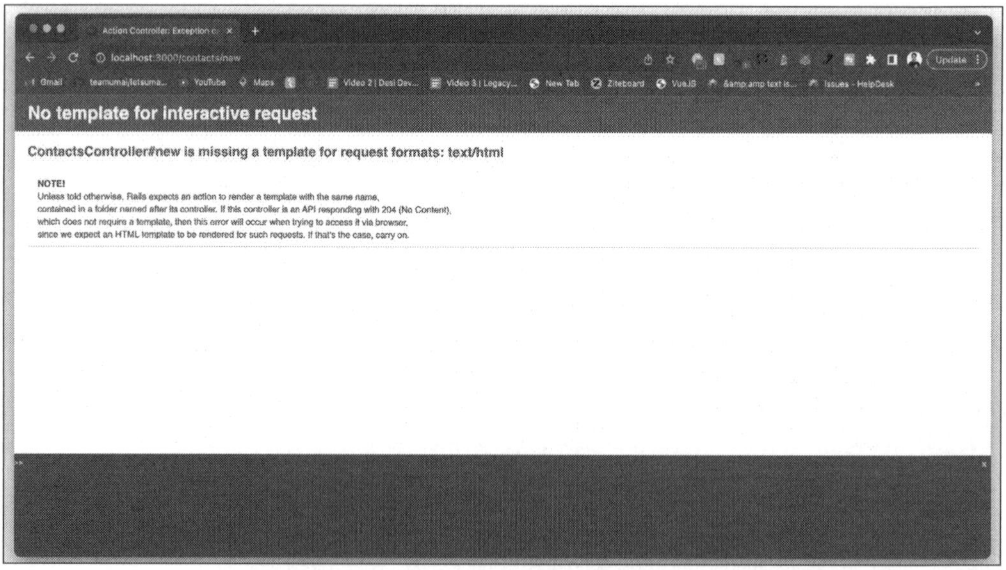

Figure 4.8: *Template missing error page*

This error occurs because we have not yet created the '`new.html.erb`' view file for the '`new`' action method. Let's create it now!

Create a new file under '**app/views/contacts/new.html.erb**' with the following content:

```
<h1>New Contact Page</h1>
```

After saving the file, refresh the error page in your browser, or navigate again to the following URL:

http://localhost:3000/contacts/new. You should see the page you just created.

Figure 4.9 shows the contacts/new page opened in the browser:

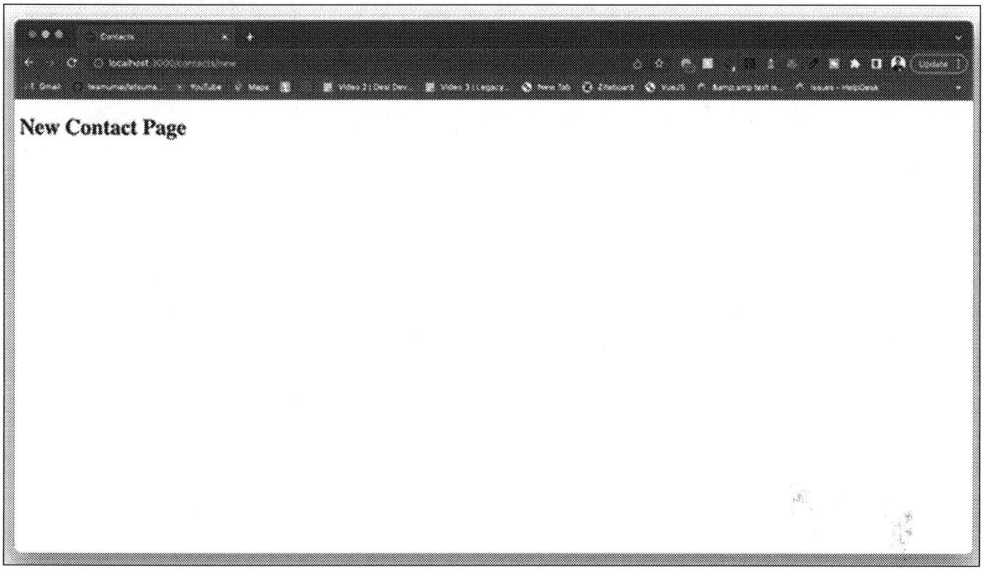

Figure 4.9: *New contact page*

Now, it's time to create a form so that users can input contact information. To do that, first, we have to initialize a new contact object and save it in an instance variable (instance variables start with '**@**' and are accessible inside the view), so that we can reference it in the view file.

Replace your existing '**new**' method inside the **contacts_controller.rb** file with the following code:

```
def new
  @contact = Contact.new
end
```

Once we have the contact object stored in an instance variable, let's use it in the view file and create a form to input the contact information. Add the following code inside the '**contacts/new.html.erb**' file:

```
<h1>New Contact</h1>

<!--form_with is a rails helper method that creates a form for a model
object.
form_with takes a model object and a url (where it will post the data)
as arguments.
contacts_path is a rails helper method that returns the path for the
contacts create action-->

<%= form_with model: @contact, url: contacts_path do |form| %>

  <!--form.label is a rails helper method that creates a label for a
form field-->
  <div class="field">
    <%= form.label :first_name %>
    <!--form.text_field is a rails helper method that creates a text field
for a form-->
    <%= form.text_field :first_name %>
  </div>

  <div class="field">
    <%= form.label :last_name %>
    <%= form.text_field :last_name %>
  </div>

  <div class="field">
    <%= form.label :email %>
    <%= form.text_field :email %>
  </div>

  <div class="field">
    <%= form.label :phone %>
    <%= form.text_field :phone %>
  </div>

  <div class="actions">
```

```
    <!--form.submit is a rails helper method that creates a submit but-
ton for a form
    submitting the form will send a POST request to the url specified in
the form_with method-->
    <%= form.submit 'Create Contact' %>
  </div>
<% end %>
```

Note: *Comments in the preceding code are only for explanation; in general, no comments are needed unless we really need them.*

Once you add the preceding code, `contacts/new.html.erb` file should look something like this:

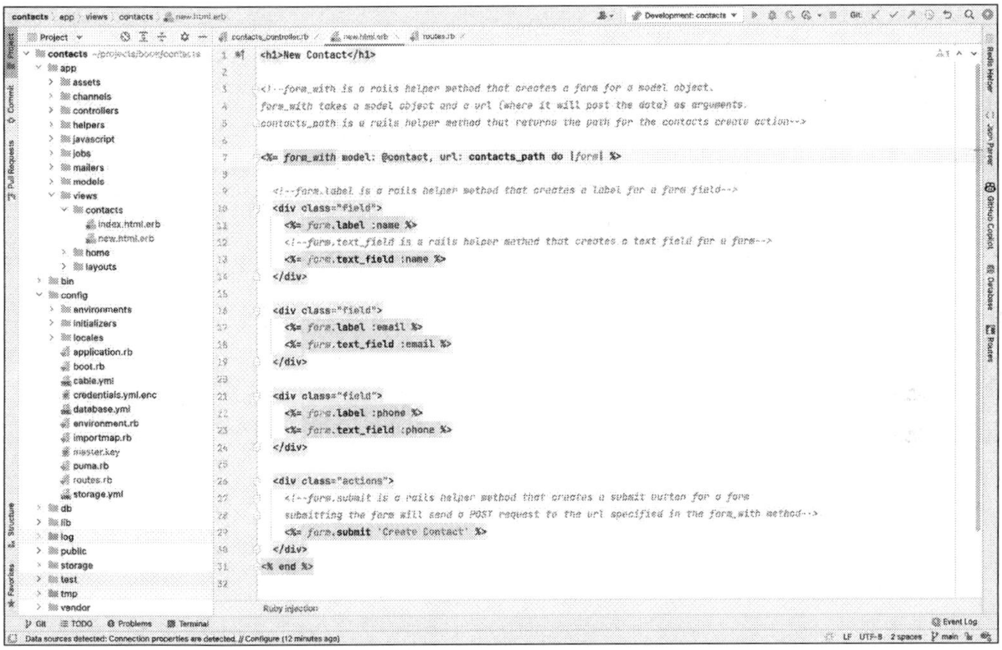

Figure 4.10: *contacts/new.html.erb file*

And the contents of "`ContactsController`" should look something like this:

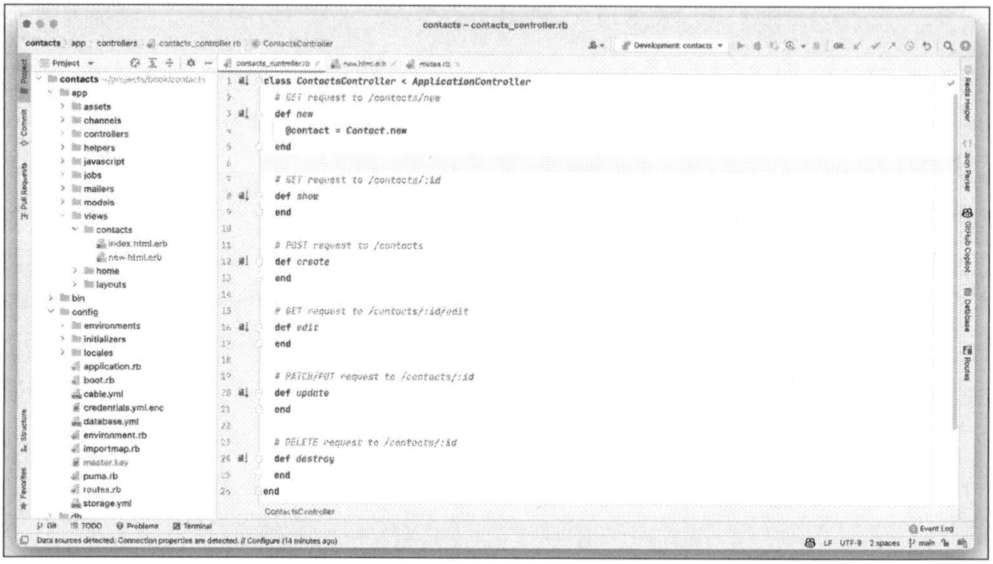

Figure 4.11: *app/controllers/contacts_controller.rb file*

At this point, the local rails server should already be running (if not, run it with the rails server command). Revisit http://localhost:3000/contacts/new URL in your browser, and you should see a contacts form where you can input contact information.

Figure 4.12 shows http://localhost:3000/contacts/new opened in the browser:

Figure 4.12: *The new contact form page*

It's not very beautiful, but will serve the purpose.

If you play around with it, you will notice that you can add the data in the input fields, but clicking submit does not do anything. Yet!

However, in reality, if you submit the form, a POST request is being made to the **`ContactsController`**'s "**`create`**" action with all the data you entered in the form. You can verify this by looking at the server logs in your terminal (where your local server is running).

Figure 4.13 shows form submission logs to **`ContactsController`** create action:

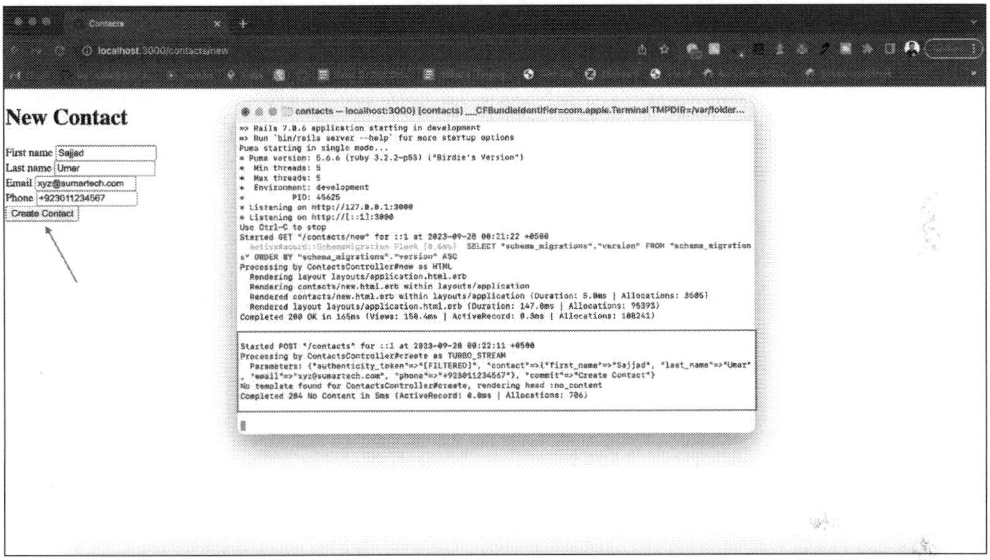

Figure 4.13: *Server logs on form submission*

If you look closely, logs suggest a POST request has been made at the "**`/contacts`**" route. The request was processed by the **`ContactsController#create`** action.

Reading further gives out that the request has the following parameters as a payload:

```
Parameters: {"authenticity_token"=>"[FILTERED]", "contact"=>{"first_
name"=>"Sajjad", "last_name"=>"Umar", "email"=>"xyz@sumartech.com",
"phone"=>"+923011234567"}, "commit"=>"Create Contact"}
```

The request has three key-value pairs, as follows:

1. **`"authenticity_token"=>"[FILTERED]"`**: This is usually a security measure to protect against cross-site request forgery (CSRF) attacks. The [**`FILTERED`**] suggests that Rails is hiding the actual token for security reasons.
2. **The contact object:** Contains **`first_name`**, **`last_name`**, **`email`**, and **`phone`**.
3. **`"commit"=>"Create Contact"`**: This part typically represents the label on the button or action that triggered the form submission. In this case, it tells the server that you want to **`"Create Contact"`**.

If you read the logs further, it shows a warning about missing templates, because the create method does not have any view and we are not redirecting to any other page. Ultimately, the request was completed with status code 204 - No Content.

Now, all we need to do is to tell Rails what to do in the "**create**" action of **ContactsController**.

Replace your "**create**" action with the following code:

```
  # POST request to /contacts
 def create
   # Mass assignment of form fields into Contact object
   # contact_prams is a method defined below
   @contact = Contact.new(contact_params)


   # Save the Contact object to the database
   if @contact.save
     # On success: redirect to the show contact page (we will implement
that shortly)
     redirect_to @contact
   else
     # On failure: render the new contact form so the user can fix the
errors
     render :new, status: :unprocessable_entity
   end
 end
```

The code has some additional comments to explain what the code is actually doing. Take some time to read all the comments to grasp every aspect of the code.

By default, all the request parameters are accessible through the `**params**` method. To create our contact object, we can use something like `**params[:contact]**` for mass-assigning the fields into the contact object. However, we are using another Rails security feature called Strong Parameters to avoid security concerns.

Strong params are a feature of Rails that allows developers to control which parameters are permitted in a controller action. This helps to prevent mass assignment vulnerabilities, which can occur when a user sends unexpected parameters to a controller action.

Mass assignment vulnerabilities can be very serious, as they can allow an attacker to take control of your application or steal sensitive data. For example, an attacker could send a parameter to a controller action that allows them to change their own user role to "**admin**."

Strong params help to prevent these vulnerabilities by requiring developers to explicitly specify which parameters are allowed to be updated. This means that even if an attacker sends unexpected parameters, they will be ignored.

So, in the preceding code, we are using the `**contact_params**` method for mass assignment. It is a private method that you need to define at the bottom of **ContactsController**. Here is the code for this method:

```
private

  def contact_params

    params.require(:contact).permit(:first_name, :last_name, :email,
:phone)

  end
```

The require method ensures that the contact parameter is present in the request. If it is not, an **ActionController::ParameterMissing** exception will be raised.

The `permit` method allows only the specified parameters to be updated. In this case, the only permitted parameters are **first_name**, **last_name**, **email**, and **phone**. Any other parameters that are sent in the request will be ignored.

Once you add this code, your controller should look something like this:

```
class ContactsController < ApplicationController

  # GET request to /contacts/new

  def new

    @contact = Contact.new

  end


  # GET request to /contacts/:id

  def show

  end


  # GET request to /contacts

  def index

  end


  # POST request to /contacts

  def create
```

```
    # Mass assignment of form fields into Contact object
    # contact_prams is a method defined below
    @contact = Contact.new(contact_params)

    # Save the Contact object to the database
    if @contact.save
      # On success: redirect to the show contact page (we will imple-
ment that shortly)
      redirect_to @contact
    else
      # On failure: render the new contact form so the user can fix the
errors
      render :new, status: :unprocessable_entity
    end
  end

  # GET request to /contacts/:id/edit
  def edit
  end

  # PATCH/PUT request to /contacts/:id
  def update
  end

  # DELETE request to /contacts/:id
  def destroy
  end

  private
  def contact_params
    params.require(:contact).permit(:first_name, :last_name, :email,
:phone)
  end
end
```

Figure 4.14 only shows what we have implemented so far. A few methods have been removed temporarily to fit everything nicely into one screenshot.

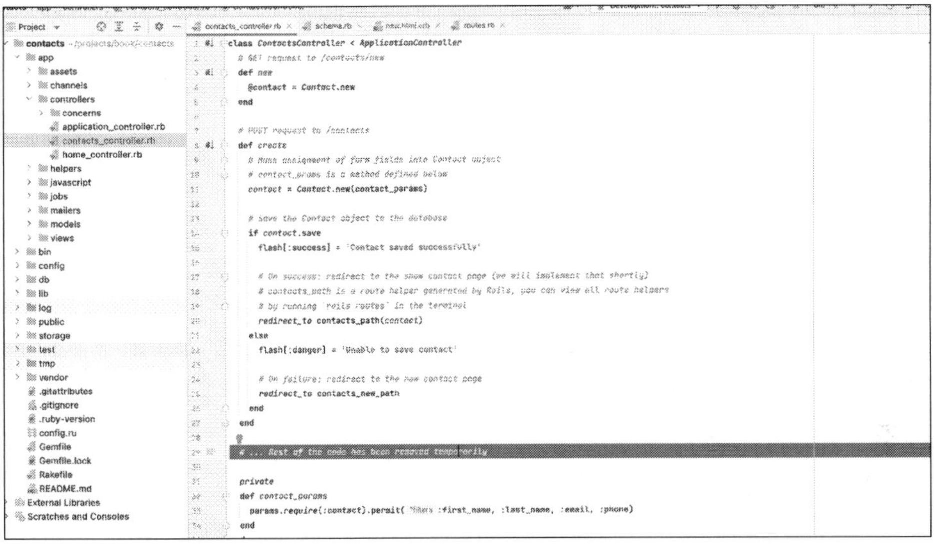

Figure 4.14: *ContactsController after adding the "create" method implementation and strong params*

Now, run the local server (if it is not already running) and revisit http://localhost:3000/contacts/new on your browser. Fill in the form data and click the "**`Create Contact`**" button. Did something happen? Probably not much visually, but if you look at the logs, quite a few things have happened.

Figure 4.15 shows logs for creating contact on form submission:

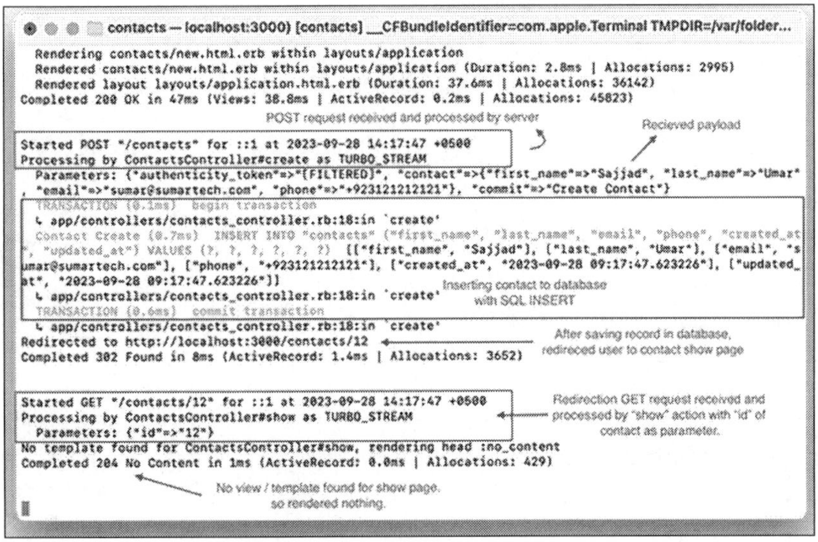

Figure 4.15: *Server logs on form submission*

Let me explain what has happened throughout the lifecycle of the form submission request:

1. The server received a POST request with all the parameters to create contact.
2. The request was processed by **`ContactsController#create`** action.
3. A new contact record was inserted into the database.
4. The user was redirected to the **`ContactsController#show`** page.
5. A **`GET`** request was received by the server and processed by the **`ContactsController#show`** page with the newly created contact ID as a parameter.
6. The request was completed with no view/template warning for the show page.

All the events are highlighted in *Figure* 4.15.

As of now, we are successfully able to present a "**`New Contact`**" form to users, and when they submit the form, we create a contact record in the “contacts” table.

Now, it’s time to implement the second part of C**R**UD, which is the read operation, that is, show and index pages.

Enabling Read Functionality

Read functionality includes reading all contacts from the database, presenting them on screen, and viewing details of any specific contact.

So, there are two controller actions that we will be using to implement these functionalities, that is, "**`show`**" and "**`index`**":

1. **`show`:** Responsible for fetching details about a specific contact with the help of contact ID, and displaying all the details on a page.
2. **`index`:** Responsible for fetching all contacts from the database, and displaying them in the form of a list.

Replace your "**`show`**" and "**`index`**" methods of your **`ContactsController`** with the following code:

```
# GET request to /contacts/:id
 def show
   # finding a contact by id from the database
   @contact = Contact.find(params[:id])
 end
```

```
 # GET request to /contacts
  def index
    # getting all contacts from the database
    @contacts = Contact.all
  end
```

Now, we need to add appropriate views to present data. First, let's add a view for "**index**" action. Create a new view file named "**app/views/contacts/index.html.erb**" and add the following code:

Note: *Take time to read the code and all the comments to understand what's happening in the code.*

```
<!-- contacts/index.html.erb -->

<!-- Display the page title -->
<h1>All Contacts</h1>

<!-- Link to create a new contact -->
<%= link_to 'New Contact', contacts_new_path %>

<!-- Create a table for displaying contacts -->
<table>
  <thead>
  <!-- Define table header row -->
  <tr>
    <!-- Column headers for contact attributes -->
    <th>First Name</th>
    <th>Last Name</th>
    <th>Email</th>
    <th>Phone</th>
    <th>Action</th>
  </tr>
  </thead>
  <tbody>
  <!-- Iterate through each contact in the @contacts list -->
  <% @contacts.each do |contact| %>
```

```
    <!-- Create a table row for each contact -->
    <tr>
      <!-- Display contact attributes in corresponding columns -->
      <td><%= contact.first_name %></td>
      <td><%= contact.last_name %></td>
      <td><%= contact.email %></td>
      <td><%= contact.phone %></td>
      <td>
        <!-- Links for showing, editing, and deleting a contact -->
        <%= link_to 'Show', contact_path(contact) %>
        <%= link_to 'Edit', edit_contact_path(contact) %>
        <%= link_to "Destroy", contact_path(contact), data: {
          turbo_method: :delete,   # Specify a Turbo Stream delete method
          turbo_confirm: "Are you sure?"  # Display a confirmation dialog
        } %>
      </td>
    </tr>
  <% end %>
  </tbody>
</table>
```

Now if you visit the following URL, you should be able to see all the contacts you have created so far: http://localhost:3000/contacts.

Figure 4.16 shows the contacts index page:

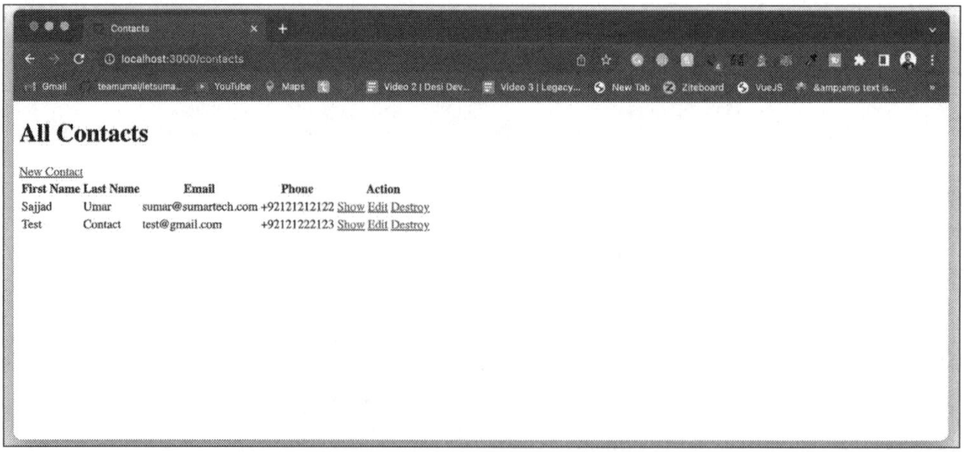

Figure 4.16: *Contacts index page*

As you can see, we have added a few action links as well. While the "**`New Contact`**" link should work already, we will implement the rest shortly.

Create a new view file at "**`app/views/contacts/show.html.erb`**" with the following code:

```
<!-- contacts/show.html.erb -->


<!-- Display the page title -->
<h1>Contact Details</h1>


<!-- Display contact attributes using @contact instance variable defined inside "show" action -->
<p><strong>First Name:</strong> <%= @contact.first_name %></p>
<p><strong>Last Name:</strong> <%= @contact.last_name %></p>
<p><strong>Email:</strong> <%= @contact.email %></p>
<p><strong>Phone:</strong> <%= @contact.phone %></p>


<!-- Link to go back to the contacts list -->
<%= link_to 'Back', contacts_path %>
```

Now, if you click the "**`Show`**" link on any of the contacts listed on the "**`index`**" page, you will be redirected to the "**`show`**" page with the details of that specific contact.

Figure 4.17 shows the contacts show page:

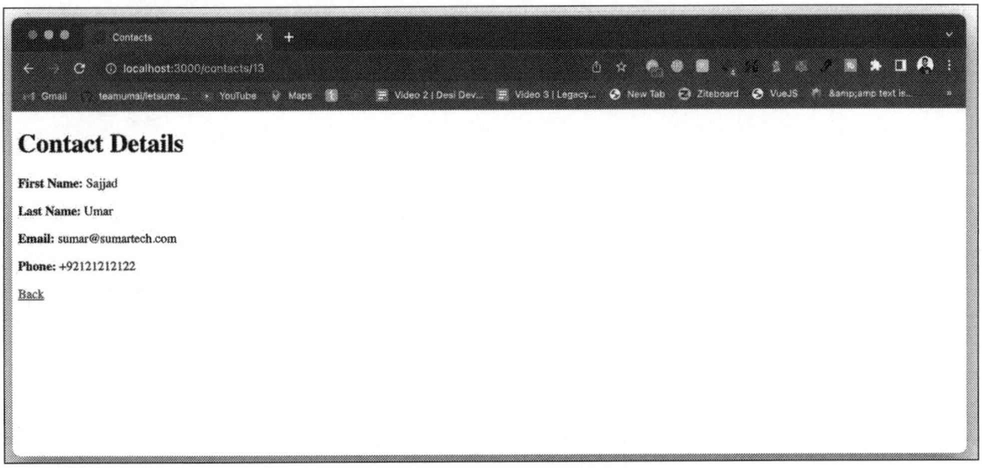

Figure 4.17: *Contacts show page*

Now the entire Read flow is complete; play around with your contacts app and celebrate the progress before we go ahead and add the Update part of CRUD operations.

At this point, our **ContactsController** code should look something like this:

```
class ContactsController < ApplicationController
  # GET request to /contacts/new
  def new
    @contact = Contact.new
  end

  # GET request to /contacts/:id
  def show
    # finding a contact by id from the database
    @contact = Contact.find(params[:id])
  end

  # GET request to /contacts
  def index
    # getting all contacts from the database
    @contacts = Contact.all
  end

  # POST request to /contacts
  def create
    # Mass assignment of form fields into Contact object
    # contact_prams is a method defined below
    @contact = Contact.new(contact_params)

    # Save the Contact object to the database
    if @contact.save
      # On success: redirect to the show contact page (we will implement
that shortly)
      redirect_to @contact
    else
      # On failure: render the new contact form so the user can fix the
errors
      render :new, status: :unprocessable_entity
```

```
    end
  end

  # GET request to /contacts/:id/edit
  def edit
  end

  # PATCH/PUT request to /contacts/:id
  def update
  end

  # DELETE request to /contacts/:id
  def destroy
  end

  private
  def contact_params
    params.require(:contact).permit(:first_name, :last_name, :email,
:phone)
  end
end
```

Upgrading with Update Functionality

To add the update functionality, first, we need to show the contact form where a user can see and edit the existing data.

Replace your "**edit**" and "**update**" actions with the following code:

```
  # GET request to /contacts/:id/edit
  def edit
    @contact = Contact.find(params[:id])
  end

  # PATCH/PUT request to /contacts/:id
  def update
    @contact = Contact.find(params[:id])
```

```
    # Mass assignment of form fields into Contact object
    # contact_prams is a method defined below
    if @contact.update(contact_params)
      redirect_to @contact
    else
      render :edit
    end
  end
```

Now, create a new view file "**app/views/contacts/edit.html.erb**" and add the following code:

```
<!-- app/views/contacts/edit.html.erb -->

<h1>Edit Contact</h1>

<%= form_with(model: @contact, local: true) do |form| %>
  <!-- Start of Form -->
  <div class="field">
    <%= form.label :first_name %>
    <%= form.text_field :first_name %>
  </div>

  <div class="field">
    <%= form.label :last_name %>
    <%= form.text_field :last_name %>
  </div>

  <div class="field">
    <%= form.label :email %>
    <%= form.text_field :email %>
  </div>

  <div class="field">
    <%= form.label :phone %>
    <%= form.text_field :phone %>
  </div>
```

```
  <div class="actions">
    <!-- Submit Button -->
    <%= form.submit 'Update Contact' %>
  </div>
  <!-- End of Form -->
<% end %>

<%= link_to 'Back', contacts_path %>
```

Now, if you visit http://localhost:3000/contacts and hit the "**`Edit`**" action, you will see a form pre-filled with the existing data, go ahead and update some of the fields and hit "**`Update Contact`**." You will be redirected to the contact details page ("**`show`**" action) with the updated contact details.

The last part of the CRUD operations is the "**`Delete`**" functionality. In the next section, we will update our "**`destroy`**" action to delete a contact from the database.

Managing Deletions with Delete Functionality

To implement the delete functionality, replace the "**`destroy`**" method in your controller with the following code:

```
# DELETE request to /contacts/:id
  def destroy
    contact = Contact.find(params[:id])
    # Destroying the contact from the database
    contact.destroy

    redirect_to contacts_path
  end
```

Now, if you hit the "**`Destroy`**" action on the contacts index page, you should be asked to reconfirm if you really want to delete the contact. Hitting the "**`Yes`**" button will delete the contact from the database.

Figure 4.18 shows the delete confirmation dialog in action:

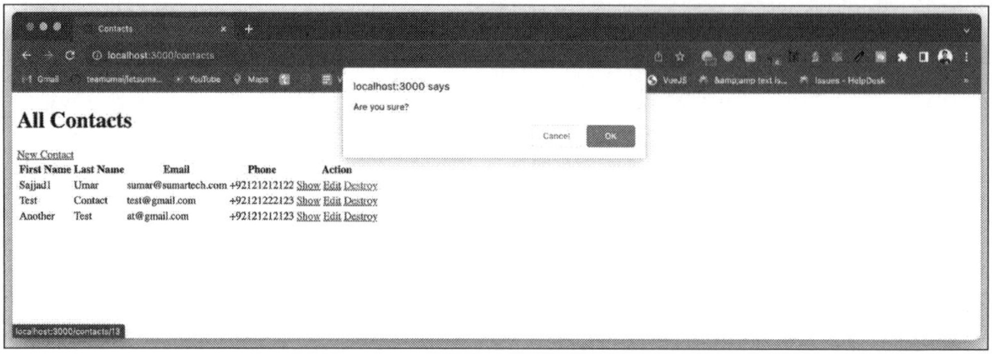

Figure 4.18: *Destroy confirmation dialog in action*

With that, pat yourself on the back and enjoy the moment as we have completed our CRUD implementation.

The last bit of optimization is to update our routes with the resourceful routes as follows:

Resourceful routes simplify the process of defining these CRUD actions in your application by providing a consistent structure. When you define resourceful routes in your Rails application, you typically use the resources method in your **`config/routes.rb`** file. For example, with the addition of resourceful routes, our **`routs.rb`** file goes from this:

```
get 'contacts/new'

get 'contacts', to: 'contacts#index'

get 'contacts/:id/edit', to: 'contacts#edit', as: 'edit_contact'

get 'contacts/:id', to: 'contacts#show', as: 'contact'

post 'contacts', to: 'contacts#create'

patch 'contacts/:id', to: 'contacts#update'

delete 'contacts/:id', to: 'contacts#destroy'
```

To this one-liner:

```
resources :contacts
```

This single line of code generates all the standard RESTful routes for the Contact resource, including routes for creating, reading, updating, and deleting contacts. It maps these routes to the corresponding controller actions.

Resourceful routes help maintain clean and organized code, improve readability, and ensure adherence to RESTful principles, making your application more predictable and easier to maintain. *Figure* 4.19 shows our entire **`routes.rb`** file:

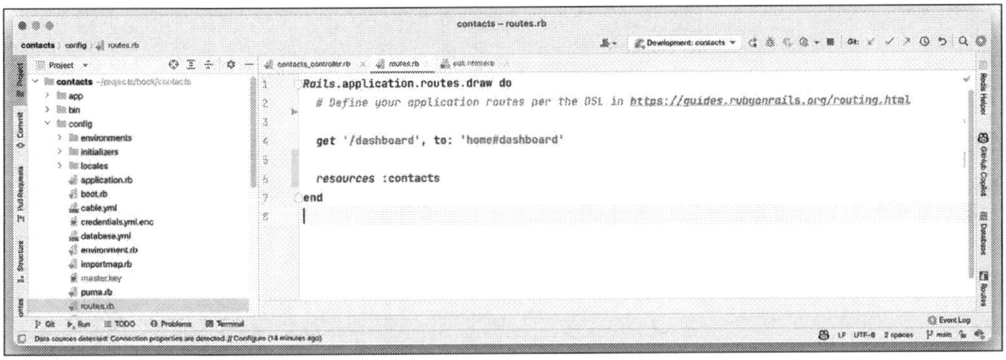

Figure 4.19: *Resourceful routes and the entire routes.rb file*

With resourceful routing, we need to adjust the **`_path`** references in our code to match the resourceful route prefixes. Let's find out the new prefixes by running the **`rails routes`** command, as shown in *Figure 4.19*.

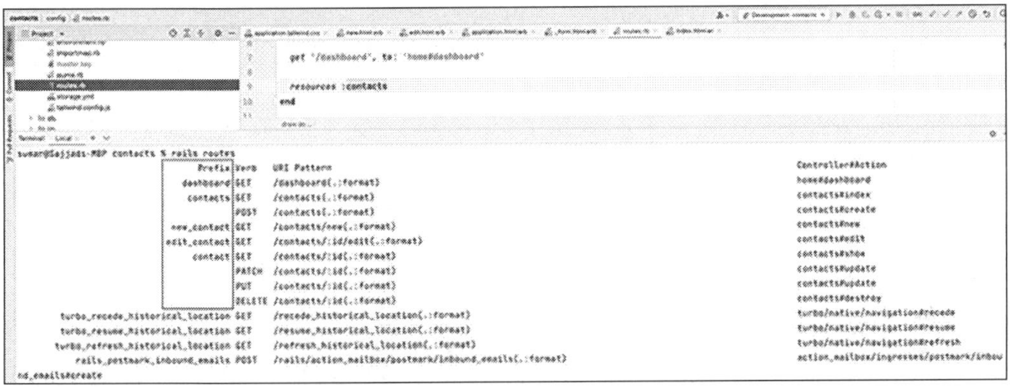

Figure 4.20: *Resourceful routes prefixes*

Now, let's quickly update the path helpers in our code:

In the **`app/views/contacts/index.html.erb`** file change:

```
<%= link_to 'New Contact', contacts_new_path %>
```

To:

```
<%= link_to 'New Contact', new_contact_path %>
```

The rest of the code is already using the resourceful routes prefixes.

Working with Associations and Relationships in Ruby on Rails

In the world of web application development, especially when dealing with databases, data relationships play a pivotal role. Data relationships allow you to connect different entities in your application, enabling you to build more complex and powerful systems. In Ruby on Rails, managing these associations and relationships is made remarkably straightforward through `ActiveRecord`, the Object-Relational Mapping (ORM) framework that comes bundled with Rails. In this section, we will delve into the concept of associations and relationships, understand why they are crucial, and explore how to leverage them effectively in a Rails application.

Understanding Data Relationships

Data relationships, in the context of a database-driven web application, refer to the connections or associations between different data models or tables. These relationships define how records in one table are related to records in another. In most relational databases, data relationships primarily fall into three categories:

- **One-to-One (1:1) Relationship:** In a one-to-one relationship, each record in one table is associated with one record in another table, and vice versa. For example, consider a scenario where you have a User model and an Address model. Each user has exactly one address, and each address belongs to only one user.
- **One-to-Many (1:N) Relationship:** In a one-to-many relationship, each record in one table can be associated with multiple records in another table, but each record in the second table is associated with only one record in the first table. For instance, think of a User model and a Post model. A user can have multiple posts, but each post is linked to a single user.
- **Many-to-Many (N:N) Relationship:** In a many-to-many relationship, multiple records in one table can be associated with multiple records in another table. To establish this type of relationship, you typically use a join table. For example, consider a Student model and a Course model. Students can enroll in multiple courses, and courses have multiple students.

Rails guide provides extensive hands-on documentation on these concepts in detail, please visit https://guides.rubyonrails.org/association_basics.html to grasp all the concepts we have discussed earlier.

Pro Tip: *Try to apply these concepts in our* `Contacts` *App as an assignment. For example, you can add an "*`Address`*" model with a one-to-many relationship, meaning one contact can have multiple addresses.*

Database Management in Ruby on Rails: Evolving Schema, Seed Data, and Data Integrity

Database management is a critical aspect of any web application, and Ruby on Rails provides a robust framework for handling it. In this section, we will explore the essential concepts of database management within Rails, focusing on how to evolve your database schema using migrations, populate your database with seed data, and ensure data integrity and efficiency.

Evolving Database Schema Using Migrations

We have covered what migrations are in this chapter already, so in this section, we will briefly summarize how to work with migrations to evolve your database over time.

To create a migration, you can use the **`rails generate migration`** command, followed by a descriptive name. For instance, `rails generate migration` **`AddDateOfBirthToContacts`** would generate a migration file for adding a **`date_of_birth`** column to the contacts table. Inside this migration file, you define the changes to be made to the database schema using the Ruby-based Domain-Specific Language (DSL) provided by Rails.

ProTip: *Do it as an assignment for your contacts app. Do not forget to add this column into strong params and all of your pages, so you can create, update, and delete it along with other attributes in your contacts model.*

Once a migration is created, you can apply it to the database using the **`rails db:migrate`** command. Rails will execute the migration, updating the schema accordingly. You can also use **`rails db:rollback`** to reverse the last migration.

Populating the Database with Seed Data

What is Seed Data?

Seed data refers to the initial data that is inserted into your database when it's created. This data is typically used to populate tables with essential records that your application needs to function correctly. Seed data can include default contacts, sample categories, or any other necessary data.

Creating Seed Data

In Rails, you can create seed data using a special file named **`seeds.rb`**. This file resides in the db directory of your Rails application. Inside **`seeds.rb`**, you can use Ruby code to define the records you want to insert into your database. In our case, let's add a few default contacts to illustrate how it works. In reality, the suitable data could be default categories, admin users, and more.

Add the following code to your **`seeds.rb`** file:

```
Contact.create(first_name: "Sajjad", last_name: "Umar", email: 
"sajjadumardev@gmail.com", phone: "1234567890")
```

To execute the seed data, you can run the **`rails db:seed`** command. This command reads the **`seeds.rb`** file and inserts the specified data into your database. It's a convenient way to ensure that your database starts with the essential data your Contacts app requires.

Ensuring Data Integrity and Efficiency

Data integrity is crucial for maintaining the quality and accuracy of your database. Rails provides various tools for enforcing data integrity, such as model validations and database constraints.

Model Validations: Model validations are rules defined within your Rails models that specify the conditions that data must meet to be considered valid. For example, you can ensure that contact email addresses are unique or that contact names are present. Validations help prevent invalid or inconsistent data from being saved to the database.

In the case of our **`Contacts`** app, we can add the following validations to our model:

```
# app/models/contact.rb


class Contact < ApplicationRecord
  # Validation for the presence of first name
  validates :first_name, presence: true


  # Validation for presence of last name
  validates :last_name, presence: true


  # Validation for email format using a regular expression
  validates :email, presence: true, format: { with: URI::MailTo::EMAIL_
REGEXP }


  # Validation for uniqueness of email
  validates :email, uniqueness: true


  # Validation for phone number format using a regular expression
  validates :phone, format: { with: /\A\+\d{1,3}\s\d{6,14}\z/, message:
"must be in the format: '+123 4567890'" }
end
```

Database Constraints: Database constraints, such as uniqueness constraints and foreign key constraints, are defined at the database level. These constraints enforce rules on the structure and relationships of the data, ensuring that the data remains consistent and accurate.

Indexing for Efficiency: Efficient database management involves optimizing query performance. One essential aspect of this optimization is indexing. Indexes are database structures that enhance the speed of data retrieval operations on database tables.

In Rails, you can add indexes to your database tables using migrations. By identifying columns that are frequently used in queries (for example, searching or sorting), you can improve query performance significantly.

Example of migration script to add an index to the email column in our contacts table:

```
# Adding an index to the 'email' column of the 'contacts' table

add_index :contacts, :email, unique: true
```

Note: *While we won't delve into every code example in the last section of this chapter, you will have the chance to explore these thoroughly as we build more applications in the upcoming chapters. To enhance your learning experience, consider experimenting with the application on your own. Try implementing various validations and database constraints to gain a deeper understanding of how they work and how they can be tailored to suit your specific project requirements. It's a fantastic way to solidify your knowledge and become a more proficient Rails developer.*

Tip: *Find all the code at:*

https://github.com/ava-orange-education/Ruby-on-Rails-for-Agile-Web-Development/tree/main/chapter04/contacts

Conclusion

In this chapter, we have embarked on an exciting journey into the heart of web development with Ruby on Rails. We have explored the fundamental concepts of CRUD operations, learned how they power web applications, and seen how to create, read, update, and delete records in our Contacts app. We have delved into the MVC architecture, dissected models, views, and controllers, and discovered how they work together to create a dynamic user experience.

We have taken our Contacts app from its infancy, adding the ability to create new contacts, view their details, edit existing data, and confidently remove entries when needed. We have even begun to grasp the intricacies of data relationships and the essential art of database management using migrations and seed data.

However, our journey is far from over. In the next chapter, *Chapter 5, Basics of Styling and Front-end Development*, we will take our Contacts app to the next level. Get ready to make it not just functional but visually stunning. We will explore the world of front-end development, learn how to style our application, and create a user interface that not only works seamlessly but looks fantastic too. So, stay tuned for an exciting exploration of the aesthetics and user experience aspects of web development. It's going to be a design journey you won't want to miss!

Short Quiz

1. **What is the primary goal of Agile development?**
   a. Centralized Routing for Unified Databases
   b. Create, Remove, Update, Delete
   c. Create, Read, Update, Delete
   d. Controller, Request, Update, Display
2. **In the context of a Rails application, what is MVC an abbreviation for?**
   a. Most Valuable Code
   b. Model, View, Controller
   c. Make Very Cool
   d. Managing Visual Components
3. **What is the primary role of a model in a Rails application?**
   a. Handling user input
   b. Displaying data to the user
   c. Storing and retrieving data from the database
   d. Defining the visual appearance of the web page
4. **Which CRUD operation involves capturing user input and saving it in the database?**
   a. Create
   b. Read
   c. Update
   d. Delete

5. **What type of functionality does the "`View Contact`" feature provide in a Rails application?**

   a. Creating new contacts

   b. Viewing individual contact details

   c. Modifying existing contact information

   d. Deleting contacts

6. **Which CRUD operation allows users to modify existing data in a Rails application?**

   a. Create

   b. Read

   c. Update

   d. Delete

7. **What does a database migration in Rails primarily do?**

   a. Populates the database with seed data

   b. Evolves the database schema

   c. Deletes all records in the database

   d. Backs up the entire database

8. **What is the purpose of seed data in a Rails database?**

   a. To provide random data for testing purposes

   b. To enhance data integrity

   c. To speed up database operations

   d. To populate the database with initial records

9. **Which file in a Rails application is used for defining model validations and associations?**

   a. schema.rb

   b. migration file

   c. seeds.rb

   d. model file

10. **In a Rails application, what does the term "resourceful routes" refer to?**
    a. Routes that take users to external resources
    b. Routes that handle CRUD operations for a resource
    c. Routes used for linking to external websites
    d. Routes that lead to the application's home page

CHAPTER 5
Basics of Styling and Front-End Development

Introduction

In the world of web development, creating a fantastic application is not just about functionality but also about appearance. In this chapter, we will dive headfirst into the captivating realm of web design and styling. We will explore the very foundation of CSS and stylesheets, providing a comprehensive understanding of core concepts and rules. Learn how to master CSS selectors and properties to breathe life into your web applications, and become proficient in arranging elements with the CSS box model. We will delve into crafting text styles and enhancing visuals through fonts, colors, backgrounds, and borders. We will also learn to efficiently position and layout elements to perfect the visual structure of your app.

We will also unveil the world of CSS frameworks, explaining why they are crucial for speeding up the design process. Discover the most popular CSS frameworks and find out how to choose the one that fits your needs best. Tailwind CSS will be our framework of choice for the Contacts App, and we will guide you through installing it, setting the application's tone with global styles, adding styles to views and elements, and creating templates for reusable, modular design.

We will wrap up the chapter by exploring responsive design techniques, ensuring your app looks and functions beautifully across various devices and screen sizes.

As we venture through this chapter, remember that all these enchanting concepts are tools you can apply to your Contacts app. You will witness your creation evolve, becoming not only efficient but visually enchanting. Your app will transform into a digital masterpiece, engaging users with both form and function.

Structure

In this chapter, we will discuss the following topics:

- Overview of CSS and Stylesheets
  - CSS Essentials: The Core Concepts you Need
  - Selectors and Properties: Mastering CSS Rules
  - Box Model and Layout: Understanding Spacing and Arrangement
  - Fonts and Colors: Crafting Text Styles
  - Backgrounds and Borders: Enhancing Visuals
  - Positioning and Layout: Arranging Elements Efficiently
- Introduction to CSS Frameworks
  - Reasons to Use CSS Frameworks
  - Popular CSS Frameworks
  - Choosing the Right Framework
  - The Framework of Choice for our Contacts App
- Styling Layouts, View and Templates
  - Installing TailwindCSS
  - Global Styles: Setting the Application's Tone
  - Adding Styles to Views and Elements
  - Templates and Partials: Reusable Modular Design
- Responsive Design Techniques

Overview of CSS and Stylesheets

Cascading Style Sheets (CSS) are an essential part of web development, defining the look and feel of a website. A CSS stylesheet is a collection of style rules that govern how elements in HTML documents should be displayed. CSS plays a crucial role in making web applications visually appealing and user-friendly.

CSS Essentials: The Core Concepts You Need

To master CSS in Rails, you need to grasp core concepts. These include selectors and properties, which help define styling rules, as well as understanding the box model and layout to control spacing and arrangement. Fonts and colors play a significant role in text styling, and backgrounds and borders enhance the visual appeal of elements. Positioning and layout are essential for arranging elements efficiently within a web page.

Selectors and Properties: Mastering CSS Rules

Selectors are used to target HTML elements for styling. They can be as broad as selecting all elements of a type or highly specific by targeting elements with particular attributes. Properties define the aspect of an element you want to style, and values determine how you want to style it. Here is an example of selecting all headings and changing their color:

```
/* Select all <h1> elements and set their color to blue */


h1 {
  color: blue;
}
```

Box Model and Layout: Understanding Spacing and Arrangement

The box model is a fundamental concept in CSS. It defines how elements are structured as boxes with content, padding, borders, and margins. Understanding this model is essential for controlling the layout of web pages. Consider a simple example that defines the width and padding of a container:

```
/* Set the width and padding for a container with the class "box" */


.box {
  width: 200px;
  padding: 20px;
}
```

Fonts and Colors: Crafting Text Styles

Typography is a crucial part of web design. CSS allows you to specify fonts, styles, sizes, and other typographical features to create visually appealing text. Here is an example of styling a class named "**`fancy`**":

```
/* Style text inside a class "fancy" */


.fancy {
  font-family: 'Arial', sans-serif;
```

```
  font-size: 18px;
  font-style: italic;
}
```

Backgrounds and Borders: Enhancing Visuals

CSS provides complete control over backgrounds, allowing you to apply gradients, colors, and patterns to elements. Borders can be added with specific styles, colors, and widths, creating visually appealing containers for your content. Here is an example of adding a border to all div elements:

```
/* Add a red dashed border to all <div> elements */


div {
  border: 2px dashed red;
}
```

Positioning and Layout: Arranging Elements Efficiently

Controlling the positioning and layout of elements is crucial for web page design. CSS offers multiple methods to arrange elements efficiently, including display property, float, and positioning. For example, creating a simple grid layout:

```
/* Create a basic two-column grid layout */


.column {
   float: left;
   width: 50%;
}
```

By mastering these core CSS concepts and utilizing them within the Rails framework, you can enhance the visual aesthetics and user experience of your web application.

Let us use one of the preceding examples and make all the H1 headings in our **`Contacts`** app orange. To do that, open '**`app/assets/stylesheets/application.css`**' and write the following code:

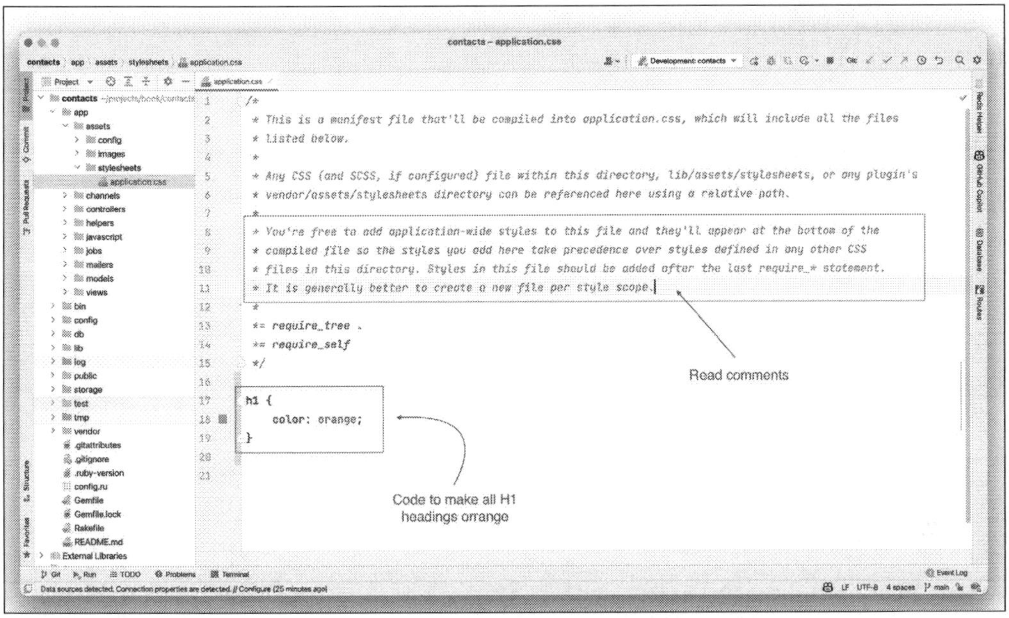

Figure 5.1: *application.css file*

Now if you reload your app, all your H1 headings should be orange as shown in *Figure* 5.2:

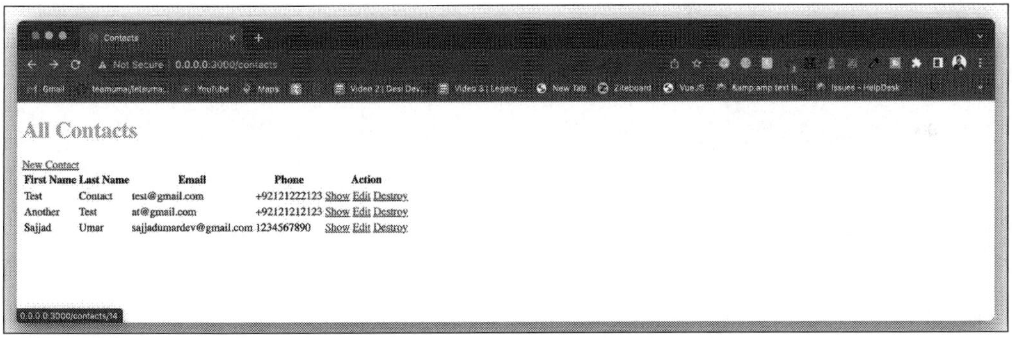

Figure 5.2: *Orange H1 headings*

Pro Tip: *Practice playing around with all the basic CSS concepts discussed so far, and learn even more about CSS at https://www.w3schools.com/css.*

Introduction to CSS Frameworks

CSS frameworks, also known as front-end frameworks or CSS libraries, are pre-prepared collections of CSS files and sometimes JavaScript files. These frameworks are designed to streamline the process of styling web applications. In essence, they provide a set of predefined styles, templates, and design components that developers can leverage to create a consistent and visually pleasing user interface without starting from scratch.

Reason to Use CSS Frameworks

The adoption of CSS frameworks offers several advantages for developers, particularly in the context of Ruby on Rails and web application development:

- **Efficiency:** Writing CSS from scratch for every project can be time-consuming. CSS frameworks eliminate the need to reinvent the wheel by providing a structured foundation. This allows developers to focus more on application functionality and less on styling.
- **Consistency:** CSS frameworks promote consistency in design. They provide a set of predefined styles and components that ensure that the application's visual elements look and behave uniformly. This is crucial for creating a professional and coherent user experience.
- **Responsive Design:** Many CSS frameworks, such as Bootstrap and Foundation, are designed with responsive web design in mind. This means that applications developed using these frameworks will adapt to different screen sizes and devices, enhancing the user experience.
- **Documentation:** CSS frameworks are often accompanied by comprehensive documentation and active developer communities. This makes it easier for developers to learn how to use the framework effectively and troubleshoot any issues they encounter.
- **Rapid Prototyping:** Some CSS frameworks, such as Tailwind CSS, follow a utility-first approach, allowing developers to apply utility classes directly in their HTML. This accelerates the process of prototyping and designing an application's user interface.

Popular CSS Frameworks

Several CSS frameworks have gained popularity in the web development community, each with its unique features and benefits. Here are a few notable examples:

- **Bootstrap:** Developed by X (formerly known as Twitter), Bootstrap is one of the most widely used CSS frameworks globally. It offers a comprehensive set of design components, including responsive grids, buttons, navigation bars, forms, and more. Bootstrap follows a mobile-first design philosophy, making it ideal for modern web applications.

  Find the official docs here https://getbootstrap.com. Rails-specific documentation can be found here https://github.com/twbs/bootstrap-rubygem.

- **Foundation:** Created by ZURB, Foundation is another highly regarded framework known for its flexibility and advanced customization options. It offers a responsive grid system and a variety of UI elements. Foundation is particularly suitable for applications where design customization is a top priority.

  Find the official docs here https://get.foundation. Rails-specific documentation can be found here https://get.foundation/sites/docs-v5/applications.html.

- **Tailwind CSS:** Tailwind CSS takes a unique approach with a utility-first philosophy. It provides utility classes that can be applied directly to HTML elements, distinguishing itself from other CSS frameworks that often rely on predefined components or stylesheets. This approach offers extreme flexibility and is ideal for web applications where speed and distinctive styling are essential.

  Find the official docs here https://tailwindcss.com. Rails-specific documentation can be found here https://tailwindcss.com/docs/guides/ruby-on-rails.

- **Bulma:** Bulma is a lightweight and straightforward CSS framework that focuses on providing a clean and minimalistic design. It is built on Flexbox, making it an excellent choice for applications that require simple yet elegant styling.

Find the official docs here https://bulma.io. Rails-specific documentation can be found here https://github.com/joshuajansen/bulma-rails.

Choosing the Right Framework

Selecting the most suitable CSS framework for your Rails application depends on the project's requirements, your familiarity with the framework, and your design preferences. Some developers prefer Bootstrap for its extensive documentation, while others opt for Tailwind CSS for its rapid prototyping capabilities. The choice should align with the goals and constraints of your specific project.

The Framework of Choice for our Contacts App

Considering Rails is great for rapid development, prototyping, and Minimal Viable Products (MVP) development. We will be using TailwindCSS for its unique utility-first approach.

Note: *This chapter will not go deep into details about TailwindCSS. You can learn all about TailwindCSS here https://tailwindcss.com.*

Styling Layouts, Views, and Templates

Let us make our Contacts App stunning as shown in *Figure* 5.3.

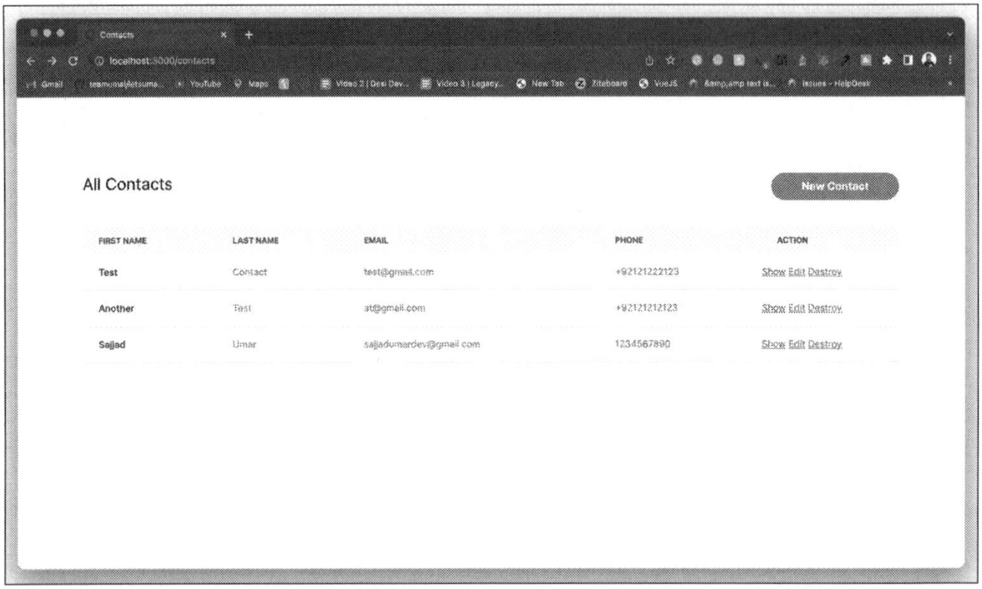

***Figure* 5.3**: *Styling Contacts App*

Installing TailwindCSS

Installing TailwindCSS is easy, all you need to do is install the **`tailwindcss-rails`** gem, and then run the install command to generate a **`tailwind.config.js`** file in the **`./config`** directory.

In the root directory of our app, run the following commands:

```
bundle add tailwindcss-rails
```

```
rails tailwindcss:install
```

These commands will take care of adding the default configuration into the **`tailwind.config.js`** and add the **`@tailwind`** directives for each of Tailwind's layers to your **`application.tailwind.css`** file located in the **`app/assets/stylesheets`** `directory`.

The last thing you need to do is to run the build process with the following command:

```
./bin/dev
```

This will start your local rails server and run rails **`tailwindcss:watch`** to dynamically build the CSS whenever you change it.

Now you are ready to use TailwindCSS. For a detailed installation process visit the official installation guide here https://tailwindcss.com/docs/guides/ruby-on-rails.

Global Styles: Setting the Application's Tone

Let us set the application's tone by adjusting some global CSS so that it applies to the entire app. In the **application.tailwind.css** file replace everything with the following code:

```
@tailwind base;
@tailwind components;
@tailwind utilities;


/* extending base with custom styles */
@layer base {
  h1 {
    @apply text-2xl;
  }

  h2 {
    @apply text-xl;
  }

  h3 {
    @apply text-lg;
  }

  a {
    @apply text-blue-600 underline hover:text-orange-400;
  }
}
```

This code is customizing the base styles of your application. Here is an explanation of what each part does:

@tailwind base;, **@tailwind components;**, **@tailwind utilities;**: These are directives that are part of the Tailwind CSS framework. They indicate the different layers of styles within your CSS file.

- **base:** The base layer provides basic, unstyled styles for common HTML elements.

- **components:** The components layer is where you can add component-specific styles. It is often used for styling custom components or third-party components.
- **utilities:** The utilities layer is for applying utility classes to elements for quick styling. It includes all the utility classes provided by Tailwind CSS.

`@layer base { ... }`: This code extends the base layer with custom styles. It allows you to define your own base styles for various HTML elements.

Now it is time to update our application layout file (**`application.html.erb`**) as follows:

```
<!DOCTYPE html>
<html>
  <head>
    <title>Contacts</title>
    <meta name="viewport" content="width=device-width,initial-scale=1">
    <%= csrf_meta_tags %>
    <%= csp_meta_tag %>
    <%= stylesheet_link_tag "tailwind", "inter-font", "data-turbo-track":
"reload" %>

    <%= stylesheet_link_tag "application", "data-turbo-track": "reload"
%>
    <%= javascript_importmap_tags %>
  </head>

  <body>
    <main class="container">
      <%= yield %>
    </main>
  </body>
</html>
```

There are two main changes in the layout, we added the tailwind **`stylesheet_link_tag`** in the head of the application layout and we added a container class to `main` element in the body tag.

Unlike bootstrap, we have to define the styling of our container class, let us do that in **`application.tailwind.css`** file.

```
.container {
  @apply mx-auto mt-28 px-5;
}
```

While we are at it, let us add few more classes:

```
.btn-primary {
  @apply text-center bg-blue-500 text-white font-bold py-2 px-4
rounded-full no-underline hover:bg-orange-400 hover:text-white;
}


.btn-secondary {
  @apply text-center bg-gray-600 text-white font-bold py-2 px-4
rounded-full no-underline hover:bg-gray-800 hover:text-white;
}


.form-label {
  @apply block mb-2 text-sm font-medium text-gray-900 dark:text-white;
}


.form-text-input {
  @apply bg-gray-50 border border-gray-300 text-gray-900 text-sm
rounded-lg focus:ring-blue-500 focus:border-blue-500 block w-full p-2.5
dark:bg-gray-700 dark:border-gray-600 dark:placeholder-gray-400
dark:text-white dark:focus:ring-blue-500 dark:focus:border-blue-500
mb-5;
}
```

We are just adding TailwindCSS classes to our basic elements, adding it in the application.tailwind.css file means we can reuse these within the entire application following DRY principle of Rails.

The entire file will look like this:

```
@tailwind base;
@tailwind components;
@tailwind utilities;


/* extending base with custom styles */
```

```
@layer base {
  h1 {
    @apply text-2xl;
  }

  h2 {
    @apply text-xl;
  }

  h3 {
    @apply text-lg;
  }

  a {
    @apply text-blue-600 underline hover:text-orange-400;
  }
}

.container {
  @apply mx-auto mt-28 px-5;
}

.btn-primary {
  @apply text-center bg-blue-500 text-white font-bold py-2 px-4 round-
ed-full no-underline hover:bg-orange-400 hover:text-white;
}

.btn-secondary {
  @apply text-center bg-gray-600 text-white font-bold py-2 px-4 round-
ed-full no-underline hover:bg-gray-800 hover:text-white;
}

.form-label {
  @apply block mb-2 text-sm font-medium text-gray-900 dark:text-white;
}

.form-text-input {
```

```
  @apply bg-gray-50 border border-gray-300 text-gray-900 text-sm
rounded-lg focus:ring-blue-500 focus:border-blue-500 block w-full p-2.5
dark:bg-gray-700 dark:border-gray-600 dark:placeholder-gray-400 dark:-
text-white dark:focus:ring-blue-500 dark:focus:border-blue-500 mb-5;
}
```

Now if you visit the http://localhost:3000/contacts in your browser (make sure you run the build process by **./bin/dev** instead of running the server via **rails server** command), you will notice some UI differences but, the page will not look similar to *Figure* 5.3 yet. To make it look similar we need to apply the TailwindCSS styles to specific views, let us do it for all the pages one by one.

Adding Styles to Views and Elements

Let us start with All Contacts page, to style like *Figure* 5.3 replace the content of **app/views/contacts/index.html.erb** file with the following code:

```
<!-- contacts/index.html.erb -->


<div class="grid grid-cols-6 gap-4 mb-10">
  <!-- Display the page title -->
  <h1 class="col-start-1 col-end-3">All Contacts</h1>

  <!-- Link to create a new contact -->
  <%= link_to 'New Contact', new_contact_path, class: 'col-end-7
col-span-1 btn-primary' %>
</div>



<!-- Create a table for displaying contacts -->
<div class="relative overflow-x-auto">
  <table class="w-full text-sm text-left text-gray-500 dark:-
text-gray-400">
    <thead class="text-xs text-gray-700 uppercase bg-gray-50
dark:bg-gray-700 dark:text-gray-400">
    <!-- Define table header row -->
    <tr>
      <!-- Column headers for contact attributes -->
      <th scope="col" class="px-6 py-3">First Name</th>
      <th scope="col" class="px-6 py-3">Last Name</th>
```

```
      <th scope="col" class="px-6 py-3">Email</th>
      <th scope="col" class="px-6 py-3">Phone</th>
      <th scope="col" class="px-6 py-3">Action</th>
    </tr>
    </thead>
    <tbody>
    <!-- Iterate through each contact in the @contacts list -->
    <% @contacts.each do |contact| %>
      <!-- Create a table row for each contact -->
      <tr class="bg-white border-b dark:bg-gray-800 dark:bor-
der-gray-700">
        <!-- Display contact attributes in corresponding columns -->
        <th scope="row" class="px-6 py-4 font-medium text-gray-900
whitespace-nowrap dark:text-white"><%= contact.first_name %></th>
        <td class="px-6 py-4"><%= contact.last_name %></td>
        <td class="px-6 py-4"><%= contact.email %></td>
        <td class="px-6 py-4"><%= contact.phone %></td>
        <td>
          <!-- Links for showing, editing, and deleting a contact -->
          <%= link_to 'Show', contact_path(contact) %>
          <%= link_to 'Edit', edit_contact_path(contact) %>
          <%= link_to "Destroy", contact_path(contact), data: {
            turbo_method: :delete,   # Specify a Turbo Stream delete
method
            turbo_confirm: "Are you sure?"  # Display a confirmation dialog
          } %>
        </td>
      </tr>
    <% end %>
    </tbody>
  </table>
</div>
```

Notice carefully that we have added quite a few CSS classes to elements inside our index view, you can study all these classes on official tailwind CSS documentation at the aforementioned link.

Now if you reload the http://localhost:3000/contacts page it should look similar to *Figure* 5.3.

Now, let us try to make our pages with forms look like this:

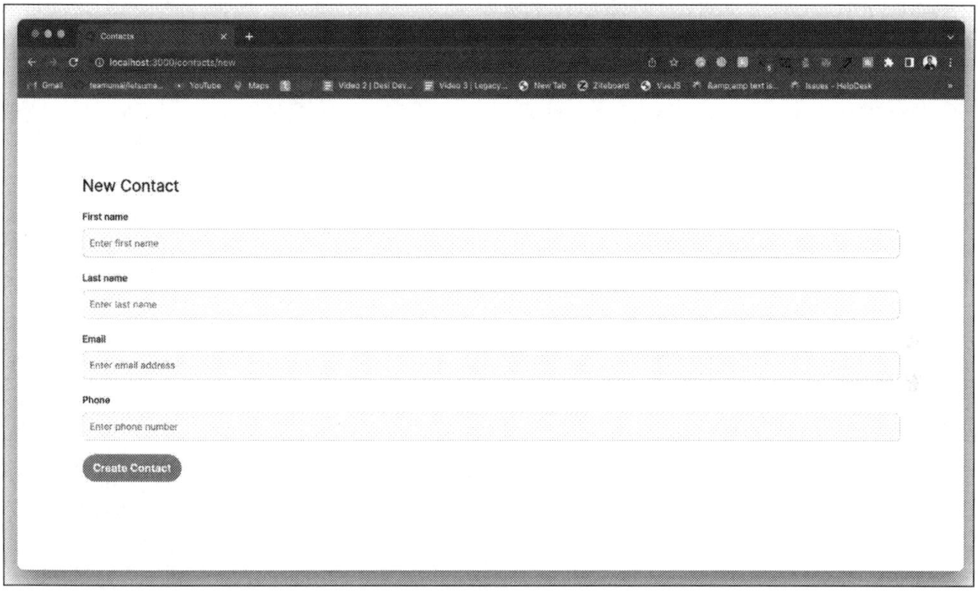

***Figure 5.4**: Pages with forms*

Replace the code of **app/views/contacts/new.html.erb** with the following code:

```
<h1 class="col-start-1 col-end-3 mb-5">New Contact</h1>


<!--form_with is a rails helper method that creates a form for a model
object.
form_with takes a model object and a url (where it will post the data)
as arguments.
contacts_path is a rails helper method that returns the path for the
contacts create action-->


<%= form_with model: @contact, url: contacts_path do |form| %>


  <!--form.label is a rails helper method that creates a label for a
form field-->
  <div class="field">
    <%= form.label :first_name, class: 'form-label'%>
    <!--form.text_field is a rails helper method that creates a text
field for a form-->
```

```
    <%= form.text_field :first_name, class: 'form-text-input', placeholder: 
'Enter first name'  %>
  </div>

  <div class="field">
    <%= form.label :last_name, class: 'form-label' %>
    <%= form.text_field :last_name, class: 'form-text-input', placeholder: 
'Enter last name' %>
  </div>

  <div class="field">
    <%= form.label :email, class: 'form-label' %>
    <%= form.text_field :email, class: 'form-text-input', placeholder: 
'Enter email address' %>
  </div>

  <div class="field">
    <%= form.label :phone, class: 'form-label' %>
    <%= form.text_field :phone, class: 'form-text-input', placeholder: 
'Enter phone number' %>
  </div>

  <div class="actions">
    <!--form.submit is a rails helper method that creates a submit button 
for a form
    submitting the form will send a POST request to the url specified in 
the form_with method-->
    <%= form.submit 'Create Contact', class: 'btn-primary' %>
  </div>
<% end %>
```

Now if you go to http://localhost:3000/contacts/new page on your browser, it will look similar to *Figure* 5.4.

Now add the following code to **app/views/contacts/edit.html.erb** to make it follow the same design language:

```
<!-- app/views/contacts/edit.html.erb -->

<h1 class="col-start-1 col-end-3 mb-5">Edit Contact</h1>
```

```
<%= form_with(model: @contact, local: true) do |form| %>
  <!-- Start of Form -->
  <div class="field">
    <%= form.label :first_name, class: 'form-label' %>
    <%= form.text_field :first_name, class: 'form-text-input', placeholder:
'Enter first name' %>
  </div>

  <div class="field">
    <%= form.label :last_name, class: 'form-label' %>
    <%= form.text_field :last_name, class: 'form-text-input', placeholder:
'Enter last name' %>
  </div>

  <div class="field">
    <%= form.label :email, class: 'form-label' %>
    <%= form.text_field :email, class: 'form-text-input', placeholder:
'Enter email address' %>
  </div>

  <div class="field">
    <%= form.label :phone, class: 'form-label' %>
    <%= form.text_field :phone, class: 'form-text-input', placeholder:
'Enter phone number' %>
  </div>

  <div class="actions">
    <!-- Submit Button -->
    <%= form.submit 'Update Contact', class: 'btn-primary mb-5' %>
  </div>
  <!-- End of Form -->
<% end %>

<%= link_to 'Back', contacts_path, class: 'btn-secondary' %>
```

Finally, we will add a bit of styling to our show page to make it look like *Figure* 5.5.

***Figure 5.5**: Styling the show page*

To achieve this style, replace the content of **app/views/contacts/show.html.erb** file with the following code:

```
<!-- app/views/contacts/show.html.erb -->


<!-- Display the page title -->
<h1 class="col-start-1 col-end-3 mb-5">Contact Details</h1>


<!-- Display contact attributes using @contact instance variable defined inside "show" action -->
<p class="mb-5"><strong class="text-blue-500">First Name:</strong> <%= @contact.first_name %></p>
<p class="mb-5"><strong class="text-blue-500">Last Name:</strong> <%= @contact.last_name %></p>
<p class="mb-5"><strong class="text-blue-500">Email:</strong> <%= @contact.email %></p>
<p class="mb-5"><strong class="text-blue-500">Phone:</strong> <%= @contact.phone %></p>


<div class="mt-5">
  <!-- Link to go back to the contacts list -->
  <%= link_to 'Go Back', contacts_path, class: 'btn-secondary' %>
</div>
```

Now if you navigate through your app; all the pages are styled as we expected.

Pro Tip: *Practice playing around with TailwindCSS classes and try to make your app unique, based on your liking.*

Templates and Partials: Reusable Modular Design

In web development, creating modular and reusable code is essential for maintaining consistency and efficiency in your projects. Templates and partials are powerful tools that help achieve this goal in Ruby on Rails, promoting a design approach that is both DRY (Don't Repeat Yourself) and highly organized.

Templates: Building Blocks for Consistency

Templates are an integral part of Rails views, providing a structured way to define the layout of a page or a section. These templates, often written in HTML with embedded Ruby code (ERB), act as blueprints for rendering dynamic content. By separating the content structure from the logic, templates facilitate a consistent and organized approach to designing your web pages.

Imagine a scenario where you want to maintain a consistent header and footer across multiple pages of your Rails application. Instead of copying and pasting the same HTML for the header and footer on each page, you can create a reusable template. This template can contain the header and footer code, and it is rendered on different pages as needed. Any changes to the header or footer are made in one place, ensuring that the modifications propagate to all pages that use the template. This not only saves time but also prevents errors and ensures a uniform design.

In our contacts, we only have one template **`app/views/layouts/application.html.erb`**. If you look closely into this file, you will notice it has the basic structure for all the pages we have in our contacts app The following code is responsible for replacing only the content inside the body with different content:

```
<body>
    <main class="container">
      <%= yield %>
    </main>
</body>
```

This helps in creating a consistent structure for web pages, ensuring that the main content of each page is wrapped in a container with specific styling.

Partials: Smaller, Reusable Components

Partials take the concept of reusability a step further by allowing you to break down your views into even smaller, manageable components. These components, often representing specific UI elements like forms, buttons, or widgets, are defined as partials. In Rails, partials are typically named with an underscore prefix (for example, **_form.html.erb**) to distinguish them from full templates.

Partials can be inserted into templates or other partials, offering a way to mix and match UI elements to construct complete views. Consider a contact form that is used in various sections of your application. You can create a contact form partial and then include it wherever needed in your views. If you ever need to update the contact form's appearance or behavior, you can do so in a single location, and the changes will be reflected throughout your application.

Furthermore, partials allow for better code organization. Your views remain clean and focused, and complex views are broken down into smaller, manageable components. This modularity enhances code readability and makes it easier for different team members to work on specific sections of your application without interfering with other parts.

If you look closely we have a form in the Contact new and edit pages that we can extract into a partial to avoid code duplication. To do that first create a new **html.erb** file at this directory **app/views/contacts/_form.html.erb** and add the following code:

```
<%= form_with model: @contact, local: true, class: 'mb-5' do |form| %>


  <!--form.label is a rails helper method that creates a label for a
form field-->
  <div class="field">
    <%= form.label :first_name, class: 'form-label'%>
    <!--form.text_field is a rails helper method that creates a text field
for a form-->
    <%= form.text_field :first_name, class: 'form-text-input', placeholder:
'Enter first name'  %>
  </div>


  <div class="field">
    <%= form.label :last_name, class: 'form-label' %>
    <%= form.text_field :last_name, class: 'form-text-input', placeholder:
'Enter last name' %>
  </div>


  <div class="field">
```

```
    <%= form.label :email, class: 'form-label' %>
    <%= form.text_field :email, class: 'form-text-input', placeholder:
'Enter email address' %>
  </div>

  <div class="field">
    <%= form.label :phone, class: 'form-label' %>
    <%= form.text_field :phone, class: 'form-text-input', placeholder:
'Enter phone number' %>
  </div>

  <div class="actions">
    <!--form.submit is a rails helper method that creates a submit button
for a form
    submitting the form will send a POST request to the url specified in
the form_with method-->
    <%= form.submit 'Save', class: 'btn-primary' %>
  </div>
<% end %>
```

With this file in place, you can change the code in the **app/views/contacts/new.html.erb** file as follows:

```
<!-- app/views/contacts/new.html.erb -->

<h1 class="col-start-1 col-end-3 mb-5">New Contact</h1>

<!--form_with is a rails helper method that creates a form for a model
object.
form_with takes a model object and a url (where it will post the data)
as arguments.
contacts_path is a rails helper method that returns the path for the
contacts create action-->

<%= render 'form' %>
```

And **app/views/contacts/edit.html.erb** file as follows:

```
<!-- app/views/contacts/edit.html.erb -->

<h1 class="col-start-1 col-end-3 mb-5">Edit Contact</h1>

<%= render 'form' %>

<%= link_to 'Back', contacts_path, class: 'btn-secondary' %>
```

If you navigate around, our forms will still function the same.

With the help of partials, we are reusing the same form on both pages. This makes our code DRY and manageable.

Responsive Design Techniques

Responsive design is a critical aspect of modern web development, ensuring that your website or web application looks and functions well across various devices and screen sizes, such as desktops, laptops, tablets, and smartphones. Tailwind CSS provides an excellent foundation for creating responsive designs with its utility-first approach.

Here are some responsive design techniques you can use with Tailwind CSS:

- **Responsive Classes**: Tailwind CSS offers responsive classes that allow you to apply different styles based on screen size breakpoints. For example, you can use classes such as **`lg:`** (large screens), **`md:`** (medium screens), and **`sm:`** (small screens) to define styles specific to each breakpoint. This is particularly useful for adjusting font sizes, margins, and padding to ensure a consistent layout across different devices.
- **Flexbox and Grid:** Tailwind CSS includes utilities for building flexible layouts. You can use classes such as flex and grid to create responsive grids and flexible containers. These make it easy to arrange elements in rows or columns and adjust the layout as the screen size changes.
- **Visibility Classes:** Tailwind CSS provides visibility classes such as hidden, block, inline, lg: hidden, and more. These classes enable you to hide or display elements based on screen size, making it simple to show or hide certain content on different devices.
- **Responsive Typography**: You can use classes like **`text-sm`**, **`text-md`**, and **`text-lg`** to adjust the font size based on screen size. This ensures that text remains readable and aesthetically pleasing on various devices.

- **Spacing Utilities:** Tailwind CSS offers classes for margin and padding adjustments. You can use **`m-`**, **`p-`**, **`mt-`**, **`mb-`**, **`ml-`**, **`mr-`**, **`pt-`**, **`pb-`**, **`pl-`**, and **`pr-`** with responsive prefixes to control spacing. This is essential for maintaining consistent spacing and alignment in responsive layouts.
- **Display Utilities:** The **`hidden`**, **`block`**, **`inline`**, **`inline-block`**, **`table`**, and **`table-cell`** classes can be combined with responsive prefixes to control the display behavior of elements on different screen sizes.
- **Responsive Images:** You can use responsive image classes like **`w-1/2`**, **`w-1/4`**, **`w-full`** to control the width of images based on screen size. This is particularly useful for optimizing image sizes for different devices.
- **Custom Breakpoints:** Tailwind CSS allows you to define custom breakpoints in your configuration to create a responsive design tailored to your project's specific requirements.

By incorporating these responsive design techniques in your Tailwind CSS application, you can ensure a consistent and user-friendly experience across a wide range of devices.

If you have not already noticed, our **`Contacts`** app is fully responsive as we have already applied responsive design techniques in our styling. *Figure* 5.6 shows the **`Edit Contact`** page running on a mobile screen.

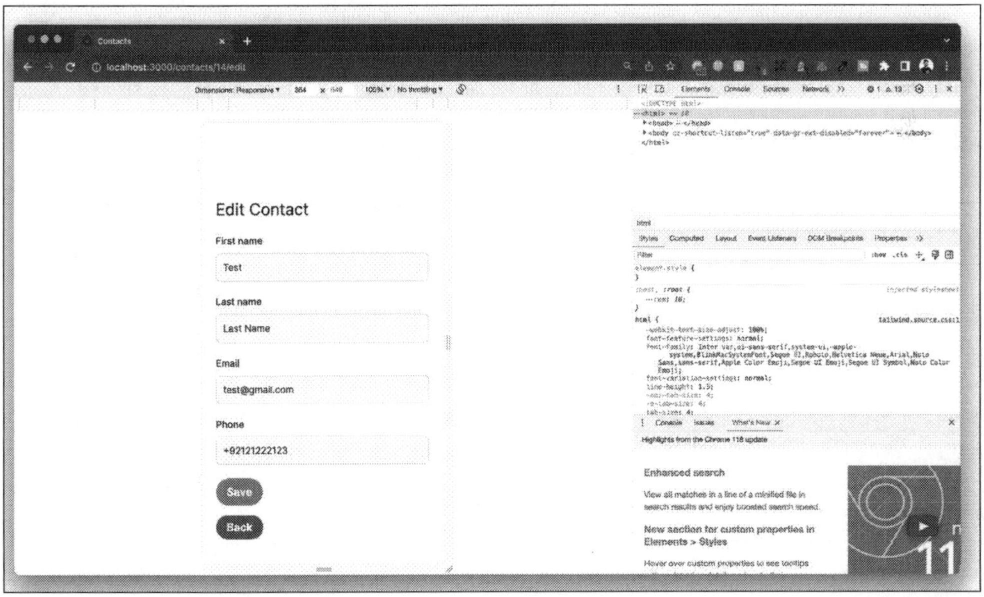

***Figure* 5.6**: *Responsive Edit Contact page*

Assignment: Read the code carefully to spot all the TailwindCSS classes being used to make our app responsive.

Pro Tip: *If you want to expand further on the contacts app here are a few suggestions:*

- *Add data validations to our contact model.*
- *Add flash and notice banners in the layout and show errors properly.*

Conclusion

In this chapter, we ventured into the fascinating world of web design and styling. We introduced you to the concept of CSS frameworks, emphasizing their importance in expediting the design process. You have explored popular CSS frameworks, with Tailwind CSS emerging as our framework of choice for the Contacts App. We covered global styles, adding styles to views and elements, and creating templates for modular design.

As you have acquired these styling skills, it is time to move forward. In the next chapter, we will embark on a new journey with a fresh Rails application, powered by PostgreSQL as our database and styled with Tailwind CSS. We will not only focus on designing the app but also dive into the critical aspects of authentication and authorization. Together, we will ensure that your web application not only looks appealing but is also secure and user-friendly. Stay tuned for an exciting learning adventure in our upcoming chapter titled *Authentication and Authorization.*

You can find all the code changes in this chapter here https://github.com/ava-orange-education/Ruby-on-Rails-for-Agile-Web-Development/tree/main/chapter05/contacts.

Short Quiz

1. **What does CSS stand for?**
   a. Creative Style Sheets
   b. Computer Style Syntax
   c. Cascading Style Sheets
   d. Content Styling System
2. **Which CSS concept is used to apply styles to specific elements on a web page?**
   a. Classes
   b. Elements
   c. ID selectors
   d. HTML tags

3. **In CSS, what is the "box model"?**
    a. A model for organizing HTML elements
    b. A way to create shadow effects
    c. A method of styling text
    d. A layout model describing how elements are rendered
4. **Which CSS property is used to set the size of fonts?**
    a. size
    b. text-size
    c. font-size
    d. letter-size
5. **What does "responsive design" refer to in web development?**
    a. A design that reacts to user interactions
    b. A design that is optimized for search engines
    c. A design that adapts to different screen sizes and devices
    d. A design that loads quickly on slow internet connections
6. **Which of the following is not a CSS framework?**
    a. Bootstrap
    b. Tailwind CSS
    c. Foundation
    d. React Native
7. **What is the primary purpose of CSS frameworks?**
    a. To build databases
    b. To improve website security
    c. To speed up web design and development
    d. To create animations
8. **Which CSS framework was chosen for the Contacts App?**
    a. Bootstrap
    b. Foundation

   c. Sass

   d. Tailwind CSS

9. **In CSS, what is the purpose of "media queries"?**

   a. To query databases for information

   b. To optimize database performance

   c. To target styles for specific devices and screen sizes

   d. To control user authentication

10. **What is the primary benefit of using a CSS framework like Bootstrap or Tailwind CSS?**

    a. Simplified web development and faster design

    b. Enhanced website security

    c. Better compatibility with older browsers

    d. Complex animations and interactions

Chapter 6
Authentication and Authorization

Introduction

Imagine you are building a magnificent fortress, but this is not just any stronghold; it is a digital castle. Inside this digital castle, you house valuable treasures: user data, sensitive information, and personalized features. But how do you guard these riches, making sure only the right people can enter the inner sanctum while keeping the wrong ones out? In this chapter, we will explore the secrets of securing your digital kingdom through the powerful principles of Authentication and Authorization.

Up until now, we have been crafting the walls and infrastructure of our castle, creating its stunning appearance with well-placed designs and responsive layouts. However, the time has come to set up the drawbridge and the gatekeepers. In this chapter, we will tackle one of the most critical aspects of web development–user authentication. We will equip our fortress with a robust system for users to register, log in, and manage their accounts securely.

But a fortress would not be complete without vigilant guards who determine who gets access to different areas. That is where authorization comes in. We will learn how to define roles and permissions for our users, ensuring they can only access what is meant for them.

With a fresh Rails application, PostgreSQL as our trusty database, and the aesthetic magic of Tailwind CSS, we will embark on a new adventure. As we dive into the world of authentication and authorization, our digital castle will become a model of security and user management.

Structure

In this chapter, we will discuss the following topics:

- Understanding the Importance of User Authentication

  - Exploring Common Authentication Methods
  - Understanding the Authentication Process in Web Development
- Implementing User Registration and Login
  - The Approach
  - The Product
  - Creating a Brand-New Rails App
  - Implementing Authentication Flow
- Role-Based Authorization in Rails
  - Key Components of Role-Based Authorization
  - Implementing Role-Based Authentication
- Making It Look Good
  - Adding Flowbite Component Library
  - Adding Theme Configuration
  - Adding Basic Styling

Understanding the Importance of User Authentication

User authentication lies at the heart of secure web applications, playing a pivotal role in confirming the identity of individuals seeking access to specific online resources or services. It is a critical mechanism employed to ensure that only authorized users can interact with and manipulate sensitive information within a system. At its core, authentication is about verifying the legitimacy of users attempting to access an application or website, typically through a process involving credentials such as usernames, passwords, or other identification methods.

Authentication is fundamental in maintaining the integrity, confidentiality, and security of digital assets. Without proper authentication measures, systems are exposed to vulnerabilities that could compromise user data, lead to unauthorized access, and facilitate malicious activities. Robust user authentication mechanisms act as gatekeepers, ensuring that only legitimate users gain entry, thereby protecting valuable information and resources from unauthorized access and misuse.

Exploring Common Authentication Methods

The domain of user authentication incorporates diverse methods tailored to varying security requirements and user preferences. These methods include:

- **Username and Password:** The traditional and widely adopted method where users input a unique username and corresponding password to access their accounts.

- **Biometric Authentication:** Leveraging unique biological traits such as fingerprints, facial recognition, or retinal scans for user identification, offering a high level of security and convenience.
- **Multi-Factor Authentication (MFA):** A layered security approach that requires users to provide multiple forms of verification (such as a password, SMS code, or fingerprint) for access and enhancing overall account security.
- **Single Sign-On (SSO):** Allowing users to access multiple applications with a single set of login credentials, streamlining the authentication process across diverse platforms.

Understanding the Authentication Process in Web Development

Let us dive deeper into how authentication works in web development:

1. **User Input:** Authentication starts when a user inputs their credentials (usually a username/email and password) into a login form on a website or application.
2. **Data Transmission:** Upon submitting the form, the provided credentials are sent to the website's server using HTTP requests. These details are typically encrypted to ensure secure transmission, often using SSL/TLS protocols.
3. **Server-Side Validation:** The server receives the credentials and verifies them against the stored user data, often stored in a database. It checks if the username exists and if the entered password matches the encrypted one stored in the database.
4. **Session Creation:** If the credentials match, the server creates a session for that user. This session is a unique identifier that confirms the user's identity. The server might also generate tokens or cookies associated with this session to maintain the user's login status.

   Cookies: *Small data files stored on the user's device by the web browser often contain session IDs or authentication tokens, enabling the identification and tracking of users across web pages and sessions.*
5. **Access Granted:** With a valid session, the user gains access to restricted areas of the website or application. They can now perform actions like viewing personal data, making purchases, or interacting with the platform.
6. **Persistent Sessions:** To prevent frequent logins, websites often use cookies or tokens to keep users logged in for a certain period, even after closing the

browser. This feature enhances user experience by eliminating the need for frequent logins.

7. **Logout:** When a user logs out, the session data on the server and the local tokens/cookies are invalidated. This action terminates the user's access to restricted areas until they log in again.
8. **Security Measures:** To ensure security, modern authentication systems employ various measures such as multi-factor authentication (MFA), CAPTCHA, and robust encryption methods to protect user data from unauthorized access or cyber threats.

In essence, authentication is the process of verifying a user's identity to grant them access to specific resources or functionalities within a website or application while maintaining their privacy and security.

Implementing User Registration and Login

While it is entirely feasible to build an entire authentication flow from scratch, leveraging existing solutions like the Devise gem in Ruby on Rails can significantly expedite and enhance the authentication process. Developing authentication mechanisms involves multiple intricate steps, such as password hashing, session management, account confirmation, and more. Using Devise, a robust authentication library, saves considerable time and effort by providing pre-built functionalities that adhere to security best practices. Devise offers features like user registration, login, password recovery, and account activation out of the box, sparing developers from reinventing these functionalities. Moreover, it is continuously maintained, with community support, updates, and security patches, ensuring a reliable and secure authentication system for your application.

We will leverage the devise gem to implement authentication into our brand-new web application.

The Approach

With an agile approach in mind, we aim to implement agile methodologies while developing a practical Software as a Service (SaaS) product. Throughout this chapter, our focus is to establish a robust foundation for the project that will be our central focus in this book's journey.

In this project, we will adopt the Kanban methodology for its adaptability and simplicity. Kanban's visual nature, emphasizing continuous delivery and workflow optimization, aligns perfectly with our goals for creating an efficient and user-centric SaaS product.

It offers a flexible approach, allowing for the management of tasks as they progress, ensuring smooth development cycles, and the ability to respond quickly to changing requirements. The simplicity of Kanban's principles enables a small team to maintain clear visibility into the project's progress, prioritize tasks effectively, and ensure a steady flow of development without overwhelming the process with unnecessary complexity.

The Product

We are constructing an HR and Employee Management Software as a Service (SaaS) solution tailored for small and medium-sized businesses. This platform aims to streamline HR processes, offering functionalities for employee onboarding, attendance tracking, leave management, and performance evaluations. It will prioritize ease of use, efficient task delegation, and secure information handling, providing HR professionals with a comprehensive tool to manage employee data effectively. Utilizing Agile methodologies, particularly the Kanban approach, we will systematically develop and enhance it, ensuring a user-friendly, efficient, and scalable product. We will call it "WagePro" and let us give it the tagline "*Empower Your HR Operations with WagePro: Simplify, Streamline, Succeed*".

The Tech Stack

- Ruby version 3.2.2
- Rails version 7.1.2
- PostgreSQL version ≥ 14.x

Benefits of Using PostgreSQL in Rails

While Rails offers compatibility with various databases, our choice for this project is PostgreSQL due to the following advantages:

- **Reliability:** PostgreSQL offers robust data integrity and supports ACID properties, ensuring consistency, reliability, and durability of data.
- **Scalability:** It can efficiently handle large volumes of data and complex workloads, making it suitable for scaling Rails applications.
- **Advanced Features:** PostgreSQL supports a wide range of data types, indexing options, and advanced features like JSONB data types, full-text search, and spatial data support.
- **Extensibility:** It allows users to create custom extensions and functions, enabling tailored functionalities to suit specific Rails application needs.
- **Compatibility:** PostgreSQL is compliant with SQL standards and integrates

well with Rails, providing seamless integration with ActiveRecord, Rails' Object-Relational Mapping (ORM) layer.

- **Security:** Offers robust security features such as SSL encryption, role-based access control (RBAC), and various authentication methods to safeguard sensitive data.

Creating a Brand-New Rails App (WagePro)

To create a Rails app with a PostgreSQL database, you need first to install it in your system. You can find instructions on how to install it on different operating systems at https://www.postgresql.org/download.

Figure 6.1 shows how you can set up your local environment for this brand-new application:

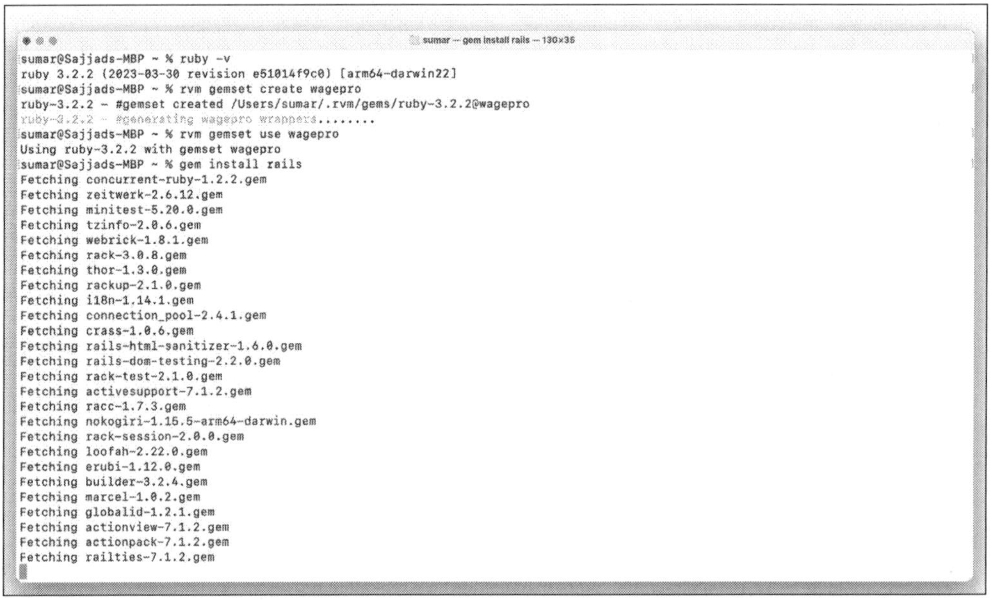

Figure 6.1: *Creating gem set and installing rails 7.1.2*

Now, let us quickly create our "*WagePro*" app with PostgreSQL database and TailwindCSS with the following command:

```
rails new wage_pro --database=postgresql --css tailwind
```

Figure 6.2 shows rails new command in action:

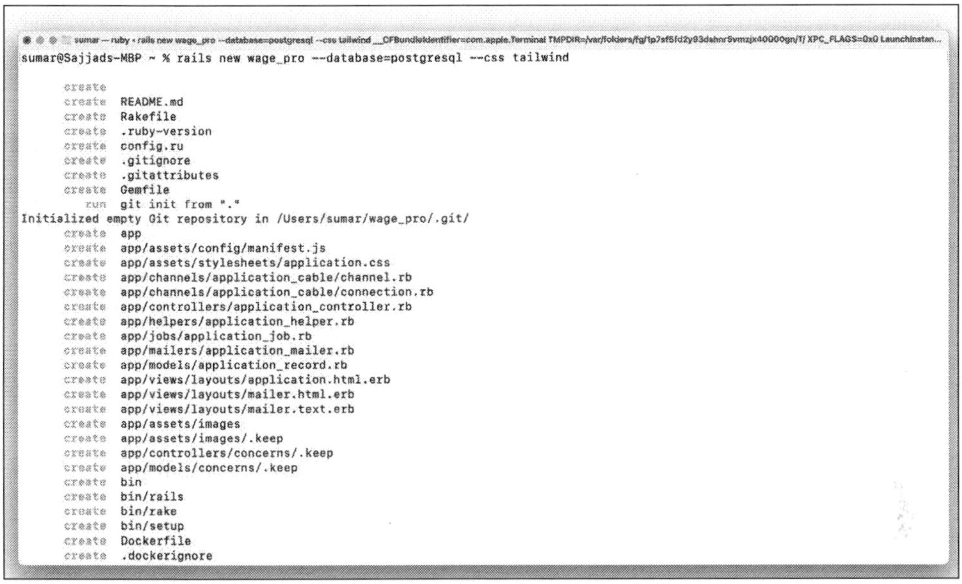

Figure 6.2: *Creating a new Rails App with Rails new command*

If you have created a username and password during your PostgreSQL installation, add it to the "`config/database.yml`" file, as shown in *Figure* 6.3.

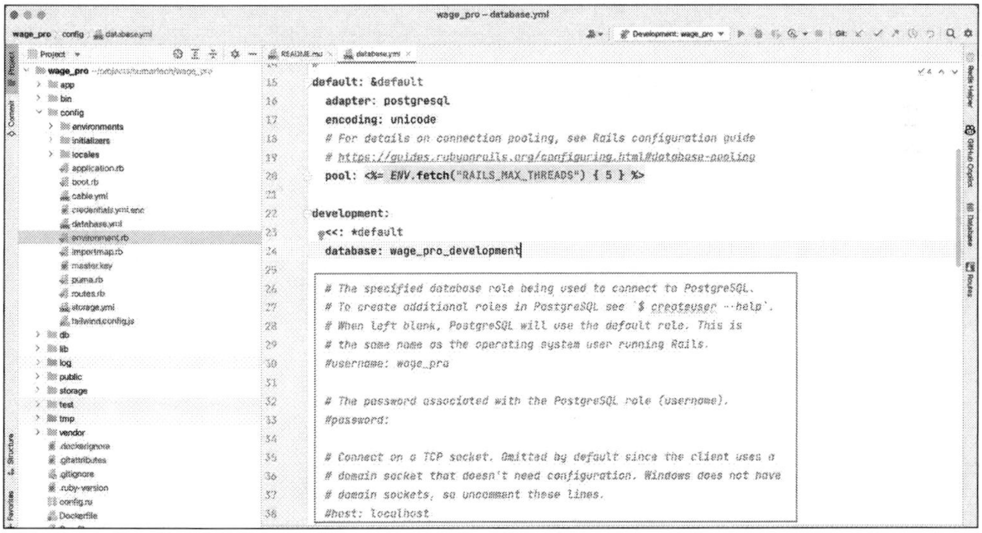

Figure 6.3: *config/database.yml file*

Now, run the following command to create the databases for your development and test environment:

```
rails db:create
```

Now, it is time to spin up our development server with **./bin/dev** command and visit the localhost:3000 URL in the browser. *Figure* 6.4 shows our brand-new app up and running on our development server.

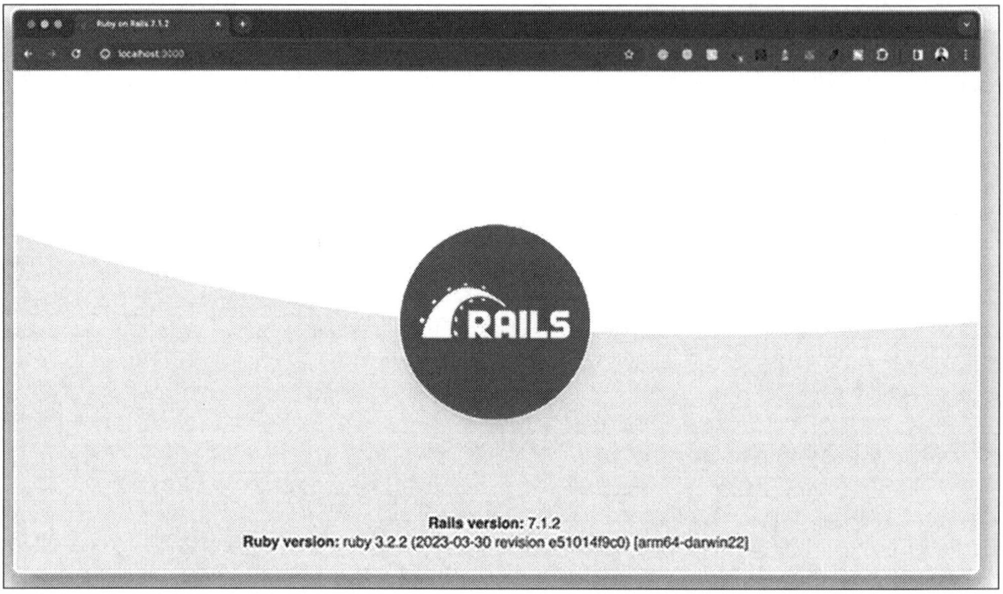

***Figure* 6.4**: *localhost:3000*

Creating a Simple Home Page

Let us quickly create a **HomeController** with an index action for our app:

```
rails generate controller home index
```

This command will take care of creating everything we need for "**HomeController**" index action. *Figure* 6.5 shows all the files created by this command:

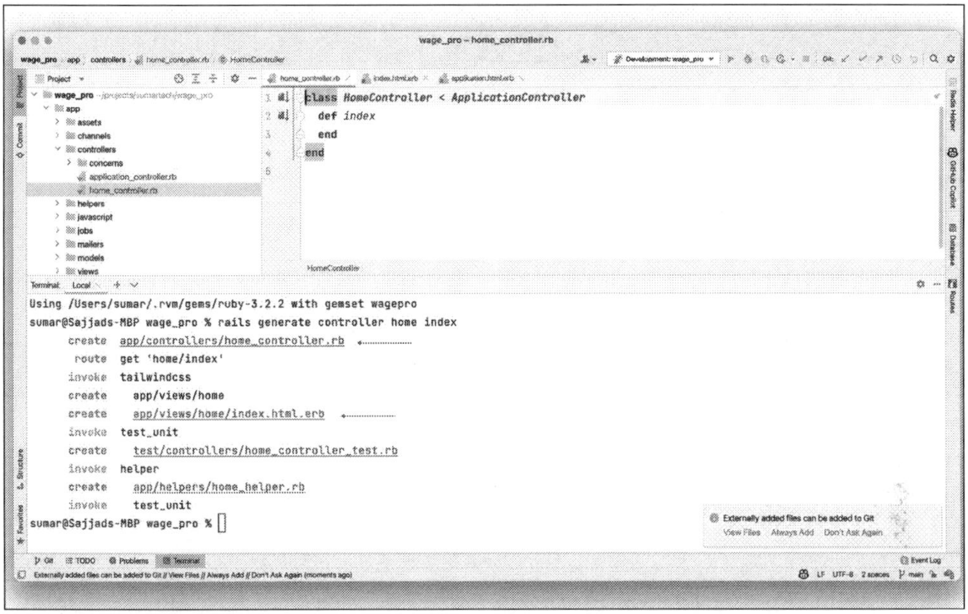

Figure 6.5: *Home controller generate command with index action*

Let us add a route for this page as a root path in our "**`config/routes.rb`**" file, as shown in *Figure* 6.6:

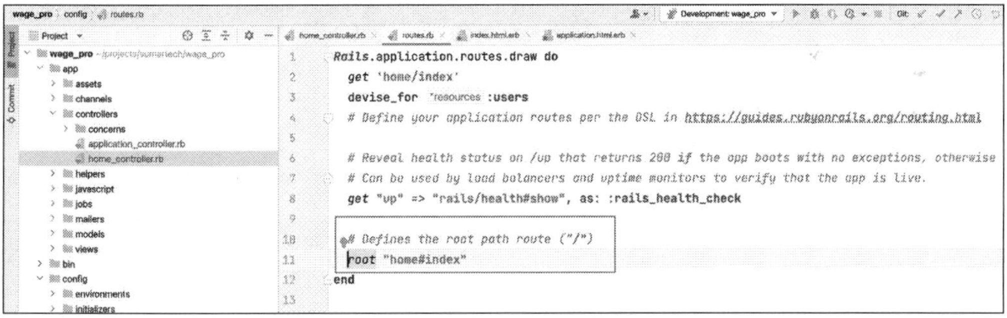

Figure 6.6: *Adding root path in routes.rb*

The root path refers to the default route or URL pattern that is mapped to the application's homepage or the main landing page.

Now, if you visit localhost:3000 on your browser, you will see your homepage in the browser. *Figure* 6.7 shows the homepage of our application:

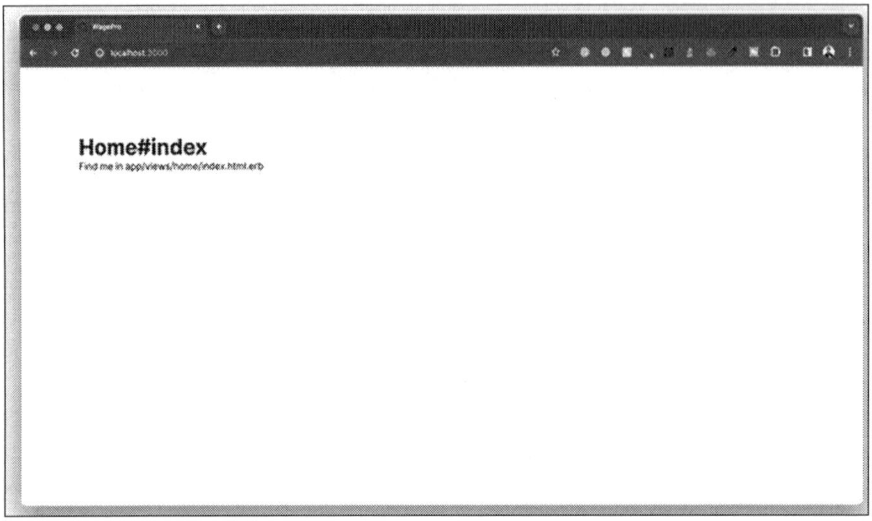

Figure 6.7: *Home page of WagePro App*

As we are following the Kanban, *Figure* 6.8 shows the very basic visualization of our project so far. We are using Jira (https://www.atlassian.com/software/jira) for project management, but you can simply use pen and paper or any other tool of your choice.

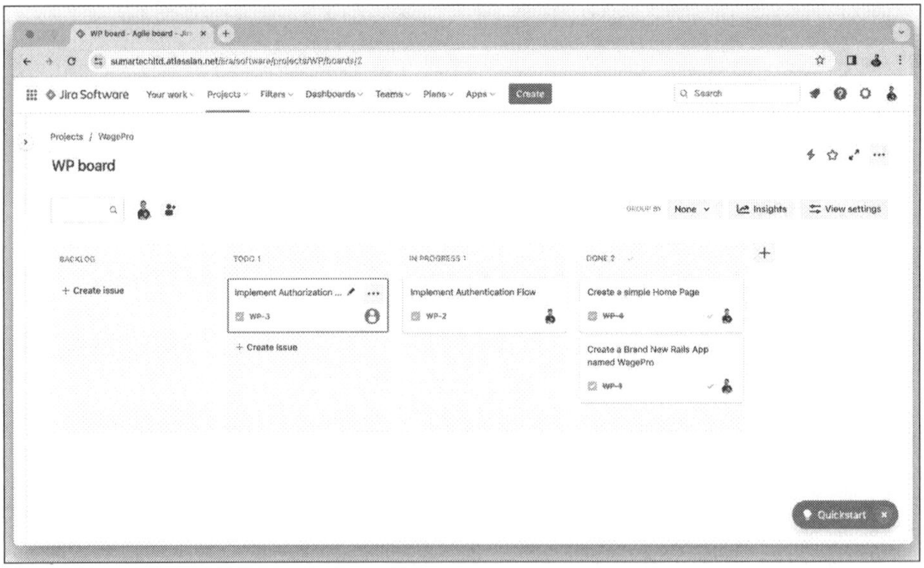

Figure 6.8: *Project visualization on Jira*

Our backlog will grow with time, but this is the time when you (as a member of an agile team) move the card labeled "`Implement Authentication Flow`" to the **`IN PROGRESS`** column so that your team has a clear idea of what is in progress.

The very first model we will introduce in our app is called the "*User*" model, and each user needs to have a way to log in to our application. This is where the devise gem shines. Devise is a flexible authentication solution for Rails. You can read about this gem at https://github.com/heartcombo/devise.

We will now follow the quick start guide from the documentation (https://github.com/heartcombo/devise#getting-started) to add it to our app.

Step 1: Install the Gem

To install the devise gem, run the following command in the terminal:

```
bundle add devise
```

Figure 6.9 shows the aforementioned command in action:

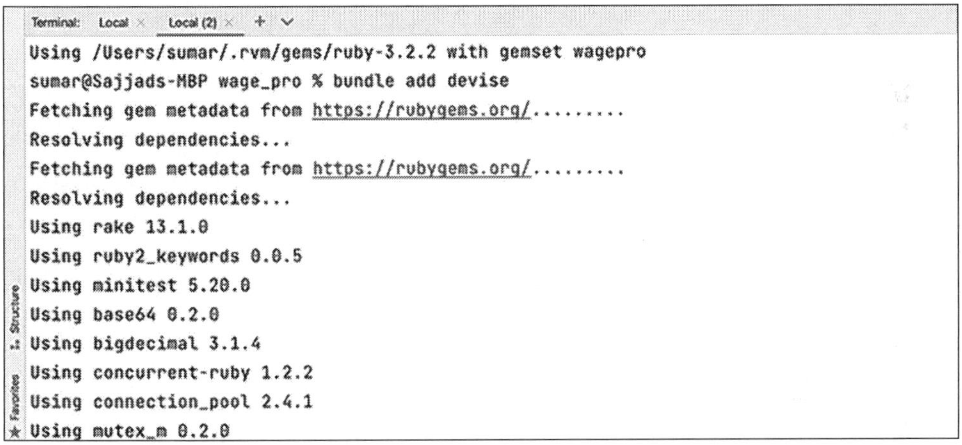

***Figure 6.9**: Installing devise gem*

Step 2: Run the Generator

Next, you need to run the generator:

```
rails generate devise:install
```

This command will print some instructions on the terminal. Let us have a look at these instructions:

Depending on your application's configuration, some manual setup may be required:

1. Ensure you have defined default URL options in your environment's files. Here is an example of **default_url_options** appropriate for a development environment in **config/environments/development.rb**:

```
        config.action_mailer.default_url_options = { host:
'localhost', port: 3000 }
```

   In production, **:host** should be set to the actual host of your application.

```
     * Required for all applications. *
```

2. Ensure you have defined **root_url** to *something* in your **config/routes.rb**.

   For example:

   ```
   root to: "home#index"
   ```

   ```
   * Not required for API-only Applications *
   ```

3. Ensure you have flash messages in **app/views/layouts/application.html.erb**.

   For example:

   ```
   <p class="notice"><%= notice %></p>
   <p class="alert"><%= alert %></p>
   ```

   ```
   * Not required for API-only Applications *
   ```

4. You can copy Devise views (for customization) to your app by running:

   ```
   rails generate devise:views
   ```

   ```
   * Not required *
   ```

ProTip: *In all rails generate commands, you can use a shorthand syntax and replace the full "generate" word with the letter "g". For example, the aforementioned command can be written in the following way as well:* ***rails g devise:views***

Read these instructions carefully and do the needful, in a nutshell, we need to add the following to "**config/environments/development.rb**":

```
config.action_mailer.default_url_options = { host: 'localhost', port: 3000 }
```

Figure 6.10 shows "**config/environments/development.rb**" with added **default_url_options**:

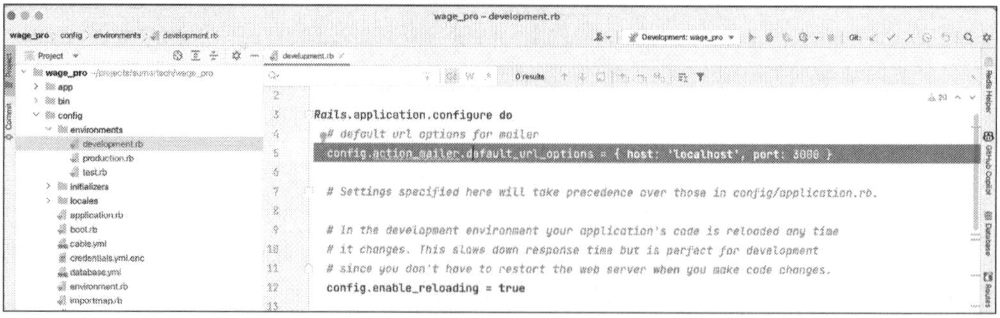

Figure 6.10: *config/environments/development.rb*

The next instruction is about adding a root URL for our application "**config/routes.rb**". We already have this in place as shown in *Figure* 6.6.

Step 3: Add Basic Flash Messages and Devise Views

To add basic flash messages, add the following code to the "**app/views/layouts/application.html.erb**":

```
<p class="notice"><%= notice %></p>

<p class="alert"><%= alert %></p>
```

Figure 6.11 shows the updated "**app/views/layouts/application.html.erb**" file:

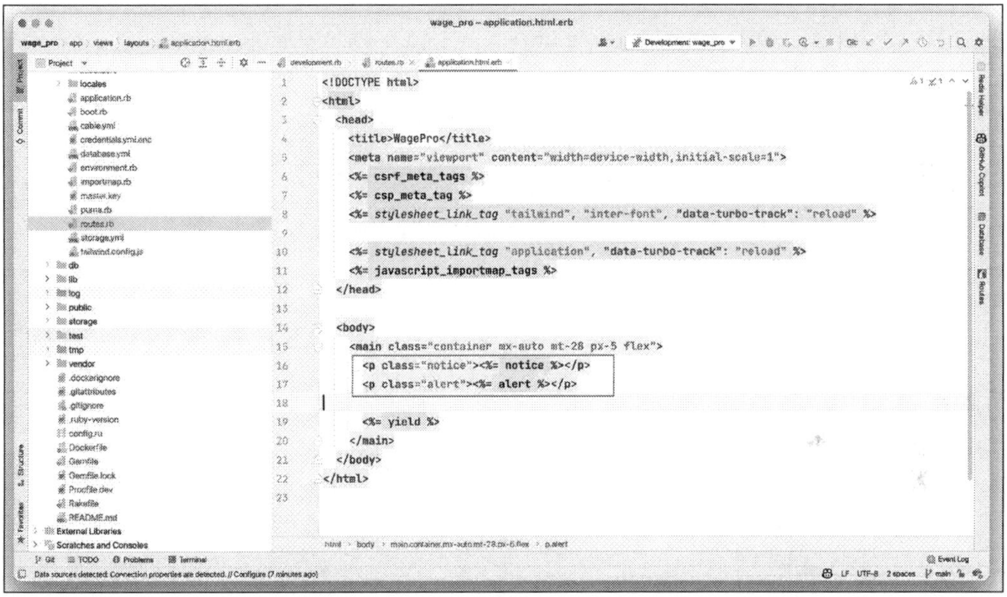

Figure 6.11: *Application Layout File*

Lastly, we can optionally add devise views for customization with the following command:

```
rails g devise:views
```

This rails generator command will add a few view files in our application, as shown in *Figure* 6.12:

```
sumar@Sajjads-MBP wage_pro % rails g devise:views
      invoke  Devise::Generators::SharedViewsGenerator
      create    app/views/devise/shared
      create    app/views/devise/shared/_error_messages.html.erb
      create    app/views/devise/shared/_links.html.erb
      invoke  form_for
      create    app/views/devise/confirmations
      create    app/views/devise/confirmations/new.html.erb
      create    app/views/devise/passwords
      create    app/views/devise/passwords/edit.html.erb
      create    app/views/devise/passwords/new.html.erb
```

Figure 6.12: *Devise views generator command*

We will customize some of these files later.

Step 4: Create the User Model with Devise

In the following command, you will replace MODEL with the class name used for the application's users (for our application, it is **`User`**, but it could be anything, such as **`Admin`**). This will create a model (if one does not exist) and configure it with the default Devise modules. The generator also configures your **`config/routes.rb`** file to point to the Devise controller.

```
rails g devise MODEL
```

Figure 6.13 shows the aforementioned command in action:

```
sumar@Sajjads-MBP wage_pro % rails g devise User
      invoke  active_record
      create    db/migrate/20231122173934_devise_create_users.rb
      create    app/models/user.rb
      invoke    test_unit
      create      test/models/user_test.rb
      create      test/fixtures/users.yml
      insert    app/models/user.rb
       route  devise_for :users
sumar@Sajjads-MBP wage_pro %
```

Figure 6.13: *Devise User model generate command*

This command has created a model, a migration, and a bunch of test files for us. Along with that, it has updated our **`routes.rb`** file and added a route pointing towards devise controllers, as shown in *Figure* 6.14:

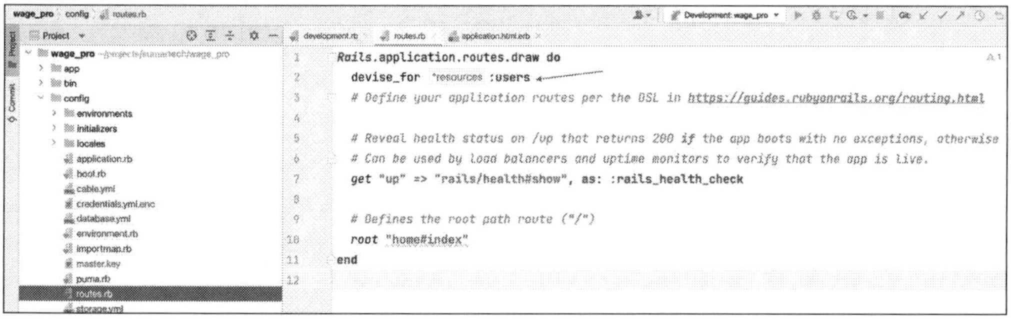

Figure 6.14: *routes.rb file with devise route*

Step 5: Run the Migration

Before we run the generated migration, we can optionally choose to add more attributes in the User model if needed, but for now, we will go with the default migration file and run the migrations with the following command:

```
rails db:migrate
```

Running the migration will add a *Users* table in our database with default attributes defined in the migration file.

All done, now run the server with **./bin/dev** and visit localhost:3000/users/sign_in URL in the browser. *Figure* 6.15 shows the aforementioned page in the browser:

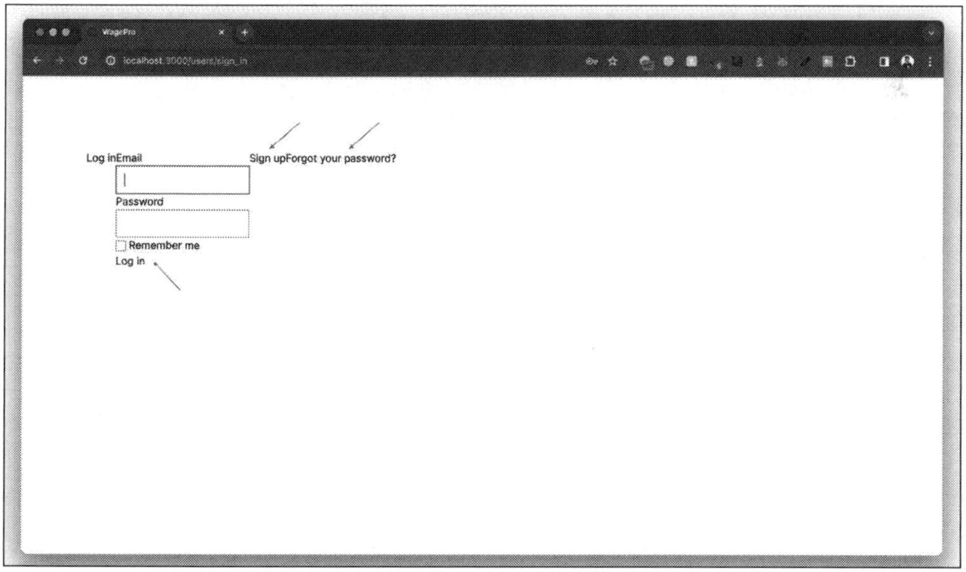

Figure 6.15: *Log-in Page*

If you look closely, this page has everything a Log-in page should have. For example:

- A link to the Sign-up page

- A link to recover your password when you forget it
- Input fields to enter Email and Password
- A checkbox to make sure you don't have to log in again and again
- A login button

Despite looking a bit clunky, it all works out of the box, try signing up with your email and password, and it will redirect you to the "**`home#index`**" action after successful sign up.

Sign Up a New User

Let us go to the Sign-up page by clicking the Sign-up link highlighted in *Figure* 6.15, and fill in the Sign-up form:

Figure 6.16 shows a filled Sign-up form in our app:

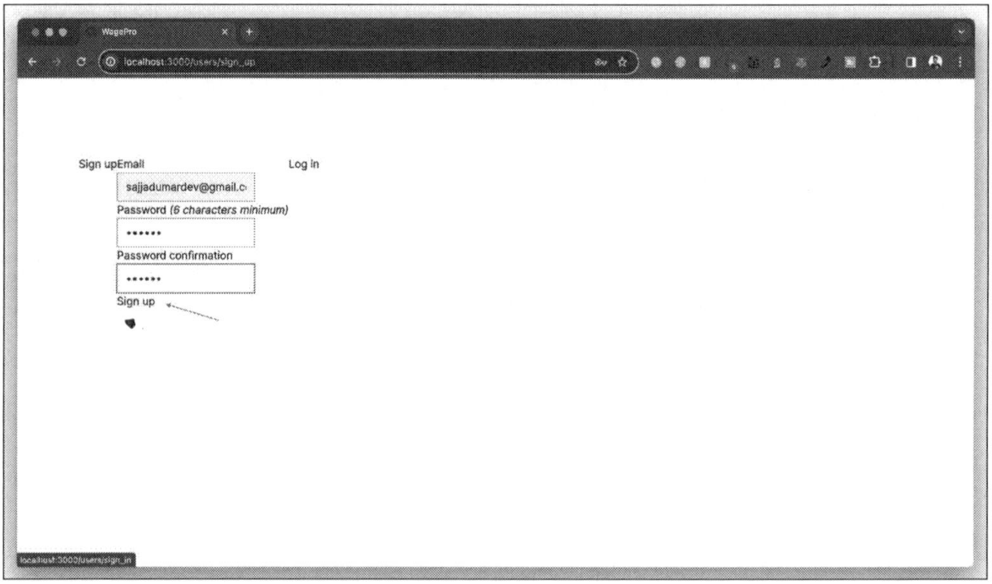

Figure 6.16: *Sign up form*

After filling in your email and password, click the Sign-up button highlighted in *Figure* 6.16. Once you click on it, a new user will be created in the database, and you will be redirected to the root path of the application which is our home page.

Figure 6.17 shows the homepage after successful user registration:

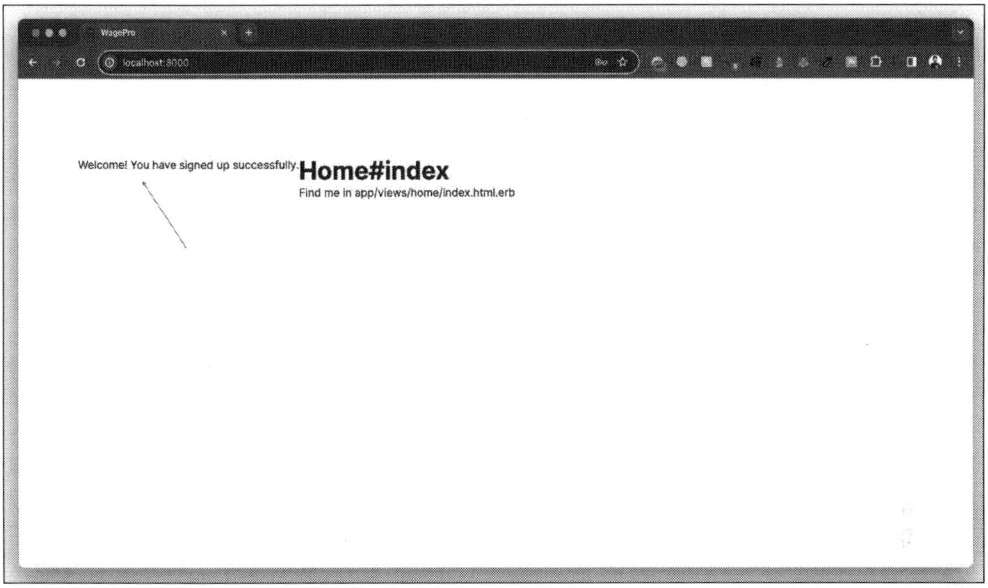

Figure 6.17: *Homepage after sign-up success*

The flash notice you see is the one we added to our application layout file (refer to *Figure* 6.11).

Let us have a look at the logs and understand what happened when you click the Sign-up button on the registration page. *Figure* 6.18 shows server logs for user registration requests.

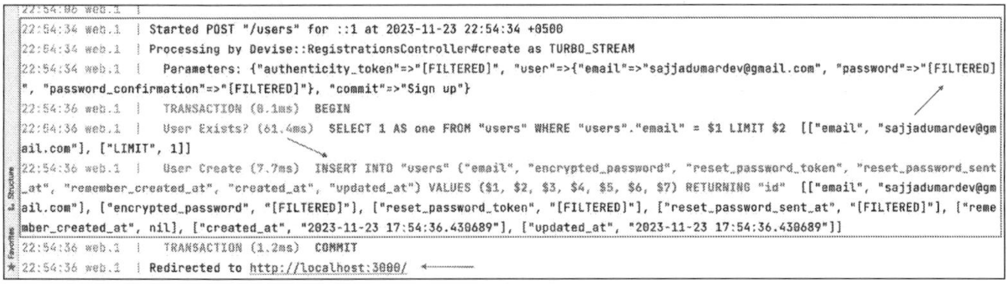

Figure 6.18: *Logs during Sign-up request*

If you look closely at *Figure* 6.18, you will notice:

- Sensitive information is automatically filtered out in logs.
- An insert quarry is made to create a user with "**encrypted_password**", this encryption of password is handled by the devise gem.
- After creating the user, the server redirected the user to http://localhost:3000

If we try to access the created user via the rails console, you will notice the sensitive information is indeed encrypted in the database to add an extra layer of security.

```
sumar@Sajjads-MBP wage_pro % rails console
Loading development environment (Rails 7.1.2)
3.2.2 :001 > user = User.last
  User Load (1.1ms)  SELECT "users".* FROM "users" ORDER BY "users"."id" DESC LIMIT $1  [["LIMIT", 1]]
 => #<User id: 1, email: "sajjadumardev@gmail.com", created_at: "2023-11-23 17:54:36.430689000 +0000", updated_at: "2023-11-23 17:5...
3.2.2 :002 > user
 => #<User id: 1, email: "sajjadumardev@gmail.com", created_at: "2023-11-23 17:54:36.430689000 +0000", updated_at: "2023-11-23 17:54:36.4
30689000 +0000">
3.2.2 :003 > user.password
 => nil
3.2.2 :004 > user.encrypted_password
 => "$2a$12$f/2qpVUcucEPlXKxxOM4N..W8xCfDT6fJ8pO1w9gdKkqjH8MveGPu"
3.2.2 :005 > 
```

Figure 6.19: *Rails console*

The Rails console, often referred to as the Rails REPL (Read-Eval-Print Loop), is a command-line tool that provides an interactive environment for interacting with your Rails application using Ruby code. It allows you to perform various operations, including accessing your application's models, querying the database, testing snippets of code, and debugging.

To access the Rails console, you typically run the following command in your terminal within the root directory of your Rails application:

```
rails console


# Short command syntax

rails c
```

This command initializes the Rails console and loads your entire Rails application, allowing you to execute Ruby code directly in the context of your application. You can interact with your models, access the database, create, read, update, or delete records, and test different functionalities of your application by writing and executing Ruby code in this environment.

Tip: *Explore and play around with the Login page and reset password flow.*

We have not done SMTP settings yet, so you will not receive any reset password email, but email instructions can be found in the server logs.

Role-Based Authorization in Rails

Role-based authorization is a security mechanism that grants access rights to users based on their assigned roles within an application. This approach organizes users into predefined groups or roles, and access privileges are granted or restricted according to these roles. It is a foundational concept in ensuring controlled access to resources within web applications.

Key Components of Role-Based Authorization

Roles:

Roles represent a set of permissions or access rights allocated to a group of users based on their responsibilities or positions. Roles are created based on common job functions or responsibilities (for example, admin, manager, employee).

Permissions:

Permissions outline the specific actions or resources that a particular role can access or manipulate. Each role is associated with a set of permissions, defining what actions are allowed or denied for users within that role.

User-Role Mapping:

Users are assigned to specific roles, dictating the permissions and functionalities they can access. A user may be assigned to multiple roles based on their responsibilities, allowing flexible access control.

Implementing Role-Based Authentication

While we can implement the role-based authentication manually from scratch, we will be using community-provided gem to make it quick and easy for us.

Creating Roles

To create roles, we will be using Rolify Gem, which is a very simple Roles library without any authorization enforcement.

You can read about it at https://github.com/RolifyCommunity/rolify.

To use this gem, we need to add it to our application, so add the following code in your gemfile:

```
gem "rolify"
```

Figure 6.20 shows the gemfile with rolify added:

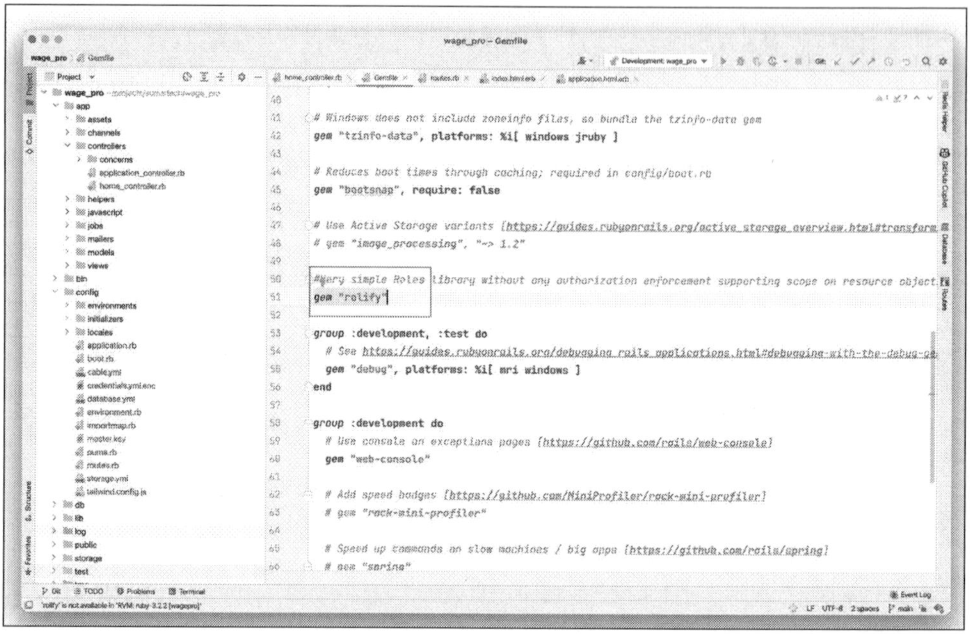

Figure 6.20: *The rolify gem added to gemfile*

Now, run the following command to install the newly added gem:

```
bundle install
```

Once done, use the generator to setup Rolify. Role and User class are the default names. However, you can specify any class name you want. For the User class name, you would probably use the one provided by your authentication solution, that is, User for our app.

Run the following command on the terminal:

```
rails g rolify Role User
```

Figure 6.21 shows the rolify generator command in action:

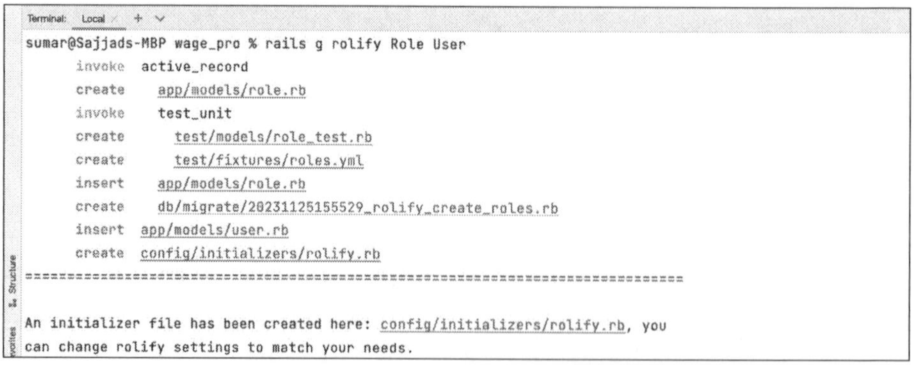

Figure 6.21: *Rolify generator in action*

Now, run the migration using the following command:

```
rails db:migrate
```

Figure 6.22 shows the migrations in action:

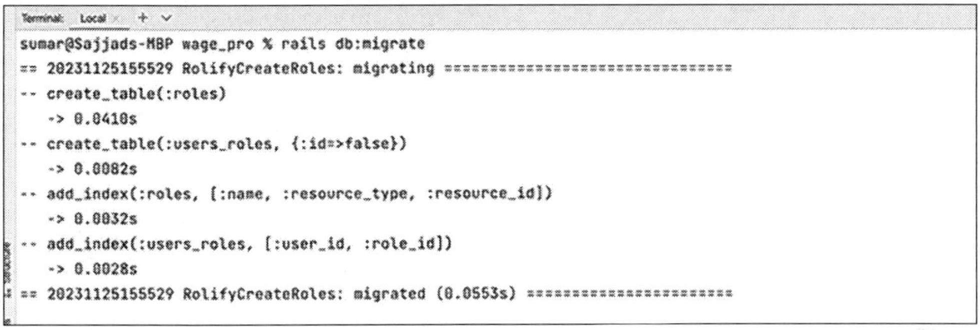

Figure 6.22: *Running migrations*

ProTip: *Open each file shown in Figure 6.21 and study all the changes made by rolify generator command.*

Now we can add roles to users, let us demonstrate this via Rails console. In the rails console, we can add an admin role to my registered user, as shown in *Figure* 6.23:

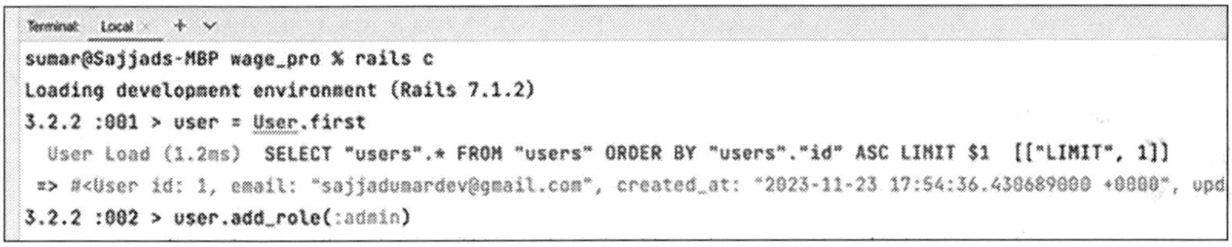

Figure 6.23: *Adding admin role to a user*

Behind the scenes, the "**`user.add_role(:admin)`**" added a new role into our "**`roles`**" table (created by rolify gem) and assigned that role to the user (using "**`user_roles`**" join table created by rolify gem).

Figure 6.24 shows the newly created role in the "**`roles`**" table and that role is successfully applied to the user:

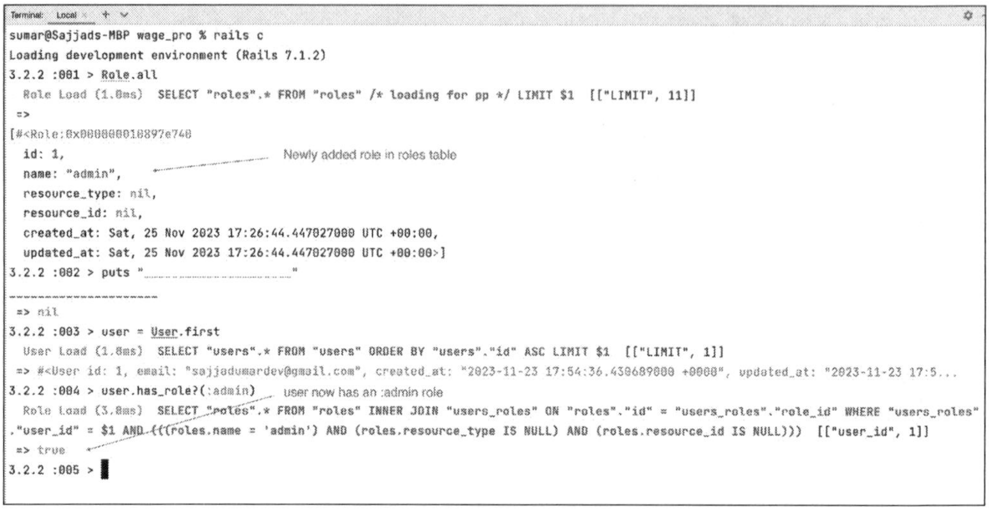

Figure 6.24: *Role applied to user*

Now that we have roles in our app and we can apply different roles to our users, the next step is to add permissions to these roles and what resources they can access.

Adding Permissions to Roles and Resources

Let us register another user as shown in *Figure* 6.16 (use incognito/private browser window if you already have a user signed in).

We have created a new user with the following email "employee@xyz.com". Now let us add a new "**employee**" role to it via console by running the following code on the rails console.

```
user = User.find_by(email: 'employee@xyz.com')
user.add_role(:employee)
```

Replace the email with the email of your newly registered user. Refer to *Figure* 6.23 if needed.

Now, we have one admin and one employee in our database.

What do we want?

We want to create a page where we display user information (a profile page), but an admin can view the profile page of any user but an employee can only view his information.

Let us quickly create a **ProfileController** with show action by running the following command:

```
rails g controller profile show
```

This will create a **ProfileController** for us (among other files). Replace the "**show**" action with the following code:

```
def show
    @user = User.find(params[:id])
end
```

In the view file "**app/views/profile/show.html.erb**", replace whatever you have with the following code:

```
<div>
  <h1 class="font-bold text-4xl">Profile</h1>
  <p>User: <%= @user.roles.pluck(:name) %></p>
  <p>Email: <%= @user.email %></p>
</div>
```

Now add route to this controller in **routes.rb** file, as shown in *Figure* 6.25:

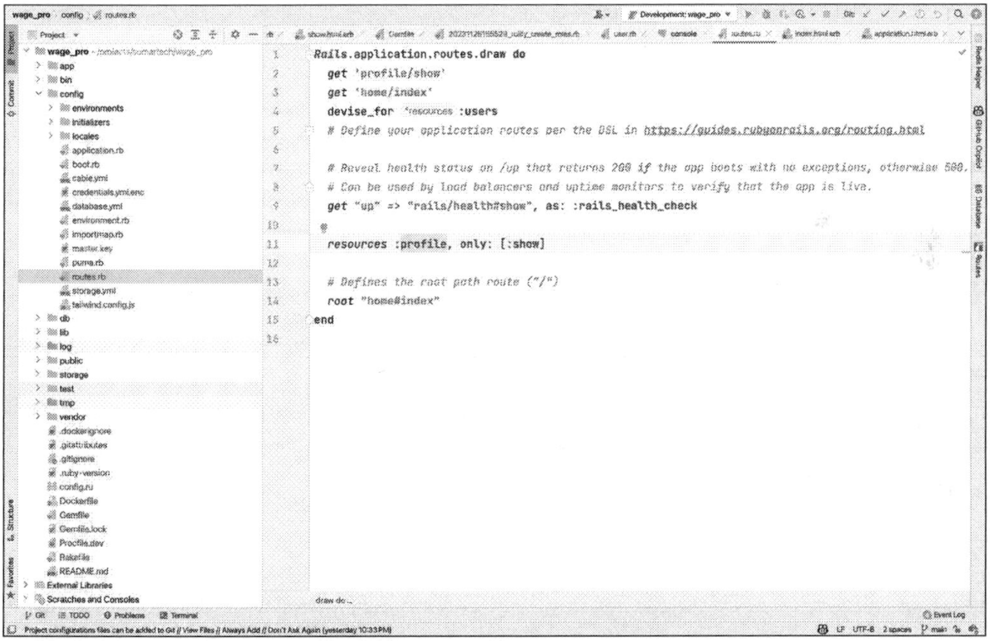

***Figure 6.25**: Adding profile route to routes.rb file*

Now, if we visit this URL in the browser "localhost:3000/profile/:id" (:id is the id of the user you want to view), you will see the profile page as shown in *Figure* 6.26:

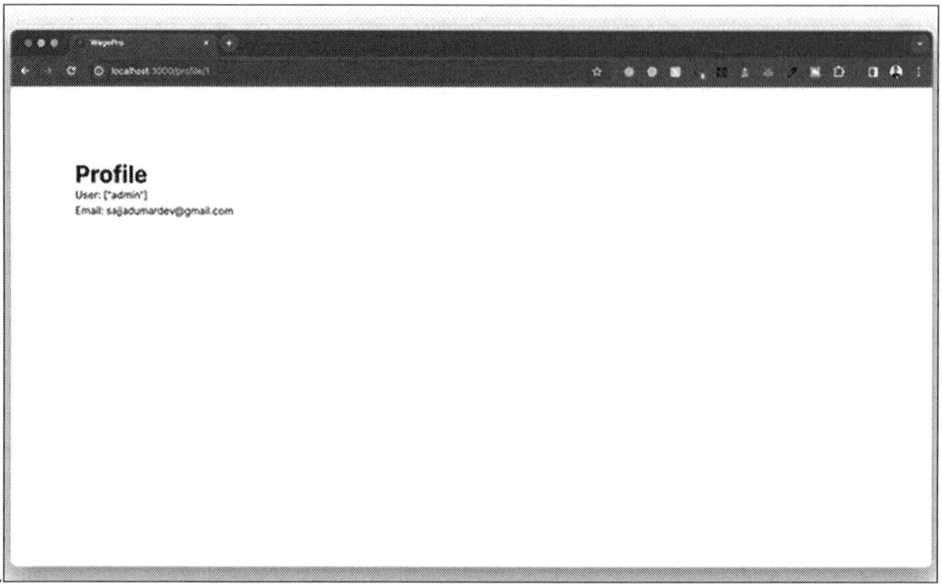

Figure 6.26: *Profile page of a user*

The problem with this page is that you can view the profile of any user by just changing the ID in the URL even if you are not logged in.

ProTip: *Try changing the ID in the profile to another user in your database without logging in. You can use an incognito or private browser window to simulate the logged-out user.*

The first problem we can simply fix by adding the following code provided by devise gem in the **ProfileController**:

```
before_action :authenticate_user!
```

The entire controller should look something like this:

```
class ProfileController < ApplicationController
  before_action :authenticate_user!


  def show
    @user = User.find(params[:id])
  end
end
```

Now if you visit the profile link without logging in (on an incognito window if needed), you will see a flash alert similar to the one shown in *Figure* 6.27.

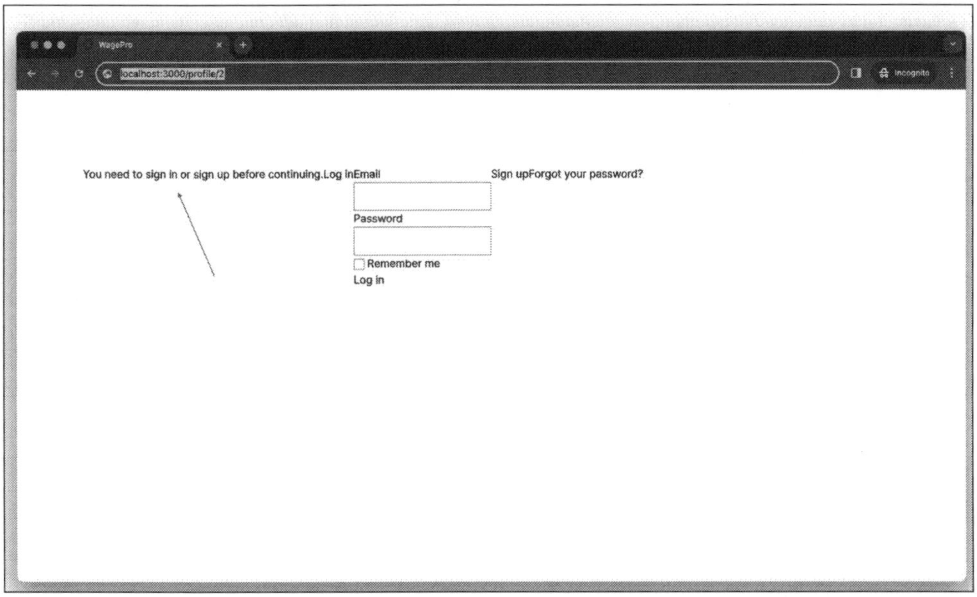

Figure 6.27: *You need to sign in or sign up before continuing*

So, now only signed-in users can see the profile page, but if you sign in with employee credentials, you will still be able to see the profile of the admin (try it on before moving forward).

To fix this issue we need authorization. Although we can implement the authorization manually from scratch, we will leverage another great authorization gem called "**pundit**".

Pundit provides a set of helpers that guide you in leveraging regular Ruby classes and object-oriented design patterns to build a straightforward, robust, and scalable authorization system.

Read all about the pundit gem at https://github.com/varvet/pundit.

Let us add the pundit gem to our app by running the following command:

```
bundle add pundit
```

This command will automatically add it to your gemfile and install it.

Once installed, run the following generator command (taken from the aforementioned gem link):

```
rails g pundit:install
```

Now modify your **ApplicationController** to look like this:

```
class ApplicationController < ActionController::Base
  include Pundit::Authorization
end
```

This concludes the installation of the pundit gem. Now let us use it in our application.

Pundit is focused on the notion of policy classes. The documentation recommends that you put these classes in the app/policies directory.

Let us add a policy class for our User model as shown in the *Figure* 6.28:

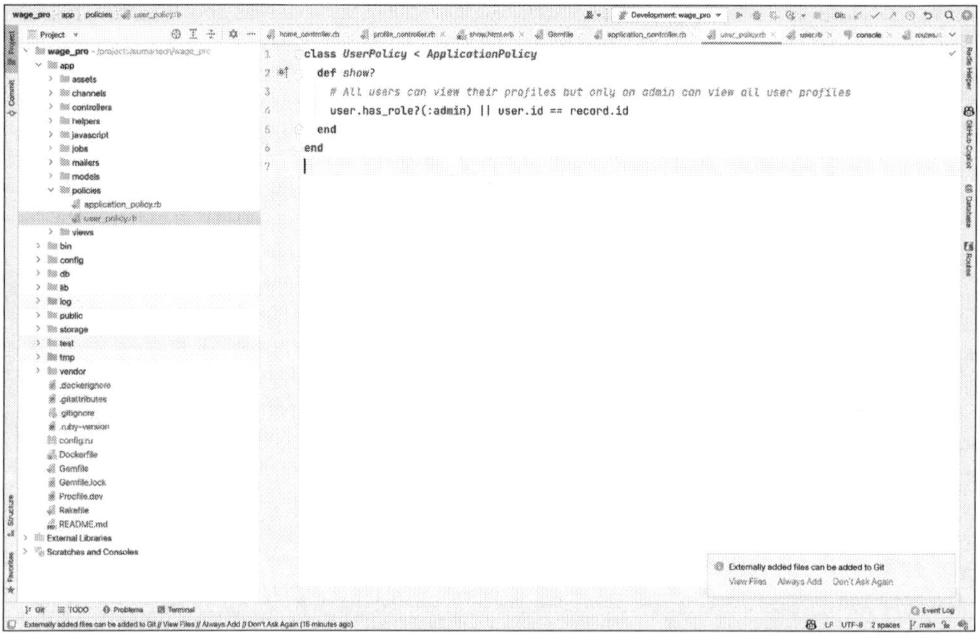

Figure 6.28: *User policy*

And modify the **ProfileController** to look like this:

```
class ProfileController < ApplicationController
  before_action :authenticate_user!


  def show
    @user = User.find(params[:id])


    authorize @user
  end
end
```

Now, restart the server so that all the newly added classes are properly loaded into our application, and try accessing the profile while logging in as an employee and admin.

Logged in as an Admin

When logged in as an admin, you can see all the profiles as shown in *Figure 6.29*:

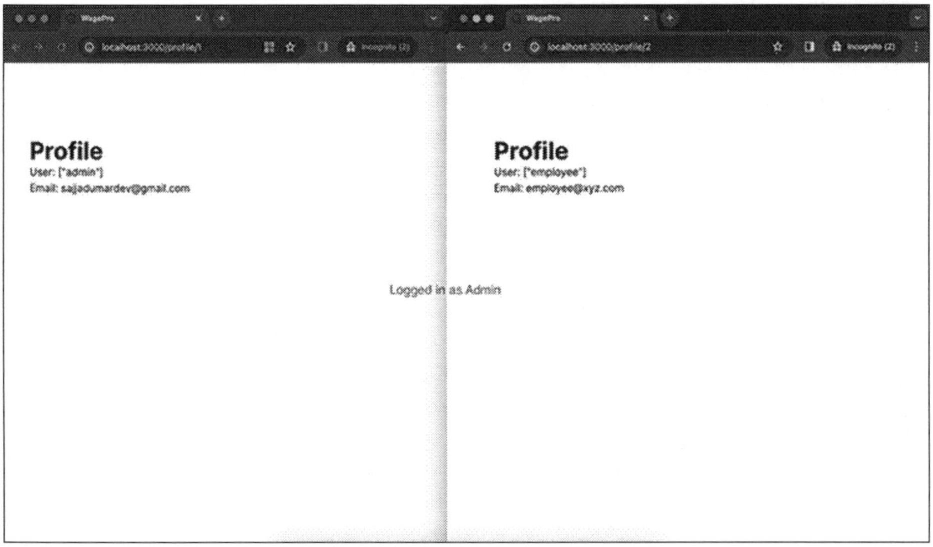

Figure 6.29: *Profile pages for admin user*

Logged in as an Employee

When logged in as an Employee, you can see only your profile, and if you try to access any other profile by changing the ID in URL, you will see an error as shown in *Figure 6.30*:

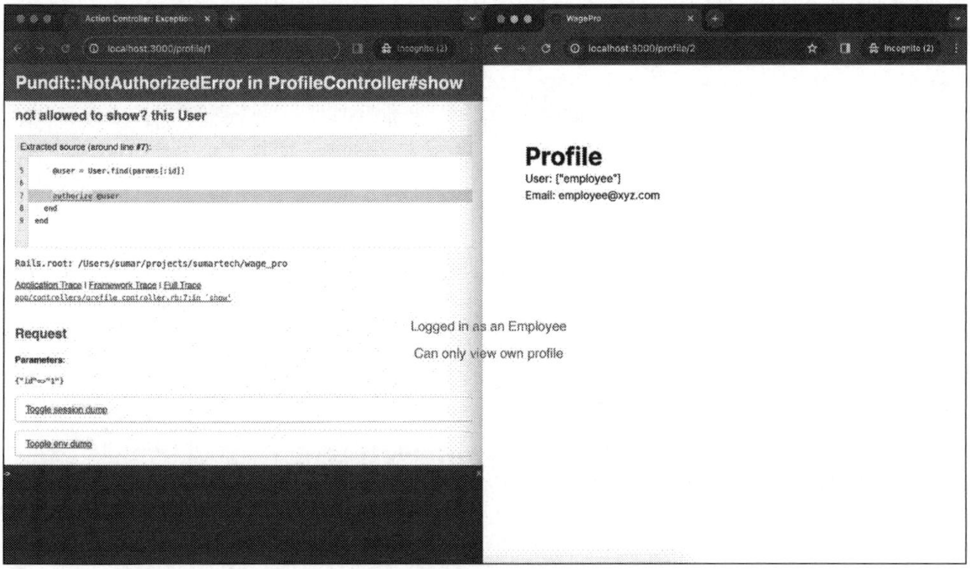

Figure 6.30: *Profile pages for employee user*

This means our authorization is working as expected.

Making It Look Good

To make this and the upcoming chapters brief, we will not go into details about styling the entire thing but we will just guide you toward our approach of styling and let you experiment with it.

To make our life easier we will be using the Flowbite components library for TailwindCSS, you can start developing with an open-source library of over 600+ UI components, sections, and pages built with the utility classes from Tailwind CSS and designed in Figma.

You can find the document for Flowbite at https://flowbite.com, and here is a link to a guide on how you can integrate Flowbite with our application: https://flowbite.com/docs/getting-started/rails.

Do not forget to look at `importmap` configurations while working with Rails 7 and above at https://flowbite.com/docs/getting-started/rails/#importmap

Once Flowbite is installed, let us set up a few things so that we are on the same page.

ProTip: *You can just copy and paste these code snippets into your application.*

Replace the code you have in "`app/assets/stylesheets/application.tailwind.css`" file with the following code to add some common style elements that we will be using on multiple pages:

```
@tailwind base;

@tailwind components;

@tailwind utilities;



.form-label {

  @apply block mb-2 text-sm font-medium text-gray-900 dark:text-white;

}


.form-text-input {

  @apply bg-gray-50 border border-gray-300 text-gray-900 sm:text-sm
rounded-lg focus:ring-primary-500 focus:border-primary-500 block w-full
p-2.5 dark:bg-gray-700 dark:border-gray-600 dark:placeholder-gray-400
dark:text-white dark:focus:ring-primary-500 dark:focus:border-prima-
ry-500;
```

```
}

.button-primary {
  @apply w-full px-3 py-3 text-base font-medium text-center text-white bg-primary-700 rounded-lg hover:bg-primary-800 focus:ring-4 focus:ring-primary-300 sm:w-auto dark:bg-primary-600 dark:hover:bg-primary-700 dark:focus:ring-primary-800;
}

.field {
  @apply mb-5;
}
```

Move out flash messages into a separate shared partial and add some styling. Create a new file "**app/views/layouts/shared/_notice_and_alert.html.erb**" and add the following code:

```
<% if notice.present? %>
  <div id="alert-1" class="flex items-center p-4 mb-4 text-blue-800 rounded-lg bg-blue-50 dark:bg-gray-800 dark:text-blue-400" role="alert">
    <svg class="flex-shrink-0 w-4 h-4" aria-hidden="true" xmlns="http://www.w3.org/2000/svg" fill="currentColor" viewBox="0 0 20 20">
      <path d="M10 .5a9.5 9.5 0 1 0 9.5 9.5A9.51 9.51 0 0 0 10 .5ZM9.5 4a1.5 1.5 0 1 1 0 3 1.5 1.5 0 0 1 0-3ZM12 15H8a1 1 0 0 1 0-2h1v-3H8a1 1 0 0 1 0-2h2a1 1 0 0 1 1 1v4h1a1 1 0 0 1 0 2Z"/>
    </svg>
    <span class="sr-only">Info</span>
    <div class="ml-3 text-sm font-medium">
      <p class="notice"><%= notice %></p>
    </div>
    <button type="button" class="ml-auto -mx-1.5 -my-1.5 bg-blue-50 text-blue-500 rounded-lg focus:ring-2 focus:ring-blue-400 p-1.5 hover:bg-blue-200 inline-flex items-center justify-center h-8 w-8 dark:bg-gray-800 dark:text-blue-400 dark:hover:bg-gray-700" data-dismiss-target="#alert-1" aria-label="Close">
      <span class="sr-only">Close</span>
      <svg class="w-3 h-3" aria-hidden="true" xmlns="http://www.w3.org/2000/svg" fill="none" viewBox="0 0 14 14">
        <path stroke="currentColor" stroke-linecap="round" stroke-linejoin="round" stroke-width="2" d="m1 1 6 6m0 0 6 6M7 7l6-6M7 7l-6 6"/>
```

```
      </svg>
    </button>
  </div>
<% end %>

<% if alert.present? %>
  <div id="alert-2" class="flex items-center p-4 mb-4 text-red-800 round-
ed-lg bg-red-50 dark:bg-gray-800 dark:text-red-400" role="alert">
    <svg class="flex-shrink-0 w-4 h-4" aria-hidden="true" xmlns="http://
www.w3.org/2000/svg" fill="currentColor" viewBox="0 0 20 20">
      <path d="M10 .5a9.5 9.5 0 1 0 9.5 9.5A9.51 9.51 0 0 0 10 .5ZM9.5
4a1.5 1.5 0 1 1 0 3 1.5 1.5 0 0 1 0-3ZM12 15H8a1 1 0 0 1 0-2h1v-3H8a1 1
0 0 1 0-2h2a1 1 0 0 1 1 1v4h1a1 1 0 0 1 0 2Z"/>
    </svg>
    <span class="sr-only">Info</span>
    <div class="ml-3 text-sm font-medium">
      <p class="alert"><%= alert %></p>
    </div>
    <button type="button" class="ml-auto -mx-1.5 -my-1.5 bg-red-50
text-red-500 rounded-lg focus:ring-2 focus:ring-red-400 p-1.5 hov-
er:bg-red-200 inline-flex items-center justify-center h-8 w-8 dark-
:bg-gray-800 dark:text-red-400 dark:hover:bg-gray-700" data-dismiss-tar-
get="#alert-2" aria-label="Close">
      <span class="sr-only">Close</span>
      <svg class="w-3 h-3" aria-hidden="true" xmlns="http://www.
w3.org/2000/svg" fill="none" viewBox="0 0 14 14">
        <path stroke="currentColor" stroke-linecap="round" stroke-line-
join="round" stroke-width="2" d="m1 1 6 6m0 0 6 6M7 7l6-6M7 7l-6 6"/>
      </svg>
    </button>
  </div>
<% end %>
```

Now modify your "**app/views/layouts/application.html.erb**" file to have the following code:

```
<!DOCTYPE html>
<html>
  <head>
```

```
    <title>Wage Pro</title>
    <meta name="viewport" content="width=device-width,initial-scale=1">
    <%= csrf_meta_tags %>
    <%= csp_meta_tag %>
    <%= stylesheet_link_tag "tailwind", "inter-font", "data-turbo-track":
"reload" %>

    <%= stylesheet_link_tag "application", "data-turbo-track": "reload"
%>
    <%= javascript_importmap_tags %>
    <script src="https://cdnjs.cloudflare.com/ajax/libs/flowbite/2.0.0/
flowbite.min.js"></script>
  </head>

  <body class="bg-gray-50">
    <main>
      <%= render 'layouts/shared/notice_and_alert' %>
      <%= yield %>
    </main>
  </body>
</html>
```

Replace the code inside "**`config/tailwind.config.js`**" with the following code:

```
const defaultTheme = require('tailwindcss/defaultTheme')

module.exports = {
  content: [
    './public/*.html',
    './app/helpers/**/*.rb',
    './app/javascript/**/*.js',
    './app/views/**/*.{erb,haml,html,slim}',
    './node_modules/flowbite/**/*.js'
  ],
  safelist: [
    'w-64',
```

```
    'w-1/2',
    'rounded-l-lg',
    'rounded-r-lg',
    'bg-gray-200',
    'grid-cols-4',
    'grid-cols-7',
    'h-6',
    'leading-6',
    'h-9',
    'leading-9',
    'shadow-lg',
    'bg-opacity-50',
    'dark:bg-opacity-80'
  ],
  theme: {
    extend: {
      colors: {
        primary: { "50": "#eff6ff", "100": "#dbeafe", "200": "#bfdbfe",
"300": "#93c5fd", "400": "#60a5fa", "500": "#3b82f6", "600": "#2563eb",
"700": "#1d4ed8", "800": "#1e40af", "900": "#1e3a8a" }
      },
      fontFamily: {
        'sans': ['Inter', 'ui-sans-serif', 'system-ui', '-apple-system',
'system-ui', 'Segoe UI', 'Roboto', 'Helvetica Neue', 'Arial', 'Noto
Sans', 'sans-serif', 'Apple Color Emoji', 'Segoe UI Emoji', 'Segoe UI
Symbol', 'Noto Color Emoji'],
        'body': ['Inter', 'ui-sans-serif', 'system-ui', '-apple-system',
'system-ui', 'Segoe UI', 'Roboto', 'Helvetica Neue', 'Arial', 'Noto
Sans', 'sans-serif', 'Apple Color Emoji', 'Segoe UI Emoji', 'Segoe UI
Symbol', 'Noto Color Emoji'],
        'mono': ['ui-monospace', 'SFMono-Regular', 'Menlo', 'Monaco',
'Consolas', 'Liberation Mono', 'Courier New', 'monospace']
      },
      transitionProperty: {
        'width': 'width'
      },
```

```
      textDecoration: ['active'],
      minWidth: {
        'kanban': '28rem'
      },
    },
  },
  plugins: [
    require('@tailwindcss/forms'),
    require('@tailwindcss/aspect-ratio'),
    require('@tailwindcss/typography'),
    require('@tailwindcss/container-queries'),
    require('flowbite/plugin')({
      charts: true,
    }),
  ]
}
```

As far as core setup and initial configuration are concerned, we are done. If you revisit the application, you will see that elements in our app now look more organized than before.

Figure 6.15 shows how our Log-in page looked before, whereas *Figure* 6.31 shows how our Log-in page looks now.

Figure 6.31: *Log-in page after initial Flowbite setup and styling*

Let us make it look like this in *Figure* 6.32 by adding the following code to "**app/views/devise/sessions/new.html.erb**" file:

```
<div class="flex flex-col items-center justify-center px-6 pt-8 mx-auto
md:h-screen pt:mt-0 dark:bg-gray-900">
```

```
  <a href="/" class="flex items-center justify-center mb-8 text-2xl font-semibold lg:mb-10 dark:text-white">
    <span>WagePro</span>
  </a>

  <!-- Card -->
  <div class="w-full max-w-xl p-6 space-y-8 sm:p-8 bg-white rounded-lg shadow dark:bg-gray-800">
    <h2 class="text-2xl font-bold text-gray-900 dark:text-white">
      Sign in to platform
    </h2>

    <%= form_for(resource, as: resource_name, url: session_path(resource_name), class: 'class="mt-8 space-y-6' ) do |f| %>
      <div class="field">
        <%= f.label :email, class: 'form-label' %>
        <%= f.email_field :email, autofocus: true, autocomplete: "email", class: 'form-text-input', placeholder: "name@company.com", required: true %>
      </div>

      <div class="field">
        <%= f.label :password, class: 'form-label' %>
        <%= f.password_field :password, autocomplete: "current-password", class: 'form-text-input', placeholder: '••••••••', required: true %>
      </div>

      <% if devise_mapping.rememberable? %>
        <div class="flex items-start">
          <div class="flex items-center h-5">
            <%= f.check_box :remember_me, class: 'w-4 h-4 border-gray-300 rounded bg-gray-50 focus:ring-3 focus:ring-primary-300 dark:focus:ring-primary-600 dark:ring-offset-gray-800 dark:bg-gray-700 dark:border-gray-600' %>
          </div>
          <div class="ml-3 text-sm">
```

```
            <%= f.label :remember_me, class: 'font-medium text-gray-900 
dark:text-white' %>
          </div>

          <%- if devise_mapping.recoverable? && controller_name != 
'passwords' && controller_name != 'registrations' %>
            <%= link_to "Lost Password?", new_password_path(resource_
name), class: 'ml-auto text-sm text-primary-700 hover:underline dark:-
text-primary-500' %>
          <% end %>
        </div>
      <% end %>

      <div class="actions mt-8 mb-8">
        <%= f.submit "Log in", class: 'button-primary' %>
      </div>

      <%- if devise_mapping.registerable? && controller_name != 
'registrations' %>
        <div class="text-sm font-medium text-gray-500 dark:-
text-gray-400">
          Not registered? <%= link_to "Create account", new_registra-
tion_path(resource_name), class: 'text-primary-700 hover:underline 
dark:text-primary-500' %>
        </div>
      <% end %>
    <% end %>
  </div>
</div>
```

Now if you refresh the Log-in page, it will look like this:

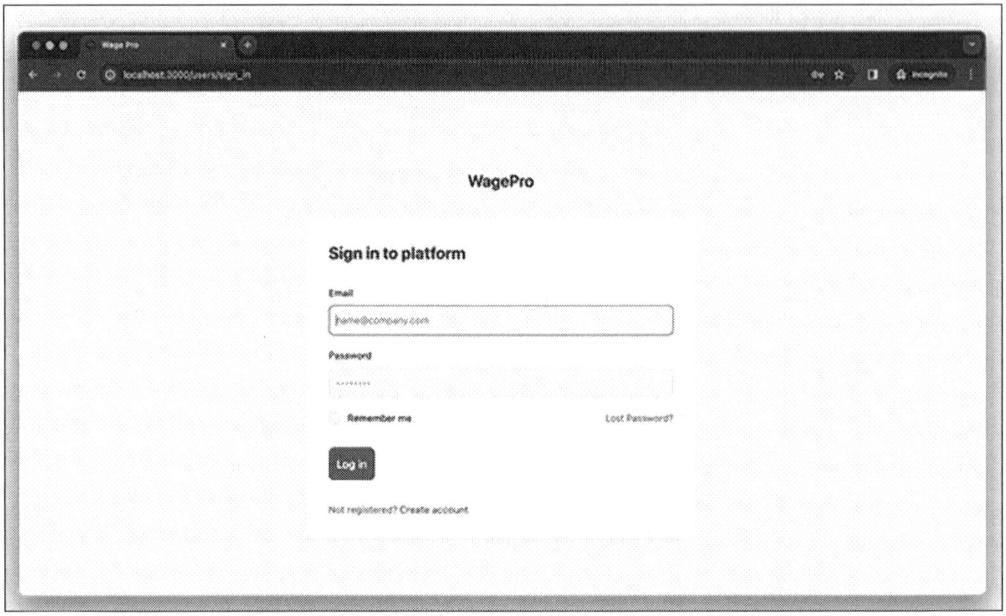

Figure 6.32: *Log-in page after adding styles*

Do It Yourself

As a practice assignment, apply the same styling to the rest of the pages of the authentication flow.

You will be touching the following devise pages:

- app/views/devise/passwords/new.html.erb
- app/views/devise/passwords/edit.html.erb
- app/views/devise/registrations/new.html.erb

Refer to the code on GitHub if you find yourself stuck somewhere. Link to all the code in this chapter: https://github.com/ava-orange-education/Ruby-on-Rails-for-Agile-Web-Development/tree/main/chapter06/wage_pro

You can get access to everything covered in the book on this GitHub repo: https://github.com/ava-orange-education/Ruby-on-Rails-for-Agile-Web-Development.

Conclusion

In this chapter, we delved into the fundamental aspect of user authentication, highlighting its crucial role in ensuring secure and personalized access within web applications. We explored various common authentication methods and comprehensively understood the authentication process in web development. By implementing user registration and login functionalities, we constructed a brand-new Rails app from scratch, establishing a solid foundation for user authentication flow. Role-based authorization was a pivotal aspect we covered, showcasing its key components and how to effectively implement this level of authentication. Additionally, we spruced up our application's appearance by integrating the Flowbite component library and applying basic styling, enhancing the user experience.

Looking ahead to the next chapter, titled *Testing and Test-Driven Development*, we will delve into the world of robust testing methodologies. Test-driven development (TDD) and its importance in crafting resilient and bug-free code will be at the forefront of our discussion. We will embark on a journey to learn the art of writing tests to ensure our application's reliability and explore best practices in creating tests that drive our development process. By understanding the significance of testing, we will empower ourselves to build more dependable and efficient software, elevate our coding skills, and fortify projects with foolproof testing methods in the upcoming chapter.

Short Quiz

1. **What is the primary purpose of user authentication in web applications?**
   a. To validate user permissions
   b. To ensure secure user data transmission
   c. To verify user identity
   d. To enhance the visual appearance of the website
2. **What authentication method involves confirming a user's identity through something they know?**
   a. Biometric authentication
   b. Two-factor authentication
   c. Password-based authentication
   d. Role-based authentication
3. **Which component is responsible for controlling access rights based on user roles?**
   a. Authentication
   b. Authorization
   c. Encryption
   d. Validation

4. **What is the primary role of user registration in the authentication process?**
   a. Granting access to admin privileges
   b. Storing user preferences
   c. Enabling user access to the system
   d. Ensuring data encryption during transmission
5. **Which authentication method requires users to provide two different authentication factors?**
   a. Single sign-on
   b. Multi-factor authentication
   c. Password less authentication
   d. OAuth authentication
6. **What is the main goal of implementing authorization in web applications?**
   a. Ensuring secure data transmission
   b. Controlling user access rights
   c. Enhancing user interface design
   d. Verifying user identity
7. **Which method controls access to various resources based on a user's role or permissions?**
   a. Role-based authorization
   b. Multi-factor authentication
   c. Password hashing
   d. Biometric authentication
8. **What is the primary function of the Pundit Gem in a Rails application?**
   a. Handling authentication
   b. Implementing database migrations
   c. Managing authorization policies
   d. Enhancing routing configurations

9. **What is the primary purpose of the Rolify Gem in a Rails application?**
   a. Handling user authentication
   b. Defining user roles and permissions
   c. Managing database migrations
   d. Implementing password encryption
10. **What is Flowbite primarily used for in web development?**
    a. Managing user authentication
    b. Designing responsive and customizable UI components
    c. Handling database migrations
    d. Implementing role-based authorization

Chapter 7
Testing and Test-Driven Development

Introduction

This chapter invites you to embark on an exploration likened to building a robust fortress to protect your web application from unforeseen storms and trials. Imagine your code as the foundation of this fortress – while creating it is crucial, ensuring its durability is equally paramount. Welcome to the world of testing in web development, where the emphasis is not only on creating the structure but also fortifying it against potential vulnerabilities and errors. Just as a skilled architect meticulously inspects each brick and mortar, testing in web development meticulously evaluates every line of code, validating its strength, reliability, and resilience. In this chapter, we will journey through the diverse landscapes of testing methodologies, where each test functions as a shield, safeguarding your application's integrity and ensuring its unwavering functionality. So, gear up to uncover the essence of testing and crafting resilient web applications that stand tall amidst the challenges of the digital realm.

Structure

In this chapter, we will discuss the following topics:

- Importance of Testing in Agile Development
  - Benefits of Testing in Agile Methodologies
  - Ensuring Software Quality and Reliability through Testing
- Types of Testing in Web Development
  - Overview of Various Types of Testing (Unit, Integration, Acceptance, and more)
  - Explaining the Purpose and Significance of Each Type
- Introduction to Testing Frameworks in Rails
  - Popular Testing Frameworks and Their Key Features

  - Choosing the Right Testing Framework
- Writing Unit Tests for Models and Controllers
  - Understanding the Importance of Unit Testing in Rails
  - Writing and Implementing Unit Tests for Models and Controllers
- Integration Testing and Acceptance Testing
  - Differentiating Between Integration and Acceptance Testing
  - Strategies for Writing Effective Integration and Acceptance Tests
- Test-Driven Development (TDD) Approach
  - Overview and Principles of TDD
  - Implementing Test-Driven Approach in WagePro

Importance of Testing in Agile Development

In the world of Agile development, testing stands as the cornerstone of ensuring software quality and reliability throughout the development lifecycle. When it comes to building web applications with Ruby on Rails, understanding the importance of testing within an Agile framework becomes fundamental to crafting robust, user-centric products.

Benefits of Testing in Agile Methodologies

Agile practices emphasize iterative development, continuous feedback, and quick adaptability. Testing plays a pivotal role in supporting these principles in the following ways:

- **Early Bug Identification:** Agile's iterative nature allows for the early detection of bugs, enabling faster resolutions and reducing the risk of major issues down the line.
- **Flexibility and Adaptability:** Testing ensures that each change or addition to the codebase does not compromise the existing functionality, maintaining the flexibility inherent in Agile development.
- **Customer Satisfaction:** Customer feedback and aligning with requirements throughout the Agile development process are crucial. Regular testing is an integral part of ensuring the product resonates with users and meets their expectations.
- **Cost-Efficiency:** Detecting defects early in the development cycle saves time and resources. Testing helps identify and rectify issues before they become costly problems.

- **Enhanced Communication:** Testing fosters collaboration among team members, encouraging discussions on requirements, potential issues, and effective solutions.

Ensuring Software Quality and Reliability through Testing

When applied to Ruby on Rails development, testing becomes an integral part of the process:

- **Comprehensive Test Coverage:** Different types of tests (unit, integration, acceptance, and so on) ensure that the Rails application functions correctly and meets high-quality standards.
- **Continuous Integration and Deployment:** Integration of testing into the development process ensures that code changes are continuously and reliably tested. This enables frequent and stable releases.
- **Test-Driven Development (TDD):** Writing tests before coding ensures that the code aligns with specific requirements, promoting better code quality.
- **Regression Testing:** Frequent iterations and updates in Agile can introduce new issues or regressions. Regular regression testing confirms that new changes have not adversely affected existing functionalities.
- **Feedback Loops:** Testing provides crucial feedback on the software's behavior and performance, enabling refinement and enhancements based on real-world usage and requirements.

In the Rails ecosystem, frameworks such as RSpec and Minitest provide the tools necessary for writing comprehensive tests across different layers of the application.

Remember, testing in Agile is not a one-time task but a continuous process integral to delivering high-quality software that meets and exceeds user expectations.

Types of Testing in Web Development

Building a fortress involves rigorous planning, construction, and testing to ensure it stands strong against potential threats. Similarly, in web development, various types of testing work together to fortify your software against vulnerabilities and ensure its resilience.

- **Unit Testing**

  Unit testing focuses on scrutinizing individual parts (units) of code in isolation. It is akin to checking each brick's quality before constructing a fortress. For instance, testing a function that calculates the total price of items in a shopping cart is like examining the quality of a brick. Developers usually perform these tests, often using frameworks like RSpec or Minitest.

- **Integration Testing**

  Integration testing examines how different units/modules work together. Think of it as assessing how various parts of a fortress, like walls, gates, and towers, coordinate with each other. It ensures these components interact seamlessly; just as different software modules must communicate effectively. Developers and specialized testers commonly handle these tests.

- **Acceptance Testing**

  Acceptance testing evaluates the entire system to confirm it meets defined requirements. It is similar to ensuring the fortress fulfills its purpose as intended. For example, testing if a user can smoothly complete a purchase from start to finish. QA testers or product owners typically conduct these tests.

- **Regression Testing**

  Regression testing verifies that recent changes have not adversely impacted existing functionalities. It is comparable to rechecking previously fortified parts after adding new sections to the fortress. Developers usually automate these tests to ensure stable performance.

- **Functional Testing**

  Functional testing ensures individual functions in the system perform as expected. It is like examining the different capabilities of the fortress, such as checking if the drawbridge functions correctly. These tests are mostly automated by developers.

- **Performance Testing**

  Performance testing assesses how the system handles various conditions like heavy traffic. It is similar to stress-testing the fortress under different scenarios to see how it holds up. Performance engineers or specialized testers perform these tests, often using tools like JMeter (JMeter is an Apache project that can be used as a load testing tool for analyzing and measuring the performance of a variety of services, with a focus on web applications).

- **Security Testing**

  Security testing seeks to identify and fix vulnerabilities to prevent breaches. It is akin to inspecting the fortress walls for potential weak points. Specialized security testers or developers conduct these tests to ensure robust protection against potential threats.

- **Usability and Accessibility Testing**

  Usability testing ensures the system is user-friendly, while accessibility testing ensures it is accessible to everyone. It is comparable to making sure the fortress is easy to navigate and accessible for everyone, including those with disabilities. These tests involve UX designers and accessibility experts to ensure an inclusive user experience.

  For efficient testing, a mix of manual and automated testing is employed based on the test type and specific requirements. This ensures comprehensive coverage and a robust, reliable final product.

Introduction to Testing Frameworks in Rails

Testing frameworks play a pivotal role in ensuring the stability, reliability, and efficiency of web applications. In the Rails ecosystem, various testing frameworks are available, each serving specific purposes and offering distinct benefits. These frameworks aid developers in automating tests, enabling them to detect bugs, errors, and inconsistencies early in the development cycle.

Popular Testing Frameworks and Their Key Features

In the dynamic world of Rails development, robust testing forms the cornerstone of a stable and high-quality application. But with a plethora of testing frameworks at hand, choosing the right one can feel like traversing a jungle.

Here are some widely used testing frameworks in Rails:

RSpec

RSpec is a behavior-driven development (BDD) framework that provides a readable and expressive syntax. It allows for easy-to-understand specifications and supports descriptive naming conventions, which can make tests more readable for both developers and stakeholders. RSpec's extensive ecosystem offers a variety of plugins and extensions for various testing needs.

Some developers might find RSpec's syntax a bit verbose compared to other testing frameworks. Additionally, due to its flexibility and the wide range of available plugins, setting up RSpec might require more initial configuration compared to other testing frameworks.

You can find all the details about RSpec at https://rspec.info.

Minitest

Minitest is included in the Ruby standard library, making it readily available without needing additional gems or dependencies. It's lightweight and provides a simple and fast testing framework suitable for smaller projects or those that require minimal overhead.

Its simplicity might be limiting for more complex testing scenarios or larger projects. Minitest might lack some advanced features and flexibility compared to other more specialized testing frameworks like RSpec.

As Minitest is the default test framework for Rails, you can read all about it on the official Rails testing guide at https://guides.rubyonrails.org/testing.html.

Capybara

Capybara is an acceptance testing framework used for simulating user interactions with the application. It allows for high-level testing of web applications through its expressive syntax, which mimics user actions like clicking buttons, filling forms, and validating page content.

Capybara tests can sometimes be slower due to their nature of emulating user interactions in the browser. Writing and maintaining Capybara tests also require a good understanding of HTML structure and page interactions, making them a bit more complex compared to unit or integration tests.

Default System tests in Rails use Capybara under the hood, you can find all about Capybara at https://github.com/teamcapybara/capybara.

Choosing the Right Testing Framework

Choosing the right testing framework often depends on the specific needs of the project, team preferences, and the nature of the tests required. For instance, RSpec might be preferred for its readability in complex scenarios, while Minitest's simplicity might be suitable for smaller projects. Capybara shines when it comes to end-to-end testing and simulating user behavior.

It is common for Rails projects to use either RSpec or Minitest along with other frameworks like Capybara to cover different types of testing: unit testing, integration testing, and acceptance testing. Moreover, the Rails community actively contributes to these frameworks, ensuring ongoing support and updates to meet evolving testing needs.

Writing Unit Tests for Models and Controllers

Unit tests are a type of software testing that focuses on validating the smallest units of code in an application, typically individual functions, methods, or modules. These tests verify that isolated parts of the codebase perform as expected by checking their inputs and outputs.

Key aspects of unit tests include:

- **Isolation:** They isolate specific components or units of code, testing them in isolation from the rest of the application. This ensures that failures or issues are contained within a particular unit and not influenced by other parts of the codebase.
- **Independence:** Unit tests should be independent of external factors such as databases, networks, or other systems. They should run consistently and produce reliable results regardless of the environment.
- **Automation:** Unit tests are automated and can be run repeatedly, making them efficient for developers to execute as part of their development workflow.
- **Granularity:** Each test should focus on a single piece of functionality or behavior within a unit of code. This granularity helps in pinpointing the source of errors quickly.

In Rails, unit tests are written using testing frameworks such as Minitest or RSpec. These tests validate the behavior of models, controllers, and other individual components of the application, ensuring that they function correctly according to the specified requirements.

Writing Unit Tests for Models

Consider the following example **Book** model:

```
# app/models/book.rb
class Book < ApplicationRecord
  validates :title, presence: true
  validates :author, presence: true

  def full_title
    "#{title} by #{author}"
  end
end
```

The **Book** model has some validations and a method. Now, let us write unit tests for it using both, Minitest and RSpec:

Minitest Unit Test

```
# test/models/book_test.rb
require 'test_helper'

class BookTest < ActiveSupport::TestCase
  test "should not save book without title" do
    book = Book.new(author: 'John Doe')
    assert_not book.save, "Saved the book without a title"
  end

  test "should not save book without author" do
    book = Book.new(title: 'Book Title')
    assert_not book.save, "Saved the book without an author"
  end

  test "should save book with title and author" do
    book = Book.new(title: 'Book Title', author: 'John Doe')
    assert book.save, "Could not save the book"
  end

  test "should return full title" do
    book = Book.new(title: 'Book Title', author: 'John Doe')
    assert_equal 'Book Title by John Doe', book.full_title, "Incorrect full title"
  end
end
```

There are four test cases written within the **BookTest** class, which are as follows:

- **Should not save book without title**

  This test examines whether a book object is prevented from being saved when lacking a title. It generates a `Book` instance devoid of a title but with an author present. The test utilizes the **assert_not** method to confirm that the book isn't stored in the database.

- **Should not save book without author**

  Similar to the first test, this test verifies if a book object is prohibited from being saved when missing an author. It generates a **Book** instance without an author but with a title and ensures that the book remains unsaved.

- **Should save book with title and author**

  This test ensures that a book with both a title and an author can be saved successfully. It creates a **Book** instance with both a title and an author, then uses the **assert** method to confirm that the book can be saved.

- **Should return full title**

  This test verifies the functionality of the **full_title** method in the **Book** model. It creates a **Book** instance with a title and an author, then uses the **assert_equal** method to compare the returned value from **book.full_title** with an expected value.

These tests aim to guarantee the expected behavior of the **Book** model. They ensure that validations for the presence of title and author work correctly, that a book can be saved with both attributes present, and that the **full_title** method returns the expected string concatenating the title and author.

The same can be achieved using RSpec as follows:

RSpec Unit Test

```
# spec/models/book_spec.rb
require 'rails_helper'

RSpec.describe Book, type: :model do
  it "is not valid without a title" do
    book = Book.new(author: 'John Doe')
    expect(book).to_not be_valid
  end

  it "is not valid without an author" do
    book = Book.new(title: 'Book Title')
    expect(book).to_not be_valid
  end
```

```
  it "is valid with title and author" do
    book = Book.new(title: 'Book Title', author: 'John Doe')
    expect(book).to be_valid
  end

  it "returns the full title" do
    book = Book.new(title: 'Book Title', author: 'John Doe')
    expect(book.full_title).to eq('Book Title by John Doe')
  end
end
```

If you look closely, RSpec uses a more descriptive language-like syntax with readable matchers, making tests appear more like plain English sentences. On the other hand, Minitest adopts a more straightforward and concise syntax without relying on additional matchers, making assertions more explicit and direct.

Writing Unit Tests for Controllers

Consider the following **`BooksController`**:

```
# app/controllers/books_controller.rb
class BooksController < ApplicationController
  before_action :set_book, only: %i[show update destroy]

  def index
    @books = Book.all
    render json: @books
  end

  def show
    render json: @book
  end

  def create
    @book = Book.new(book_params)
    if @book.save
      render json: @book, status: :created
    else
```

```
      render json: @book.errors, status: :unprocessable_entity
    end
  end

  def update
    if @book.update(book_params)
      render json: @book
    else
      render json: @book.errors, status: :unprocessable_entity
    end
  end

  def destroy
    @book.destroy
    head :no_content
  end

  private

  def set_book
    @book = Book.find(params[:id])
  end

  def book_params
    params.require(:book).permit(:title, :author)
  end
end
```

It has the usual CRUD actions for the book. Now, let us write some Unit tests for this controller using both Minitest and RSpec:

Minitest Unit Test

```
# test/controllers/books_controller_test.rb
require 'test_helper'

class BooksControllerTest < ActionController::TestCase
```

```
  test "should get index" do
    get :index
    assert_response :success
    assert_not_nil assigns(:books)
  end

  test "should show book" do
    book = books(:one)
    get :show, params: { id: book.id }
    assert_response :success
  end

  test "should create book" do
    assert_difference('Book.count') do
      post :create, params: { book: { title: 'New Book', author: 'John
Doe' } }
    end
    assert_response :success
  end

  test "should update book" do
    book = books(:one)
    patch :update, params: { id: book.id, book: { title: 'Updated Title'
} }
    assert_response :success
    book.reload
    assert_equal 'Updated Title', book.title
  end

  test "should destroy book" do
    book = books(:one)
    assert_difference('Book.count', -1) do
      delete :destroy, params: { id: book.id }
    end
    assert_response :success
  end
end
```

RSpec Unit Test

```
# spec/controllers/books_controller_spec.rb
require 'rails_helper'

RSpec.describe BooksController, type: :controller do
  describe "GET #index" do
    it "returns a success response" do
      get :index, format: :json
      expect(response).to be_successful
    end
  end

  describe "GET #show" do
    it "returns a success response" do
      book = create(:book)
      get :show, params: { id: book.id }, format: :json
      expect(response).to be_successful
    end
  end

  describe "POST #create" do
    context "with valid params" do
      it "creates a new book" do
        expect {
          post :create, params: { book: { title: 'New Book', author:
'John Doe' } }, format: :json
        }.to change(Book, :count).by(1)
        expect(response).to be_successful
      end
    end
  end

  describe "PATCH #update" do
```

```
    context "with valid params" do
      it "updates the requested book" do
        book = create(:book)
        patch :update, params: { id: book.id, book: { title: 'Updated
Title' } }, format: :json
        book.reload
        expect(book.title).to eq('Updated Title')
      end
    end
  end

  describe "DELETE #destroy" do
    it "destroys the requested book" do
      book = create(:book)
      expect {
        delete :destroy, params: { id: book.id }, format: :json
      }.to change(Book, :count).by(-1)
      expect(response).to be_successful
    end
  end
end
```

These tests serve multiple purposes. They check if the controller actions function as expected, confirming that these actions return the appropriate HTTP responses. Additionally, they validate the behavior of the application when creating, updating, showing, and deleting books, ensuring the correct interaction with the database.

Integration Testing and Acceptance Testing

Integration testing is a level of software testing where individual units or components of a system are combined and tested together as a group. Its primary aim is to uncover interface issues between these integrated units. This process verifies that different parts of the system work together as intended. Integration testing can be conducted using various strategies such as top-down, bottom-up, or a combination of both, ensuring that the integrated modules function correctly as a whole.

Acceptance testing, also known as User Acceptance Testing (UAT), is performed to determine whether a system meets the specified requirements and is acceptable for delivery to the end-users or stakeholders. This testing phase validates the software against business requirements and user expectations. It is usually the final phase of testing before the software is released. Acceptance testing can include alpha testing (in-house testing) and beta testing (real-world testing by end-users), ensuring that the software meets the needs of its intended audience.

The integration test for **BooksController** can look something like this:

Integration Test Using RSpec

```
# spec/requests/books_integration_spec.rb
require 'rails_helper'


RSpec.describe 'Books API', type: :request do
  describe 'GET /books' do
    it 'returns all books' do
      create_list(:book, 5)

      get '/books'

      expect(response).to have_http_status(:success)
      expect(JSON.parse(response.body).size).to eq(5)
    end
  end

  describe 'GET /books/:id' do
    it 'returns a book' do
      book = create(:book)

      get "/books/#{book.id}"

      expect(response).to have_http_status(:success)
      expect(JSON.parse(response.body)['title']).to eq(book.title)
    end
```

```
  end

  describe 'POST /books' do
    context 'with valid params' do
      it 'creates a new book' do
        book_params = { title: 'New Book Title', author: 'New Book
Author' }

        post '/books', params: { book: book_params }

        expect(response).to have_http_status(:created)
        expect(Book.last.title).to eq('New Book Title')
      end
    end

    context 'with invalid params' do
      it 'does not create a new book' do
        post '/books', params: { book: { title: nil, author: 'Invalid
Author' } }

        expect(response).to have_http_status(:unprocessable_entity)
      end
    end
  end

  describe 'PATCH /books/:id' do
    it 'updates a book' do
      book = create(:book)
      updated_title = 'Updated Book Title'

      patch "/books/#{book.id}", params: { book: { title: updated_title
} }

      expect(response).to have_http_status(:success)
```

```
      expect(Book.find(book.id).title).to eq(updated_title)
    end
  end

  describe 'DELETE /books/:id' do
    it 'deletes a book' do
      book = create(:book)

      delete "/books/#{book.id}"

      expect(response).to have_http_status(:no_content)
      expect { Book.find(book.id) }.to raise_error(ActiveRecord::Record-
NotFound)
    end
  end
end
```

Acceptance Tests Using Capybara with RSpec

```
# spec/features/book_actions_spec.rb
require 'rails_helper'

RSpec.describe 'Book actions', type: :feature do
  before(:each) do
    @book = create(:book, title: 'Sample Book', author: 'Sample Author')
  end

  it 'displays all books on the index page' do
    visit '/books'

    expect(page).to have_content('Sample Book')
    expect(page).to have_content('Sample Author')
  end

  it 'displays a book on its show page' do
```

```
    visit "/books/#{@book.id}"

    expect(page).to have_content('Sample Book')
    expect(page).to have_content('Sample Author')
  end

  it 'creates a new book' do
    visit '/books/new'

    fill_in 'Title', with: 'New Book Title'
    fill_in 'Author', with: 'New Book Author'
    click_button 'Create Book'

    expect(page).to have_content('Book was successfully created.')
    expect(page).to have_content('New Book Title')
    expect(page).to have_content('New Book Author')
  end

  it 'updates a book' do
    visit "/books/#{@book.id}"

    click_link 'Edit'
    fill_in 'Title', with: 'Updated Book Title'
    fill_in 'Author', with: 'Updated Book Author'
    click_button 'Update Book'

    expect(page).to have_content('Book was successfully updated.')
    expect(page).to have_content('Updated Book Title')
    expect(page).to have_content('Updated Book Author')
  end

  it 'deletes a book' do
    visit '/books'
```

```
    click_link 'Destroy'

    expect(page).to have_content('Book was successfully destroyed.')
    expect(page).not_to have_content('Sample Book')
    expect(page).not_to have_content('Sample Author')
  end
end
```

We can also write acceptance tests (also known as System tests) using Minitest and Capybara as follows:

Acceptance/System Test Using Minitest

```
# test/system/book_actions_test.rb
require "application_system_test_case"

class BookActionsTest < ApplicationSystemTestCase
  setup do
    @book = books(:one)
  end

  test "display all books on index page" do
    visit books_url

    assert_text @book.title
    assert_text @book.author
  end

  test "display a book on its show page" do
    visit book_url(@book)

    assert_text @book.title
    assert_text @book.author
  end

  test "create a new book" do
    visit new_book_url
```

```
    fill_in "Title", with: "New Book Title"
    fill_in "Author", with: "New Book Author"
    click_on "Create Book"

    assert_text "Book was successfully created."
    assert_text "New Book Title"
    assert_text "New Book Author"
  end

  test "update a book" do
    visit edit_book_url(@book)

    fill_in "Title", with: "Updated Book Title"
    fill_in "Author", with: "Updated Book Author"
    click_on "Update Book"

    assert_text "Book was successfully updated."
    assert_text "Updated Book Title"
    assert_text "Updated Book Author"
  end

  test "delete a book" do
    visit books_url

    accept_confirm do
      click_on "Destroy", match: :first
    end

    assert_text "Book was successfully destroyed."
    assert_no_text @book.title
    assert_no_text @book.author
  end
end
```

These tests mirror the functionality tested in the previous examples using RSpec, but written in a Minitest syntax. They ensure that the web application behaves as expected when users interact with it and perform various CRUD actions on the books.

Test-Driven Development (TDD) Approach

Test-Driven Development (TDD) is a software development approach that emphasizes writing tests before writing the actual code. It follows a cycle known as the Red-Green-Refactor cycle.

Principles of TDD

The principles of TDD are as follows:

- **Write Tests First:** Developers start by writing tests that describe the desired behavior of a feature or functionality before writing any code.
- **Test Often:** Tests are run frequently, ideally after every small change or addition to ensure that new code does not break existing functionality.
- **Fail Tests Initially (Red Phase):** Initially, the tests are expected to fail because the corresponding code has not been written yet.
- **Write the Minimum Code to Pass Tests (Green Phase):** Implement the simplest code possible to make the failing tests pass.
- **Refactor:** Once the tests are passing, refactor the code to improve its structure, readability, and maintainability while keeping the tests passing.

Advantages of TDD

Test-driven development encompasses several advantages, including:

- **Code Quality:** TDD encourages writing modular, clean, and maintainable code. Since each piece of code is tested, it tends to be more reliable.
- **Improved Design:** Writing tests upfront forces developers to think about the usage and requirements of the code, leading to better-designed software.
- **Regression Testing:** TDD ensures that changes or additions to the codebase do not break existing functionalities. The suite of tests acts as a safety net.
- **Faster Debugging:** When a test fails, it pinpoints the exact location of the problem, making debugging more efficient.

The Red-Green-Refactor Cycle

The Red-Green-Refactor cycle is a fundamental practice in test-driven development. It involves three steps:

- **Red Phase (Write a Failing Test):** Start by writing a test that describes the desired behavior of the code. Since the code does not exist yet, the test should fail.

- **Green Phase (Write the Minimum Code to Pass the Test):** Implement the simplest code to make the failing test pass. This code might not be optimal but should make the test succeed.
- **Refactor Phase (Improve Code Quality):** Enhance the code without changing its behavior. Refactoring includes improving readability, removing duplication, and optimizing performance.

Figure 7.1 shows the Red, Green, and Refactor cycle:

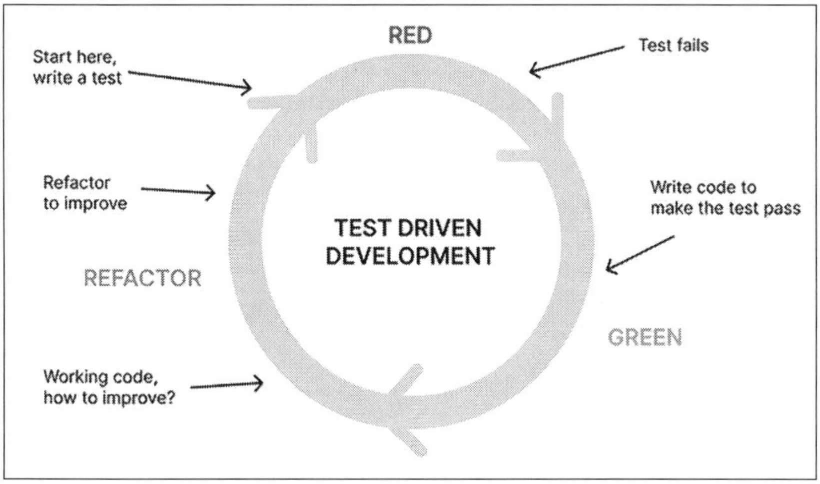

Figure 7.1: *Red, Green, and Refactor Cycle*

When implementing Test-Driven Development (TDD), it is essential to start with small, discrete functionalities or components by crafting tests that define their expected behavior. This approach involves cycling through the Red-Green-Refactor steps repeatedly, focusing on individual tests to write the simplest code that passes them and then refining the code without altering its behavior. Balancing the testing effort is crucial, avoiding extremes of excessive or insufficient testing by prioritizing critical functionalities and addressing edge cases. However, TDD does present some challenges, notably an initial learning curve where writing tests upfront might initially slow down development until developers familiarize themselves with the methodology. Additionally, TDD might not seamlessly fit scenarios characterized by highly dynamic requirements or in situations requiring exploratory development methods.

Let us see this approach in action with our WagePro app (discussed in the previous chapters).

Implementing Test-Driven Approach in WagePro

Currently, in WagePro we have Users who can have different roles, for example, Admin,

Manager, or Employee. Now, let us add an Organization model so that an Admin User can create multiple organizations.

Requirements

Let us say our requirements are as follows:

- Create an Organization model
- An organization must have a unique name
- An organization must belong to an Admin User
- An organization cannot belong to a non-admin user
- An Admin User can have multiple organizations

ProTip: *At this point, when the requirements are clear and we want to start working on this Task, we will move the Task in our Kanban board to the In Progress column so that everybody in the team can track the progress. Figure 7.2 shows the current state of our Kanban Board.*

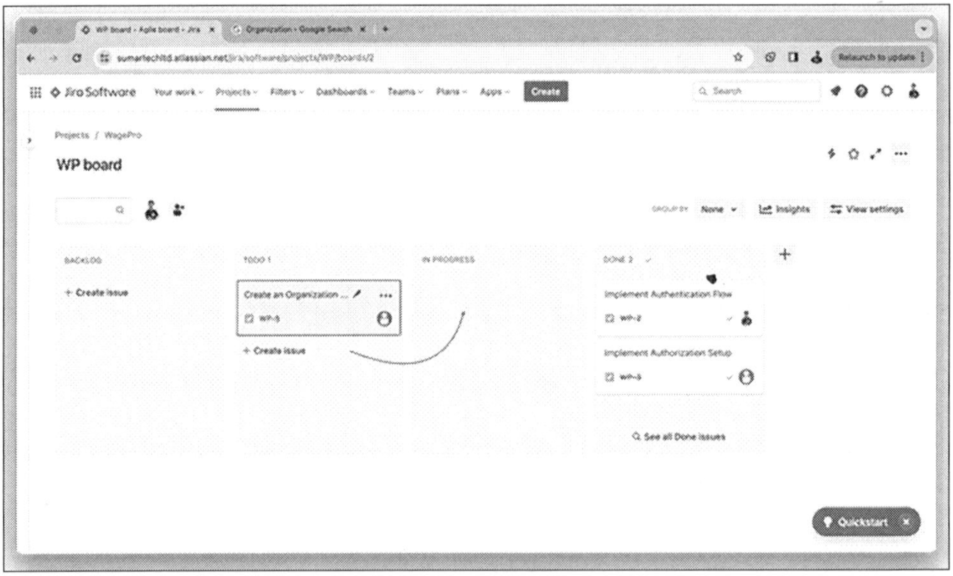

Figure 7.2: *WagePro Kanban Board*

Once this task is in progress, we can start working on it. Let us quickly create a Department model with the following command:

```
rails g model Organization
```

This command will create an Organization model and all the files we need to write tests for this model with Minitest. *Figure* 7.3 shows all the files created by the aforementioned command and highlights the test file for the Organization model.

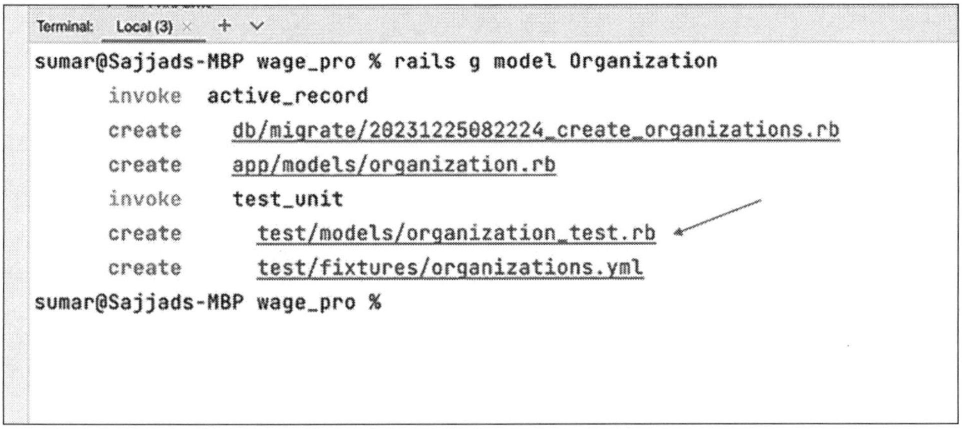

***Figure 7.3**: Test file for Organization model*

Now let us open the **test/models/organization_test.rb** file and write unit tests for the following requirements:

- The organization must have a name
- The organization name must be unique

Add the following code to your test file:

```
require "test_helper"


class OrganizationTest < ActiveSupport::TestCase
  test "organization should have a name" do
    organization = Organization.new
    assert_not organization.valid?, "Saved the organization without a
name"
  end
end
```

This code is checking for the requirement where an organization must have a name. Now if we run the tests using the **rails test** command, it will say you have some pending migrations as shown in *Figure 7.4*:

```
sumar@Sajjads-MBP wage_pro % rails test

Rebuilding...

Done in 265ms.
Migrations are pending. To resolve this issue, run:

        bin/rails db:migrate

You have 1 pending migration:

db/migrate/20231225082224_create_organizations.rb
```

Figure 7.4: *Pending Migrations*

To fix the issue, run the suggested **`rails db:migrate`** command and rerun the tests with the following command:

```
rails test test/models/organization_test.rb
```

Now you will see your test failed, this is called the Red State in the Red-Green-Refactor Cycle. This test failed because the Organization must not be saved without a name, but it did as we do not have any name attribute in the database nor do we have any validations for it. *Figure* 7.5 shows our first failing test:

```
Using /Users/sumar/.rvm/gems/ruby-3.2.2 with gemset wagepro
sumar@Sajjads-MBP wage_pro % rails test test/models/organization_test.rb
Running 1 tests in a single process (parallelization threshold is 50)
Run options: --seed 10629

# Running:

F

Failure:
OrganizationTest#test_organization_should_have_a_name [/Users/sumar/projects/sumartech/wage_pro/test/models/organization_test.rb:6]:
Saved the organization without a name  <-- The Red State

bin/rails test test/models/organization_test.rb:4



Finished in 0.048362s, 20.6774 runs/s, 20.6774 assertions/s.
1 runs, 1 assertions, 1 failures, 0 errors, 0 skips
```

Figure 7.5: *The Failing Test (Red State)*

Note: *If you get any other error besides the failing test, have a look at your fixtures and comment out all the code inside. These fixtures can throw errors as they are not yet updated based on our current schema.*

Now, let us begin the green state of the Red-Green-Refactor Cycle. The idea is to write enough code to make the test pass.

So, we will roll back our last migration to undo the table creation in the database with the following command:

```
rails db:rollback
```

Once done, we will add a name attribute in the migration file and run the migration as shown in *Figure 7.6*:

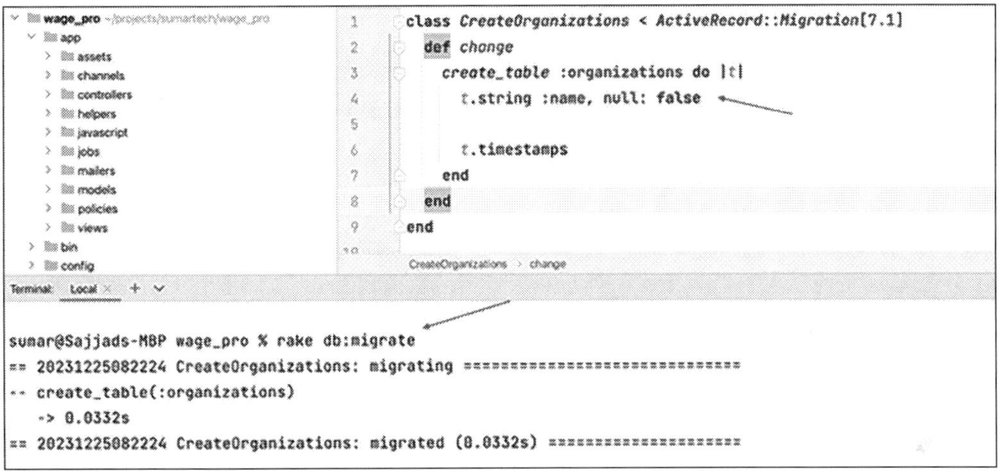

Figure 7.6: *Adding name to Organization*

Now, we need to add a validation in Organization model as follows to make sure the name is indeed present when we create an organization:

```
class Organization < ApplicationRecord
  validates :name, presence: true
end
```

Now if you run the tests with the following command, the test will pass, as shown in *Figure 7.7*:

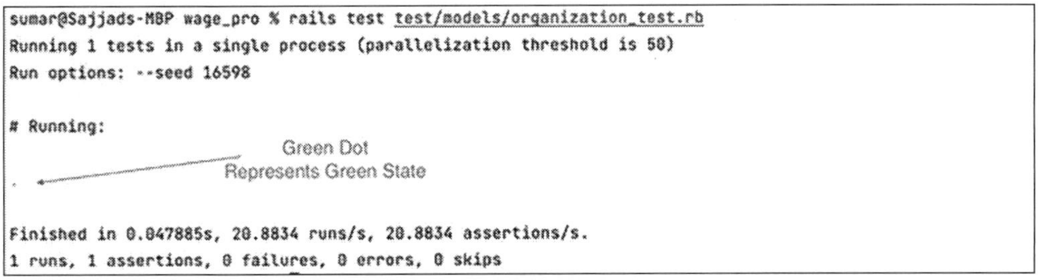

Figure 7.7: *The Green State*

Note: *If you get any other error while running the tests, have a look at your fixtures and comment out all the code inside. These fixtures can throw errors as they are not yet updated based on our current schema.*

We will skip the Refactor stage as our code is already optimized.

Now let us move to our second requirement "*The organization name must be unique*". Add the following test in our **`organization_test.rb`** file under the existing test:

```
test "organization name should be unique" do
    Organization.create(name: "Existing Org")
    organization = Organization.new(name: "Existing Org")
    assert_not organization.valid?
end
```

This test will fail, as shown in *Figure 7.8*:

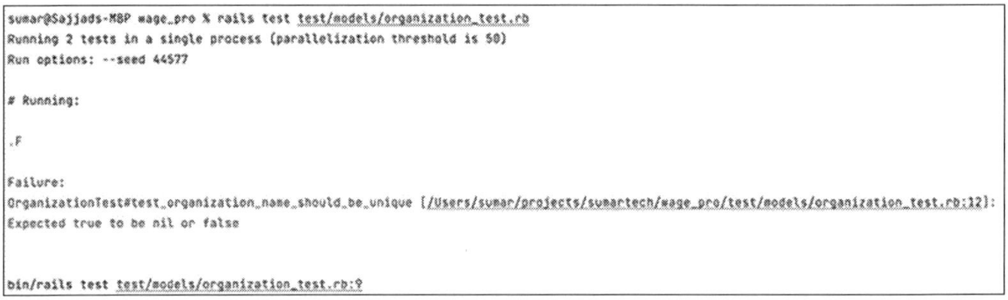

```
sumar@Sajjads-MBP wage_pro % rails test test/models/organization_test.rb
Running 2 tests in a single process (parallelization threshold is 50)
Run options: --seed 44577

# Running:

.F

Failure:
OrganizationTest#test_organization_name_should_be_unique [/Users/sumar/projects/sumartech/wage_pro/test/models/organization_test.rb:12]:
Expected true to be nil or false


bin/rails test test/models/organization_test.rb:9
```

Figure 7.8: *Failing test for unique name*

To make this test pass, modify the name validation in your model to add uniqueness as follows:

```
class Organization < ApplicationRecord
  validates :name, presence: true, uniqueness: true
end
```

Now your tests should pass again, as shown in *Figure 7.9*:

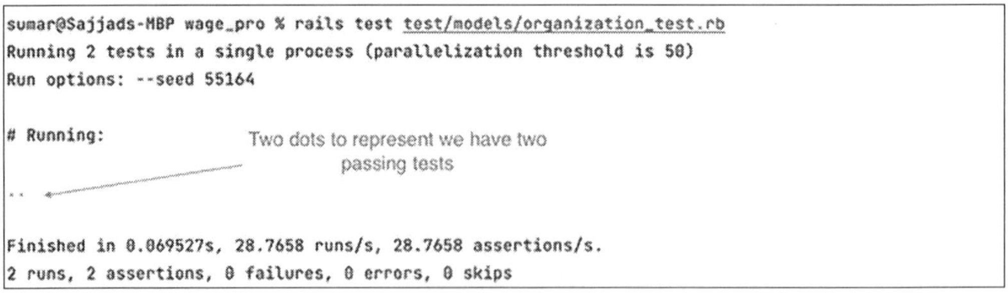

```
sumar@Sajjads-MBP wage_pro % rails test test/models/organization_test.rb
Running 2 tests in a single process (parallelization threshold is 50)
Run options: --seed 55164

# Running:

..

Finished in 0.069527s, 28.7658 runs/s, 28.7658 assertions/s.
2 runs, 2 assertions, 0 failures, 0 errors, 0 skips
```


Figure 7.9: *Passing tests*

We will repeat the process until all our requirements are complete. Here is the final failing test file for our organization model:

```
require 'test_helper'

class OrganizationTest < ActiveSupport::TestCase
  def setup
    @admin_user = User.create(email: 'admin@example.com', password:
'password', password_confirmation: 'password')
    @admin_user.add_role(:admin)

    @non_admin_user = User.create(email: 'user@example.com', password:
'password', password_confirmation: 'password')
  end

  test "organization should be valid" do
    organization = Organization.new(name: "Test Org", admin_user: @ad-
min_user)
    assert organization.valid?
  end

  test "organization should have a name" do
    organization = Organization.new(admin_user: @admin_user)
    assert_not organization.valid?
  end

  test "organization name should be unique" do
    Organization.create(name: "Existing Org", admin_user: @admin_user)
    organization = Organization.new(name: "Existing Org", admin_user: @
admin_user)
    assert_not organization.valid?
  end

  test "organization should belong to an admin user" do
    organization = Organization.new(name: "Test Org", admin_user: @non_
admin_user)
    assert_not organization.valid?
  end
```

```
  test "admin user should have multiple organizations" do
    Organization.create(name: "Org 1", admin_user: @admin_user)
    Organization.create(name: "Org 2", admin_user: @admin_user)
    assert_equal 2, @admin_user.organizations.count
  end
end
```

As an assignment, try to write a code to make these tests pass. If you get stuck, feel free to get help from the following GitHub repo where we have provided all the necessary changes to make these tests pass.

Hint: *Consider modifying the User model to establish a has_many relationship between a User and an Organization.*

The GitHub link provided contains the commit associated with all the code demonstrated in this chapter: https://github.com/ava-orange-education/Ruby-on-Rails-for-Agile-Web-Development/tree/main/chapter07/wage_pro

You can get access to everything covered in the book on this GitHub repo: https://github.com/ava-orange-education/Ruby-on-Rails-for-Agile-Web-Development.

Conclusion

In this chapter, we delved into the fundamental aspects of testing and test-driven development (TDD) within the context of Ruby on Rails applications. We explored the significance of testing in Agile development, understanding the diverse types of testing in web development, and delved into the world of testing frameworks. Additionally, we walked through writing unit tests for models and controllers, emphasizing the importance of these tests in ensuring the reliability and functionality of the application. Moreover, by crafting tests for a hypothetical BooksController, we demonstrated the practical implementation of Minitest and RSpec for comprehensive testing, ensuring that each action of the controller operates as expected. Finally, we added some Unit tests to our WagePro app using the default testing framework of Rails called MiniTest.

Looking ahead, the next chapter, titled *RESTful APIs and Web Services*, promises to be an exciting dive into building efficient and scalable APIs for web applications. We will explore the world of APIs, understand RESTful principles, and master the creation of web services, all essential for modern web development. Stay tuned for an insightful journey into the world of APIs and the seamless integration of services into web applications.

Short Quiz

1. **What is the primary purpose of using testing frameworks in Rails?**
    a. To increase the application's complexity
    b. To simplify the code structure
    c. To ensure the reliability of the application
    d. To improve the visual design
2. **Which testing frameworks were explored in this chapter for testing Rails applications?**
    a. Django and Flask
    b. RSpec and Minitest
    c. Selenium and Protractor
    d. Jasmine and Karma
3. **In Rails, which testing framework follows a more Behavior-Driven Development (BDD) style?**
    a. Minitest
    b. RSpec
    c. Cucumber
    d. Jasmine
4. **What is the primary difference between RSpec and Minitest in terms of syntax?**
    a. RSpec has more specific assertions than Minitest
    b. Minitest has a more compact and traditional syntax compared to RSpec
    c. RSpec allows more parallel testing than Minitest
    d. Minitest has more detailed reporting capabilities than RSpec
5. **What does the "Red" phase signify in the Red-Green-Refactor cycle?**
    a. Implementing new features
    b. Writing tests that fail
    c. Refactoring existing code
    d. Analyzing test coverage

6. **What is the purpose of using the expect keyword in RSpec tests?**
   a. To set up the testing environment
   b. To define the expected behavior or outcome
   c. To generate sample data for the tests
   d. To measure the time taken by each test
7. **What is the significance of writing unit tests for models in Rails applications?**
   a. To ensure the application's visual appearance
   b. To test the functionality of controller actions
   c. To verify the behavior of model methods
   d. To check the internet connection of the application
8. **In the Red-Green-Refactor cycle, what is the primary goal of the "Green" phase?**
   a. Writing tests that pass
   b. Fixing existing bugs
   c. Analyzing code complexity
   d. Adding new features
9. **What is the purpose of the "Refactor" phase in the Red-Green-Refactor cycle?**
   a. Writing additional tests
   b. Improving code structure without altering functionality
   c. Redesigning the UI components
   d. Enhancing database performance
10. **What defines System testing in the context of software development?**
    a. Testing individual components or modules of the system
    b. Evaluating the functionality of the entire system as a whole
    c. Focusing solely on user interface testing
    d. Conducting load testing for performance assessment

CHAPTER 8

RESTful APIs and Web Services

Introduction

Welcome to the dynamic world of RESTful APIs and Web Services in Ruby on Rails! In this chapter, we will embark on a journey to unravel the magic behind modern web communication. Imagine your Rails application is not just serving web pages but also seamlessly interacting with external systems, sharing and consuming data effortlessly. We will demystify the concept of RESTful architecture, guiding you through the creation of robust API endpoints within your Rails projects. Beyond this, we will explore how Rails applications can communicate with external APIs, empowering your app to connect, retrieve, and utilize information from diverse sources. But that is not all; we will delve into the crucial realms of authentication and authorization, ensuring that your APIs stay secure. By the end, you will be adept at harnessing the power of Rails to create, consume, and secure APIs, enriching your applications with boundless possibilities. Let us start with understanding what are Web Services and APIs:

Web Services are a type of technology that enables different systems or applications to communicate with each other over the Internet. They provide a standardized way for software components to interact, share data, and access functionalities regardless of the platforms or programming languages they use. Web services are essentially a broader concept that encompasses various methods of communication between applications.

APIs, on the other hand, are interfaces that allow different software systems to interact with each other. An API defines the methods and protocols that enable communication between different software components. APIs can exist within a single application or system (internal APIs) or be exposed to the outside world for external use (external APIs).

Structure

In this chapter, we will discuss the following topics:

- Understanding RESTful Architecture
  - Key Components of RESTful Architecture
  - Principles of RESTful Design
  - Benefits of REST in Web Development
- Building API Endpoints in Rails
  - Setting Up Rails for API Development
  - Creating RESTful Routes and Controllers
- Consuming APIs in Rails Applications
  - Making HTTP Requests in Rails
  - Handling API Responses
  - Parsing Data from External APIs
  - Integrating External Data into Rails Models
- Authentication and Authorization for APIs
  - Introduction to API Authentication
  - Token-Based Authentication (JWT, OAuth)
  - Implementing Authentication in Rails APIs
  - Securing API Endpoints with Authorization

Understanding RESTful Architecture

Understanding RESTful architecture is fundamental for designing robust and scalable web systems. REST, or Representational State Transfer, is an architectural style that defines a set of principles guiding the creation of web services. At its core, REST simplifies communication between different software systems by leveraging the familiarity and ubiquity of HTTP and adopting a resource-centric approach.

Key Components of RESTful Architecture

The key components of RESTful architecture are as follows:

- **Resources**

  In RESTful architecture, everything is treated as a resource. A resource can be any entity that can be accessed or manipulated – a piece of data, an object, or even a service. These resources are identified by unique Uniform Resource Identifiers (URI).

- **Uniform Interface**

  A cornerstone of REST is its uniform interface. It employs a standardized set of operations (HTTP methods) to perform actions on resources:

  GET: Retrieve a resource.

  POST: Create a new resource.

  PUT: Update an existing resource.

  DELETE: Remove a resource.

  These HTTP methods, combined with URIs, form a consistent and predictable way to interact with resources.

- **Statelessness**

  RESTful architecture is stateless, meaning each request from a client to the server contains all the information necessary to process that request. The server does not retain any client context between requests. This simplifies server management and enhances scalability.

- **Representation**

  Resources in REST are represented in various formats like JSON or XML. Clients can request different representations of the same resource based on their needs. For example, a client might prefer JSON over XML for data exchange.

- **Hypermedia as the Engine of Application State (HATEOAS)**

  This principle suggests that the server should provide navigational links dynamically in responses to guide the client on what actions can be performed next. HATEOAS enhances the discoverability and flexibility of the API.

Benefits of RESTful Architecture

Using RESTful architecture comes with several benefits as follows:

- **Scalability**

  The stateless nature of REST allows for easy scaling. Servers can handle requests without holding session information, making it simpler to add more servers or nodes.

- **Simplicity and Understandability**

  RESTful APIs are intuitive and easy to comprehend due to their uniform interface and resource-centric approach. Developers can quickly grasp how to interact with the API.

- **Interoperability**

  REST leverages standard protocols like HTTP, making it interoperable across various platforms and devices. This promotes compatibility and ease of integration.

- **Flexibility**

  Its resource-based approach enables flexibility in data representation and manipulation. Clients can request specific representations of resources.

By adhering to these principles, you can create systems that are intuitive, interoperable, and adaptable to evolving requirements.

Building API Endpoints in Rails

In our WagePro application (discussed in previous chapters), imagine we want to build an API that allows an organization to access their departmental information and team member details so that they can display it on their company website. This API will serve as a secure means for companies to retrieve and display information about their departments and team members such as names, roles, and profiles. The API should provide this data in a structured format like JSON, ensuring that only authorized organizations can access it.

To save us some time, we have made some changes to our database schema. *Figure 8.1* highlights all the changes made to the database:

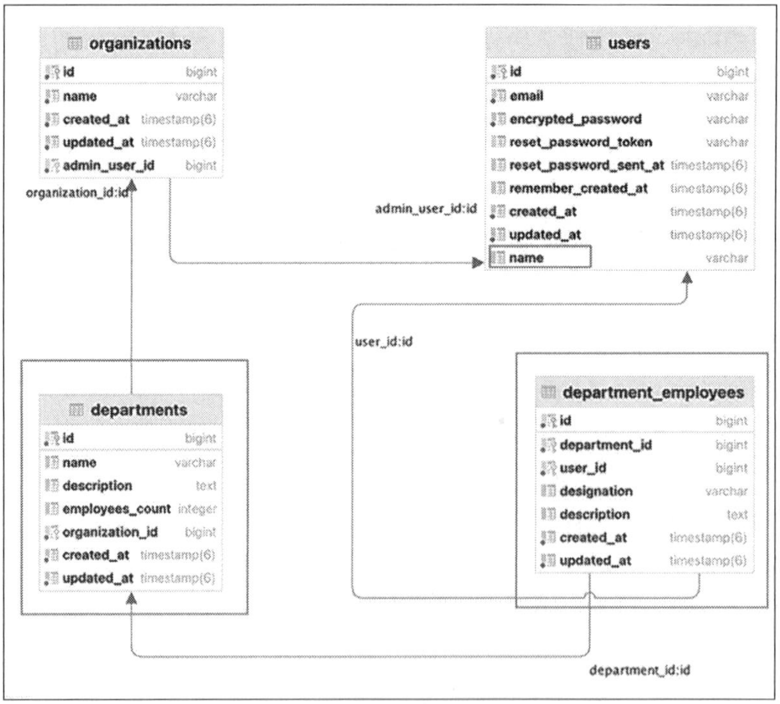

Figure 8.1: *Schema diagram of database changes*

We have added the '**departments**' table and '**department_employees**' table to establish the following associations:

- Organizations can have multiple departments.
- Departments can have multiple employees through the '**department_employees**' table.
- Employees can belong to multiple departments.

You can follow all the changes done so far at this GitHub link: https://github.com/ava-orange-education/Ruby-on-Rails-for-Agile-Web-Development/tree/main/chapter08/wage_pro

At this stage, we want to add a scoped uniqueness validation on the Organization name and Department name, which means we do not want our organization and department name to be unique throughout the table. Instead, we want all organizations by a single admin User to have a unique name, and all departments within an organization to have a unique name.

We can achieve this by replacing the following line in the Organization model:

```
validates :name, presence: true, uniqueness: true
```

with the following line:

```
validates :name, presence: true, uniqueness: { scope: :admin_user_id }
```

Similarly, for Departments model, replace:

```
validates :name, presence: true, uniqueness: true
```

with:

```
validates :name, presence: true,  uniqueness: { scope: :organization_id }
```

Now, we are ready to implement our API.

RESTful APIs Implementation

To implement the APIs, we need an **OrganizationsController**. To make APIs easier to manage, we will create all our API controllers in the directory '**app/controllers/api/v1**. So, let us quickly create that with the following command:

```
rails g controller 'api/v1/organizations'
```

This command will create our **OrganizationsController** inside api/v1 directory.

To make our APIs more configurable, we will also create an **ApiController** that will inherit from **ActionController::Base** (same as **ApplicationController**).

```
rails g controller 'api/v1/api'
```

This will create an **ApiController** for us. Now let's inherit it from **ActionController::Base**. To do that, replace the content of **ApiController** with the following code:

```
class Api::V1::ApiController < ActionController::Base
end
```

Also, let's inherit our **OrganizationsController** from our newly created **ApiController**, and replace the content of **OrganizationsController** with the following code:

```
class Api::V1::OrganizationsController < Api::V1::ApiController
end
```

Now that we have assembled all the necessary components for our APIs, it is time to augment the organizations controller with an index action. This action will fetch and present a comprehensive list of organizations, incorporating all departments within each organization. For each department, it will include details of all employees working within that specific department.

First of all, let's add the following route in **routes.rb** file with the default format set to "JSON".

```
  namespace :api, defaults: {format: :json} do
    namespace :v1 do
      resources :organizations, only: [:index]
    end
  end
```

This will create the following route for us:

```
api_v1_organizations_index
GET /api/v1/organizations(.:format) api/v1/organizations#index {:for-
mat=>:json}
```

Figure 8.2 shows us the **routes.rb** file along with the generated route.

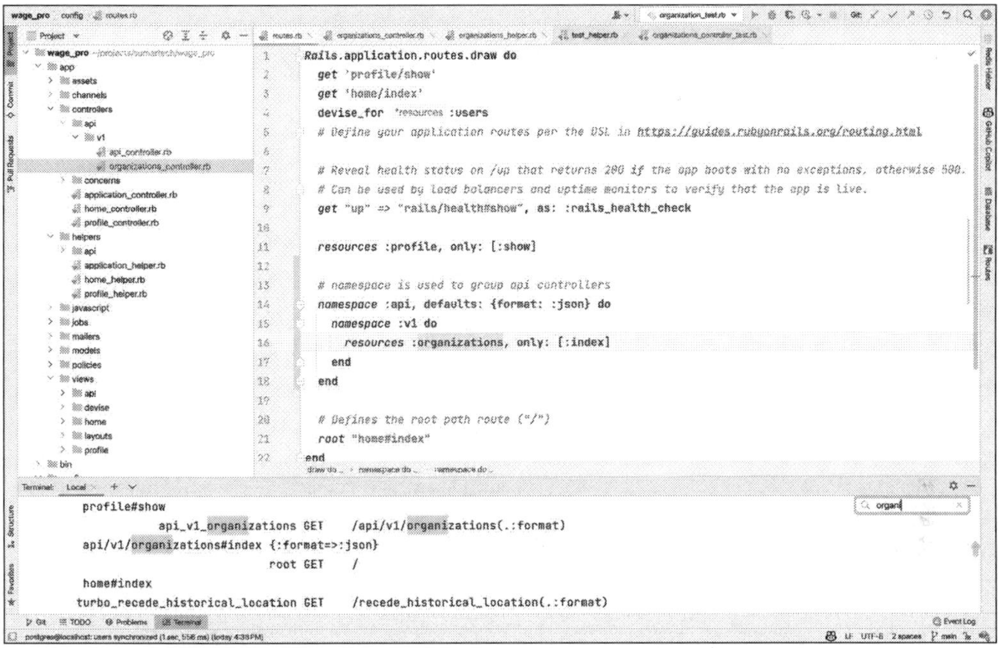

Figure 8.2: *Route for index action for OrganizationsController*

Now add the following index action to the **OrganizationsController**:

```
def index
    @organizations = Organization.all

    render json: @organizations.as_json(only: [:id, :name], include: {
      departments: {
        only: [:id, :name, :description, :employees_count],
        include: {
          department_employees: {
            only: [:id, :designation, :description],
            include: {
              user: {
                only: [:name, :email]
              }
            }
          }
        }
      }
    })
  end
```

Figure 8.3 highlights what is happening in the index action:

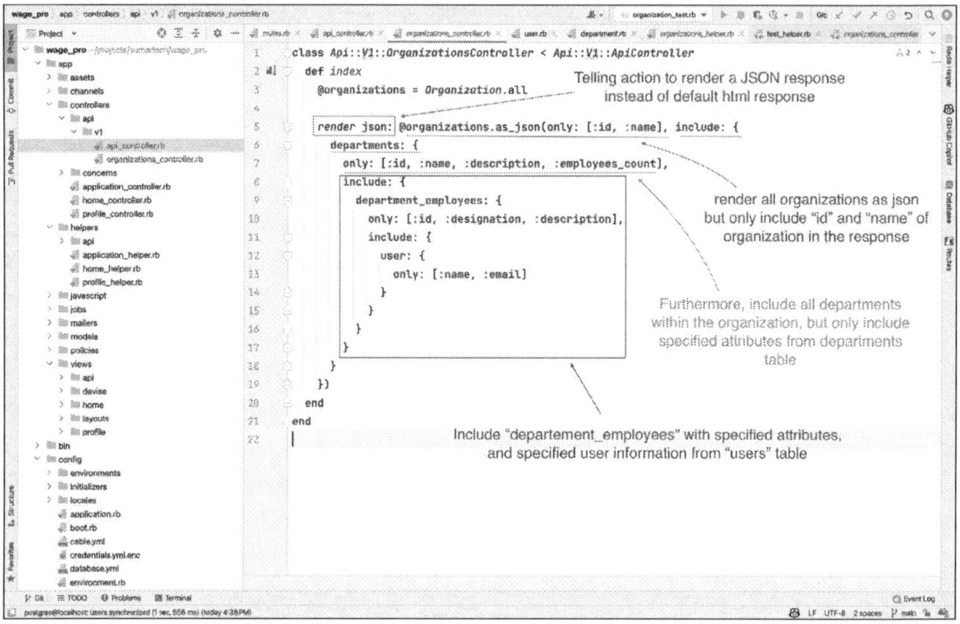

Figure 8.3: *Breakdown of index action*

Now if you run the server using **`./bin/dev`** command, and send a GET request to this action using the Postman API platform, you will get a JSON response somewhat similar to the one in *Figure* 8.4:

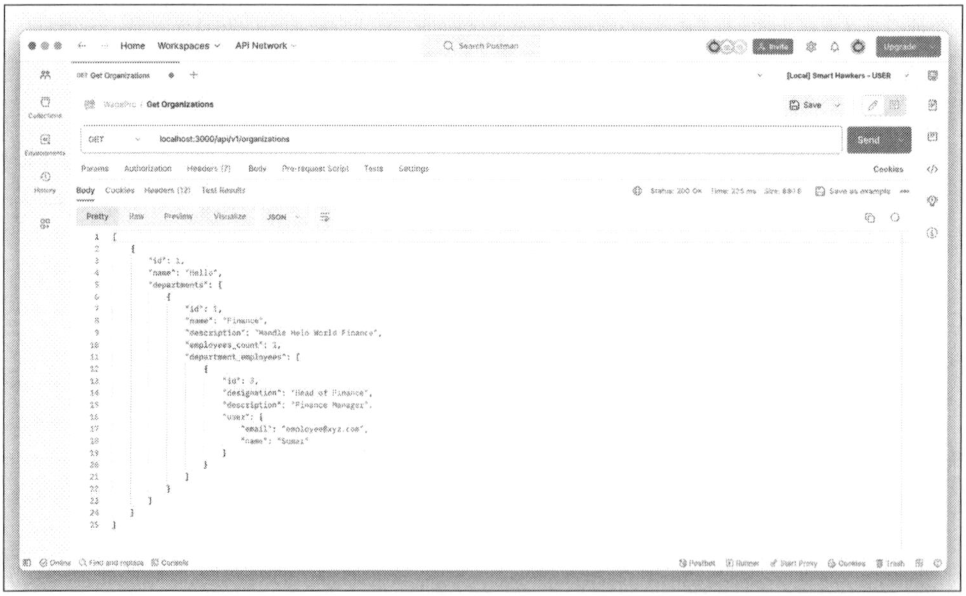

Figure 8.4: *GET organizations via API using Postman*

Note: *Your response can be different based on the data you have in your database, but the response structure will exactly match the one in Figure 8.4.*

Postman is a helpful tool that makes it easy to test, debug, and document APIs. With its easy-to-use interface, you can build and send API requests, see the responses, and manage your APIs. Check out Postman's official website at https://www.postman.com.

You can add data to your database using the rails console or **`seeds.rb`** file.

Using the rails console, you can do:

```
# get the first user from the database, or create a new one
user = User.first


# create an organization of user
organization = user.organizations.create(name: "SUMAR TECH LTD.")


# create a department within organization
department = organization.departments.create(name: 'Finance',
description: 'Handle Finance Related Matters')


# create an employee user
employee = User.create(name: 'SUMAR', email: 'sumar@sumartech.com',
password: '12345678', password_confirmation: '12345678')


# add employee role to user
employee.add_role :employee


# add the employee user to the department created above
department.department_employees.create(user_id: employee.id,
designation: 'Finance Manager', description: 'Head of Finance')
```

Now if you hit the same API again using Postman, you should get some data in the response similar to *Figure* 8.4.

Our API is ready but, at the moment it is a public API and it returns all Organizations without any security measures. Later in this chapter, we will make it secure. But before that let's see how we can consume external APIs in our Rails application.

Consuming APIs in Rails Applications

Imagine an organization hiring globally from different parts of the world, we want our WagePro application to show salaries in the local currency of each employee. For that, our application will need currency exchange rates.

We will be using the free version of **ExchangeRate** API (https://www.exchangerate-api.com/docs/free) to get the latest exchange rates.

You will find a link similar to this on the **ExchangeRate** API website: https://open.er-api.com/v6/latest/<BASE_CURRENCY>. We will replace the <BASE_CURRENCY> with USD because we want to fetch the exchange rate from USD to other currencies. The URL will become as follows:

https://open.er-api.com/v6/latest/USD

Once you open this URL in your browser, you will get a response similar to the one shown in *Figure 8.5*:

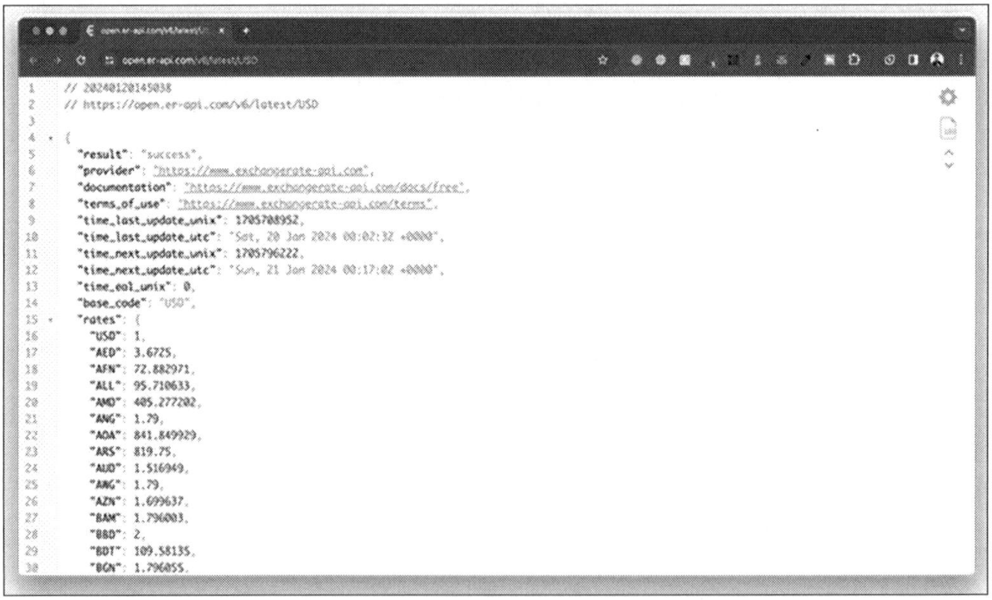

***Figure 8.5**: Response from ExchangeRate API*

As you can see, it has rates from **base_code** "USD" to all other currencies. Now let's see how we can use this API in our Rails application.

The first thing that might come to mind is where to put this code so we can easily use it whenever the need arises. It is a good question, and the solution lies in a common approach used in the Rails community called Service Objects.

Service Objects in a Ruby on Rails application are classes that encapsulate a specific piece of business logic or a service. They act as a way to organize and isolate complex logic, making the codebase more modular, readable, and maintainable.

Here are some characteristics of Service Objects:

- **Encapsulation:** Service Objects encapsulate a specific service or business logic, isolating it from the rest of the application. This promotes a clean separation of concerns.
- **Reusability:** By organizing logic into Service Objects, you create modular components that can be easily reused across different parts of your application. This enhances code reuse and reduces redundancy.
- **Readability:** Complex operations or services can be challenging to understand when scattered throughout the codebase. Service Objects provide a structured and dedicated place for such logic, improving code readability.
- **Maintainability:** Isolating specific functionalities into Service Objects simplifies maintenance. When updates or changes are needed, you can focus on the relevant Service Object without affecting other parts of the application.

The first step is to create a services directory under "**`app/services`**" and put our very first service inside it, "**`app/services/exchange_rate_api_service.rb`**", as shown in *Figure* 8.6:

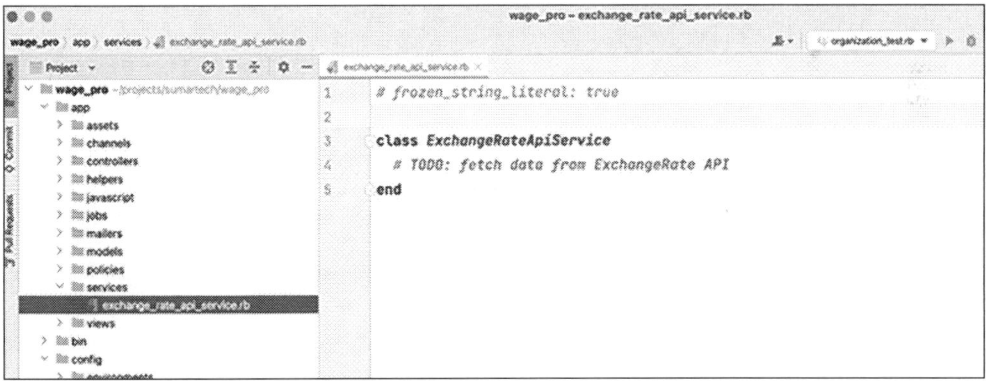

***Figure 8.6**: app/services/exchange_rate_api_service.rb*

Now add the following code:

```
# frozen_string_literal: true
require 'net/http'


class ExchangeRateApiService
  def self.get_exchange_rates(from = 'USD')
```

```
    uri = URI("https://open.er-api.com/v6/latest/#{from}")
    response = Net::HTTP.get_response(uri)
    return nil unless response.is_a?(Net::HTTPSuccess)

    JSON.parse(response.body)
  end
end
```

Figure 8.7 shows the entire file, with some additional comments to explain what is happening in the code:

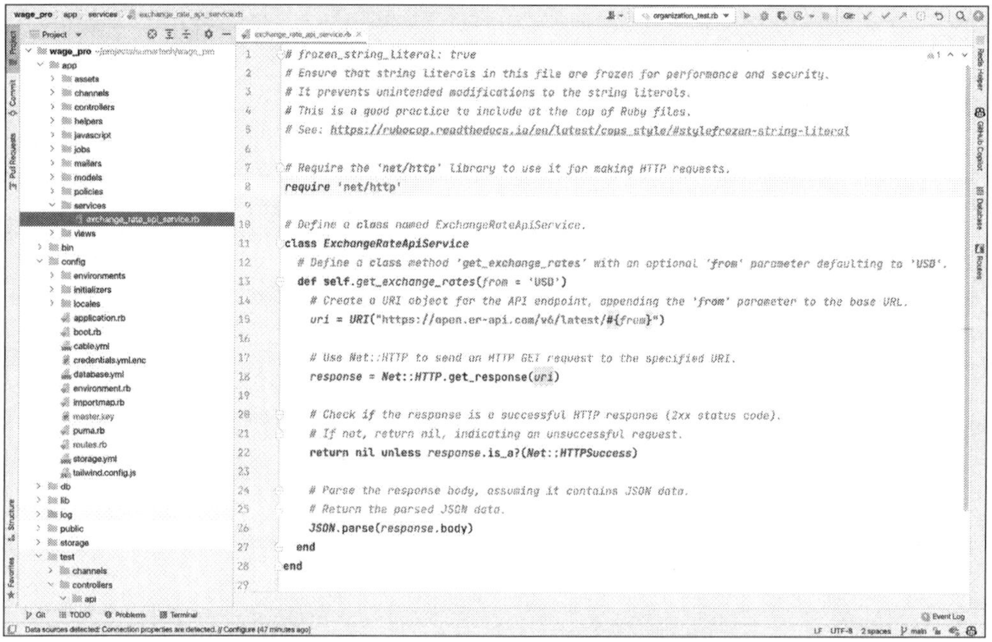

***Figure 8.7**: "app/services/exchange_rate_api_service.rb" with additional comments*

With that, our **ExchangeRate** API service is ready; let's try it in the rails console. Run the following command to initiate the console:

```
rails console
```

OR the shorthand:

```
rails c
```

Once the console is ready, run the following code to fetch data using **ExchangeRate** API:

```
ExchangeRateApiService.get_exchange_rates
```

You can optionally pass a base currency code to fetch rates for that specific currency, as shown in *Figure* 8.8:

```
Terminal: Local
sumar@Sajjads-MBP wage_pro % rails c
Loading development environment (Rails 7.1.2)
3.2.2 :001 > ExchangeRateApiService.get_exchange_rates('PKR')
 =>
{"result"=>"success",
 "provider"=>"https://www.exchangerate-api.com",
 "documentation"=>"https://www.exchangerate-api.com/docs/free",
 "terms_of_use"=>"https://www.exchangerate-api.com/terms",
 "time_last_update_unix"=>1705708952,
 "time_last_update_utc"=>"Sat, 20 Jan 2024 00:02:32 +0000",
 "time_next_update_unix"=>1705796542,
 "time_next_update_utc"=>"Sun, 21 Jan 2024 00:22:22 +0000",
 "time_eol_unix"=>0,
 "base_code"=>"PKR",
 "rates"=>
  {"PKR"=>1,
   "AED"=>0.013265,
   "AFN"=>0.262544,
```

Figure 8.8: *Using ExchangeRateApiService to fetch exchange rates in the console*

Note: *In this service, we are making an HTTP GET request to the* **`ExchangeRate`** *API to fetch data using the default* **`Net::HTTP`** *library that comes with Ruby, you can use* **`Net::HTTP`** *to make GET, POST, PUT, PATCH, DELETE requests. Read all about* **`Net::HTTP`** *at https://docs.ruby-lang.org/en/master/Net/HTTP.html*

Now our service is ready, and we can use it anywhere throughout the application.

Authentication and Authorization for APIs

API Authentication is a crucial aspect of securing interactions between different software applications, ensuring that only authorized users or systems can access or modify data through an API. It involves validating the identity of the entity making a request to an API, typically through the exchange of credentials or tokens. As APIs are stateless, API authentication requires authentication details to be included with each request.

Web Authentication typically involves session-based authentication using cookies or other session storage mechanisms. Whereas API authentication involves token-based authentication, API keys, or OAuth.

Token-Based Authentication

Token-based authentication is a method of authenticating users or systems in which a unique token is issued to an authenticated entity after successful login or authentication. This token, often a string of characters, is then included in subsequent requests to prove the identity of the entity making the request. This approach is commonly used in web development, APIs, and mobile applications.

How Token-Based Authentication Works:

Here's how Token-Based authentication typically works:

1. **User Authentication**

   The process begins with the user providing valid credentials (such as a username and password) during the authentication or login process.

2. **Token Generation**

   Upon successful authentication, the server generates a unique token associated with the authenticated user. This token is cryptographically signed to ensure its integrity.

3. **Token Issuance**

   The server issues the token to the client, typically in the form of a response to the authentication request. This token serves as proof of the user's identity.

4. **Token Storage**

   The client (for example, a web browser or a mobile app) stores the token locally. Common storage locations include cookies, local storage, or device storage, depending on the platform.

5. **Token Inclusion in Requests**

   For subsequent requests that require authentication, the client includes the token in the request header or as a parameter. This is commonly done using the "`Authorization`" header, prefixed with a specific scheme (for example, "`Bearer`").

6. **Server Verification**

   Upon receiving a request, the server verifies the authenticity of the token. This involves checking the token's integrity, expiration, and the signature created during the token generation.

7. **Granting Access**

   If the token is valid, the server grants access to the requested resource or operation. The server uses the information embedded in the token, such as user roles or permissions, to determine what actions the authenticated user is authorized to perform.

8. **Token Refresh (Optional)**

   Tokens may have a limited lifespan for security reasons. In some systems, a refresh token is issued alongside the access token. The client can use the refresh token to obtain a new access token without requiring the user to re-enter their credentials.

Token-based authentication is widely adopted in modern web development due to its flexibility, security, and scalability. It enhances the user experience by allowing for seamless, stateless authentication across various types of applications and services.

Although we can do all this manually, why reinvent the wheel when we can use battle-tested gems? There are quite a few popular options that seamlessly work with the devise (our authentication system). For example:

- **Devise Token Auth**

  Devise Token Auth is an extension of Devise specifically designed to work with token-based authentication. It allows you to use tokens alongside your Devise models, making it easy to secure your API endpoints.

  Checkout the documentation for more details: https://devise-token-auth.gitbook.io/devise-token-auth

- **JSON Web Token (JWT)**

  While not specifically designed for Devise, the JWT gem allows you to work with JSON Web Tokens. You can use it alongside Devise to implement token-based authentication in your Rails application.

  Checkout the documentation for more details: https://github.com/jwt/ruby-jwt

API Key-Based Authentication

API key-based authentication is a simple yet effective method of securing access to an API. In this approach, a unique API key is issued to each client (user, application, or system) that wants to interact with the API. The API key serves as a credential, allowing the server to identify and authenticate the requesting entity.

How Token-Based Authentication Works

Here is how API key-based authentication typically works:

1. **API Key Generation**

   The API provider generates a unique API key for each client that requests access to the API. This key is typically a long alphanumeric string.

2. **API Key Distribution**

   The API key is securely provided to the client, often through a registration or onboarding process. It can be sent via email, displayed on a dashboard, or delivered through another secure method.

3. **Inclusion in Requests**

   When making requests to the API, the client includes the API key in the request. This can be done through various means:

   - In the request header (for example, Authorization: `API_KEY`)
   - As a query parameter (for example, https://api.example.com/resource?api_key=API_KEY)

4. **Server Verification**

   Upon receiving a request, the server checks the included API key for validity. This verification process typically involves comparing the provided key against a list of authorized keys maintained by the API server.

5. **Granting Access**

   If the API key is valid, the server grants access to the requested resource or operation. If the key is invalid, expired, or lacks the necessary permissions, access is denied.

API key-based authentication is straightforward to implement and suitable for various use cases, especially when simplicity and ease of use are priorities. However, it may lack some features found in more complex authentication methods, such as user-specific permissions or delegation of access. Choosing the right authentication method depends on the specific requirements and security considerations of the API and its users.

OAuth-Based Authentication

Open Authorization (OAuth) is an open standard for access delegation commonly used for authentication and authorization in the context of web applications and APIs. It enables a user to grant a third-party application limited access to their resources (such as profiles, photos, or data) without sharing their credentials. OAuth operates on the principle of delegation, allowing users to authorize a service to act on their behalf.

Key Components of OAuth:

- **Resource Owner (User)**

  The resource owner is the user who possesses the resource (for example, a user with an account on a social media platform).

- **Client (Third-Party Application)**

  The client is a third-party application that requests access to the user's resources. It can be a mobile app, a web application, or any other software that wants to interact with the user's data.

- **Authorization Server**

  The authorization server is responsible for authenticating the user and obtaining their consent for the client to access specific resources. It issues access tokens after successful authentication and authorization.

- **Resource Server**

  The resource server hosts the protected resources (user data). It validates the access tokens and serves the requested resources to the client if the token is valid.

- **Access Token**

  An access token is a credential that represents the authorization granted to the client. It allows the client to access specific resources on behalf of the user. Access tokens have a limited lifespan.

OAuth Flow (Authorization Code Grant)

The most common OAuth flow is the Authorization Code Grant, which involves the following steps:

1. **User Authorization**

   The client redirects the user to the authorization server's login page, asking the user to grant permission for the client to access their resources.

2. **User Authentication**

   The user logs in and authenticates on the authorization server's page.

3. **Authorization Code**

   After successful authentication, the authorization server redirects the user back to the client's redirect URI with an authorization code.

4. **Token Request**

   The client sends a request to the authorization server, including the authorization code obtained in the previous step.

5. **Access Token Issuance**

   The authorization server verifies the authorization code, authenticates the client, and issues an access token to the client.

6. **Resource Request**

   The client uses the obtained access token to make requests to the resource server on behalf of the user.

7. **Resource Access**

   The resource server validates the access token, and if valid, it provides the client with the requested resources.

OAuth is widely used by major platforms and services, including social media networks, cloud services, and APIs, to enable secure and delegated access to user resources.

"`Sign in with Google`" and "`Sign in with Apple`" are examples of authentication systems that use OAuth as part of their underlying technology. These systems allow users to sign in to third-party applications or websites using their existing Google or Apple credentials without sharing their username and password with the third-party service.

There are many popular gems available to utilize OAuth based authentication including but not limited to OminAuth (https://github.com/omniauth/omniauth) with Devise and Doorkeeper (https://github.com/doorkeeper-gem/doorkeeper).

For demonstration in our WagePro application, we will be using API key-based Authentication to secure the API we created earlier in this chapter.

Implementing API Key-Based Authentication

To implement API key-based authentication, let us follow the aforementioned steps:

1. **API Key Generation**

   On creating the User, we will generate a random access token and Rails has a convenient way to do it. In the User model, add the following code:

   ```
   has_secure_token :api_key
   ```

   Now, we need to add the **`api_key`** attribute to User, and create a new migration as follows:

   ```
   rails g migration addApiKeyToUser
   ```

   Add the following code to the migration file to create the **`api_key`** attribute and add a unique index to it:

   ```
   def change
       add_column :users, :api_key, :string
       add_index :users, :api_key, unique: true
   end
   ```

Figure 8.9 shows the entire migration file:

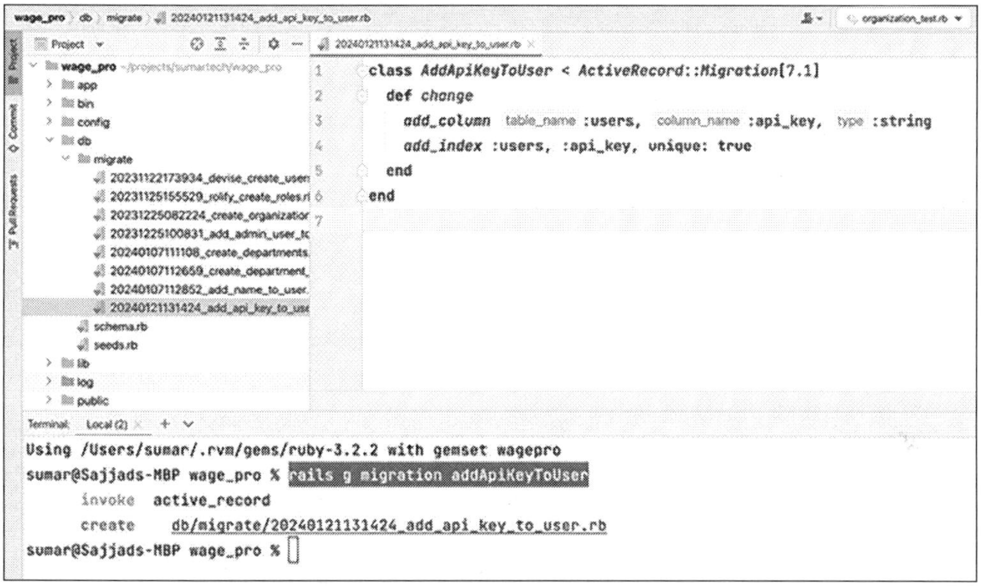

***Figure 8.9**: Migration for adding API key to the User model*

Now, run the migration with the following command:

```
rails db:migrate
```

We are done, this will add the **`api_key`** attribute to our User model, and it will automatically create a secure random API key whenever a User object is initialized.

You can learn more about **`has_secure_token`** at https://api.rubyonrails.org/classes/ActiveRecord/SecureToken/ClassMethods.html

2. **API Key Distribution**

   Ideally, we need a user interface where we will show this API key to logged-in users so that they can copy and use it. But, for now, we will access it from the rails console.

   For new users, the key will be generated automatically. However for existing users, we can generate the key using the following method:

   ```
   user.regenerate_<attribute_name>
   ```

   As our attribute name is "**`api_key`**", the preceding code will be:

   ```
   user.regenerate_api_key
   ```

Figure 8.10 shows the creation of the API key of an existing user, and how to get it using the rails console:

```
sumar@Sajjads-MBP wage_pro % rails c
Loading development environment (Rails 7.1.2)
3.2.2 :001 > user = User.first
  User Load (1.8ms)  SELECT "users".* FROM "users" ORDER BY "users"."id" ASC LIMIT $1  [["LIMIT", 1]]
 => #<User id: 1, email: "sajjadumardev@gmail.com", created_at: "2023-11-23 17:54:36.430689000 +0000", updated_at: "2023-11-23 17:5...
3.2.2 :002 > user.regenerate_api_key
  TRANSACTION (1.1ms)  BEGIN
  User Update (10.8ms)  UPDATE "users" SET "updated_at" = $1, "api_key" = $2 WHERE "users"."id" = $3  [["updated_at", "2024-01-21 13:58:2
2.076186"], ["api_key", "[FILTERED]"], ["id", 1]]
  TRANSACTION (3.0ms)  COMMIT
 => true
3.2.2 :003 > user.api_key
 => "iAcBWwQ95cUp94Q9TQ73aDq9"
3.2.2 :004 >
```

Figure 8.10: *Generating key for the existing user and accessing it from the console*

Note: *Your API key will be different than what is shown in Figure 8.10.*

3. **Inclusion in Requests**

   We will use Postman to make a GET request to our API and include the generated API key in the request Authorization header in the following format:

   `Authorization`: "***`Bearer <API KEY>`***"

Figure 8.11 shows how we can add the API key to the **`Authorization`** header of the request:

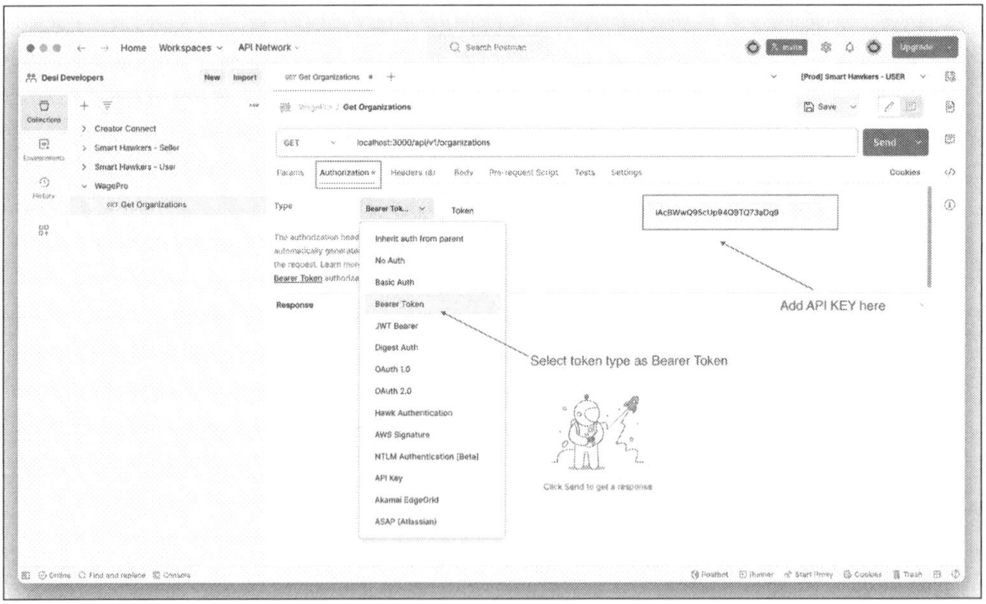

Figure 8.11: *Adding Authorization Header to Request*

Bearer tokens are a type of authentication scheme used to identify the type of token being used for authentication and authorization.

Postman will add our API KEY to request headers as shown in *Figure* 8.12:

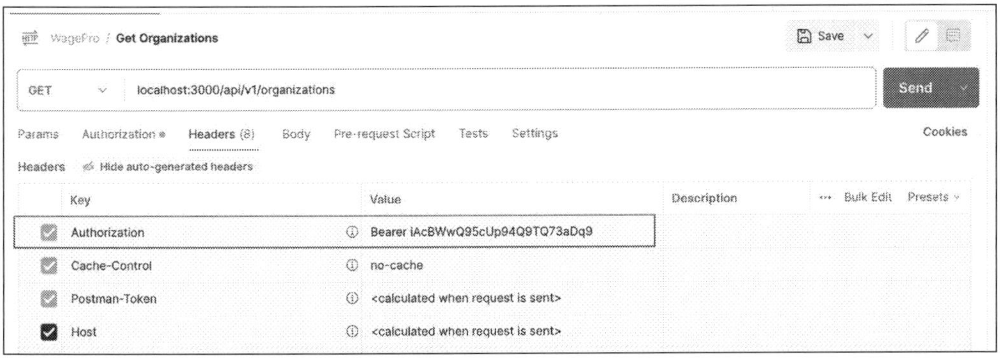

***Figure 8.12**: API key added to request headers*

Make sure your application server is running, and hit Send on Postman to send a GET request to our application.

You can verify if the request indeed has the **`Authorization`** header attached by adding the following code to your **`Api::V1::OrganizationsController#index`** method as shown in *Figure* 8.13:

```
puts "__________PRINTING HEADERS___________"
puts request.headers['Authorization']
```

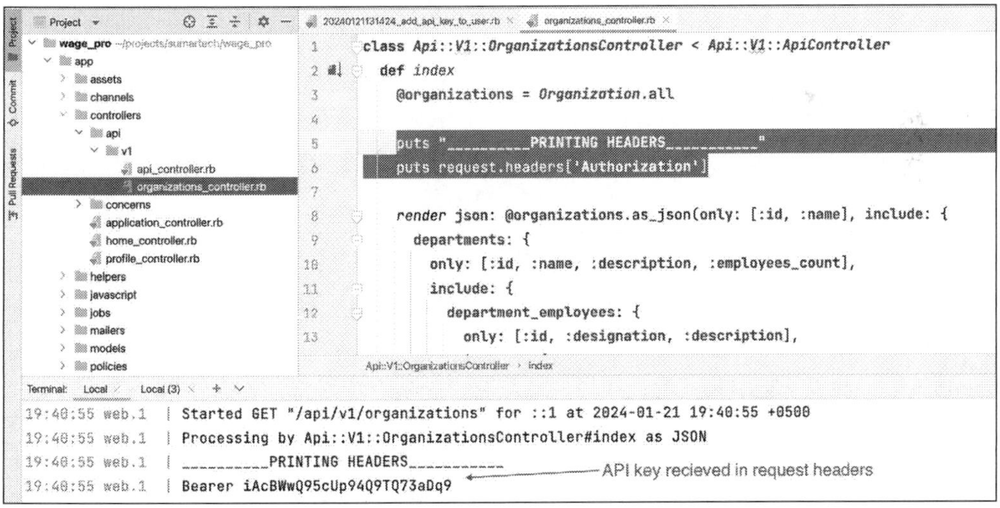

***Figure 8.13**: API key received by our application/server*

4. **Server Verification**

   It is time to verify the API key received via the **`Authorization`** header and check if it is valid.

We can do that by adding the following code in our **Api::V1::ApiController**:

```
class Api::V1::ApiController < ActionController::Base
  before_action :authenticate_with_api_token!

  attr_reader :current_user

  private

  def authenticate_with_api_token!
    authenticate_or_request_with_http_token do |token, _options|
      @current_user = User.find_by(api_key: token)

      @current_user || render_unauthorized
    end
  end

  def render_unauthorized
    render json: { error: 'Invalid API Key' }, status: :unautho-
rized
  end
end
```

Figure 8.14 shows the **ApiController** with some additional comments to explain what is happening in the code:

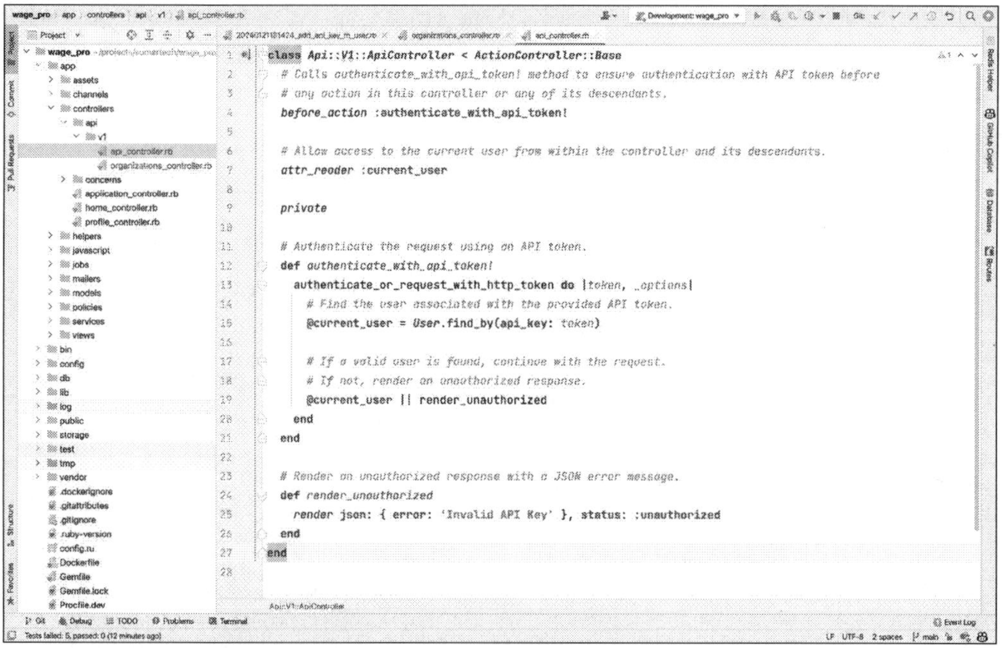

Figure 8.14: *Performing API key-based authentication in ApiController*

Now if you send another request from Postman it will go through an API key-based authentication process. You will not see any difference unless you send an invalid API Key, or you do not send any key at all. *Figure* 8.15 shows the response in case of an invalid API key in Authorization headers:

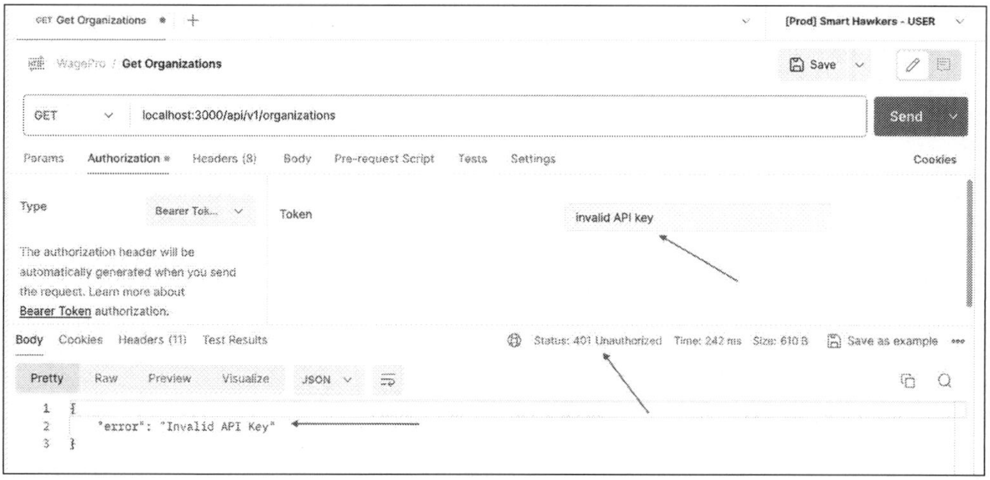

Figure 8.15: *API response for invalid API Key*

At this point you will notice if you send a valid API Key, our API is still sending data of all organizations; in reality, it should only send organizations that our authenticated user is authorized to access.

5. **Granting Access (Authorization)**

   Now it is time to send only what the current user is authorized to access. As we already have pundit (authorization gem), we will make use of it.

   First, create a new policy class "**app/policies/organizaion_policy.rb**" and add the following code:

```
class OrganizationPolicy < ApplicationPolicy
  class Scope < ApplicationPolicy::Scope
    def resolve
      if user.has_role?(:admin)
        admin_scope
      else
        non_admin_user_scope
      end
    end

    private

    def non_admin_user_scope
      scope.joins(:departments).where(departments: { id: user.
department_ids })
    end

    def admin_scope
      scope.joins(:departments).where(admin_user_id: user.id).
or(non_admin_user_scope)
    end
  end
end
```

Figure 8.16 shows the **oragnization_policy.rb** file with additional comments to explain what is happening in this class:

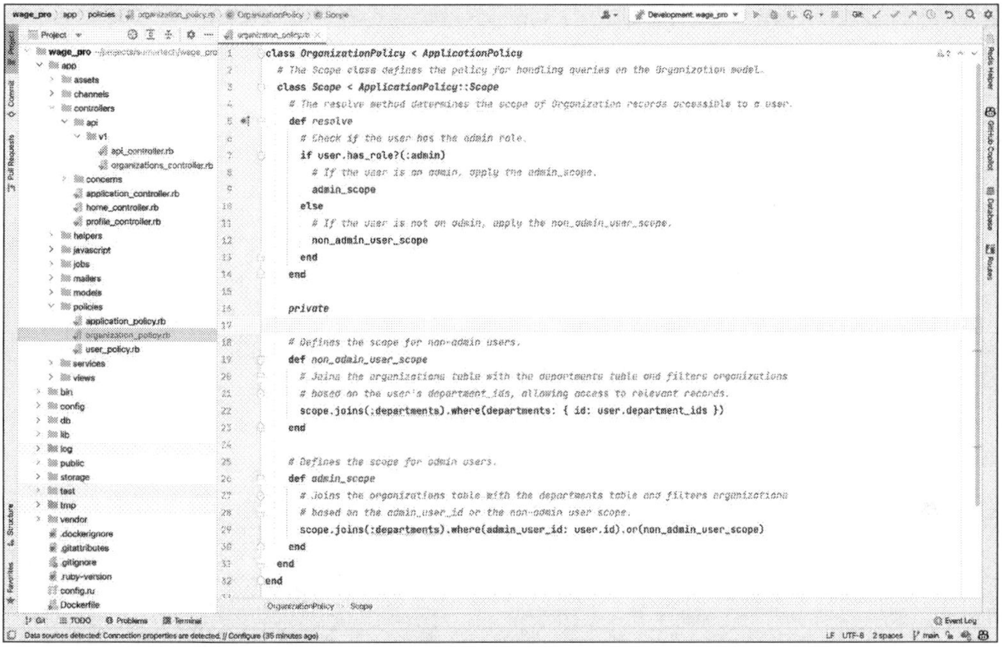

Figure 8.16: *Organization policy file with additional comments*

In the organization policy, we are using another feature of pundit gem called scopes. You can read more about scopes on the official documentation of Pundit Gem at https://github.com/varvet/pundit?tab=readme-ov-file#scopes.

That's all, if you test the API, it will only return organizations a User is authorized to access.

Figure 8.17 shows finding a User from the database who only has an "**`employee`**" role in one organization's department and creating its API key:

```
Loading development environment (Rails 7.1.2)
3.2.2 :001 > user = User.last
  User Load (1.4ms)  SELECT "users".* FROM "users" ORDER BY "users"."id" DESC LIMIT $1  [["LIMIT", 1]]
 => #<User id: 3, email: "sumar@sumartech.com", created_at: "2024-01-11 17:47:39.639555000 +0000", updated_at: "2024-01-11 17:47:39...
3.2.2 :002 > user.roles_name
  Role Pluck (2.7ms)  SELECT "roles"."name" FROM "roles" INNER JOIN "users_roles" ON "roles"."id" = "users_roles"."role_id" WHERE "users_
roles"."user_id" = $1  [["user_id", 3]]
 => ["employee"]
3.2.2 :003 > user.department_ids
  Department Pluck (2.0ms)  SELECT "departments"."id" FROM "departments" INNER JOIN "department_employees" ON "departments"."id" = "depar
tment_employees"."department_id" WHERE "department_employees"."user_id" = $1  [["user_id", 3]]
 => [2]
3.2.2 :004 > user.regenerate_api_key
  TRANSACTION (1.3ms)  BEGIN
  User Update (9.4ms)  UPDATE "users" SET "updated_at" = $1, "api_key" = $2 WHERE "users"."id" = $3  [["updated_at", "2024-01-23 14:18:51
.791935"], ["api_key", "[FILTERED]"], ["id", 3]]
  TRANSACTION (2.2ms)  COMMIT
 => true
3.2.2 :005 > user.api_key
 => "g325NLWEVdHvz8Mqjhqr92UM"
3.2.2 :006 >
```

Figure 8.17: *Getting API key for a user with an employee role*

Let's make a GET request to our API from Postman with the API key shown in *Figure* 8.17.

Figure 8.18 shows the API only returns one organization in response, which means it is working as expected:

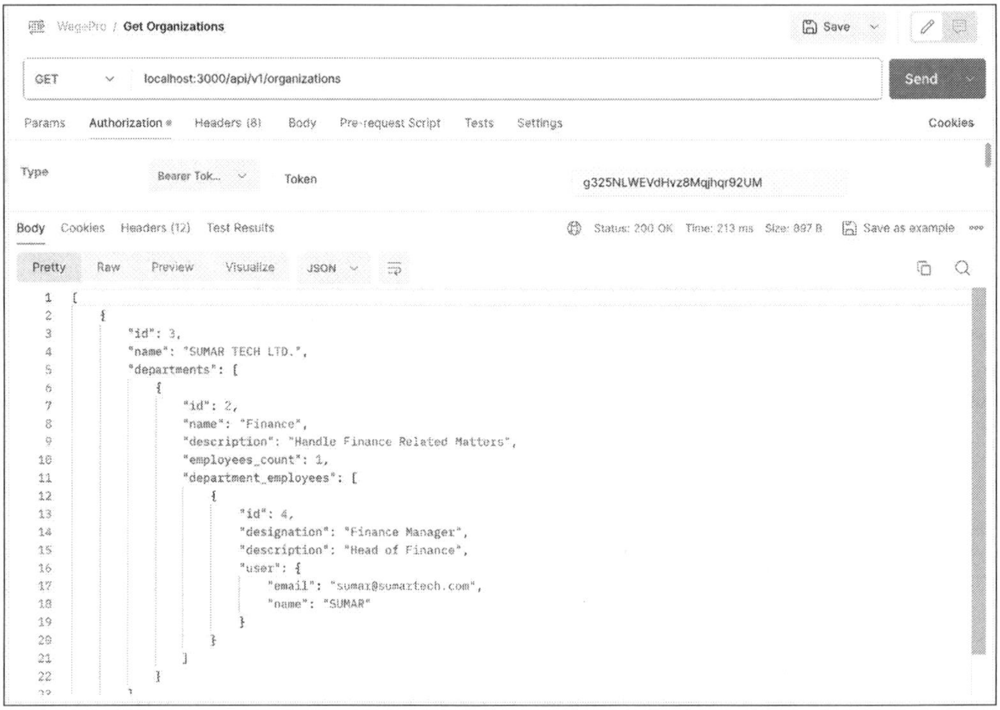

Figure 8.18: *API response that returns only one organization's information*

The GitHub link provided contains the commit associated with all the code demonstrated in this chapter: https://github.com/ava-orange-education/Ruby-on-Rails-for-Agile-Web-Development/tree/main/chapter08/wage_pro

You can get access to everything covered in the book on this GitHub repo: https://github.com/ava-orange-education/Ruby-on-Rails-for-Agile-Web-Development.

Conclusion

In this chapter, we looked into RESTful APIs and web services, unraveling the intricacies of designing, building, and securing APIs in Ruby on Rails. We explored the fundamental principles of RESTful architecture, building API endpoints, consuming external web services, and implementing authentication mechanisms. Now, as we venture into *Chapter* 9, *Deployment and Scaling*, we will transition from the development phase to the deployment phase of our journey. In this chapter, we will guide you through the essential steps of preparing your application for deployment, deploying it to a popular hosting provider, and addressing the challenges of scaling Rails applications. We will also delve into monitoring and performance optimization and discuss the concepts of continuous integration and deployment. This chapter will equip you with the knowledge and skills needed to successfully take your Ruby on Rails application from the development environment to a live and scalable production setting.

Short Quiz

1. **What does REST stand for in the context of web services?**
   a. Remote Entity State Transfer
   b. Representational State Transfer
   c. Responsive Entity State Transfer
   d. Responsive Stateful Transfer
2. **What are the core principles of RESTful design?**
   a. Independence, Simplicity, Efficiency
   b. Scalability, Security, Flexibility
   c. Statelessness, Client-Server, Uniform Interface
   d. Authentication, Authorization, Encryption
3. **Which HTTP method is commonly used to retrieve resource representation in RESTful architecture?**
   a. POST
   b. GET
   c. PUT
   d. DELETE
4. **What is the purpose of creating RESTful routes and controllers in Rails API development?**
   a. To handle database migrations
   b. To define different user roles
   c. To structure API endpoints and manage resource actions
   d. To integrate external data into models
5. **How do you make HTTP requests in Rails when consuming external APIs?**
   a. Using rails `api:request` command
   b. Using curl in the terminal

   c. Using the `Net::HTTP` library or HTTP client gems
   d. Making direct SQL queries

6. **What is token-based authentication, and how is it commonly implemented in Rails APIs?**
   a. Storing user credentials in plain text
   b. Using API keys for authentication
   c. Tokenizing database entries
   d. Utilizing JWT or OAuth to issue and verify tokens

7. **What is the purpose of implementing authentication in Rails APIs?**
   a. To generate API documentation
   b. To secure API endpoints and verify the identity of users or clients
   c. To handle database queries
   d. To parse data from external APIs

8. **How can API endpoints in Rails be secured with authorization?**
   a. Using Devise gem
   b. Applying SSL certificates
   c. Validating user roles and permissions
   d. Using JavaScript frameworks

9. **What is API key-based authentication in the context of web services?**
   a. A method for storing passwords securely
   b. A technique for encrypting API responses
   c. An approach to validate user identities using biometrics
   d. A mechanism where clients include a unique key in their requests for authentication

10. **How does API key-based authentication work in Rails applications?**
   a. By using QR codes for authentication
   b. By sending user credentials in the request body
   c. By including a unique API key in the request headers
   d. By relying on session cookies for authentication

Chapter 9
Deployment and Scaling

Introduction

In this chapter of our Ruby on Rails adventure, it's time to unveil the secrets of "*Deployment and Scaling*." Imagine your Rails application as a rocket ready for liftoff–this chapter is where we fuel it up and launch it into the digital cosmos.

We're about to embark on the journey from your computer to the vast world of users. In simple terms, deploying is like releasing your app into the wild, letting it spread its wings beyond the development nest. We'll guide you through this process, making sure your app lands softly and operates smoothly.

Ever heard of Render and AWS? Think of them as the launch pads for your rocket. We'll show you how to send your app to these platforms, ensuring it gets the attention it deserves. But that's not all; we're not just sending your app out there–we're also giving it the power to grow.

Scaling is like providing your rocket with turbo boosters. We'll share tips on how to make your app handle more users without breaking a sweat. Imagine your app going from a cozy neighborhood to a bustling metropolis–scaling helps it thrive in the bustling digital city.

Monitoring and performance optimization? Picture it as having a dashboard in your rocket that tells you how smoothly it's sailing through the digital skies. We'll guide you on how to keep an eye on things and tweak your app to be as fast and efficient as possible.

Lastly, we're going to introduce you to a magical tool called GitHub Actions. It's like having a team of digital assistants who help you build, test, and deploy your app automatically. Less hassle, more magic!

So, buckle up! This chapter is where we turn your Rails app into a digital superstar, ready to conquer the vast and dynamic universe of the internet. Let's make your app soar!

Structure

In this chapter, we will discuss the following topics:

- Understanding Deployment Basics
- Deploying Rails Application
- Continuous Integration and Deployment (CI/CD)
- Scaling Rails Applications
  - Understanding the Need for Scaling
  - Tips for Effective Scaling
- Monitoring and Performance Optimization
  - The Importance of Monitoring
  - Strategies for Performance Optimization

Understanding Deployment Basics

Deployment is the pivotal transition from the development phase to a live, accessible environment for your Rails application. It involves making the application available to users beyond the local development setup.

Let's discuss and understand some key deployment concepts before we deploy our application.

Key Concepts

When deploying an application, several components come into play:

- **Web Server:** Acts as a gateway, handling user requests and forwarding them to the application server.

  Common web servers include Nginx and Apache. They handle static content and forward dynamic requests to the application server.

- **Application Server:** Executes the application code and communicates with the web server.

  Puma, Unicorn, and Passenger are popular choices for running Rails applications. They interpret Ruby code, manage application processes, and communicate with the web server.

- **Database:** Stores and retrieves data necessary for the application's functionality.

  Various databases are supported, such as PostgreSQL and MySQL. Configuring the database ensures seamless data transactions.

- **Dependencies:** External components such as gems and libraries your application relies on. Properly managing these dependencies is crucial to avoid compatibility issues.

Understanding the interaction among these components is crucial for a seamless deployment, ensuring a smooth user experience.

Deployment Strategies

To deploy a Rails Application, we can implement one or a combination of the following strategies:

Continuous Deployment

Continuous Deployment is a dynamic approach to deploying software changes seamlessly and rapidly. In this strategy, the deployment process is automated and initiated automatically after a successful run of automated tests. The goal is to ensure that as soon as a new feature or bug fix is implemented and passes all tests, it is swiftly deployed to the production environment without manual intervention.

Key Points:

- **Automation:** The deployment process is fully automated, reducing the likelihood of human error and ensuring consistency.
- **Rapid Rollouts:** New features and bug fixes are rolled out promptly, providing users with the latest improvements.
- **Immediate Feedback:** Automated tests serve as a gatekeeper, providing immediate feedback on the code's stability and functionality.

Blue-Green Deployment

Blue-Green Deployment is a strategy designed to minimize downtime and mitigate risks during the deployment of updates or changes. It involves running two separate, nearly identical production environments: one (Blue) hosting the current version of the application, and the other (Green) hosting the updated version. The transition between the two environments is seamless, reducing the impact on users.

Key Points:

- **Parallel Environments:** Blue and Green environments coexist, with one serving as the active production environment while the other is preparing for the update.
- **Switching Mechanism:** Once the Green environment is ready, a switch is made to redirect user traffic from the Blue to the Green environment without downtime.

- **Rollback Capability:** In case issues arise after the switch, rolling back to the previous version (Blue) is immediate and requires minimal effort.

Canary Releases

Canary Releases involve a cautious and gradual rollout of new features or updates by exposing them to a subset of users before a full release. The concept is akin to sending a canary into a coal mine – it serves as an early warning system. In this strategy, a small percentage of users experience the changes, allowing for real-time performance monitoring and user feedback before a broader release.

Key Points:

- **Gradual Exposure:** New features are incrementally introduced to a limited audience before reaching the entire user base.
- **Performance Monitoring:** The subset of users acts as a test group, providing insights into the new features' performance, stability, and user satisfaction.
- **Risk Mitigation:** Identifying issues early on allows for adjustments or rollbacks before a full-scale release, reducing the impact of potential problems.

These deployment strategies offer flexibility and risk management, ensuring that software changes are introduced smoothly and with a focus on user experience and system reliability.

Now we know a bit about deployment, let's jump straight into the deployment and deploy a Ruby on Rails application to the Cloud so that it is available for the world to use.

Deployment

Let us deploy our application on a fully managed Platform as a Service (PaaS) solution. Among the widely used options are Heroku (https://www.heroku.com), AWS Elastic Beanstalk (https://aws.amazon.com/elasticbeanstalk), and Render (https://render.com). For this chapter, we've chosen Render due to its availability of a free tier.

Subsequently, you can also deploy your applications to an Infrastructure as a Service (IaaS) platform. Commonly favored choices encompass Amazon Elastic Compute Cloud (https://aws.amazon.com/ec2), DigitalOcean Droplets (https://www.digitalocean.com), and Hetzner (https://www.hetzner.com). To keep this chapter concise, we will only cover deployment on PaaS.

Deploying Your Rails App on Render

To demonstrate deployment on Render we are going to create a simple brand-new Rails application.

We will be using Ruby 3.2.2, Rails 7.1.3, and the latest version of the PostgreSQL database for our new application.

Let's quickly create our "**`simple_blog`**" application using the following command:

```
rails new simple_blog --database=postgresql -c tailwind
```

This command will create our new "**`simple_blog`**" application with PostgreSQL database and tailwind CSS, as shown in *Figure* 9.1:

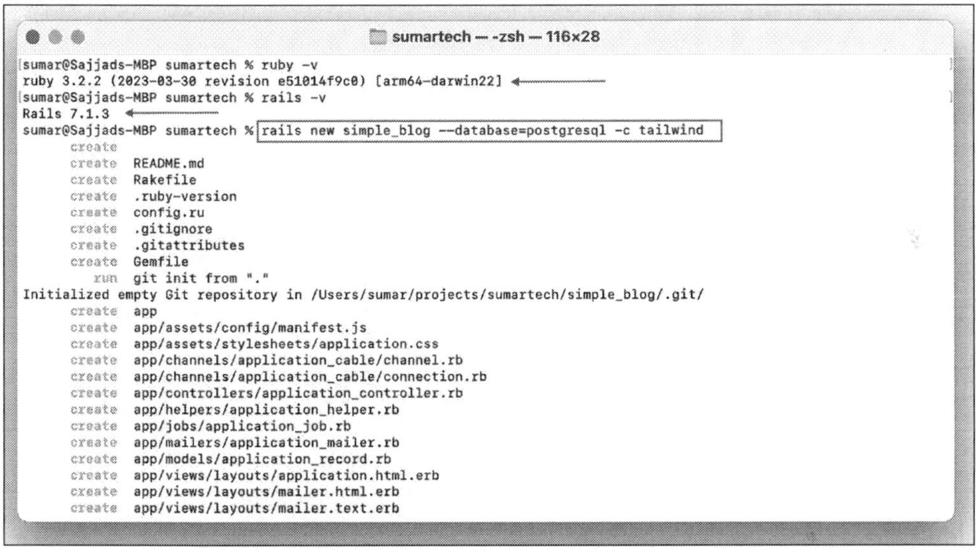

Figure 9.1: *Creating a new "simple_blog" rails app*

Note: *If you are on a different version of Ruby and Rails, please follow the instructions given in the section "Installing Ruby and Rails" in Chapter 3, "Getting Started with Ruby on Rails".*

Now inside the root directly of your newly created app, run the following command to scaffold a Post.

```
rails g scaffold post title:string content:text
```

Now last thing we need is to uncomment/add the following route to our **`routes.rb`** file:

```
root "posts#index"
```

After that, just run the following commands one by one:

1. `rails db:create db:migrate`
2. `./bin/dev`

These are the only commands we need to have our basic application up and running, as shown in *Figure* 9.2.

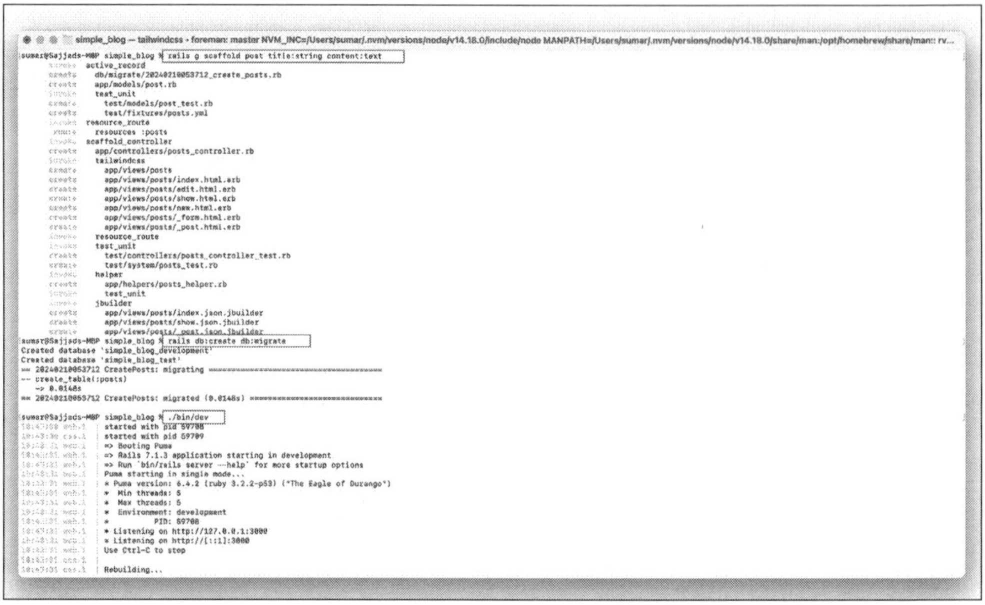

Figure 9.2: *Scaffolding, Prepared Database, and Running Server*

Note: *If you face any issues with database connections, please review the "`config/database.yml`" file of your newly created application.*

Once our newly created app is up and running, you can visit `localhost:3000` to view it in your browser, as shown in *Figure* 9.3:

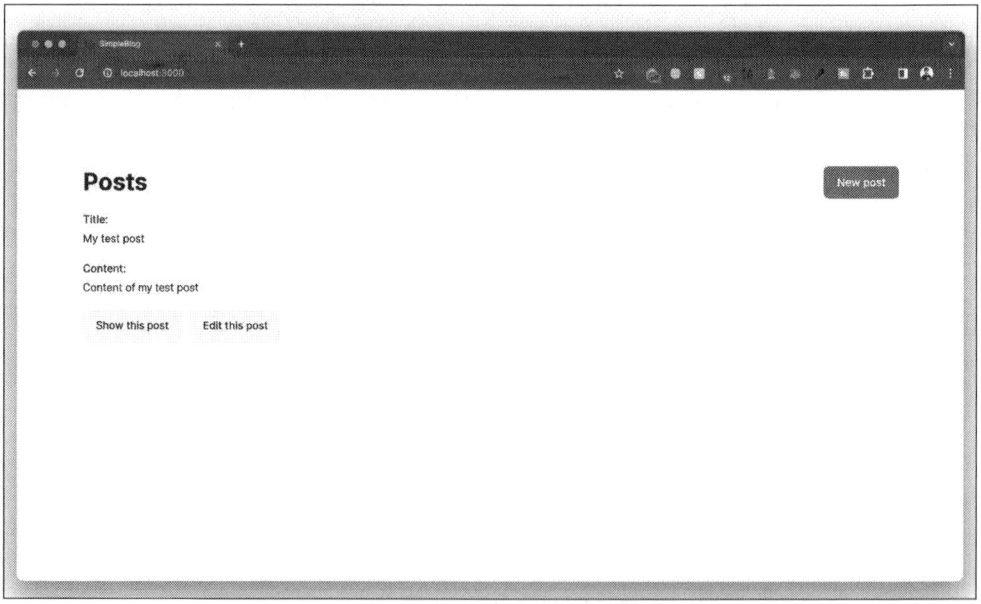

Figure 9.3: *Exploring our new app on localhost:3000*

Note: *Figure 9.3 shows that we have also created a test post in our application, please go ahead and create one on your own to explore the app.*

Now let's deploy it!

There are two ways to deploy on Render:

- Automatic deployment using **`render.yaml`** file
- Manual deployment

In this chapter, we will cover automatic deployment as it handles most things automatically. If you want to do the manual deployment, please study the official render documentation: https://docs.render.com/deploy-rails#deploy-manually.

Automatic Deployment Using `render.yaml`

Render builds your project before each deployment by running a **`build`** command that you specify. Let's create a script to use for this command.

Create a file named **`bin/render-build.sh`** in your repo's bin directory. Paste the following into it and save:

```
#!/usr/bin/env bash

# exit on error

set -o errexit


bundle install

./bin/rails assets:precompile

./bin/rails assets:clean

bundle exec rails db:migrate

bundle exec rails db:seed
```

Ensure the script is executable before committing it to Git, let's do that by running the following command:

```
chmod a+x bin/render-build.sh
```

Figure 9.4 shows the above file and the execution of the preceding command on the terminal.

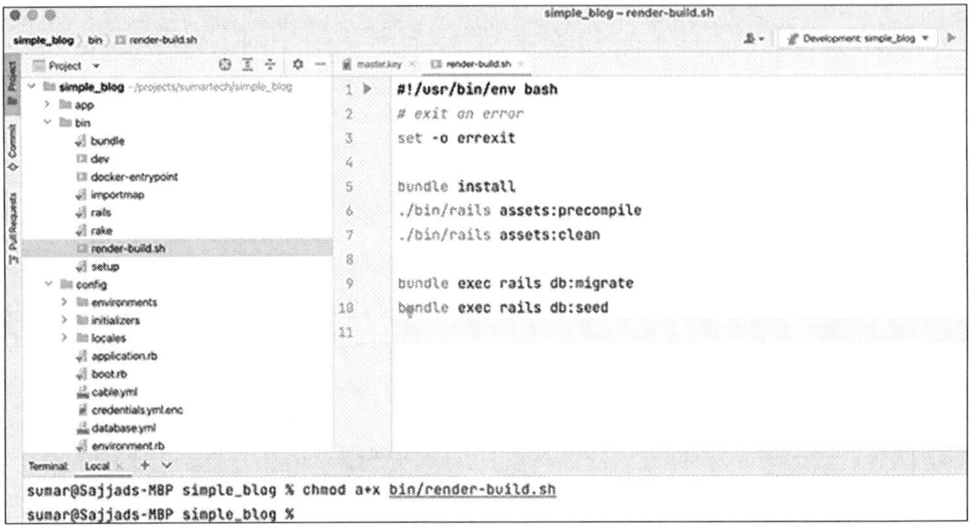

Figure 9.4: *bin/render-build.sh file and setting appropriate permission*

Now create a file named **`render.yaml`** at the root of your directory and paste in the YAML content below. This defines information about your Rails web service, along with the database that it connects to:

```
databases:
  - name: simple_blog_production
    databaseName: simple_blog_production
    user: sumar # change it with your username
    plan: free


services:
  - type: web
    name: simple_blog
    runtime: ruby
    plan: free
    buildCommand: "./bin/render-build.sh"
    # preDeployCommand: "./bin/rails db:migrate" # preDeployCommand only available on paid instance types
    startCommand: "./bin/rails server"
    envVars:
      - key: DATABASE_URL
        fromDatabase:
          name: simple_blog_production
```

```
          property: connectionString
      - key: RAILS_MASTER_KEY
        sync: false
      - key: WEB_CONCURRENCY
        value: 2 # sensible default
```

Figure 9.5 shows **`render.yaml`** file with the above code.

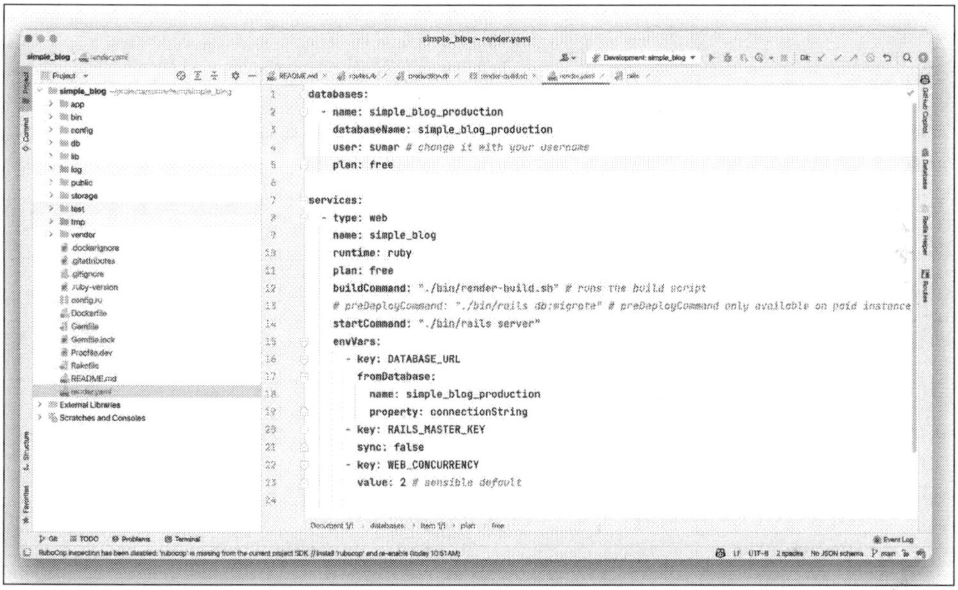

Figure 9.5: *render.yaml file*

Note: *If you don't set* **`WEB_CONCURRENCY`**, *Rails determines a value based on the runtime's physical CPU count. This might result in your application running out of memory immediately on boot. Render recommends setting this value to 2 as a default, but also optimizing this value for your own application.*

Now we need to deploy our application to GitHub, so that we can authorize render to get the latest version from your GitHub account.

This book does not cover how to push your code to GitHub, but you can find all the instructions here on the official GitHub documentation https://docs.github.com/en/get-started/using-git. Spoiler alert, it is pretty easy!

Once you have pushed your code to GitHub, it is time to get an account on render, you can sign on the following link: https://dashboard.render.com/register.

Once you have a render account, go to Blueprints (https://dashboard.render.com/blueprints) page and create a new Blueprint instance. *Figure* 9.6 shows the blueprints page.

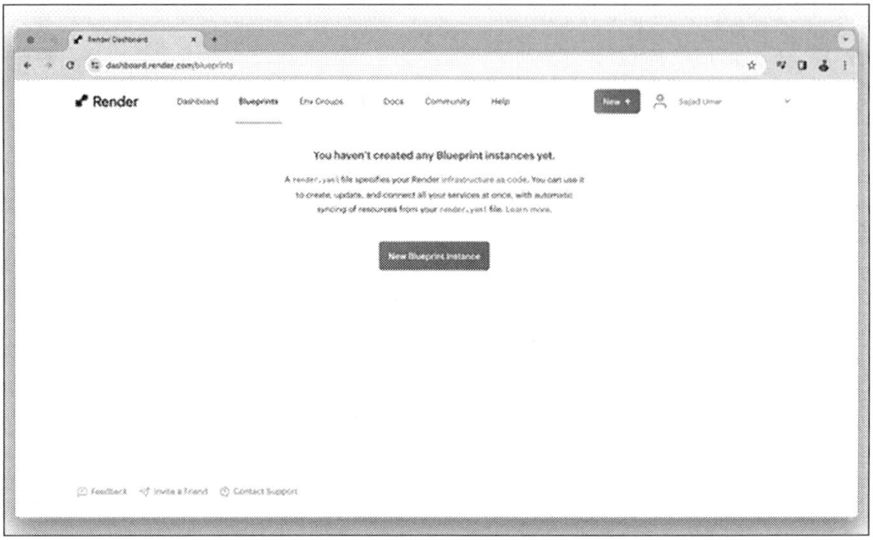

Figure 9.6: *Blueprints page on Render*

Note: *Render might ask you to provide your payment information to create a new Blueprint Instance, go ahead and add it, but for this application, we will be using the free plan of Render.*

Once you click on the New Blueprint Instance button shown in *Figure* 9.6, render will ask you to connect your GitHub account, go ahead and authorize render to access your GitHub account and repositories.

Now, select the repository of your **`simple_blog`** application from GitHub on the next screen, as shown in *Figure* 9.7:

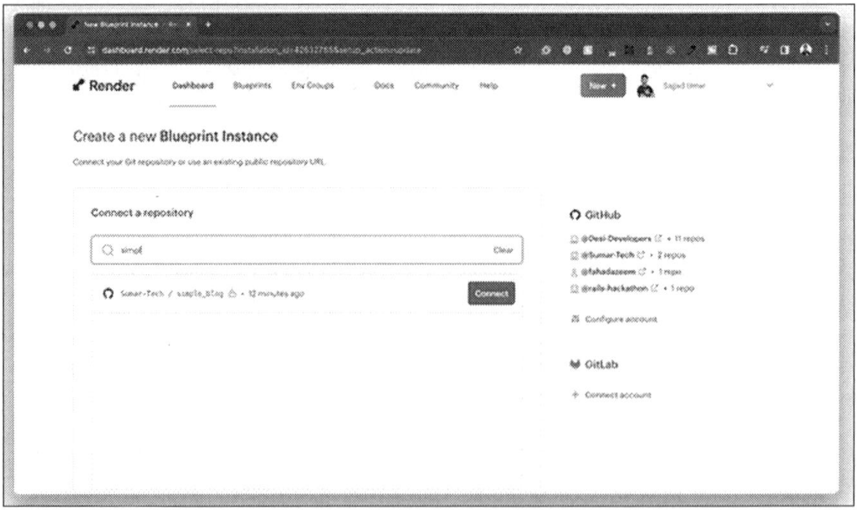

Figure 9.7: *Connecting GitHub Repo to Render Blueprint Instance*

Once you hit connect, render will ask you to give your instance a unique name, and provide **`RAILS_MASTER_KEY`**, you can find your **`RAILS_MASTER_KEY`** in the "**`config/master.key`**" file of your application. Go ahead and give a name and put in the master key of your application.

The **`master.key`** file is a crucial part of the encrypted credentials system introduced in Rails 5.2. It is used to decrypt the **`credentials.yml.enc`** file, which stores sensitive information such as API keys, database passwords, and other configuration details securely.

Here's how it works:

- **`credentials.yml.enc`**: This file contains encrypted sensitive information. It's typically located in the config directory of a Rails application.
- **`master.key`**: This file is the decryption key for **`credentials.yml.enc`**. It's kept secret and should never be shared or exposed in version control.

During development and deployment, Rails uses the `master.key` to decrypt `credentials.yml.enc` and access the sensitive information stored within it.

It's essential to keep the **`master.key`** secure, especially in production environments, to prevent unauthorized access to sensitive data. If the **`master.key`** is lost or compromised, you won't be able to decrypt **`credentials.yml.enc`**, potentially leading to service disruptions or security breaches.

Figure 9.8 shows assigning a name and adding **`RAILS_MASTER_KEY`** to the **`Render Blueprint`**.

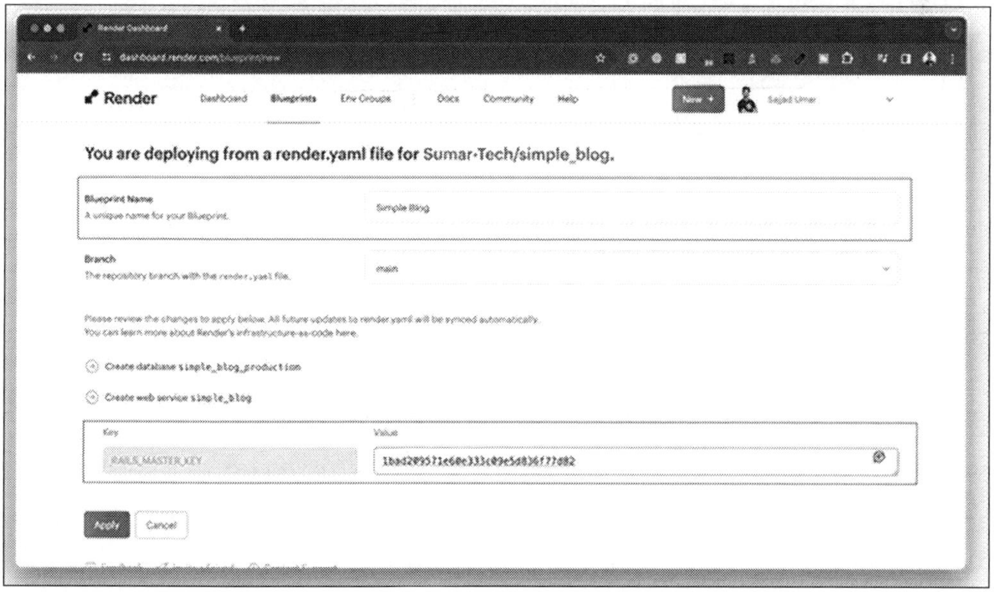

Figure 9.8: *Assigning name and adding RAILS_MASTER_KEY to Render Blueprint*

Once you hit apply, Render will start doing its magic and it will deploy your application to the Blueprint instance as shown in *Figure* 9.9:

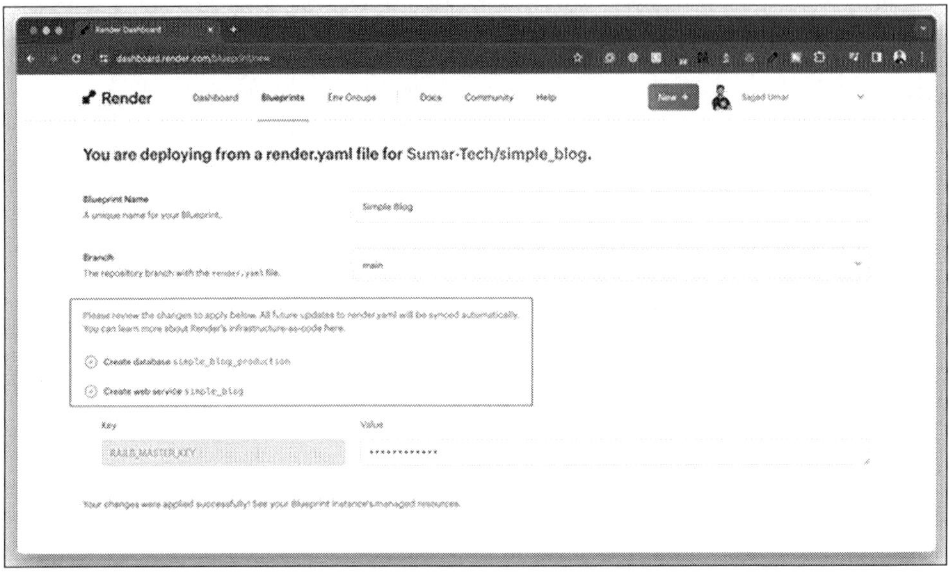

***Figure* 9.9:** *Render deploying your application*

On the **`Dashboard`** page (https://dashboard.render.com) you will be able to see your application is deployed successfully and your database is live and available for your application.

Figure 9.10 shows your deployed services on the render **`Dashboard`** page.

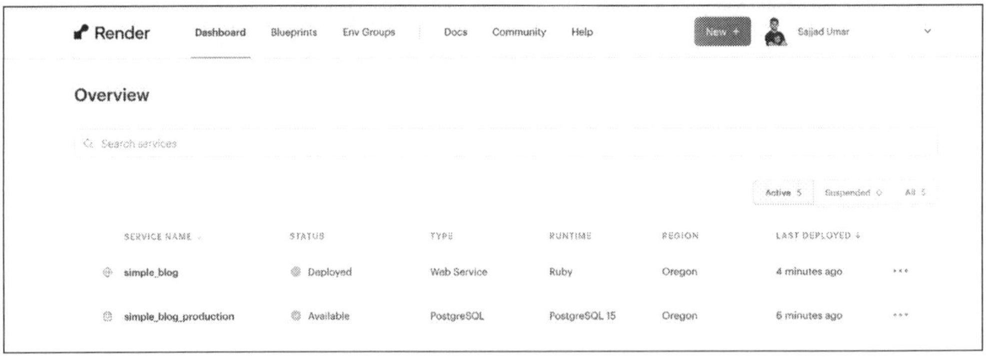

***Figure* 9.10**: *Render Dashboard*

Now click on the **`simple_blog`** service and get your application URL as shown in *Figure* 9.11:

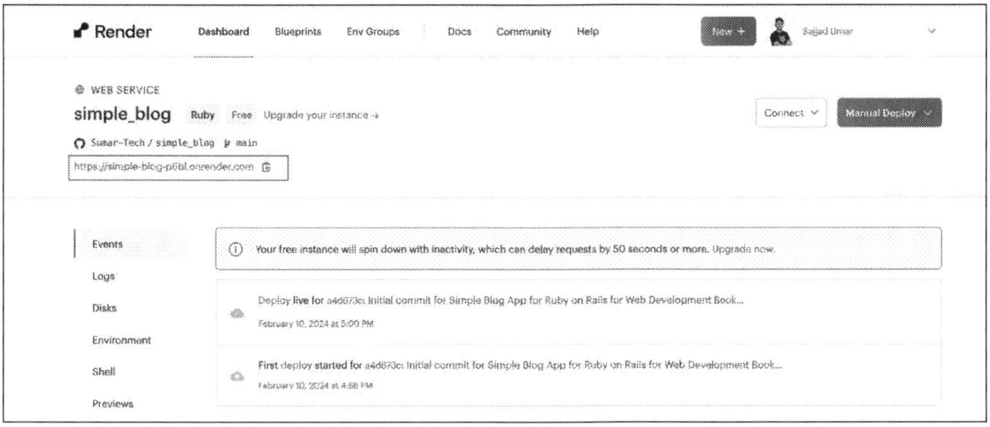

Figure 9.11: *Application URL*

Now open this URL in the browser of your choice and you will see your application up and running. Your application is now live and ready to serve real users!

Figure 9.12 shows our **`simple_blog`** application running on **`Render`**.

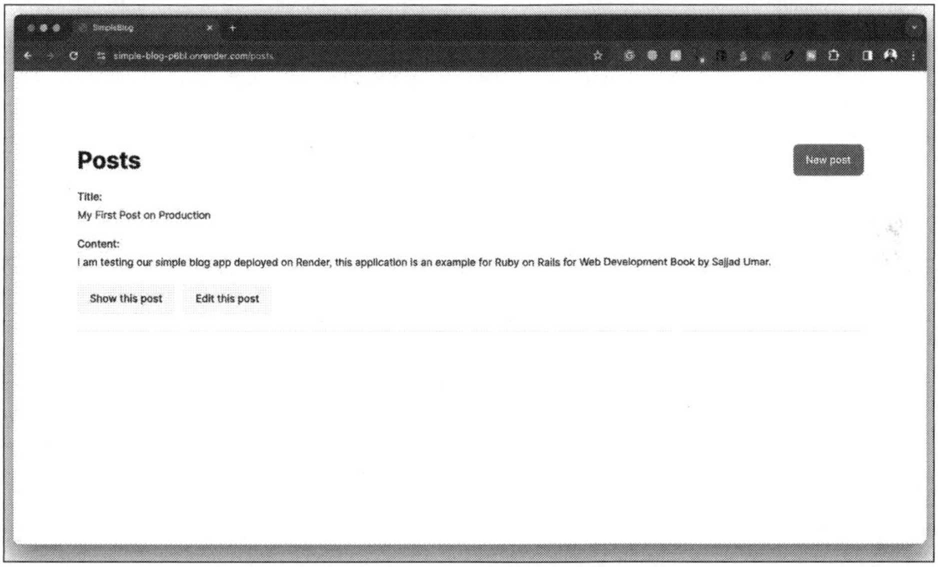

Figure 9.12: *Live application on Render*

Continuous Integration and Deployment (CI/CD)

Now we have a live application, ready to serve real users. The next step is to ease the deployment process with Continuous Integration and Deployment.

- **Continuous Integration (CI)**: CI is a software development practice where developers frequently integrate their code changes into a shared repository. With each integration, an automated build process is triggered followed by a suite of automated tests. The primary goal of CI is to detect integration errors and ensure that the codebase remains stable, even as developers make frequent changes. By facilitating rapid feedback loops, CI fosters collaboration among team members, reduces integration issues, and maintains high code quality.
- **Continuous Deployment (CD):** CD is an extension of CI that automates the deployment of code changes to production or staging environments after passing through a series of automated tests. In Continuous Deployment, code changes are automatically deployed to production environments without manual intervention, ensuring rapid and frequent releases.

CI/CD practices enable teams to develop, test, and deploy software with greater efficiency, reliability, and speed.

Render Blueprints comes with an inbuilt auto-deployment feature, which means, whenever you push changes to the branch you specified during the setup process (default to "*main*" branch). Render will start the deployment process automatically.

Note: *Try triggering an automatic deployment by pushing any change to your version control repository.*

This works great unless you want to run tests before the deployment. This is where we need a more advanced CI/CD platform.

Several popular CI/CD platforms are widely used by developers and organizations to automate the build, test, and deployment processes of software applications. Some of these platforms include:

- **GitHub Actions:** Provided by GitHub, GitHub Actions allows developers to automate workflows directly within their GitHub repositories. It offers seamless integration with GitHub's version control system and supports a wide range of actions and integrations.
- **GitLab CI/CD:** GitLab CI/CD is an integral part of the GitLab platform, offering native CI/CD capabilities for GitLab repositories. It enables developers to define and manage CI/CD pipelines using YAML configuration files and provides features for testing, code quality analysis, and deployment.
- **Travis CI:** Travis CI is a cloud-based CI/CD platform that integrates with GitHub and Bitbucket repositories. It supports automatic testing and deployment of projects in various programming languages and environments, making it a popular choice among open-source projects.

- **CircleCI:** CircleCI is a CI/CD platform that provides continuous integration and delivery for software applications. It offers customizable workflows, parallel testing, and integration with popular version control systems like GitHub and Bitbucket.
- **Jenkins:** Jenkins is an open-source automation server widely used for CI/CD. It offers extensibility through a vast ecosystem of plugins and supports building, testing, and deploying applications across different environments.
- **Azure Pipelines:** Azure Pipelines is a cloud-based CI/CD service provided by Microsoft Azure. It enables developers to build, test, and deploy applications across a variety of platforms and integrates seamlessly with Azure DevOps and GitHub repositories.
- **AWS CodePipeline:** AWS CodePipeline is a fully managed CI/CD service offered by Amazon Web Services (AWS). It allows developers to automate the release process of their applications, including building, testing, and deploying code changes across different AWS services.

These platforms offer various features and integrations to streamline the software development lifecycle and facilitate efficient and reliable delivery of software updates. As we are using GitHub for our **`simple_blog`** app, we will be using GitHub Actions for CI/CD.

GitHub Action Terminologies

Before we jump into creating GitHub Actions workflows, let's learn some terminologies:

- **Trigger:** Specifies the events that trigger the workflow, such as code pushes or pull requests
- **Jobs:** Define one or more jobs, each consisting of a sequence of steps to be executed
- **Steps:** Configure individual steps, such as checking out code, running tests, building artifacts, and deploying to environments
- **Environment Variables:** Define environment variables to store sensitive information or configuration settings used in the workflow
- **Caching:** Optionally, configure caching to improve build performance by storing dependencies or intermediate build artifacts between workflow runs

Now, let's build some CI/CD workflows for our application as follows:

Whenever a code is merged, or a pull request is created against the "**`main`**" of our repository, our workflow should trigger and do the following:

1. Run all the tests
2. If tests pass, start the deployment

3. If tests fail, the workflow should fail without any deployment

But, we don't have any tests in our application as of now, so let's add the following code to our application:

Add some validations in our Post model:

```
class Post < ApplicationRecord
  validates :title, :content, presence: true
end
```

Now, add the following unit tests for the Post model at "**test/models/post_test.rb**":

```
require "test_helper"

class PostTest < ActiveSupport::TestCase
  # test the presence of the title and content
  test "should not save post without title" do
    post = Post.new
    assert_not post.save, "Saved the post without a title"
  end

  test "should not save post without content" do
    post = Post.new
    assert_not post.save, "Saved the post without content"
  end

  test "should save post with title and content" do
    post = Post.new(title: "Title", content: "Content")
    assert post.save, "Could not save the post with title and content"
  end
end
```

Now try running these tests locally by running the following command in the terminal:

```
rails test
```

Figure 9.13 shows all our newly added tests are passing.

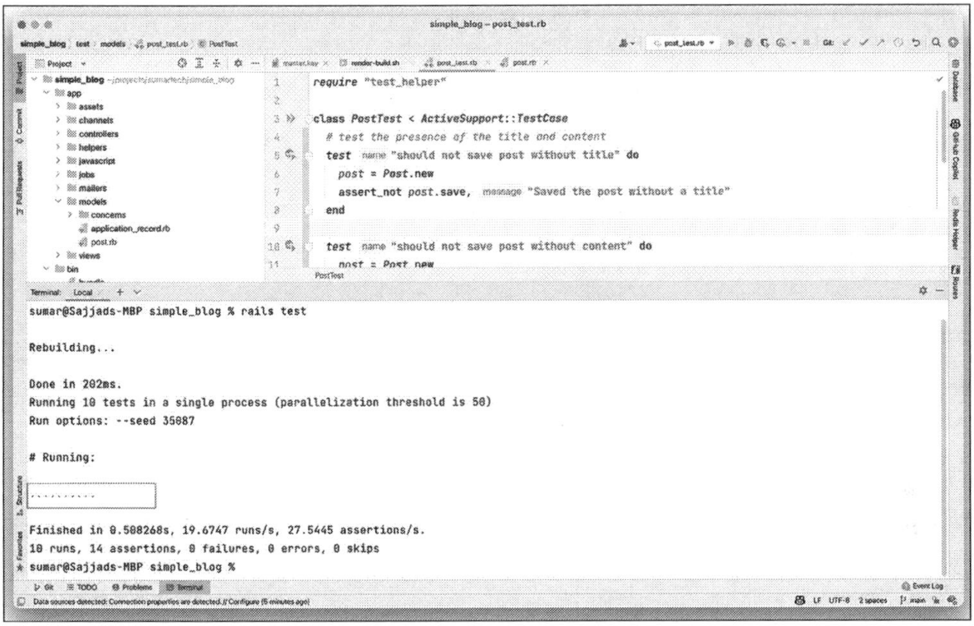

Figure 9.13: *Running tests locally*

Don't forget to push these changes to GitHub (Render will automatically trigger a deployment).

Now, open your GitHub repository in the browser, and navigate to the Actions tab as shown in *Figure* 9.14:

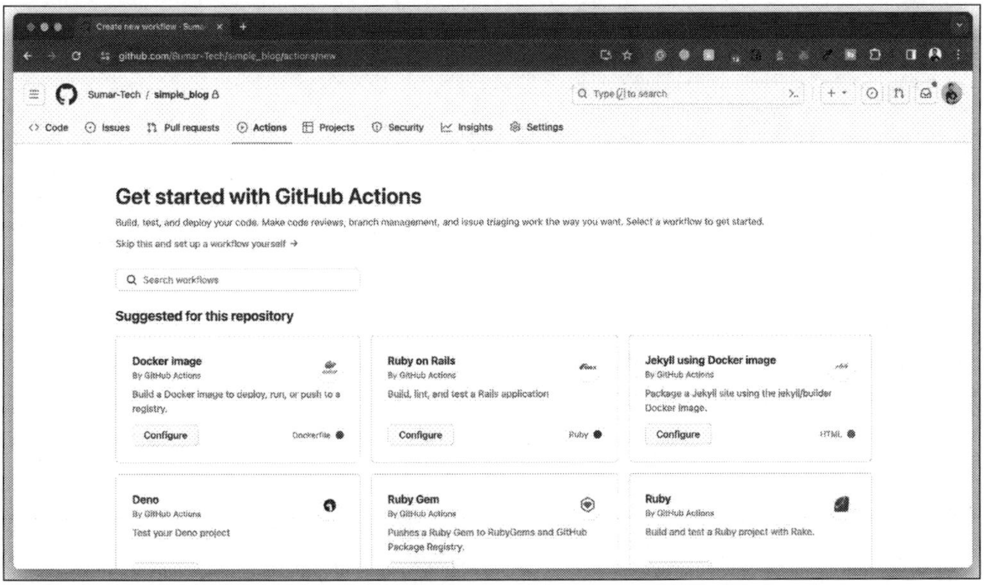

Figure 9.14: *Actions tab of our simple_blog GitHub repository*

Now search for Ruby on Rails in the search bar to find the community-provided workflow template for Ruby on Rails applications as shown in *Figure 9.15*:

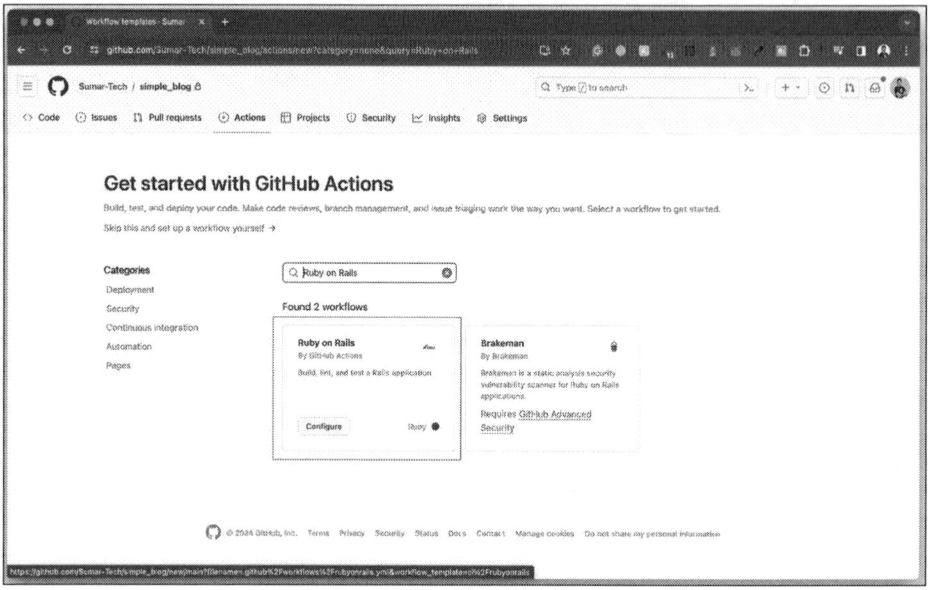

Figure 9.15: *Ruby on Rails template for GitHub Actions workflow*

Select the highlighted template and press **Configure**, which will give us a jumpstart, and we will customize this template based on our needs.

Figure 9.16 shows the default Ruby on Rails workflow.

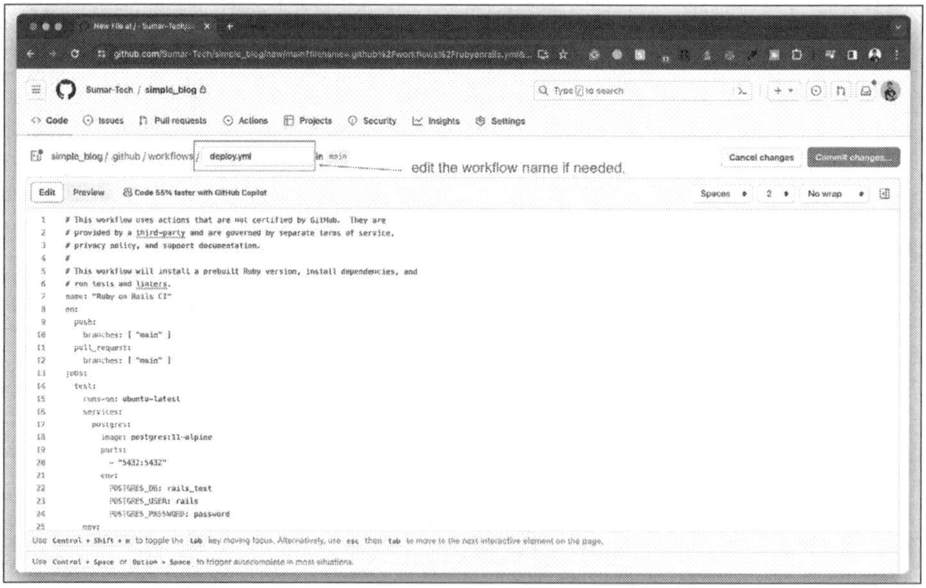

Figure 9.16: *Default community-provided workflow*

Replace the existing code with the following YML code:

```
name: "CI/CD for SimpleBlog production"
on:
  push:
    branches: [ "main" ]
  pull_request:
    branches: [ "main" ]
jobs:
  test_and_deploy:
    runs-on: ubuntu-latest
    services:
      postgres:
        image: postgres:11-alpine
        ports:
          - "5432:5432"
        env:
          POSTGRES_DB: rails_test
          POSTGRES_USER: rails
          POSTGRES_PASSWORD: password
    env:
      RAILS_ENV: test
      DATABASE_URL: "postgres://rails:password@localhost:5432/rails_
test"
    steps:
      - name: Checkout code
        uses: actions/checkout@v3
      - name: Install Ruby and gems
        uses: ruby/setup-ruby@55283cc23133118229fd3f97f9336ee23a179fcf #
v1.146.0
        with:
          ruby-version: 3.2.2
          bundler-cache: true
      - name: Set up database schema
        run: bin/rails db:schema:load
      - name: Run tests
        run: bundle exec rails test
```

```
    - name: Trigger deployment on Render
      uses: tyrrrz/action-http-request@master
      with:
        url: https://api.render.com/deploy/your-unique-hook?key=your-
unique-key
```

Let's break down what's happening step by step:

1. **Workflow Setup:**
    a. The workflow is named "**`CI/CD for SimpleBlog production`**"
    b. It is triggered on push events to the main branch and pull requests targeting the main branch
2. **Jobs:**
    a. The workflow defines a single job named "**`test_and_deploy`**"
    b. This job runs on an Ubuntu environment provided by GitHub Actions
3. **Services:**
    a. A PostgreSQL service is defined to provide a database for running tests. It uses the **`postgres:11-alpine`** Docker image
    b. The service exposes port 5432, allowing the SimpleBlog application to connect to the PostgreSQL database
    c. Environment variables are set for the PostgreSQL database name, username, and password
4. **Environment Variables:** Environment variables are set for the Rails environment (**`RAILS_ENV`**) and the database URL (**`DATABASE_URL`**). These variables are used by the SimpleBlog application during testing

Steps:

1. **Checkout code:** The workflow checks out the code of the SimpleBlog application
2. **Install Ruby and gems:** Ruby and necessary gems are installed using the **`ruby/setup-ruby`** action. The specified Ruby version is 3.2.2, and bundler caching is enabled
3. **Set up database schema:** The database schema is set up by running the **`bin/rails db:schema:load`** command. This prepares the database for testing
4. **Run tests:** Tests for the SimpleBlog application are executed using the bundle exec rails **`test`** command

5. **Trigger deployment on Render:** Finally, the workflow triggers a deployment on the Render platform using an HTTP request. This action sends a request to Render's API endpoint with deployment details, such as the service name and API key.

Figure 9.17 shows the updated workflow file:

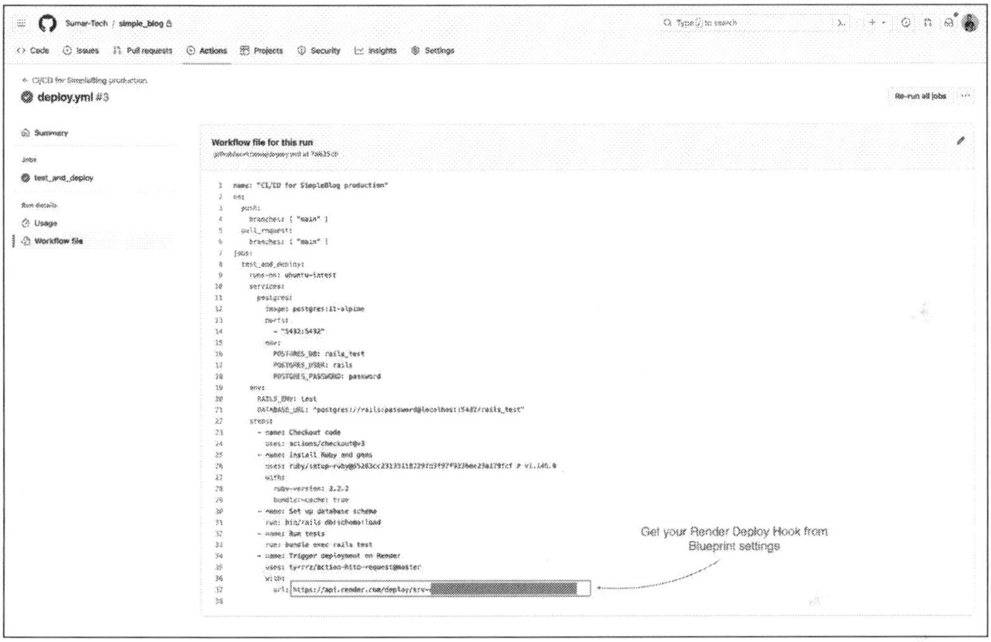

Figure 9.17: *GitHub actions workflow file*

On Render, navigate to **`simple_blog`** service settings and turn off Render Auto-Deploy. You will also find your unique **`Deploy Hook`** on that page, copy it, and add it to your GitHub Actions workflow as highlighted in *Figure* 9.17.

Figure 9.18 shows the **`Render`** settings where you can find the Auto-Deploy toggle and your unique deploy hook. Remember to keep this hook secret.

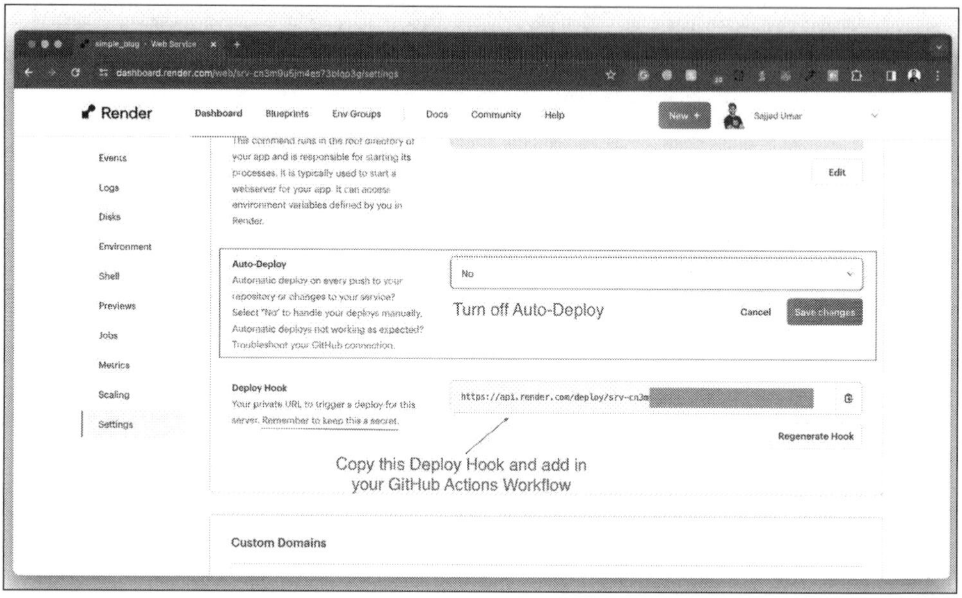

Figure 9.18: *Auto-Deploy and Deploy Hook settings*

Once you commit the workflow file, navigate to the **`Actions`** tab again. You will notice a workflow has been triggered as shown in *Figure 9.19*:

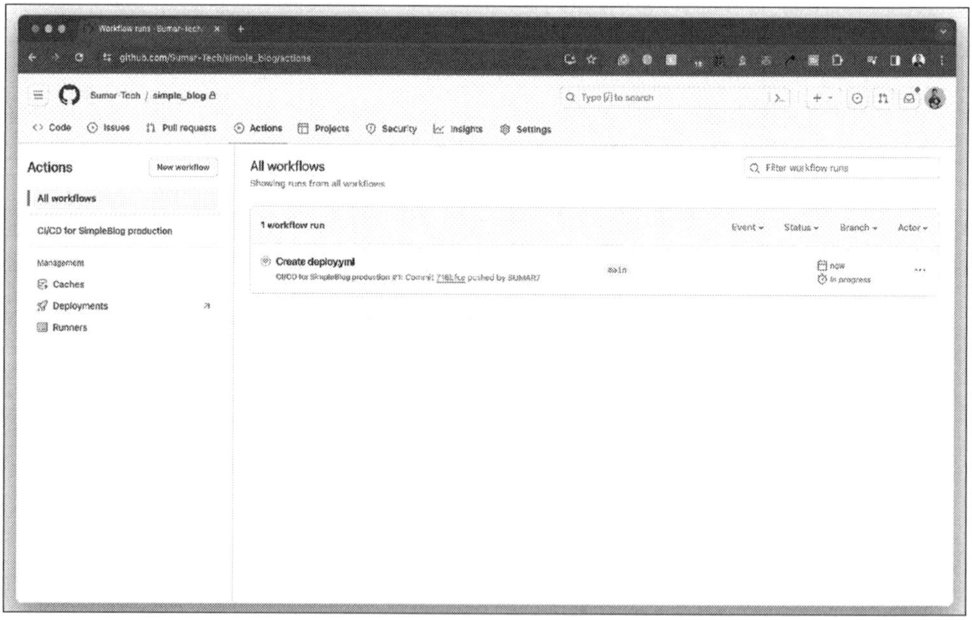

Figure 9.19: *CI/CD workflow in progress*

By clicking on the workflow, you can view all the steps being executed. Once all steps are executed, each should display a checkmark, and the entire job should exhibit a green checkmark, signifying the successful completion of both the job and all its steps, as illustrated in *Figure* 9.20:

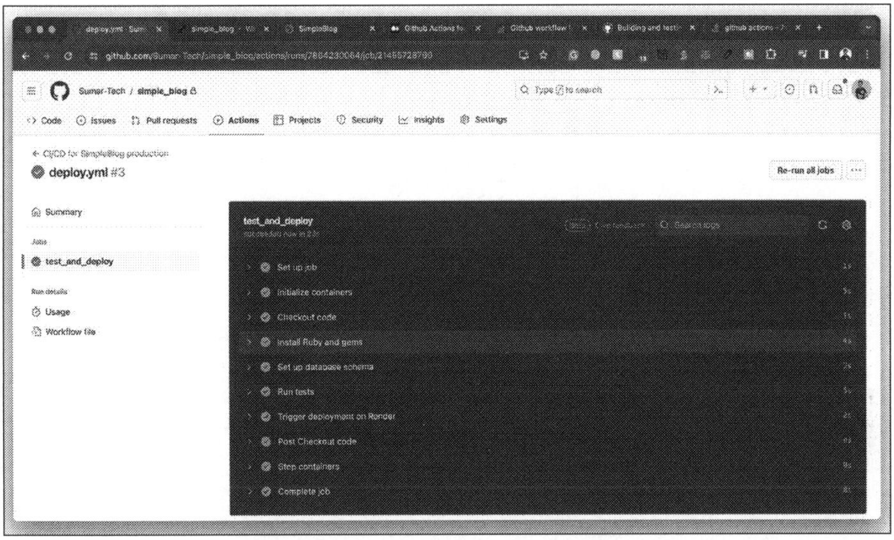

Figure 9.20: *Successful CI/CD workflow*

Once the job is complete, you can verify that a deployment has indeed started on the `Render` dashboard.

If the job fails for any reason, for example, due to failure of test cases, the job will show a red cross sign indicating that the job has failed. You will also notice that the deployment step has not been run as shown in *Figure* 9.21.

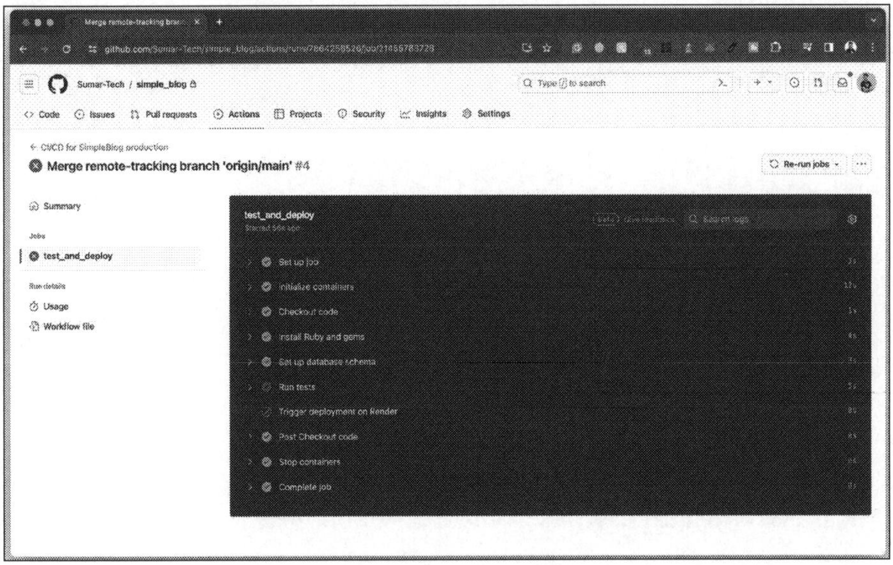

Figure 9.21: *Filed job due to failing tests*

Note: *We deliberately introduced a failing test to demonstrate the failing job in Figure 9.21. You can find the failing test code as follows:*

```
test "should not save post without title" do
  post = Post.new
  # TODO: assert should be assert_not
  assert post.save, "Saved the post without a title"
end
```

Your job will fail if you push this failing test for the `Post` model to the main branch of your GitHub repository as shown in *Figure* 9.21.

Note: *Don't forget to remove the failing test once you verify everything is working as expected.*

With this, our CI/CD workflow is complete, you can go deeper into GitHub actions and do a lot of cool stuff with it. Find the official documentation for GitHub Actions here https://docs.github.com/en/actions.

Find all the code for our "`simple_blog`" application here: https://github.com/ava-orange-education/Ruby-on-Rails-for-Agile-Web-Development/tree/main/chapter09/simple_blog.

Scaling Rails Applications

Scaling Rails applications refers to the process of adjusting the application's architecture, infrastructure, and resources to handle increased loads and accommodate growing user demands. As applications gain popularity and user bases expand, they may experience performance bottlenecks and resource constraints, necessitating scaling strategies to maintain responsiveness and reliability.

Understanding the Need for Scaling

An application may need scaling due to multiple factors such as:

- **Increased Traffic:** As an application gains popularity, it experiences higher levels of traffic, leading to increased demand on server resources such as CPU, memory, and network bandwidth.
- **Performance Degradation:** Without proper scaling measures, an application may suffer from performance degradation, resulting in slow response times, timeouts, and errors, ultimately impacting user experience and satisfaction.
- **Seasonal or Sporadic Peaks:** Some applications may experience periodic spikes in traffic due to seasonal events, marketing campaigns, or sudden bursts of

viral content. Scaling ensures the application can handle these peaks without downtime or service interruptions.

- **Business Growth:** Scaling is essential for accommodating business growth and expansion. As a company acquires more users, enters new markets, or introduces additional features, the application must be able to scale to meet the growing demands.

Tips for Effective Scaling

By adopting some of the following scaling strategies and best practices, Rails applications can effectively accommodate growing user bases, handle increased traffic loads, and maintain optimal performance and reliability over time.

- **Vertical Scaling:** Increase the capacity of individual server instances by upgrading hardware resources such as CPU, RAM, and storage. Vertical scaling is often a quick and straightforward solution but may have limitations in terms of scalability and cost-effectiveness.
- **Horizontal Scaling:** Distribute the load across multiple server instances by adding more servers or instances to the application's infrastructure. Horizontal scaling offers better scalability and fault tolerance by distributing the workload, but it may require load balancing and synchronization mechanisms.
- **Database Scaling:** Optimize database performance and scalability by employing techniques, such as sharding, replication, and caching. Sharding involves partitioning the database across multiple servers based on specific criteria, while replication replicates data across multiple database instances for redundancy and improved read performance.
- **Caching Strategies:** Implement caching mechanisms to reduce database load and improve application responsiveness. Use caching solutions like Memcached or Redis to store frequently accessed data in memory, reducing the need for repeated database queries.
- **Content Delivery Networks (CDNs):** Offload static assets and content to CDN providers to improve delivery speed and reduce server load. CDNs cache content on edge servers located closer to the user, resulting in faster loading times and reduced latency.
- **Monitoring and Optimization:** Continuously monitor application performance metrics, server health, and user behavior to identify bottlenecks and areas for optimization. Utilize tools like New Relic, Datadog, or Prometheus for comprehensive monitoring and performance analysis.
- **Auto-Scaling:** Implement auto-scaling policies that automatically adjust the number of server instances based on predefined criteria such as CPU utilization, network traffic, or request latency. Auto-scaling ensures that

the application can dynamically respond to fluctuations in demand without manual intervention.

Here are some of the scaling options provided by Render.

- **Vertical Scaling**

  Upgrade the performance tier of your Render service to increase the capacity of individual server instances. You can easily adjust the CPU, memory, and disk resources from the Render dashboard.

  Navigate to the "`Resources`" tab of your Render service and choose a higher plan with more resources to scale vertically.

- **Horizontal Scaling**

  Add more instances to your Render service to distribute the load across multiple server instances. Horizontal scaling improves scalability and fault tolerance by spreading the workload.

  Navigate to the "`Settings`" tab of your Render service and adjust the "`Instance Count`" to add more instances. Render automatically load balances traffic across all instances.

- **Database Scaling**

  Optimize your database performance and scalability by using managed database solutions offered by Render, such as Render PostgreSQL or Render MySQL.

  Upgrade the database instance size or enable auto-scaling to automatically adjust the database resources based on demand.

- **Caching Strategies**

  Implement caching mechanisms to reduce database load and improve application responsiveness. Use in-memory caching solutions like Redis or Memcached, supported by Render.

  Configure caching layers within your application code or use managed caching services available on Render.

- **Content Delivery Networks (CDNs)**

  Offload static assets and content to a CDN provider to improve delivery speed and reduce server load. Render integrates seamlessly with CDN providers like Cloudflare.

  Configure CDN settings through the Render dashboard or CDN-specific configurations in your application code.

- **Auto-Scaling**

  Enable auto-scaling for your Render service to automatically adjust the number of server instances based on predefined criteria such as CPU utilization or request throughput.

  Navigate to the "`Settings`" tab of your Render service and enable "`Autoscaling`" to activate auto-scaling capabilities.

Monitoring and Performance Optimization

Monitoring and performance optimization are crucial aspects of maintaining health, reliability, and efficiency of a Rails application. By monitoring application metrics closely and continuously optimizing performance, developers can identify bottlenecks, improve responsiveness, and enhance user experience.

The Importance of Monitoring

Here are some importance of monitoring optimization:

- **Early Detection of Issues:** Monitoring allows developers to detect and identify performance issues, errors, and anomalies in real-time. Early detection enables prompt investigation and mitigation, minimizing the impact on users and preventing potential downtime.
- **Proactive Problem Resolution:** Monitoring provides insights into application health, resource utilization, and user interactions, enabling proactive problem resolution before issues escalate. By addressing issues proactively, developers can maintain optimal application performance and reliability.
- **Optimization Opportunities:** Monitoring helps identify areas for performance optimization by tracking key metrics such as response times, throughput, and resource utilization. Insights from monitoring tools guide optimization efforts, allowing developers to streamline code, improve database queries, and enhance overall application performance.

Strategies for Performance Optimization

Here are the strategies listed for performance optimization:

- **Code Optimization Techniques:**

  Identify and eliminate performance bottlenecks in application code by profiling and analyzing code execution. Use profiling tools like Ruby Prof or

StackProf to identify slow-running code segments and optimize them for better performance.

Implement caching mechanisms to reduce database queries, network requests, and computation overhead. Utilize fragment caching, page caching, or action caching to cache frequently accessed data and improve response times.

- **Database Optimization Tips:**

  Optimize database queries by indexing frequently accessed columns, avoiding N+1 queries, and minimizing unnecessary database operations. Use database query analyzers like `EXPLAIN` to analyze query execution plans and identify optimization opportunities.

  Consider database scaling options, such as sharding, replication, or using managed database services to improve database performance and scalability.

- **Infrastructure Optimization:**

  Optimize server configurations, including CPU, memory, and disk settings, to ensure efficient resource utilization and maximum performance. Use server monitoring tools to track resource usage and adjust configurations as needed.

  Implement load balancing and auto-scaling mechanisms to distribute traffic evenly across server instances and dynamically adjust resources based on demand.

- **Application Profiling and Monitoring:**

  Monitor application metrics, such as response times, error rates, and throughput using monitoring tools, such as New Relic, Datadog, or Prometheus. Set up alerts to notify stakeholders of performance issues or anomalies in real-time.

  Conduct regular performance audits and reviews to identify areas for optimization and track improvements over time. Continuously monitor and optimize performance to ensure optimal application health and user experience.

By implementing these strategies for monitoring and performance optimization, developers can ensure that their Rails applications deliver optimal performance, scalability, and reliability, meeting the demands of users and business requirements effectively.

In *Chapter* 11, titled "*Advanced Topics in Ruby on Rails*," we will delve further into some of these concepts.

The GitHub link given here contains all the code demonstrated in this chapter: https://github.com/ava-orange-education/Ruby-on-Rails-for-Agile-Web-Development/tree/main/chapter09/simple_blog.

You can access everything covered in the book on this GitHub repo: https://github.com/ava-orange-education/Ruby-on-Rails-for-Agile-Web-Development.

Conclusion

In this chapter, we have discussed essential aspects of deploying, scaling, and optimizing Ruby on Rails applications to ensure their reliability, performance, and scalability. We began by understanding the basics of deployment, covering the essential preparations needed before deploying a Rails application. We then explored the deployment process, leveraging platforms like Render and utilizing Continuous Integration and Deployment (CI/CD) workflows with GitHub Actions to automate the deployment process efficiently.

Scaling Rails applications became our next focus, where we discussed the importance of scaling to accommodate increased traffic and user demands. We outlined effective scaling strategies and shared tips for optimizing application performance.

As we conclude this chapter, we have equipped ourselves with valuable insights and strategies for deploying, scaling, and optimizing Ruby on Rails applications. In the next chapter, titled "*Building a Real-World Ruby on Rails Application*," we will embark on a journey to develop a real-world Ruby on Rails application, exploring various features, functionalities, and development methodologies to create a robust and functional application from start to finish. Join us as we dive into the exciting world of building Ruby on Rails applications that make a real impact.

Short Quiz

1. **Which deployment strategy involves running two identical production environments simultaneously?**

    a. Continuous Deployment

    b. Blue-Green Deployment

    c. Canary Releases

    d. Vertical Scaling

2. **Which database optimization technique involves partitioning the database across multiple servers?**

    a. Indexing

    b. Sharding

    c. Replication

    d. Fragmentation

3. **What is the primary advantage of using a Content Delivery Network (CDN) for Rails applications?**
    a. Reducing server costs
    b. Improving database performance
    c. Offloading static assets for faster delivery
    d. Scaling server instances dynamically
4. **What is the primary purpose of auto-scaling mechanisms in Rails applications?**
    a. Reducing deployment time
    b. Dynamically adjusting server resources based on demand
    c. Optimizing database queries
    d. Minimizing downtime during updates
5. **What is the main goal of Continuous Integration (CI) in Rails application development?**
    a. Automating the deployment process
    b. Identifying and resolving performance issues
    c. Ensuring that changes integrate smoothly with the main codebase
    d. Scaling server instances dynamically
6. **What is one way to optimize database performance in Rails applications?**
    a. Running N+1 queries
    b. Avoiding indexing
    c. Using database scaling options like sharding
    d. Disabling caching mechanisms
7. **Which technique involves analyzing code execution to identify slow-running segments?**
    a. Caching
    b. Code Optimization
    c. Database Sharding
    d. Continuous Integration

8. **What is one of the key reasons for scaling Rails applications?**
   a. Ensuring backward compatibility
   b. Handling increased traffic and user demands
   c. Reducing server costs
   d. Limiting feature updates
9. **Which cloud service provides users with virtualized computing resources, allowing them to control and manage the underlying infrastructure?**
   a. Platform as a Service (PaaS)
   b. Infrastructure as a Service (IaaS)
   c. Software as a Service (SaaS)
   d. Function as a Service (FaaS)
10. **What is the primary advantage of using a Platform as a Service (PaaS) solution for deploying a Rails application?**
   a. Complete control over the underlying infrastructure
   b. Simplified deployment process and management of application resources
   c. Low-level access to hardware resources for performance optimization
   d. Ability to customize and configure server environments according to specific requirements

Further Reading

- Sajjad Umar, presented a keynote session, titled "*Creating 10X Faster Ruby on Rails Applications*" at the Ruby on Rails Global Summit 2023 by Geekle.us. The written version of that talk is available for more insights into some of these advanced topics.

  https://medium.com/@sajjadumar/creating-10x-faster-ruby-on-rails-applications-my-talk-at-global-ruby-on-rails-summit-2023-by-bca96906f42d.

CHAPTER 10
Building A Real-World Rails Application

Introduction

In the preceding chapters, we have established the groundwork for the WagePro application. Now, we are embarking on a more dynamic journey, transforming WagePro into a full-fledged Rails application, embodying the essence of a Minimum Viable Product (MVP).

This chapter moves swiftly, focusing on essential modules while omitting redundant details. Though more technical in nature, comprehensive code samples will be provided for deeper understanding and reference.

So far, the schema of our WagePro application looks as shown in *Figure 10.1*:

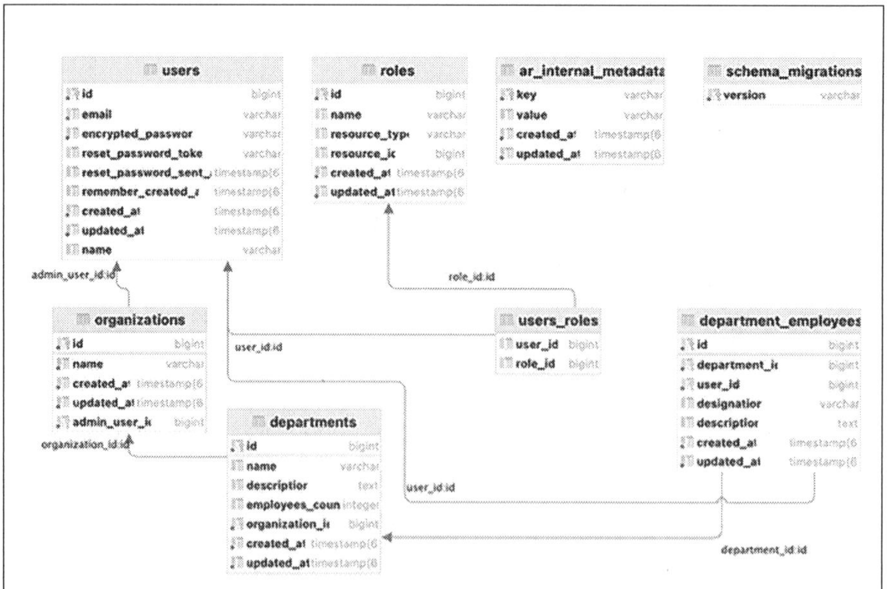

Figure 10.1: *Schema diagram of WagePro application*

We will expand this database to add more tables so that we can build all the features included in MVP.

Structure

In this chapter, we will cover the following topics:

- Establishing MVP Requirements
- Database Expansion to Meet MVP Requirements
- Roles Management and Authorization
    - Development of a Simple yet Functional User Interface
- Implementation of Access Management for Users
- Integration of Core Features Essential to MVP

Establishing MVP Requirements

We aim to enhance the WagePro application, evolving it into a Minimum Viable Product (MVP) that we can launch and refine further in response to user feedback. Our MVP will have the following features:

- **Simple UI:** A simple but functional User Interface
- **Organizations Management:** Manages multiple organizations
- **Department Management**: Manages departments for each organization
- **Employee Management:** Manages employees and their employment profile
- **Access Management:** Manage access roles for employees
- **Salary Slip Management:** Generates and distributes salary slips monthly.

Without any further ado, let's add a few more tables to our database.

Database Expansion

We need to arrange our database based on *Figure* 10.2.

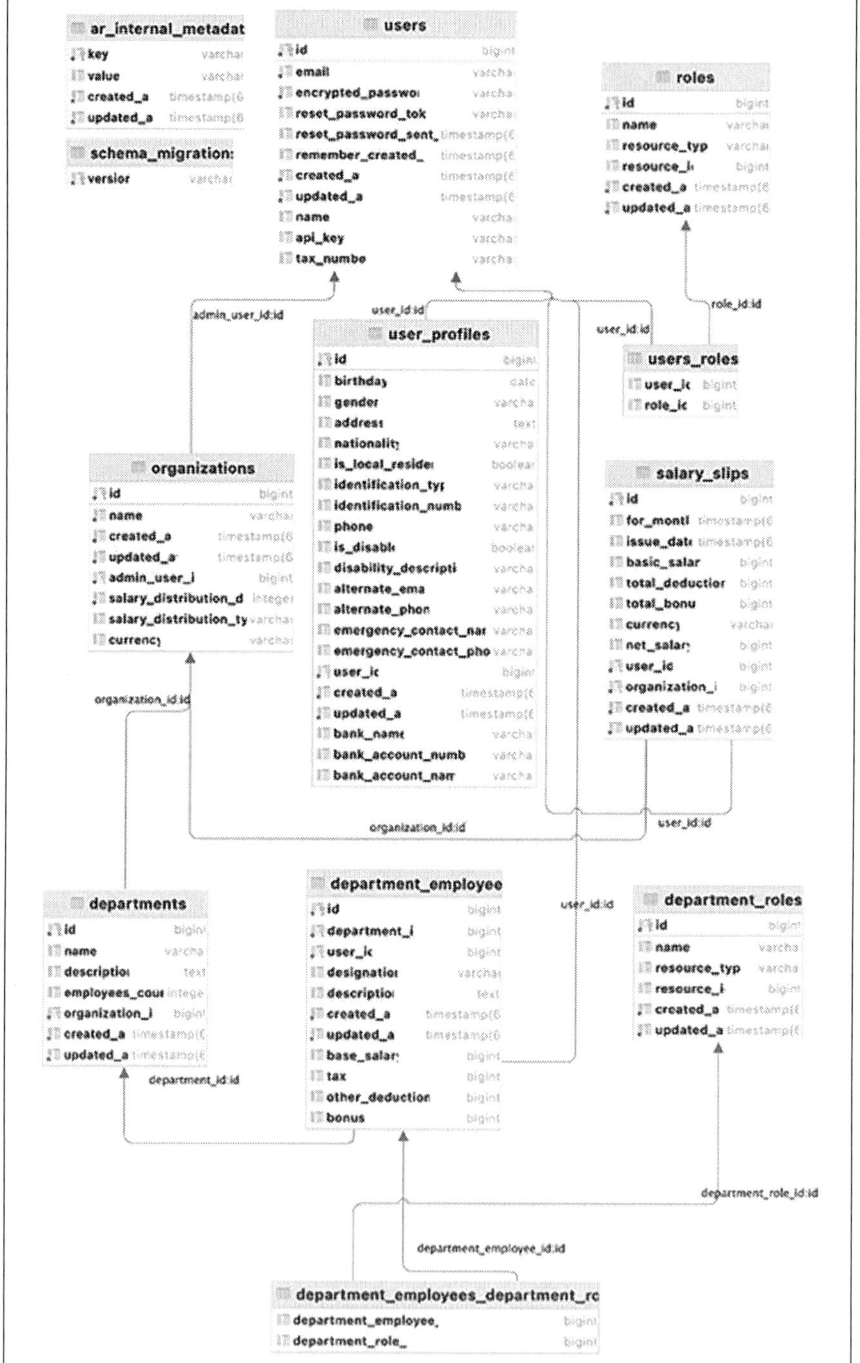

Figure 10.2: *New Schema diagram of WagePro application*

Look closely at *Figure* 10.2 and you will notice that we have made the following rearrangements to the database:

- **User Profile**: Added to save profile information for each user
- **User**: Added tax number attribute to the Users table
- **Organization**: Added more attributes to save salary distribution information
- **Salary Slips:** Added to store salary slip information of employees
- **Department Roles**: Added to support department-specific roles for each user using Rolify Gem

You can find all the migrations for the above changes under the **`db/migrate`** folder in the WagePro GitHub repository mentioned at the start of this chapter.

Now it is time to define relations between our models, and here is what we need to add to our models.

User:

```
has_one :user_profile, dependent: :destroy
```

UserProfile:

```
belongs_to :user
```

Organization:

```
has_many :department_employees, through: :departments

has_many :employees, through: :department_employees, source: :user
```

You can find all the associations under the app/model folder in the WagePro GitHub repository provided at the start of this chapter.

That is all for now, we will keep updating our models as we progress.

Pagination

Pagination in web development refers to dividing a large set of data into smaller, manageable chunks or pages. This allows users to navigate the data more efficiently, as they can view one page of results at a time rather than being overwhelmed by a single large dataset. Pagination is commonly used in applications that display lists of items, such as search results, product listings, or social media feeds. It enhances user experience by improving loading times, reducing clutter, and making it easier for users to find the information needed.

We are going to utilize "**`pagy`**" gem to paginate our listings. Let's quickly add it to our **`Gemfile`**:

```
# for pagination functionality

gem 'pagy', '~> 7.0'
```

Read more about pagy Gem at https://rubygems.org/gems/pagy.

Employee Search

We are also going to build a search functionality to effortlessly search employees by name or email address, for that we are going to utilize the "**pg_search**" gem. Let's quickly add it to the **Gemfile** as well.

```
# for search functionality

gem 'pg_search', '~> 2.3', '>= 2.3.6'
```

Read more about **pg_search** Gem at https://rubygems.org/gems/pg_search.

Once these gems are added, run the "**bundle install**" command to install them.

Roles Management and Authorization

To manage roles, we use Rolify and for authorization, Pundit Gem, and using these gems we have added policies under the policies folder, as shown in *Figure* 10.3. Get the code for these policies from the GitHub link in the end of this chapter and add it to your code.

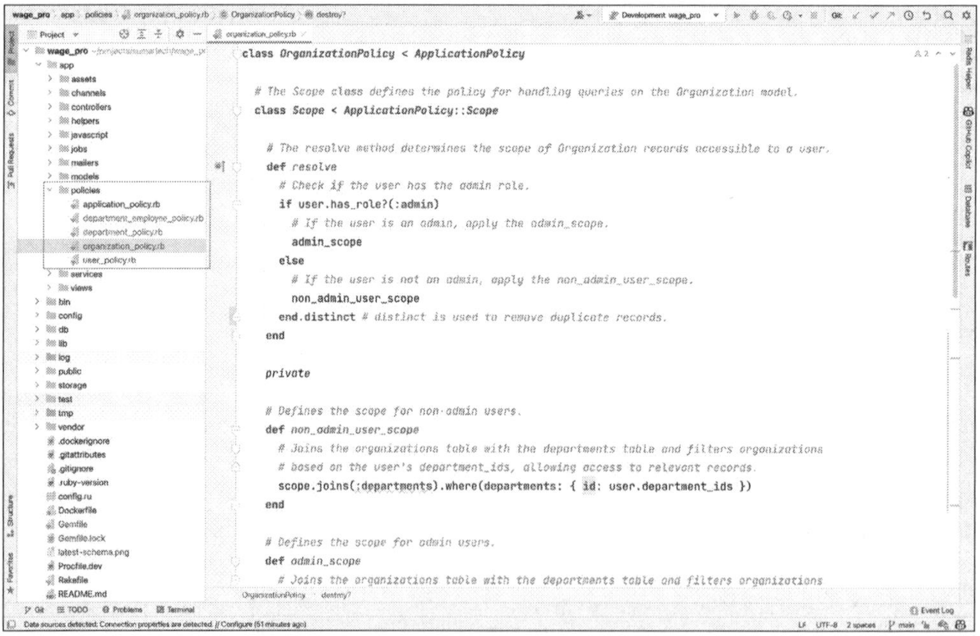

Figure 10.3: *Organization policy (policies)*

Take some time to read through all the comments added in these files to understand these policies well.

Now let's start adding some UI to our application.

Organization Management

In this section, we will build a *simple yet functional user interface* where an admin user can manage multiple organizations.

Functionality includes:

- A global layout with side navigation
- Ability to create Organizations
- Ability to view single or all organizations
- Ability to update or delete organizations

Let's first create a new layout file with side navigation to do that, create a new file at `` `app/views/layouts/dashboard.html.erb` `` and add the code provided at the following GitHub link: https://github.com/ava-orange-education/Ruby-on-Rails-for-Agile-Web-Development/tree/main/chapter10/wage_pro.

Next, we will add our **`OrganizationController`** with the following code:

```
class OrganizationsController < ApplicationController
  layout 'dashboard'


  def index
    @pagy, @organizations = pagy(policy_scope(Organization))
  end


  def show
    @organization = policy_scope(Organization).includes(:departments).
find(params[:id])
  end


  def new
    @organization = Organization.new
    authorize @organization
  end


  def edit
```

```
    @organization = policy_scope(Organization).find(params[:id])
    authorize @organization
  end

  def create
    @organization = current_user.organizations.new(organization_params)
    authorize @organization

    if @organization.save
      redirect_to organizations_path, notice: 'Organization was
successfully created.'
    else
      flash[:alert] = @organization.errors.full_messages.join(', ')
      render :new
    end
  end

  def update
    @organization = policy_scope(Organization).find(params[:id])
    authorize @organization

    if @organization.update(organization_params)
      redirect_to organization_path(@organization), notice:
'Organization was successfully updated.'
    else
      flash[:alert] = @organization.errors.full_messages.join(', ')
      render :edit
    end
  end

  def destroy
    @organization = policy_scope(Organization).find(params[:id])
    @organization.destroy
```

```
    redirect_to organizations_path, notice: 'Organization was
successfully deleted.'
  end


  private


  def organization_params
    params.require(:organization).permit(:name, :salary_distribution_
day)
  end
end
```

You can locate all the codes on the GitHub URL referenced at the end of this chapter.

`layout 'dashboard'` line in our code will ensure that the newly created layout file is used for our controller.

Next, *Figure 10.4* illustrates the complete set of views required for managing all CRUD operations associated with organizations.

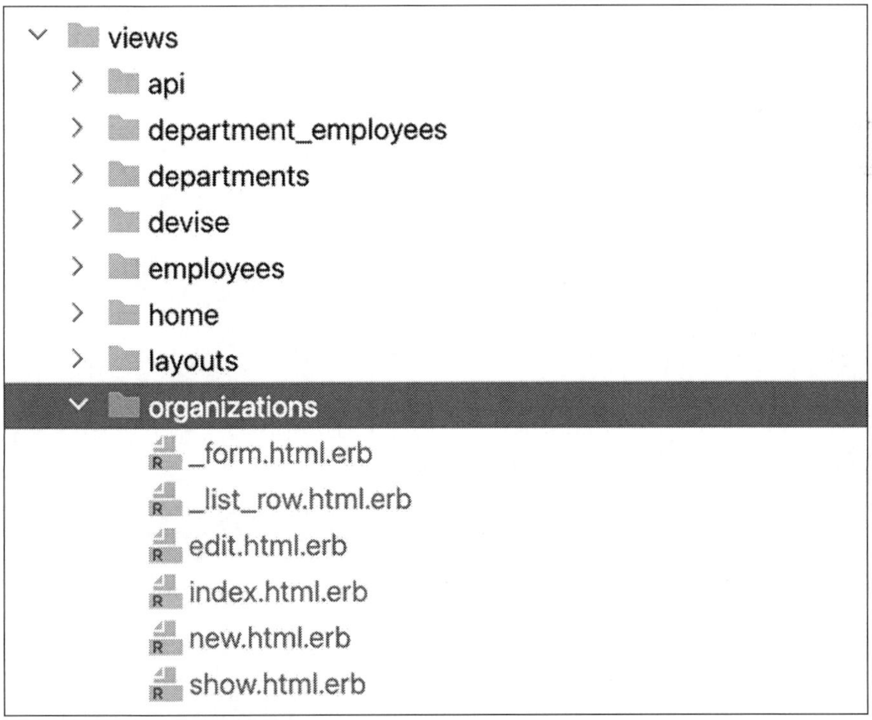

Figure 10.4*: Views for OrganizationController*

Let's delve into the code within these views independently. You'll notice that the **_list_row.html.erb** and **_form.html.erb** partials are utilized across multiple views, aiming to minimize repetition and adhere to the DRY (Don't Repeat Yourself) principle.

You will also find the usage of pagination in the "**index.html.erb**" file, *Figure* 10.5 highlights all the pagination-specific changes we need to make the pagination work (except the use of pagy in **organizations_controller**).

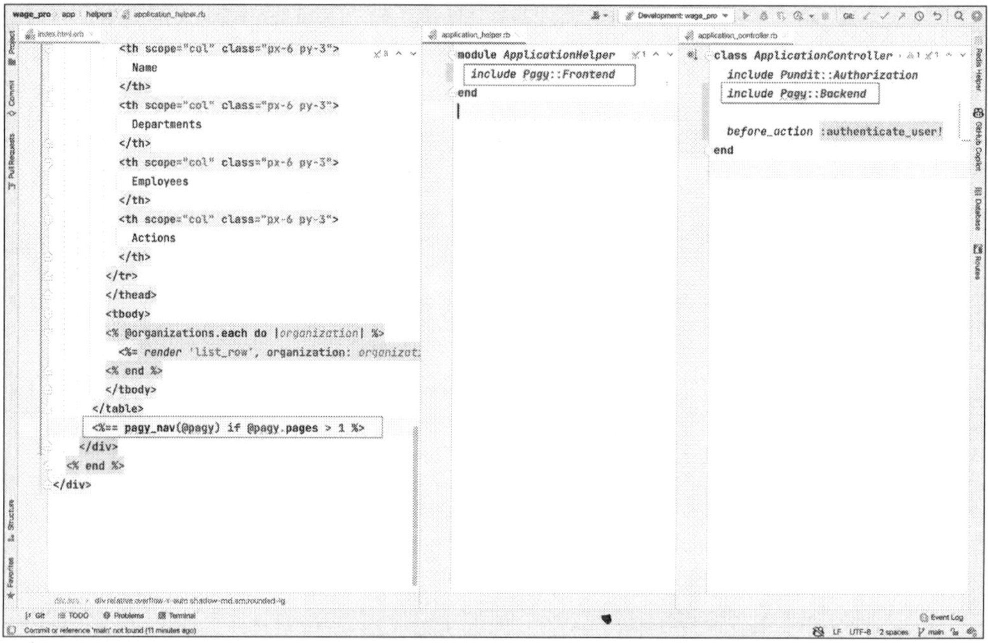

***Figure 10.5**: Using pagy Gem for pagination*

Once we have everything set up, the pagination links should automatically appear once the list items on the page exceed the default 20 items per page.

The "**pagy**" docs in the preceding *Figure* 10.5 have all the information on how you can adjust the defaults based on your needs.

Adding Required Routes

Now replace your **routes.rb** file with the following code so that you have everything needed to build all the pages.

```
Rails.application.routes.draw do
  get 'home/index'
  devise_for :users
  # Define your application routes per the DSL in https://guides.
rubyonrails.org/routing.html
```

```
  # Reveal health status on /up that returns 200 if the app boots with
no exceptions, otherwise 500.
  # Can be used by load balancers and uptime monitors to verify that
the app is live.
  get "up" => "rails/health#show", as: :rails_health_check

  resources :profile, only: [:show] do
    member do
      get :new_profile
      post :create_new_profile
      put :update_profile
      patch :update_profile
      get :edit_profile
    end
  end

  resources :organizations do
    resources :departments do
      resources :department_employees
    end
  end
  resources :employees

  # namespace is used to group api controllers
  namespace :api, defaults: {format: :json} do
    namespace :v1 do
      resources :organizations, only: [:index]
    end
  end

  # Defines the root path route ("/")
  root "home#index"
end
```

As our root path is the **home#index**, let's quickly make **HomeConroller** use the dashboard layout as follows:

```
class HomeController < ApplicationController
  layout 'dashboard'


  def index
  end
end
```

The last thing before we run our app is to add a shared partial we are using in some of our views to show a click-to-action (CTA) button when there is no record in the database. *Figure* 10.6 shows where to place this file in the code.

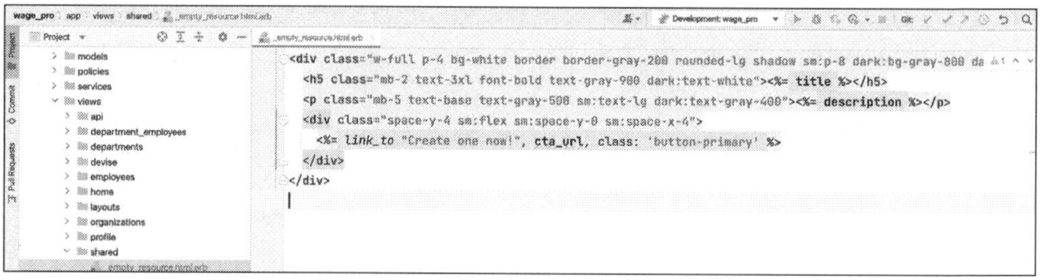

Figure 10.6: *shared/_empty_resource.html.erb*

Now if you run the app with the following command, you will be able to sign in and land on the home page, as shown in *Figure* 10.7.

```
./bin/dev
```

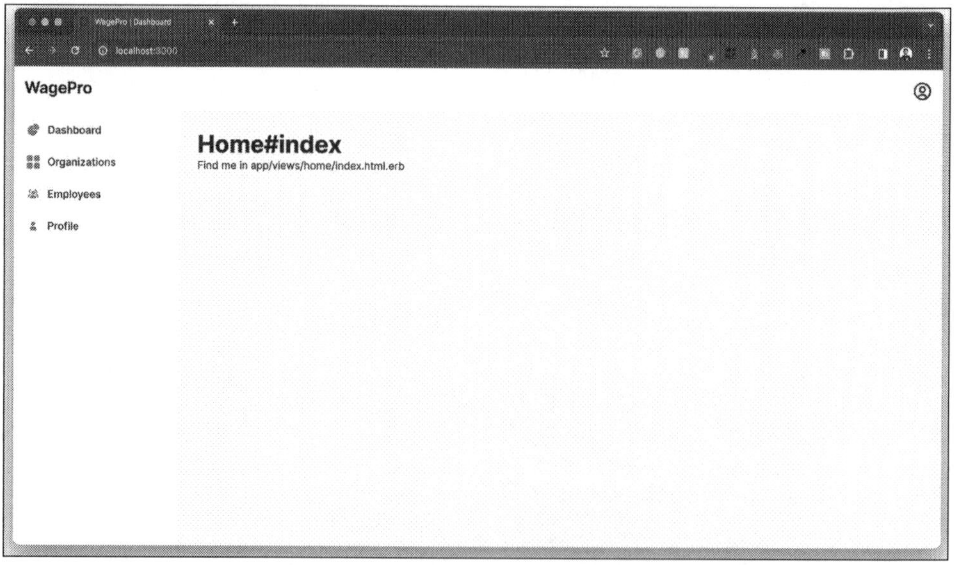

Figure 10.7: *Index page of HomeController (dashboard page)*

Now navigate to the Organizations page from side navigation, you will see the index page of **`OrganizationsController`** as shown in *Figure* 10.8.

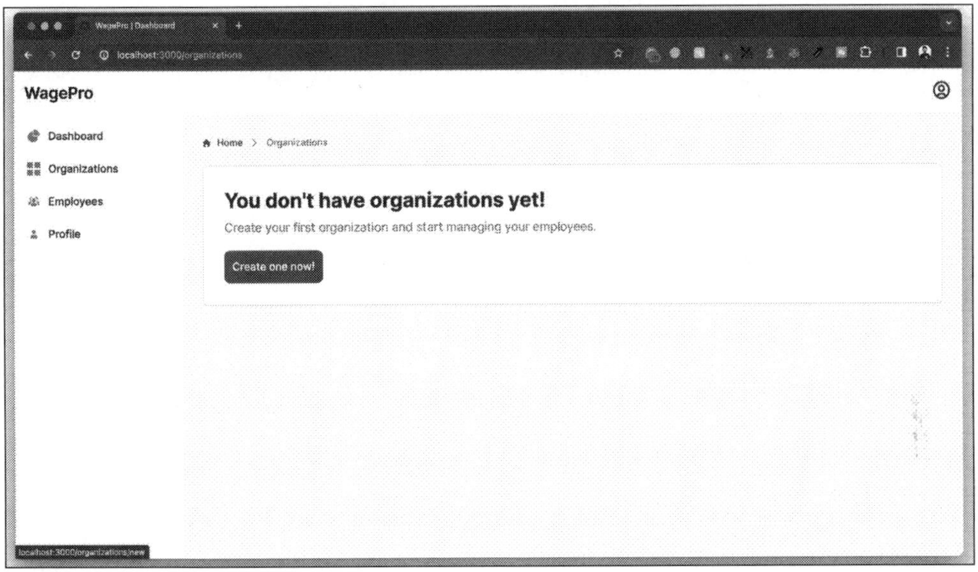

Figure* 10.8**: *Organizations page with* ***`_empty_resource.html.erb` *visible on the screen*

Click on the blue button "**`Create one now!`**" CTA to create a new organization; clicking moves you to the **`OrganizationsController#new`** action. *Figure* 10.9 shows a form to create a new organization.

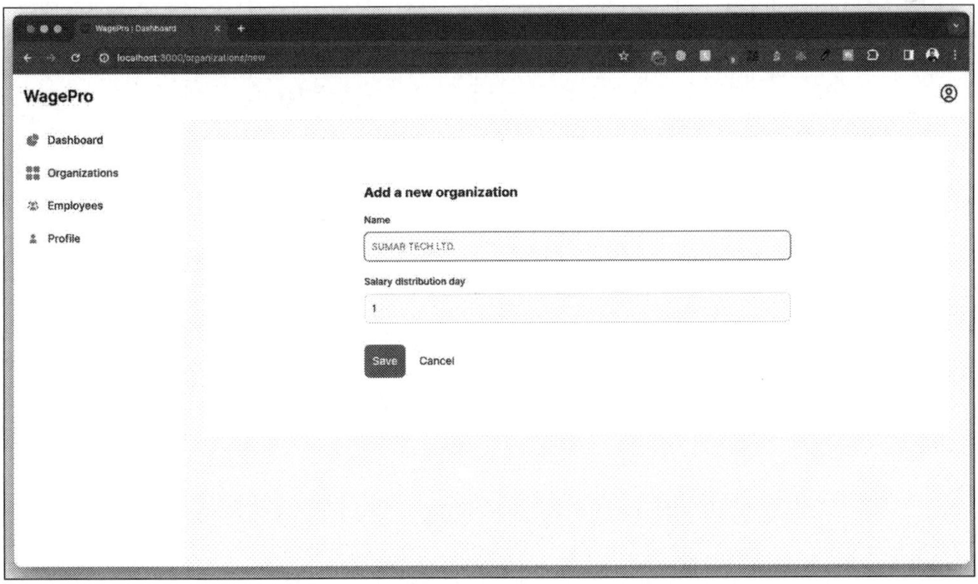

***Figure* 10.9**: *Form to create an organization*

Before you fill in the information and hit save, let's ensure your organization model is ready to do the needful as shown in *Figure 10.10*.

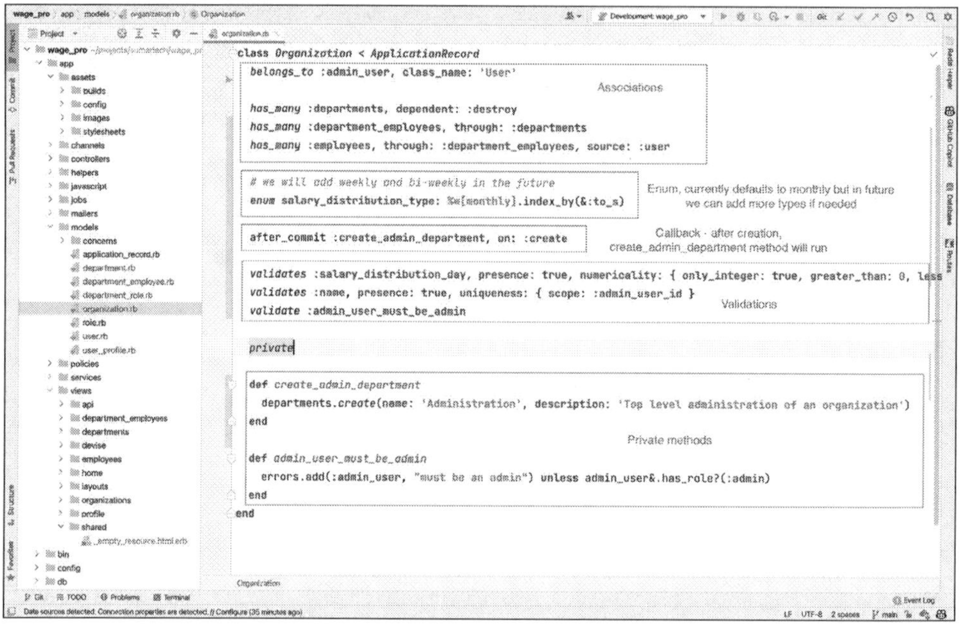

Figure 10.10: *Organization model*

Please find all the codes in the GitHub URL mentioned at the end of this chapter.

Now, if you fill in the form shown in *Figure 10.9* and hit save, your very first organization will be created as shown in *Figure 10.11*:

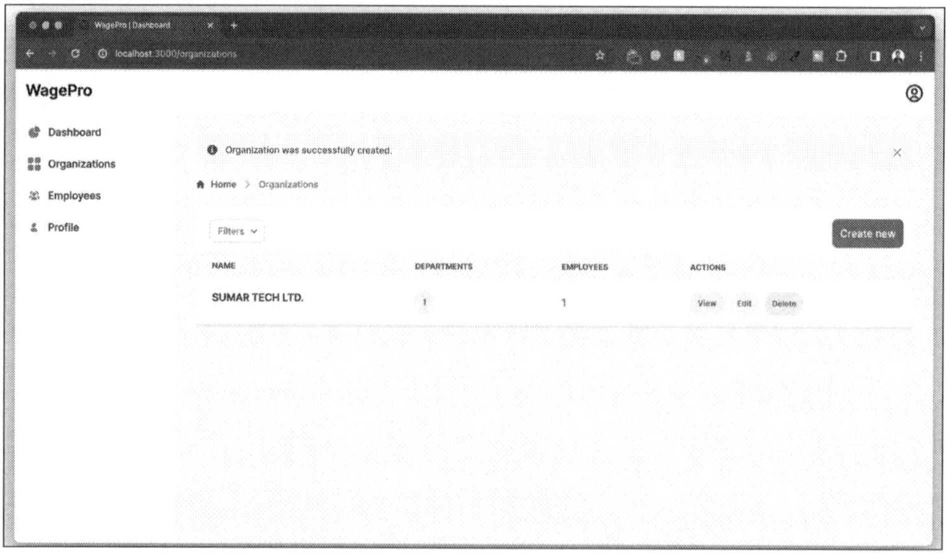

Figure 10.11: *Organizations listing (index) page*

At this point the **Edit** and **Delete** buttons for the organization are working. Try these on your own to understand the flow.

Before you can click "**view**" and see details for your organization, repeat all the steps starting after *Figure* 10.3 for the following controllers:

- `DepartmentsController`
- `DepartmentEmployeesController`
- `EmployeesController`
- `ProfileController`

Also, look at the rest of the controllers shown in *Figure* 10.12 and update your code accordingly.

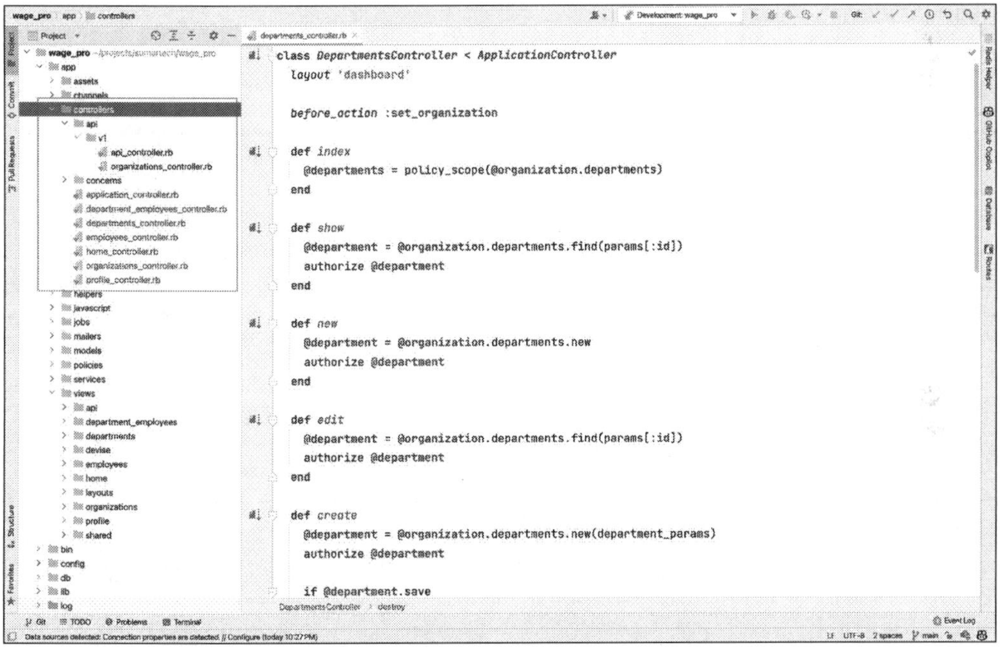

Figure 10.12: *Adding all controllers to the codebase*

Please find all the code in the GitHub URL mentioned at the end of this chapter.

Once you have everything, you can now click "**View**" in the organization listing shown in *Figure* 10.11 to visit the details page shown in *Figure* 10.13.

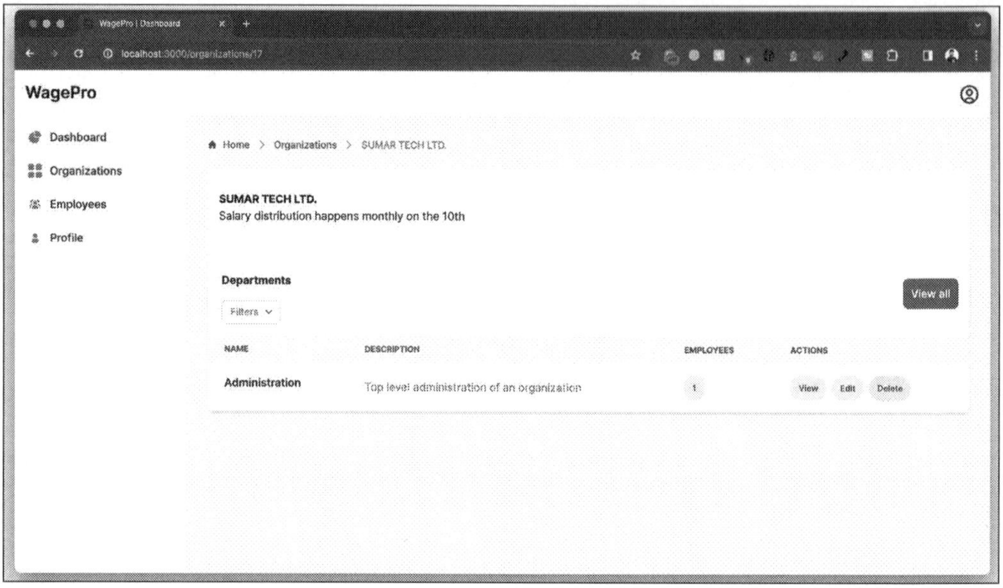

Figure 10.13: *Organization detail page (show action)*

You will notice the "**`Administration`**" department is automatically created by the callbacks highlighted in *Figure* 10.10, and the currently logged-in user has been added to this department with the help of another callback in the department model.

```
after_commit :add_admin_to_department, if: -> { name ==
'Administration' }, on: :create
```

Now that you have everything in place, you can do the following:

1. Manage departments within an organization (*Figure* 10.14)
2. Add employees to departments (*Figure* 10.15)
3. Assign roles to employees for different access levels (*Figure* 10.16)
4. View and Search employees across all organizations (*Figure* 10.17)
5. Manage your employment profile (*Figure* 10.18)

Figure 10.14 shows a screen where you can manage departments within an organization.

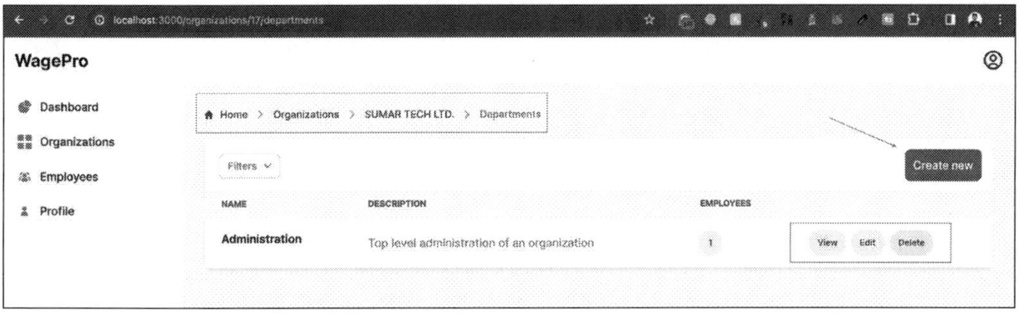

Figure 10.14: *Manage Departments*

Figure 10.15 shows a screen where you can manage employees within a department.

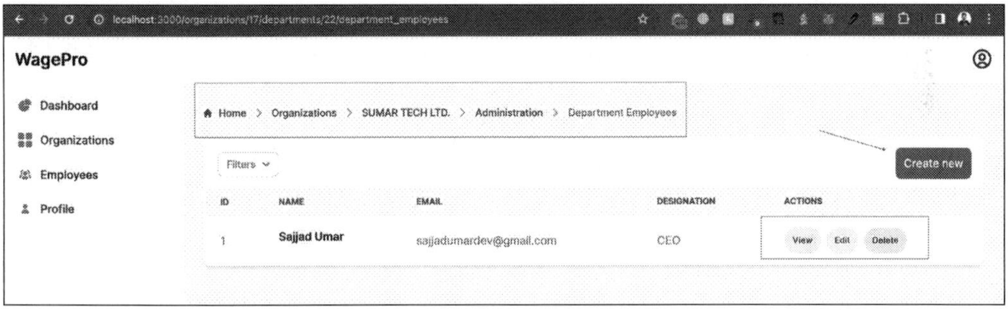

Figure 10.15: *Manage Employees within a department*

Figure 10.16 shows a section of a form where you can create employees within a department and assign roles.

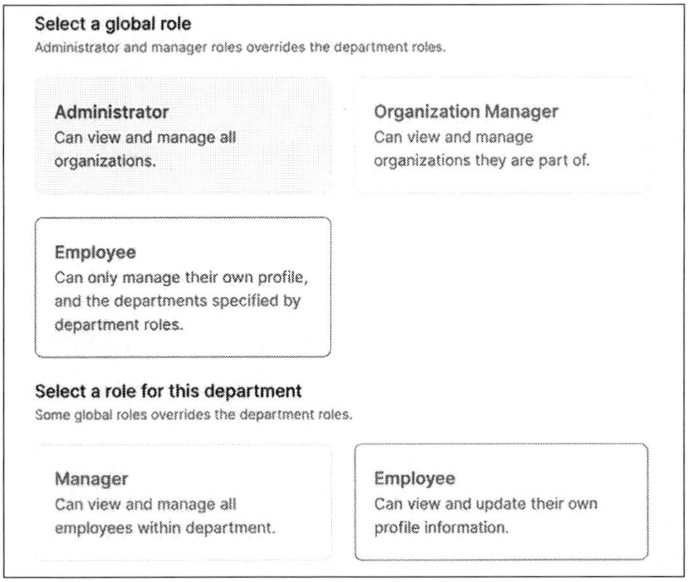

Figure 10.16: *Assign Roles*

Figure 10.17 shows a screen where you can view and manage employees across all organizations. You can view them, edit them, and if you have access, you can delete them and view their personal and employment profile.

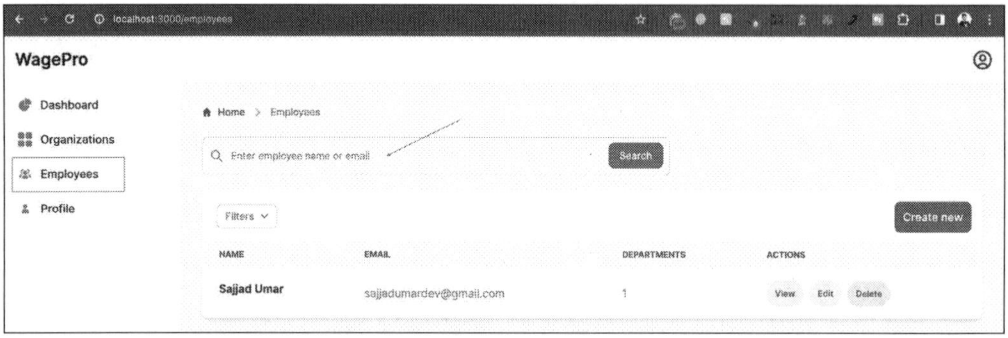

Figure 10.17: *Search employees across all your organizations*

Figure 10.18 shows a screen where users can view their profile which contains all the details about the employee.

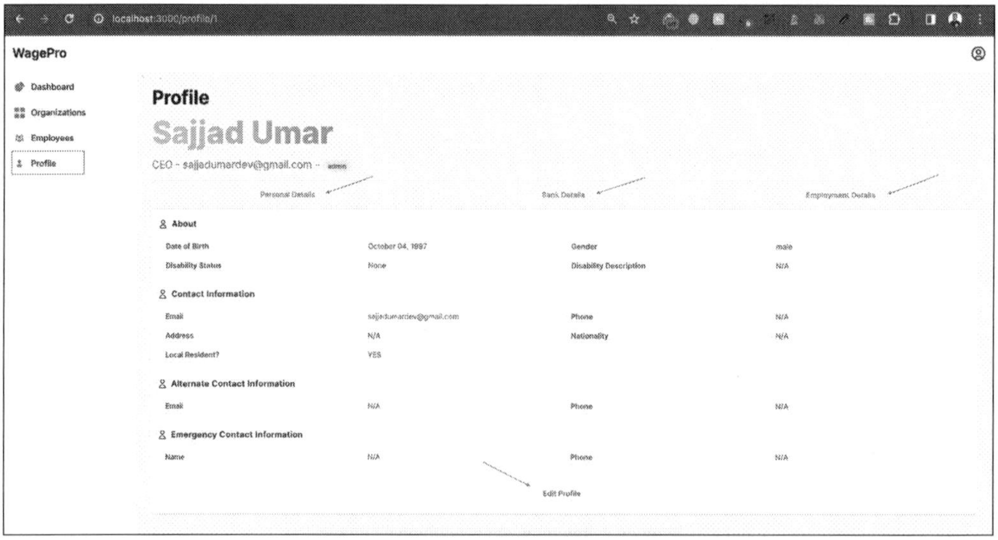

Figure 10.18: *Employment Profile*

Pro Tip: *Try logging in from different roles to see how different users have different access levels, and based on their access they can only do certain actions within the application.*

Salary Slip Management

WagePro will automatically create salary slips for each employee within an organization on the salary distribution day, and employees can view their salary slips and download them as a PDF.

Associations

We have defined the following relations between SalarySlip, Organization, and User model.

- An employee (user) has many salary slips
- An organization has many salary slips
- SalarySlip belongs to a user and an organization

The user model has the following line of code:

```
has_many :salary_slips, dependent: :destroy
```

The organization model has the following line of code:

```
has_many :salary_slips, dependent: :destroy
```

The SalarySlip model has the following lines of code:

```
belongs_to :user

belongs_to :organization
```

PDF Creation

To create a SalarySlip PDF, we will be using the following gems:

1. Prawn: Prawn is a fast, tiny, and nimble PDF generator for Ruby (https://rubygems.org/gems/prawn)
2. Prawn-Table: **`Prawn::Table`** provides tables for the Prawn PDF toolkit (https://rubygems.org/gems/prawn-table)

Now, let's implement a service to create a salary slip PDF as shown in *Figure* 10.19.

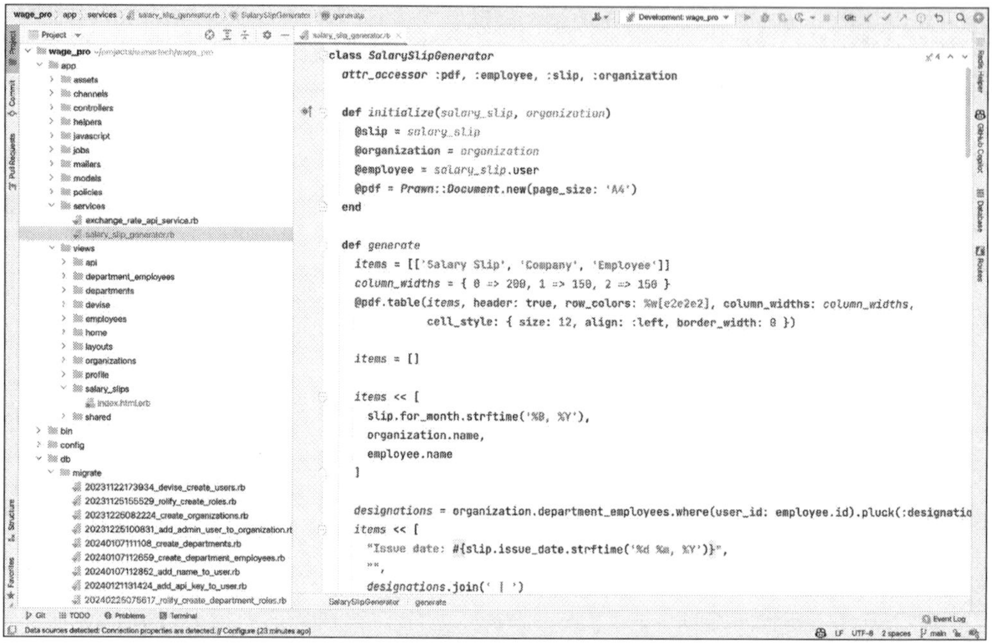

Figure 10.19: *SalarySlipGenerator service*

Please find all the codes in the GitHub URL mentioned at the end of this chapter.

This service takes a **salary_slip** object and an organization object as parameters and generates a salary slip PDF.

But before we create a **salary_slip**, we need the salary slip object to be saved in the **SalarySlip** model. Let's create an ActiveJob which we will schedule to run each day and automatically create salary slip objects for each organization based on the salary distribution date set in the organization model.

ActiveJob: ActiveJob is a framework for declaring jobs and making them run on a variety of queuing backends. These jobs can be everything from regularly scheduled clean-ups to billing charges, to mailings, anything that can be chopped up into small units of work and run in parallel.

Run the following command:

```
rails generate job salary_creation_job
```

Figure 10.20 shows the **SalaryCreationJob** file.

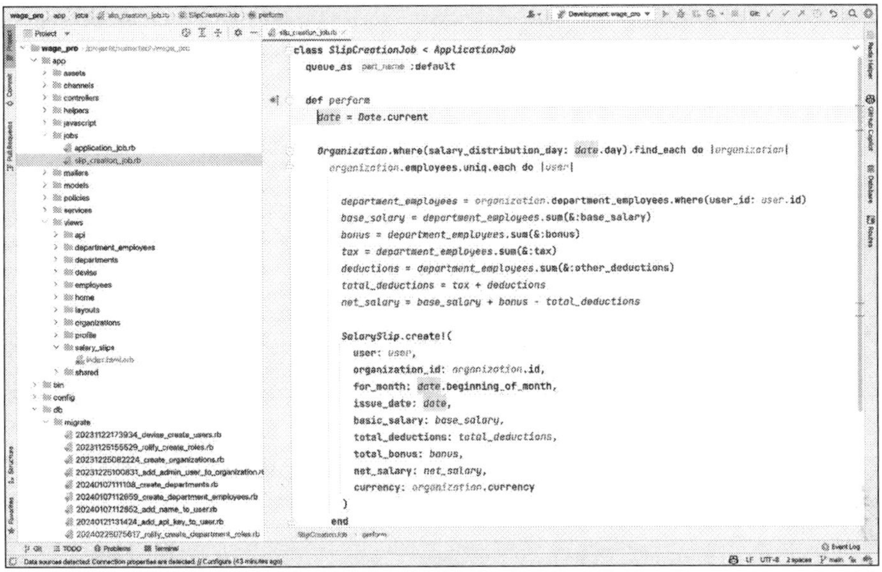

Figure 10.20: *SlipCreationJob file*

For now, we will be running this via the console, but in the next chapter, we will cover how to run jobs with queuing frameworks and periodically run jobs in the background.

SalarySlipsController

Figure 10.21 shows the **`SalarySlipsController`** which has an index and a show actions to list and show salary slips.

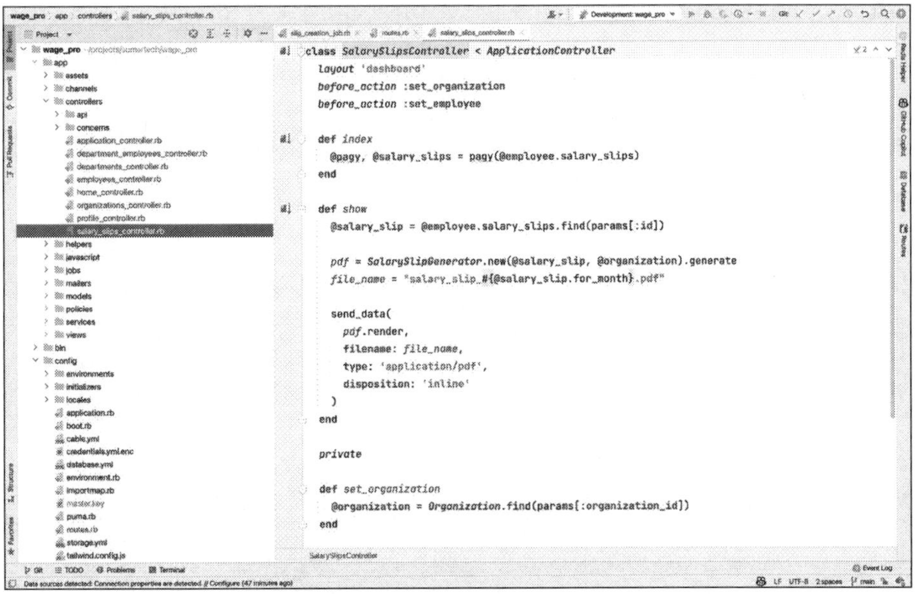

Figure 10.21: *SalarySlipsController*

The show action is creating a PDF on the fly using the **`SalarySlipGenerator`** service and sending it back to the browser to view with an option to download.

In the **`routes`** file, we have added the following code inside organization resource routes:

```
resources :employees, only: [] do
  resources :salary_slips
end
```

Along with that, we have also added the **`index.html.erb`** view file for index action and added links to view the salary slips of an employee on the profile page, as shown in *Figure 10.22*.

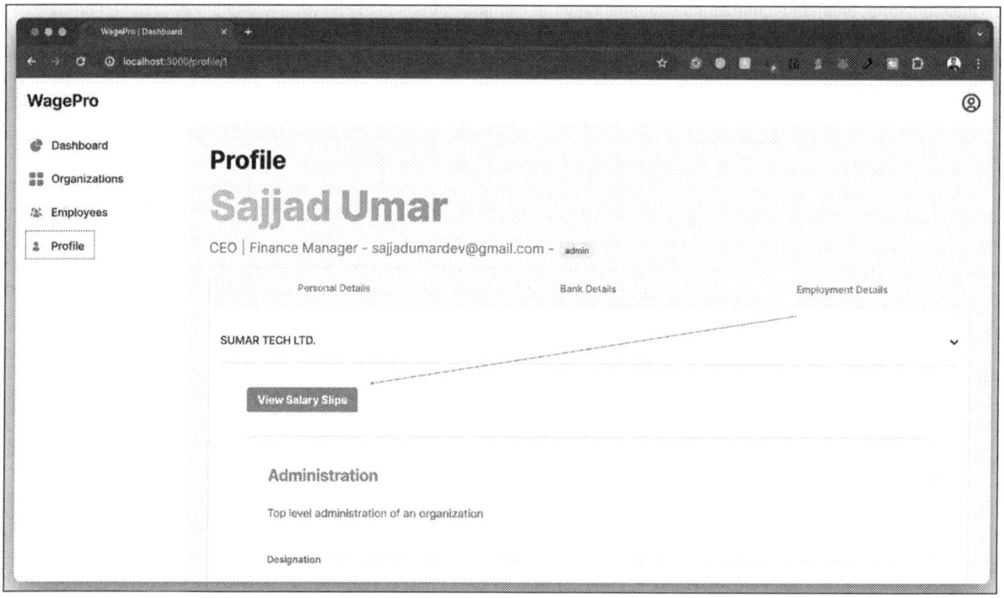

Figure 10.22: *Button to View Salary Slips*

Now, all you need to do is, edit the department employee and add the salary information as shown in *Figure 10.23*.

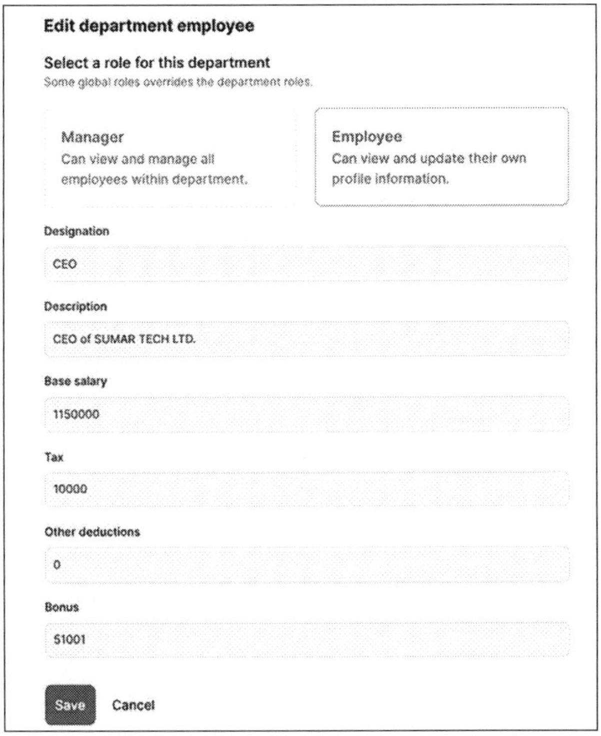

***Figure 10.23**: Adding salary information to a department employee*

Once added, edit the organization itself to add today's date as salary distribution day for your organization as shown in *Figure 10.24*.

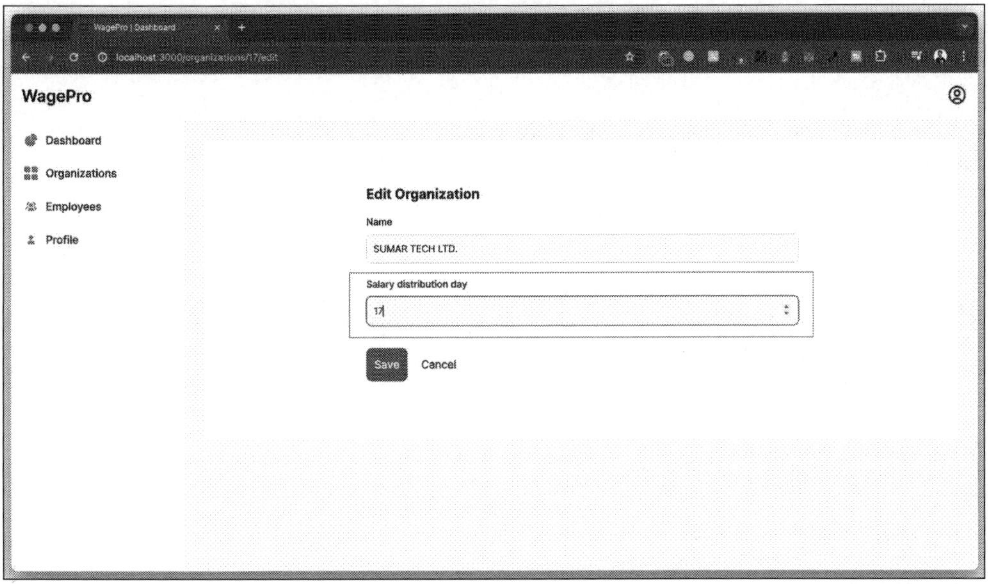

***Figure 10.24**: Add/edit salary distribution day to the organization*

Now, let's run our slip creation job from the console (rails c) using the following command:

```
SlipCreationJob.perform_now
```

This will create a salary slip object for all employees of each organization with a matching salary distribution day.

Now if you click on the "**View Salary Slips**" button highlighted in *Figure* 10.22, you will be presented with all the salary slips of the currently logged-in user, as shown in *Figure* 10.25.

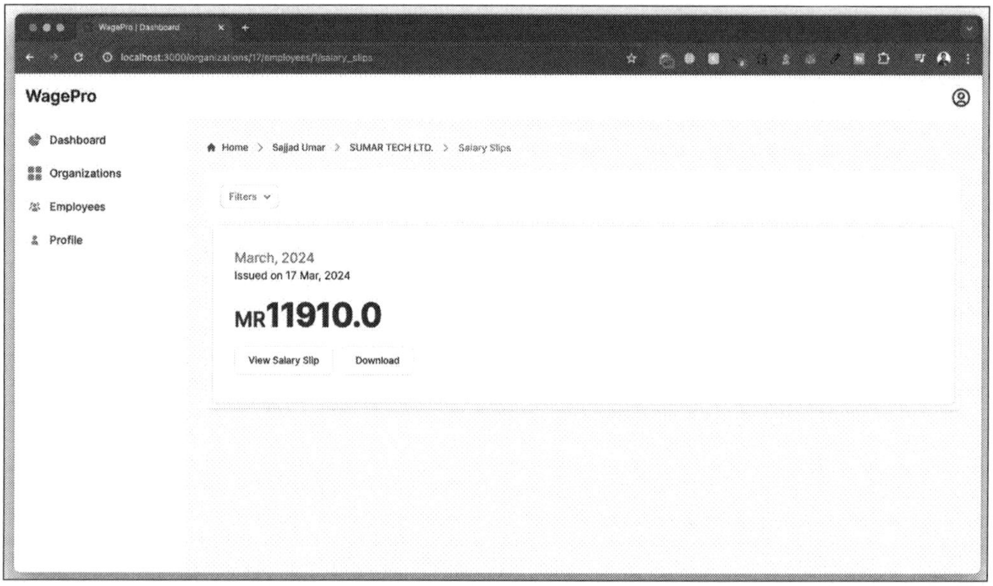

Figure 10.25: *Salary slips for logged-in user*

Clicking **View Salary Slip** or **Download** will create the Slip in PDF form and present it in the browser. *Figure* 10.26 shows a salary slip created by WagePro.

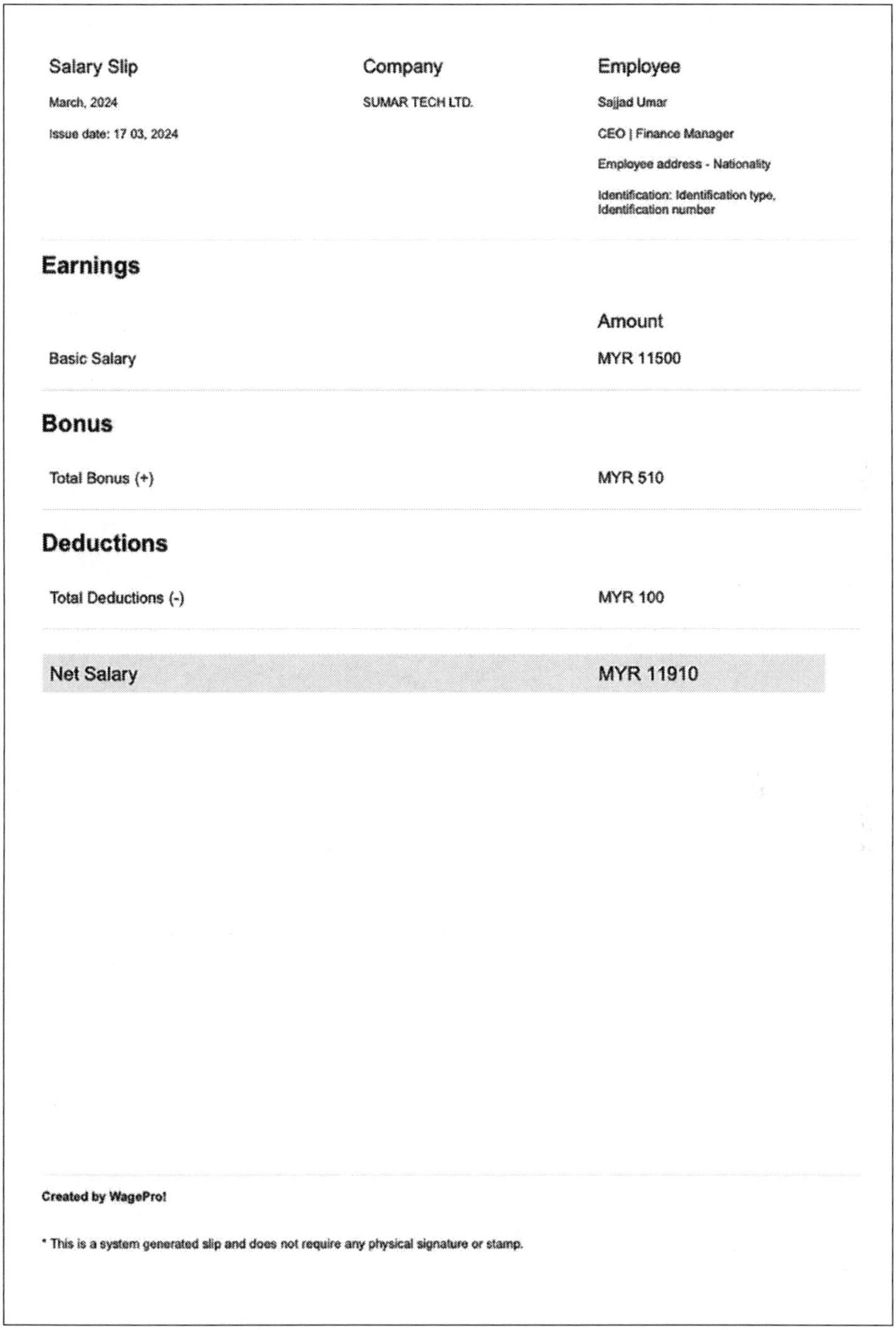
Salary Slip

March, 2024

Issue date: 17 03, 2024

Company

SUMAR TECH LTD.

Employee

Sajjad Umar

CEO | Finance Manager

Employee address - Nationality

Identification: Identification type, Identification number

Earnings

	Amount
Basic Salary	MYR 11500

Bonus

Total Bonus (+)	MYR 510

Deductions

Total Deductions (-)	MYR 100
Net Salary	MYR 11910

Created by WagePro!

* This is a system generated slip and does not require any physical signature or stamp.

Figure 10.26: *Salary slip PDF generated by WagePro*

We have a functional MVP of WagePro, that you can expand on as a practice assignment.

The GitHub link provided contains all the code demonstrated in this chapter: https://github.com/ava-orange-education/Ruby-on-Rails-for-Agile-Web-Development/tree/main/chapter10/wage_pro

You can get access to everything covered in the book on this GitHub repo: https://github.com/ava-orange-education/Ruby-on-Rails-for-Agile-Web-Development.

Conclusion

In this chapter, we embarked on a transformative journey, expanding the WagePro application into a Minimum Viable Product (MVP) that is almost ready for launch. We began by defining the requirements for our MVP and expanded our database accordingly to meet these needs. With a focus on user experience, we implemented a simple yet functional user interface, ensuring seamless navigation and interaction.

Furthermore, we addressed access management for users, ensuring that appropriate permissions are in place to safeguard sensitive data and functionalities. By integrating core features essential to our MVP, we laid a solid foundation for future enhancements and iterations based on user feedback.

As we conclude this chapter, we've witnessed the evolution of WagePro into a robust application poised for launch. In the next chapter, titled "*Advanced Topics in Ruby on Rails*," we will delve into more complex and sophisticated concepts and techniques within the Rails framework. Join us as we explore advanced topics that will elevate your Rails development skills to new heights.

Short Quiz

1. **What is the purpose of expanding the database in a Rails application when transitioning to an MVP?**
    a. To increase application performance
    b. To introduce unnecessary complexity
    c. To meet the requirements of the Minimum Viable Product (MVP)
    d. To decrease the application's scalability
2. **Which principle advocates for minimizing code repetition in software development?**
    a. DRY (Don't Repeat Yourself)
    b. KISS (Keep It Simple, Stupid)
    c. YAGNI (You Ain't Gonna Need It)
    d. SOLID (Single Responsibility, Open-Closed, Liskov Substitution, Interface Segregation, Dependency Inversion)

3. **What is the purpose of utilizing partials in Rails views?**
    a. To complicate the codebase
    b. To increase the number of views
    c. To reduce code repetition and maintainability
    d. To slow down the rendering speed
4. **Which term refers to the principle of allowing only authorized users to access certain parts of an application?**
    a. Code Optimization
    b. Access Management
    c. Performance Monitoring
    d. Deployment Strategy
5. **What is the purpose of schema in a Rails application?**
    a. To define database structure and relationships between tables
    b. To generate PDF documents
    c. To schedule background jobs
    d. To authenticate users
6. **Which command is used to generate a migration file for creating a new table in Rails?**
    a. rails generate model
    b. rails generate controller
    c. rails generate migration
    d. rails generate scaffold
7. **Which ActiveRecord association represents a one-to-many relationship in Rails?**
    a. `belongs_to`
    b. `has_one`
    c. `has_many`
    d. `has_and_belongs_to_many`

8. **Which gem is commonly used in Rails for generating PDF documents?**
   a. Prawn
   b. CarrierWave
   c. Devise
   d. Sidekiq
9. **What is the purpose of ActiveJob in Rails?**
   a. To generate PDF documents
   b. To schedule background jobs
   c. To manage database migrations
   d. To handle authentication
10. **Which method is used in this chapter to run ActiveJob from the console?**
   a. `perform_now`
   b. `perform_later`
   c. `perform_async`
   d. `perform_in`

Chapter 11
Advanced Topics in Ruby on Rails

Introduction

If you have made it this far in your Rails journey, congratulations – you are about to level up your skills and unlock a whole new world of possibilities. Think of this chapter as your secret stash of power-ups, where you will learn how to turbocharge your Rails applications with cutting-edge techniques.

First, we will dive into the world of background jobs and asynchronous processing. Imagine being able to handle time-consuming tasks in the background while your app continues to run smoothly – that's the magic of background jobs. With Active Job in Rails, you will learn how to queue up tasks and let your workers handle them behind the scenes, freeing up your app to do more important things.

Next, we will explore the art of caching and performance optimization. Picture your app running at lightning speed, thanks to clever caching strategies that store frequently accessed data for quick retrieval. From fragment caching to HTTP caching, you will discover a treasure trove of techniques to boost performance and delight your users with snappy response times.

But that's not all – we will also delve into the fascinating world of internationalization and localization. Ever wanted to make your app speak multiple languages? With Rails' built-in internationalization features, you will learn how to translate your app's content into different languages, opening new markets and reaching a global audience.

Let's not forget about security – a topic near and dear to every developer's heart. In this chapter, we will cover common security vulnerabilities in web applications and show you how to fortify your Rails app against cyber threats. From implementing authentication and authorization to managing security patches and updates, you will learn how to keep your app safe and secure in an ever-changing digital landscape.

So, buckle up, and get ready to level up and become the Rails master you were always meant to be!

Structure

In this chapter, we will be discussing the following topics:

- Background Jobs and Asynchronous Processing
  - Active Job in Rails
  - Queuing Systems and Workers
- Caching and Performance Optimization Techniques
  - Page Caching
  - Action Caching
  - Fragment Caching
  - Low-Level Caching
  - Performance Optimization Strategies
- Sending Emails
- Introduction to Internationalization and Localization
- Introduction to JavaScript Frameworks with Rails
- Securing Rails Application
- File Uploads

Background Jobs and Asynchronous Processing

In web development, certain tasks can take a significant amount of time to complete, such as sending emails, processing large datasets, or generating reports. Traditionally, these tasks are performed synchronously, meaning the user has to wait for them to finish before they can continue using the application. However, this can lead to poor user experience, as users may become frustrated with long loading times or unresponsive pages.

Background jobs offer a solution to this problem by allowing these time-consuming tasks to be performed asynchronously, in the background, without blocking the main thread of execution. This means that users can continue using the application while the task is being processed, leading to a smoother and more responsive user experience.

Active Job in Rails

Active Job is a framework in Ruby on Rails that provides a unified interface for working with background jobs. It abstracts away the details of different queuing systems, allowing developers to write job code once and run it on different queuing backends, such as SolidQueue, Sidekiq, DelayedJob, or Resque.

Active Job, as a framework within Ruby on Rails, empowers developers with the ability to encapsulate background tasks into dedicated job classes. These job classes serve as containers for the specific tasks that need to be executed asynchronously. Once defined, these job classes can be seamlessly enqueued into a queuing system, where they await processing by a dedicated worker process.

Active Job offers a suite of features to enhance the robustness and flexibility of background processing systems. For instance, developers can configure job retries to automatically retry failed jobs, ensuring fault tolerance and resilience against transient errors. Additionally, Active Job supports job scheduling, enabling developers to schedule jobs to run at specific times or intervals. This capability is invaluable for handling recurring tasks, such as periodic data synchronization or report generation.

Furthermore, Active Job facilitates the implementation of priority queues, allowing developers to prioritize the execution of critical tasks over less important ones. This ensures that high-priority tasks are processed promptly, even during periods of heavy workload.

Queuing Systems and Workers

Queuing systems are an essential component of background job processing. They manage the storage and execution of queued jobs, ensuring that they are processed in the order they were enqueued and that no jobs are lost if a worker process crashes.

Worker processes are responsible for fetching jobs from the queue and executing them. In Rails applications, worker processes are typically separate from the web server and run asynchronously in the background. This allows them to handle long-running tasks without impacting the responsiveness of the application.

We have several options when it comes to choosing a queuing system for background job processing. Among the most popular choices are Sidekiq, DelayedJob, Resque, and the newly introduced SolidQueue. Each of these queuing systems offers unique features and capabilities, catering to different use cases and scalability requirements.

- **Sidekiq:** Sidekiq is a popular background job processing framework for Ruby on Rails applications. It leverages multithreading and Redis for efficient job execution, making it well-suited for high-throughput environments. Sidekiq offers advanced features such as job retries, scheduling, and prioritization, providing developers with a robust and scalable solution for handling asynchronous tasks.

  Read more about Sidekiq here: https://github.com/sidekiq/sidekiq.

- **DelayedJob:** DelayedJob is a simple and easy-to-use background job processing framework for Ruby on Rails applications. Unlike Sidekiq, which relies on multithreading and Redis, DelayedJob stores job metadata in the database itself, simplifying setup and integration. This makes it a preferred choice for smaller applications or projects with straightforward background processing requirements. However, DelayedJob's single-threaded architecture may limit its scalability compared to Sidekiq, especially for applications with high concurrency demands. Despite this difference, both DelayedJob and Sidekiq offer essential features like job retries, scheduling, and prioritization, catering to different use cases and development preferences.

  Read more about DelayedJob here: https://github.com/collectiveidea/delayed_job.

- **Resque:** Resque utilizes Redis as its backend for job storage and execution. It operates on a pool of worker processes, providing scalability and reliability for handling asynchronous tasks. Resque offers features such as job retries, failure handling, and job dependencies, making it suitable for complex job processing workflows.

  Compared to Sidekiq, Resque has a different architecture, relying on separate worker processes rather than multithreading. While Sidekiq offers higher concurrency with its multithreaded approach, Resque excels in horizontal scalability by adding more worker processes as needed. Additionally, Resque's reliance on Redis ensures fast and reliable job execution, while Sidekiq relies on Redis for job storage but uses its own multithreaded processing for execution.

  Read more about Resque here: https://github.com/resque/resque.

- **SolidQueue**: Inspired by Resque and GoodJob (another queuing framework), Solid Queue is a DB-based queuing backend for Active Job, designed with simplicity and performance in mind.

  Read more about Resque here: https://github.com/rails/solid_queue.

The choice of queuing framework for your project depends on various factors, such as the complexity of your background job processing needs, scalability requirements, infrastructure setup, and personal preferences.

In our WagePro application, we will use SolidQueue as it has got quite a hype in the market and nicely fits into our application needs.

Add "**`solid_queue`**"gem in your **`Gemfile`** and run **`bundle install`** as shown in *Figure 11.1*:

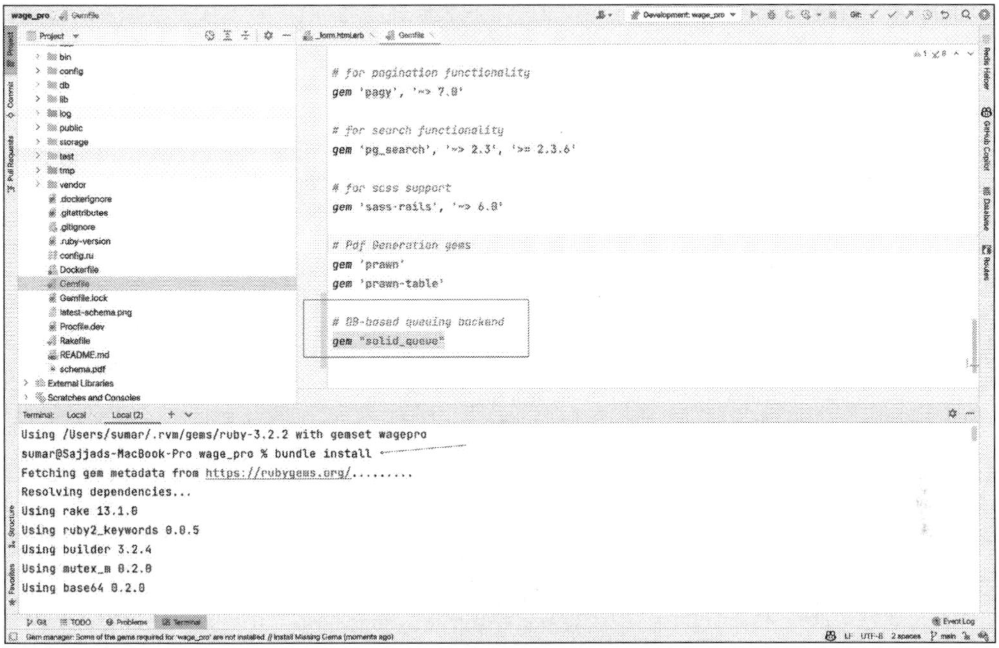

Figure 11.1: *Installing SolidQueue Gem*

Now, it's time to set up the required migrations and configure the Active Job adapter. You can handle both tasks simultaneously by using the provided generator:

```
bin/rails generate solid_queue:install
```

Figure 11.2 shows running the **solid_queue** generator.

```
sumar@Sajjads-MacBook-Pro wage_pro % bin/rails generate solid_queue:install
        gsub  config/environments/production.rb
      create  config/solid_queue.yml
       rails  railties:install:migrations FROM=solid_queue
Copied migration 20240328161438_create_solid_queue_tables.solid_queue.rb from solid_queue
Copied migration 20240328161439_add_missing_index_to_blocked_executions.solid_queue.rb from solid_queue
Copied migration 20240328161440_create_recurring_executions.solid_queue.rb from solid_queue
sumar@Sajjads-MacBook-Pro wage_pro %
```

Figure 11.2: *Running solid_queue generator*

By executing this command, you'll configure the Active Job adapter to use **solid_queue** in production and automatically copy over the necessary migration files to your application.

Now run the migrations with the following command:

```
bin/rails db:migrate
```

After completing this step, you'll be all set to add jobs to the queue using Solid Queue.

Just remember, it's essential to launch Solid Queue's supervisor before jobs can be executed. You can do that with the following command:

```
bundle exec rake solid_queue:start
```

This will start processing jobs in all queues using the default configuration. Read all about SolidQueue and default configurations here: https://github.com/rails/solid_queue.

In smaller projects, you have the option to operate Solid Queue on the same machine as your web server. As your project grows and scalability becomes a priority, Solid Queue offers seamless horizontal scaling capabilities. You can easily deploy Solid Queue on a separate server from your web server, or alternatively, execute **`bundle exec rake solid_queue:start`** on multiple machines simultaneously.

For now, we will run it on the same machine as our webserver with the preceding command.

Figure 11.3 shows a terminal running Solid Queue supervisor.

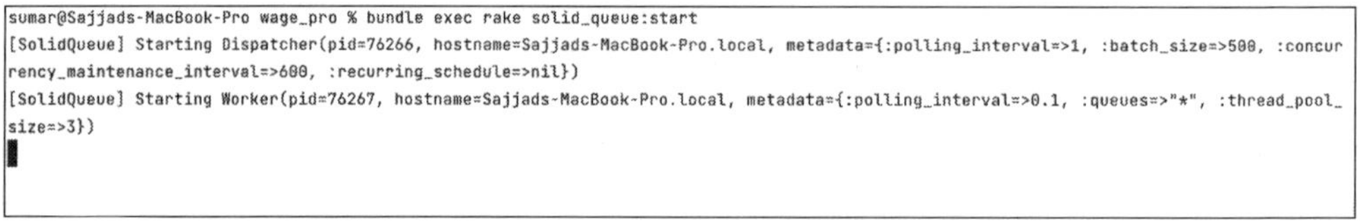

Figure 11.3: *Running sold_queue supervisor*

To test our setup locally, we need to add the following line of code in **`config/environments/development.rb`** file, as shown in *Figure* 11.4.

```
# making the active job use the solid queue adapter in development
config.active_job.queue_adapter = :solid_queue
```

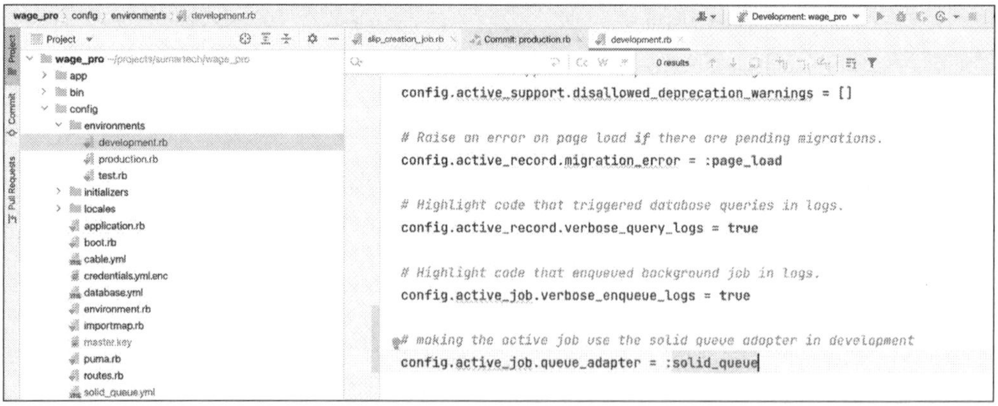

Figure 11.4: *Configuring solid_queue as ActiveJob adapter for development environment*

Now let's try to enqueue our **`SlipCreationJob`** in the background by running the following command in the rails console and see if it gets picket by the **`SolidQueue`** supervisor.

```
SlipCreationJob.perform_later
```

Figure 11.5 shows our **`SlipCreationJob`** being picked up and processed by Solid Queue.

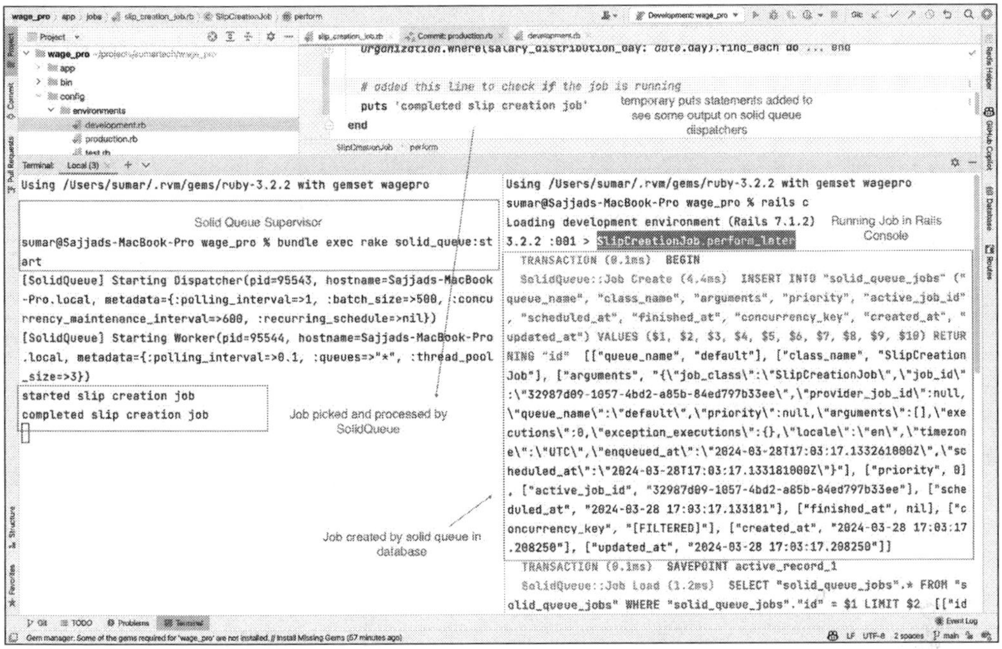

Figure 11.5: *Solid Queue running SlipCreationJob in the background*

In the WagePro application, we need to run this job automatically every day at a specific time like a cron job. SolidQueue provides an option to run jobs periodically.

Cron Job: A cron job, short for "*chronograph job*," is a scheduled task or command executed automatically at specified intervals by the cron daemon, a system service found in Unix-like operating systems. These tasks can be set to run hourly, daily, weekly, monthly, or at custom intervals defined by the user. Cron jobs are commonly used for automating repetitive tasks, such as data backups, system maintenance, log rotation, and batch processing. They are defined in a cron table file (typically located at **`/etc/crontab`** or in a user's crontab file), where users can specify the command to be executed, the schedule for execution, and any additional parameters or conditions. Once configured, the cron daemon runs these tasks in the background according to the defined schedule, providing a convenient way to automate routine administrative tasks on Unix-like systems.

As an assignment, create a recurring task in Solid Queue to run our **`SlipCreationJob`** every day at 10 AM.

You can get information about recurring tasks from the official SolidQueue documentation here: https://github.com/rails/solid_queue?tab=readme-ov-file#recurring-tasks.

You can also find the implementation of recurring tasks in the "**config/solid_queue.yml**" file at the GitHub URL provided at the end of this chapter.

Caching and Performance Optimization Techniques

Caching is a technique used to store frequently accessed data in memory or a faster storage system, thereby reducing the need to regenerate the data from its source each time it's requested. This can significantly improve the performance and responsiveness of web applications. Rails provides various caching mechanisms to help developers optimize their applications.

Page Caching

Page caching involves storing entire HTML pages in a cache and serving them directly to users without executing the corresponding controller action. This is the fastest form of caching but is only suitable for static pages that don't require dynamic content. Example:

```
class ProductsController < ApplicationController
  def show
    @product = Product.find(params[:id])
    expires_in 1.hour, public: true
  end
end
```

Action Caching

Action caching caches the output of controller actions, allowing subsequent requests to be served directly from the cache without re-executing the action. This is useful for dynamic pages with relatively stable content. Example:

```
class ProductsController < ApplicationController
  before_action :set_cache_control_headers, only: :show

  def show
    @product = Product.find(params[:id])
```

```
  end

  private

  def set_cache_control_headers
    expires_in 1.hour, public: true
  end
end
```

Fragment Caching

Fragment caching involves caching specific parts of a view or template, allowing for more granular caching of dynamic content within a page. This is useful for caching individual components or sections of a page that are expensive to render. Example:

```
<% cache @product do %>
  <div class="product">
    <h2><%= @product.name %></h2>
    <p><%= @product.description %></p>
    <p><%= @product.price %></p>
  </div>
<% end %>
```

Low-Level Caching

Rails provides low-level caching mechanisms such as **`Rails.cache.fetch`** and **`Rails.cache.read/write`** for caching arbitrary data in memory or a configured cache store. This is useful for caching database queries, API responses, or any other computationally expensive operations. Example:

```
class ProductsController < ApplicationController
  def index
    @products = Rails.cache.fetch('products', expires_in: 1.hour) do
      Product.all
    end
  end
end
```

There is a lot more to caching than what is described here. Rails has an extensive guide on caching; consider reading it and applying different techniques to our WagePro application. Here is the link to the official caching guide: https://guides.rubyonrails.org/caching_with_rails.html.

Performance Optimization Strategies

Performance optimization in Rails is a multifaceted approach aimed at enhancing your application's speed, responsiveness, and scalability. By identifying and addressing bottlenecks across various layers of the stack, you can significantly improve the overall performance and user experience. Here's a detailed look at some key performance optimization techniques in Rails, along with examples:

Database Optimization

Database optimization is crucial for improving the performance and efficiency of your application. By optimizing database operations, you can reduce latency, minimize resource consumption, and enhance the overall user experience. While optimizing the database, focus on:

1. **Efficient Queries:** Use ActiveRecord query methods to construct efficient database queries. Methods, such as **`where`**, **`joins`**, **`includes`**, and **`select`** allow you to retrieve only the necessary data and avoid loading unnecessary records.

    ```
    # Example of an optimized query using `includes`
    @posts = Post.includes(:comments).where(published: true)
    ```

2. **Indexes**: Add indexes to database columns that are frequently used in queries to speed up data retrieval. Indexes allow the database engine to quickly locate and retrieve rows based on indexed columns.

    ```
    # Example of adding an index to a column in a database migration file
    add_index :users, :email
    ```

3. **Data Cleanup**: Regularly clean up unused or obsolete data from the database to improve performance and maintain database health. This includes deleting expired sessions, removing old logs, and purging obsolete records.

    ```
    # Example of cleaning up expired sessions
    Session.where('expires_at < ?', Time.now).destroy_all
    ```

4. **Database Sharding**: Divide large databases into smaller, more manageable shards to distribute the workload and improve scalability. Sharding involves splitting data across multiple databases or database servers based on a predetermined sharding key.

```
# Example of sharding users across multiple databases
class User < ApplicationRecord
  self.abstract_class = true
  establish_connection "#{Rails.env}_users"
end
```

5. **Optimized Database Configuration:** Set the size of the database connection pool appropriately to handle database connections effectively and avoid resource depletion. Fine-tune buffer sizes and cache configurations to enhance database memory utilization and optimize disk I/O operations.

6. **Database Replication:** Database replication offers several benefits in improving the scalability, performance, and reliability of your application's database infrastructure. One approach is through read replicas, which involve duplicating the database across multiple replica servers. By doing so, read-only queries can be distributed among these replicas, effectively reducing the load on the primary database server and enhancing overall read performance. Another replication strategy is master-slave replication, where data from the primary (master) database server is replicated to one or more secondary (slave) servers. This setup ensures redundancy and scalability by allowing read and write operations to be distributed across multiple servers, thereby increasing fault tolerance and accommodating growing workloads. Overall, database replication plays a crucial role in optimizing resource utilization, improving query responsiveness, and ensuring the high availability of your database infrastructure.

These methods only scratch the surface, and there's much more to discover within each technique to effectively optimize your database according to the specific requirements of your application.

In addition to optimizing the database, we can leverage caching, asset optimization, code optimization, background jobs, and asynchronous processing to enhance the performance of our Rails applications.

Sending Emails

Sending emails in any application is a common requirement for various purposes such as user notifications, password resets, marketing campaigns, and more. Rails provides built-in support for sending emails through Action Mailer, simplifying the process.

Here's a basic overview of how to send emails in a Rails app:

- **Set Up Email Configuration:** First, configure the email settings in your Rails application, which includes specifying the SMTP server details or using third-party email services, such as SendGrid, Mailgun, or Amazon SES. You typically configure these settings in the **config/environments/*.rb** files, such as **development.rb** for the development environment and **production.rb** for the production environment.

- **Create Email Templates:** Next, create email templates using HTML or plain text format. These templates reside in the **app/views** directory and are typically organized within a folder named after the mailer class. For example, if you have a mailer named **UserMailer**, you would create corresponding view templates in the **app/views/user_mailer** directory.
- **Define Mailer Class:** Create a mailer class in the **app/mailers** directory. This class extends **ActionMailer::Base** and contains methods for generating and sending emails. Each method corresponds to a specific email that your application sends. Within these methods, specify the email subject, recipient, and sender, and render the appropriate email template.
- **Trigger Emails:** Call the mailer method from your controllers or other parts of your application where you want to send emails. Pass any necessary data as parameters to the mailer method, which can be used within the email template.
- **Delivery:** Once the mailer method is invoked, Action Mailer generates the email and delivers it using the configured delivery method (SMTP server or third-party service). Action Mailer handles the processes, such as connecting to the email server, formatting the email, and sending it to the recipient.

Here's a basic example demonstrating these steps:

```
# 1. Configure email settings in config/environments/*.rb

# config/environments/development.rb
config.action_mailer.delivery_method = :smtp
config.action_mailer.smtp_settings = {
  address: 'smtp.example.com',
  port: 587,
  user_name: 'username',
  password: 'password',
  authentication: 'plain',
  enable_starttls_auto: true
}

# 2. Create email template in app/views/user_mailer/welcome_email.html.
erb
# app/views/user_mailer/welcome_email.text.erb
```

```
# 3. Define mailer class in app/mailers/user_mailer.rb
class UserMailer < ApplicationMailer
  def welcome_email(user)
    @user = user
    mail(to: @user.email, subject: 'Welcome to Our App')
  end
end

# 4. Trigger email in a controller or service
class UsersController < ApplicationController
  def create
    @user = User.new(user_params)
    if @user.save
      UserMailer.welcome_email(@user).deliver_now # use ".deliver_later"-
to send via ActiveJob in the background.
      redirect_to @user, notice: 'User was successfully created.'
    else
      render :new
    end
  end
end
```

This is a basic overview, and you can customize the email content, delivery settings, and other aspects based on your application's requirements. Additionally, Rails provides support for advanced features like attachments, inline images, email previews, and more through Action Mailer.

Read the official documentation for ActionMailer on Rails guides here https://guides.rubyonrails.org/action_mailer_basics.html.

Note: *As an assignment, implement sending an email to employees whenever a new salary slip is generated for them in the WagePro application.*

Introduction to Internationalization and Localization

Internationalization refers to the process of designing and developing applications in a way that allows them to be easily adapted to different languages and cultures without requiring significant code changes. The primary goal of internationalization is to make an application flexible enough to support multiple languages and cultural conventions. This involves separating user interface (UI) text, date formats, currency symbols, and other locale-specific elements from the application code.

Localization is the process of customizing an application for a specific locale or region by translating and adapting its content, UI elements, and functionality to suit the language, cultural norms, and preferences of the target audience. Localization goes beyond language translation and may involve modifying date formats, numeric representations, currency symbols, and other aspects of the application to align with the local conventions and standards of the target region.

Rails provides an I18n framework to easily internationalize and localize Rails applications.

Rails Internationalization (I18n) API

The Ruby I18n gem, an abbreviation for internationalization, comes bundled with Ruby on Rails (from Rails 2.2 onwards). It offers a user-friendly and adaptable framework for translating your application into a custom language besides English or for implementing multi-language support seamlessly.

How I18n in Ruby on Rails Works

Internationalization is a complex problem. Natural languages differ in so many ways (for example, in pluralization rules) that it is hard to provide tools for solving all problems at once. For that reason, the Rails I18n API focuses on:

- Providing support for English and similar languages out of the box
- Making it easy to customize and extend everything for other languages

As part of this solution, every static string in the Rails framework – for example, Active Record validation messages, time, and date formats - has been internationalized.

The most important methods of the I18n API are:

```
translate # Lookup text translations
localize  # Localize Date and Time objects to local formats
```

These have the aliases #t and #l so you can use them like this:

```
I18n.t 'store.title'
I18n.l Time.now
```

Key Components of Internationalization and Localization

Here are some of the key concepts of internationalization and localization:

- **Language Files:** Internationalization involves storing language-specific text strings in separate resource files or dictionaries, commonly known as language files. These files contain translations of UI text and messages for different languages, allowing developers to easily switch between languages without modifying the application code.
- **Locale Management:** Locale management is the process of identifying the user's preferred language and region settings and configuring the application to display content accordingly. This typically involves detecting the user's locale based on browser settings or user preferences and loading the appropriate language resources.
- **Translation Workflow:** Localization requires a systematic workflow for translating and managing language resources. This may involve collaborating with professional translators or using automated translation tools to generate translations for different languages. Additionally, localization workflows often include validation and quality assurance processes to ensure the accuracy and consistency of translations.

Benefits of Internationalization and Localization

Here are some of the benefits of internationalizing and localizing your app:

- **Expanded Market Reach:** By supporting multiple languages and regions, internationalized and localized applications can reach a broader audience and penetrate new markets.
- **Enhanced User Experience:** Providing content in the user's preferred language and format improves the overall user experience and engagement, leading to higher user satisfaction and retention.
- **Cultural Sensitivity:** Localization allows applications to adapt to cultural nuances and preferences, making them more relatable and appealing to users in different regions.
- **Compliance with Regulations:** In some cases, internationalization and localization are necessary to comply with legal and regulatory requirements governing language usage and accessibility in specific regions or industries.

Rails guides has a detailed documentation on how to set up your application for Internationalization, get all the details here: https://guides.rubyonrails.org/i18n.html.

Introduction to JavaScript Frameworks with Rails

JavaScript frameworks have become integral components of modern web development, offering powerful tools and libraries for building dynamic and interactive user interfaces. When integrated with Ruby on Rails, these frameworks enhance the frontend capabilities of Rails applications, enabling developers to create rich, responsive, and engaging user experiences. Let's explore the intersection of JavaScript frameworks and Rails in more detail.

Evolution of JavaScript Frameworks

JavaScript frameworks have evolved significantly over the years, providing developers with robust solutions for frontend development. Frameworks such as React, Vue.js, and Angular have gained widespread adoption due to their flexibility, performance, and developer-friendly features. These frameworks offer components, state management, routing, and other essential functionalities for building modern web applications.

Integrating JavaScript Frameworks with Rails

Ruby on Rails traditionally emphasizes server-side rendering and follows the MVC (Model-View-Controller) architecture for building web applications. However, with the rise of client-side rendering and single-page applications (SPAs), Rails developers often integrate JavaScript frameworks to enhance the frontend capabilities of their applications. This integration allows Rails applications to leverage the strengths of JavaScript frameworks while benefiting from Rails' conventions and backend functionalities.

Benefits of Using JavaScript Frameworks with Rails

Here are some benefits of using JavaScript frameworks with Rails:

- **Enhanced User Experience:** JavaScript frameworks enable developers to create dynamic, interactive user interfaces that respond to user actions in real-time, providing a seamless and engaging experience
- **Improved Performance:** Client-side rendering offered by JavaScript frameworks can enhance application performance by reducing server load and minimizing page load times, especially for SPAs
- **Modular Development:** JavaScript frameworks promote modular development by offering components and reusable UI elements, allowing developers to build complex interfaces more efficiently
- **Ecosystem Support:** JavaScript frameworks have vibrant ecosystems with extensive documentation, community support, and third-party libraries, making it easier for Rails developers to find solutions and resources for frontend development

Drawbacks of Using JavaScript Frameworks with Rails

Using JavaScript frameworks with Rails comes with some drawbacks as well.

- **Increased Complexity:** Integrating JavaScript frameworks with Rails introduces additional complexity to the development stack. Developers need to manage two separate codebases, handle communication between frontend and backend components, and ensure compatibility between different technologies. This complexity can lead to a steeper learning curve and require additional effort for maintenance and debugging.
- **Performance Overhead:** While JavaScript frameworks offer powerful frontend capabilities, they also introduce performance overhead, especially for client-side rendering. SPAs built with JavaScript frameworks may require significant initial loading times and consume more system resources, impacting the overall performance of the application. Additionally, managing client-side state and routing can lead to increased memory usage and slower page rendering.
- **SEO Challenges:** Client-side rendering used in JavaScript frameworks can pose challenges for search engine optimization (SEO). Search engines may have difficulty indexing content generated dynamically by JavaScript, leading to lower search engine rankings and reduced visibility for the application. Implementing server-side rendering or pre-rendering techniques can mitigate this issue but adds complexity to the development process.
- **Compatibility Issues:** JavaScript frameworks evolve rapidly, introducing new features, updates, and breaking changes over time. Ensuring compatibility between Rails and the chosen JavaScript framework, as well as managing dependencies and versioning can be challenging. Additionally, changes in browser support and compatibility may require updates to the application codebase to maintain optimal performance and functionality.
- **Learning Curve:** Learning and mastering a JavaScript framework alongside Ruby on Rails can be daunting for developers, especially those with limited frontend development experience. Each framework has its own syntax, concepts, and best practices, requiring additional time and effort for training and skill acquisition. This learning curve can slow down development velocity and may result in suboptimal implementation choices during the initial stages of integration.

That said, there's also a widely embraced approach for creating modern user interfaces, which is Hotwire (HTML over the wire), recommended and built by the Rails core team.

Hotwire

Hotwire is an alternative approach to building modern web applications without using much JavaScript by sending HTML instead of JSON over the wire. This makes for fast first-load pages, keeps template rendering on the server, and allows for a simpler, more productive development experience in any programming language, without sacrificing any speed or responsiveness associated with a traditional single-page application.

Here is the link to the official Hotwire documentation: https://hotwired.dev.

The team at 37Signals (the company behind the Rails framework, https://37signals.com/) has created some handy hotwire-supported frameworks; they work together, complementing each other to give you a complete solution across all platforms:

- **Turbo:** The heart of Hotwire is Turbo. A set of complementary techniques for speeding up page changes and form submissions, dividing complex pages into components, and streaming partial page updates over WebSocket. All without writing any JavaScript at all. Designed from the start to integrate perfectly with native hybrid applications for iOS and Android.

  Head over to official documentation for more details on turbo here: https://turbo.hotwired.dev.

- **Stimulus:** While Turbo usually takes care of at least 80% of the interactivity that traditionally would have required JavaScript, there are still cases where a dash of custom code is required. Stimulus makes this easy with an HTML-centric approach to state and wiring.

  Learn more about stimulus here: https://stimulus.hotwired.dev.

- **Strada:** Standardizes the way web and native parts of a mobile hybrid application talk to each other via HTML bridge attributes. This makes it easy to progressively level up web interactions with native replacements.

  You can find official documentation for STRADA here:
  https://strada.hotwired.dev.

Securing Rails Application

Securing a Rails application is a critical aspect of the development process to safeguard sensitive data, prevent unauthorized access, and mitigate potential security risks.

Web application frameworks serve as valuable tools for developers to streamline the process of building web applications, offering assistance in various aspects, including security. While it's important to recognize that no framework inherently provides superior security over another, the key lies in utilizing the framework effectively. Ruby on Rails, for instance, offers a range of helpful methods to combat vulnerabilities like SQL injection, thus mitigating potential risks.

However, it's essential to understand that achieving robust security isn't as simple as plugging in a framework. Security is contingent upon numerous factors, including the expertise of the individuals utilizing the framework and the development methodologies employed. Furthermore, security encompasses all layers of the web application environment, encompassing the backend storage, web server, and the application itself, among others.

Research conducted by the Gartner Group indicates that a significant portion of cyberattacks target the web application layer, with a staggering percentage of audited sites found to be vulnerable. Web applications are susceptible to exploitation due to their inherent simplicity, making them easily comprehensible and manipulable, even for non-experts.

The array of threats facing web applications includes user account hijacking, circumvention of access controls, unauthorized access to sensitive data, and the dissemination of fraudulent content. Attackers may also seek to install malicious software or engage in activities aimed at financial gain or tarnishing a company's reputation. To safeguard against these threats, it's imperative to comprehend various attack vectors and implement appropriate countermeasures effectively.

Developing secure web applications necessitates staying abreast of advancements across every layer of the technology stack and understanding potential adversaries. Engaging with security mailing lists, reading security-related blogs, and integrating regular updates and security checks into development practices are crucial steps. Manual assessment remains indispensable for uncovering intricate security vulnerabilities that may evade automated detection mechanisms.

Here are some essential practices and techniques for securing a Rails application:

- **Authentication and Authorization:** Implement robust authentication mechanisms to verify the identity of users accessing the application. Use secure password hashing algorithms, such as bcrypt to store user passwords securely. Additionally, enforce authorization controls to restrict access to sensitive resources based on user roles and permissions.
- **Parameter Sanitization and Validation:** Sanitize and validate user input to prevent common security vulnerabilities, such as SQL injection, cross-site scripting (XSS), and cross-site request forgery (CSRF). Utilize Rails' built-in features, such as strong parameters and validation helpers to ensure incoming data is safe and adheres to expected formats.
- **HTTPS Encryption:** Enable HTTPS encryption to secure data transmission between the client and server. Use SSL/TLS certificates to encrypt HTTP traffic, protecting sensitive information from interception and tampering by

malicious actors. Configure Rails to enforce HTTPS connections for all web requests to ensure end-to-end encryption.

- **Cross-Site Scripting (XSS) Protection:** Employ measures to mitigate cross-site scripting attacks by escaping and encoding user-generated content displayed on web pages. Utilize Rails' built-in XSS protection mechanisms, such as the sanitize helper method and content security policy (CSP), to sanitize and filter potentially malicious scripts embedded in user input.
- **Cross-Site Request Forgery (CSRF) Protection:** Implement CSRF protection mechanisms to prevent unauthorized requests from being executed on behalf of authenticated users. Rails provides built-in CSRF protection by generating unique tokens for each session and verifying the authenticity of requests submitted via forms or AJAX calls.
- **Secure Session Management:** Implement secure session management practices to protect user sessions from session fixation, session hijacking, and session replay attacks. Use secure HTTP cookies with appropriate settings, such as the secure and `HttpOnly` flags, to prevent cookie-based attacks and enforce secure communication between the client and server.
- **Content Security Policy (CSP):** Configure a CSP to mitigate the risks associated with XSS and other code injection attacks. Define a whitelist of trusted sources for scripts, stylesheets, fonts, and other resources to prevent unauthorized execution of inline scripts and mitigate the impact of XSS vulnerabilities.
- **Regular Security Audits and Vulnerability Scanning:** Conduct regular security audits and vulnerability assessments to identify and address potential security vulnerabilities in the application codebase. Utilize automated security scanning tools and manual code reviews to detect and remediate security flaws, ensuring ongoing protection against emerging threats.

Rails guides has detailed documentation on securing rails applications and you can read it at the following URL: https://guides.rubyonrails.org/security.html.

The author of this book has delivered a comprehensive learning session on securing rails applications on his YouTube channel where he specifically discussed about securing rails applications from SQL injections. Here is the link to the recording of that session: https://youtu.be/p6V7UKM4-O0?si=jcTlTa2_acIC12Ii.

File Uploads

File upload functionality is a common requirement in web applications, and Ruby on Rails simplifies this task with its built-in feature called Active Storage. Introduced in Rails 5.2, Active Storage provides a seamless way to upload files to cloud storage services like Amazon S3, Google Cloud Storage, or even local disk storage.

Active Storage is typically included in Rails applications by default, starting from version 5.2. However, if you're using an older Rails version, you may need to add the **active_storage** gem to your Gemfile and run bundle install to set it up.

Configuring Storage Services

Configure Active Storage to use the desired storage service(s). This involves adding configuration settings for cloud storage services like Amazon S3 or Google Cloud Storage in the **config/storage.yml** file.

Attaching Files to a Model

In your model, let's say **user.rb** model file, use the **has_one_attached** method to specify which files can be attached to instances of the User model. For example, let's attach a **profile_image**:

```
class User < ApplicationRecord
  has_one_attached :profile_image
end
```

Creating the File Upload Form

Create a form in your Rails views to allow users to upload profile images. Use the **file_field** form helper to generate a file input field:

```
<%= form_with model: @user, local: true do |form| %>


  <%= form.label :profile_image %>
  <%= form.file_field :profile_image %>


  <%= form.submit 'Upload Profile Image' %>
<% end %>
```

Handling File Upload in the Controller

In your controller, permit the **profile_image** parameter and attach the uploaded file to the User model instance:

```
def create
  @user = User.new(user_params)
  if @user.save
    redirect_to @user, notice: 'User created successfully.'
```

```
  else
    render :new
  end
end

private

def user_params
  params.require(:user).permit(:profile_image)
end
```

Displaying Uploaded Profile Images

Finally, display the uploaded profile images in your views using the appropriate helpers provided by Active Storage. For example, you can use the **image_tag** helper to display profile images:

```
<%= image_tag @user.profile_image %>
```

Ensure you validate file uploads and implement any necessary security measures to protect against malicious file uploads, such as validating file types, enforcing file size limits, and sanitizing file names.

You can read all about Active Storage here https://guides.rubyonrails.org/active_storage_overview.html.

You can access everything covered in the book on this GitHub repo: https://github.com/ava-orange-education/Ruby-on-Rails-for-Agile-Web-Development.

Conclusion

In this chapter, we have delved into several advanced topics in Ruby on Rails, essential for creating production-ready applications. We explored background jobs and asynchronous processing, caching and performance optimization techniques, internationalization and localization, integrating JavaScript frameworks with Rails, handling security and vulnerability management, sending emails with ActionMailer, and file uploads with Active Storage.

Throughout our exploration, we learned about the importance of background jobs for handling long-running tasks and improving application responsiveness. We discussed various queuing systems like Sidekiq, DelayedJob, Resque, and SolidQueue, each offering unique features and capabilities. Additionally, we explored caching strategies to enhance application performance and internationalization techniques to make our applications accessible to a global audience.

Furthermore, we covered best practices for integrating JavaScript frameworks like Hotwire and securing Rails applications against common vulnerabilities. We also discussed about emailing using ActionMailer and facilitating file uploads using Active Storage, enriching our understanding of building robust and feature-rich Rails applications.

As we wrap up this chapter, we encourage you to continue exploring and experimenting with these advanced topics to deepen your expertise in Ruby on Rails development. In the final chapter of this book, titled "*Conclusion*", we will provide some next steps for your Ruby on Rails journey, along with additional resources and references to further enhance your skills and knowledge.

Short Quiz

1. **What is the purpose of background jobs in Ruby on Rails applications?**
    a. Enhancing frontend performance
    b. Handling long-running tasks asynchronously
    c. Simplifying database queries
    d. Managing user authentication
2. **Which of the following is not a popular queuing system used in Rails applications?**
    a. Sidekiq
    b. DelayedJob
    c. Resque
    d. Firebase
3. **What is the primary advantage of using caching in Rails applications?**
    a. Reducing database queries
    b. Increasing server load
    c. Decreasing security vulnerabilities
    d. Enhancing code readability

4. **What is the purpose of internationalization and localization in Rails applications?**
    a. Optimizing database performance
    b. Translating the application into multiple languages
    c. Improving security measures
    d. Handling background jobs
5. **What is the main drawback of using JavaScript frameworks with Rails applications?**
    a. Limited browser compatibility
    b. Increased complexity and learning curve
    c. Poor performance
    d. Lack of community support
6. **What gem is commonly used for sending emails in Rails applications?**
    a. MailerGem
    b. EmailSender
    c. Mailgun
    d. ActionMailer
7. **What is the purpose of Active Storage in Rails applications?**
    a. Managing database connections
    b. Sending HTTP requests
    c. Handling file uploads
    d. Storing user sessions
8. **Which of the following is not a security consideration for Rails applications?**
    a. SQL injection
    b. Cross-Site Scripting (XSS)
    c. Internationalization
    d. Cross-Site Request Forgery (CSRF)

9. **What is the primary advantage of using SolidQueue in Rails applications?**
   a. Simplifying database migrations
   b. Handling long-running tasks
   c. Enhancing code readability
   d. Improving database replication
10. **What is the primary purpose of a cron job in a Rails application?**
    a. To optimize database queries
    b. To handle background job processing
    c. To schedule recurring tasks at specific intervals
    d. To translate the application into multiple languages

Further Reading

- Sajjad Umar, delivered a presentation on "*Strategies for Building Rails Applications with 10x Faster Performance*" during one of their instructional sessions. Dive into the written rendition of this session to delve deeper into optimization techniques and enrich your understanding. You can access the article at the following URL: https://medium.com/@sajjadumar/creating-10x-faster-ruby-on-rails-applications-my-talk-at-global-ruby-on-rails-summit-2023-by-bca96906f42d.

CHAPTER 12
Conclusion

Introduction

In this final chapter, we reach the culmination of our journey through Ruby on Rails. Having delved into various aspects of web development using this powerful framework, it's time to reflect on what we've learned and consider the next steps in your Rails journey. From mastering the basics to exploring advanced topics, this chapter serves as a guidepost for further learning and growth. Additionally, we provide a curated list of additional resources and references to aid you in your ongoing exploration of Ruby on Rails. Let's take a moment to review our accomplishments and chart a course for future endeavors in the dynamic world of web development.

Structure

In this chapter, we will cover the following topics:

- A Short Recap
- Next Steps in Your Ruby on Rails Journey
- Additional Resources and References
- Answers to All Short Quizzes

A Short Recap

Throughout this journey, we embarked on a comprehensive exploration of Ruby on Rails, covering a wide array of topics essential for building robust web applications. We began with an introduction to Agile development fundamentals, setting the stage for our journey into the world of Rails.

In the early chapters, we laid down the foundational principles of Rails development, mastering CRUD operations, database management, and basic front-end styling. With these skills in hand, we delved into the intricacies of authentication and authorization, ensuring the security and integrity of our applications.

As our journey progressed, we ventured into the realm of testing and test-driven development, learning how to write reliable and maintainable code through automated testing practices. We then explored the intricacies of building RESTful APIs and consuming external web services, enabling seamless communication between different parts of our applications.

Deployment and scaling became our focus in the latter chapters, as we learned how to prepare our applications for deployment, deploy them to various platforms, and optimize their performance to handle increased traffic and user demands effectively.

Our journey culminated in the creation of a real-world Rails application, WagePro, where we applied our newfound knowledge and skills to build a fully functional application from scratch. Along the way, we tackled advanced topics in Rails, including background jobs, caching, internationalization, and integration with JavaScript frameworks.

As we reflect on our journey through the chapters of this book, we've gained valuable insights and practical experience that will serve us well in our future endeavors as Ruby on Rails developers. From Agile development principles to advanced deployment strategies, we've covered a wide range of topics, equipping ourselves with the tools and knowledge needed to thrive in the world of Rails development.

Next Steps in Your Ruby on Rails Journey

On reading this book, you become well-equipped to continue your journey as a Ruby on Rails developer. A few steps you can take next to further enhance your skills and expertise are as follows:

1. **Build more projects:** Practice makes perfect. Continue building projects of varying complexity to solidify your understanding of Rails concepts and refine your development skills.

2. **Contribute to open-source projects:** Get involved in the Rails community by contributing to open-source projects. Not only will you gain valuable experience, but you'll also have the opportunity to collaborate with other developers and give back to the community.

3. **Read open-source projects:** Reading the code of open-source projects is an excellent way to learn new techniques, best practices, and patterns used by experienced developers, providing valuable insights into real-world applications and fostering continuous improvement in your coding skills.

4. **Explore advanced topics:** Dive deeper into advanced Rails topics such as performance optimization, security, concurrency, and microservices architecture. Expand your knowledge and explore new techniques to become a more proficient developer.

5. **Attend conferences and meetups:** Stay connected with the Rails community by attending conferences, workshops, and meetups. These events provide valuable learning opportunities, networking opportunities, and a chance to stay updated on the latest trends and developments in Rails.
6. **Continue learning:** The world of technology is constantly evolving, so it's important to stay curious and keep learning. Explore online tutorials, courses, books, and documentation to deepen your understanding of Rails and stay up-to-date with new features and best practices.
7. **Build your portfolio:** Showcase your projects, contributions, and achievements in a portfolio website or GitHub repository. A strong portfolio demonstrates your capabilities to potential employers and clients and can help you land new opportunities.

By following these next steps, you'll continue to grow and evolve as a Ruby on Rails developer, positioning yourself for success in your career.

Advance Topics to Explore

While we've delved into advanced topics in this book, the journey doesn't end here. There's still much to discover in the world of Ruby on Rails. To further your learning journey, consider exploring these additional topics, to help you deepen your understanding and mastery of the framework.

- **ActiveRecord:** There is a lot more to ActiveRecord than what we have covered in this book, so go through the official Rails guides to learn more about ActiveRecord here https://guides.rubyonrails.org/active_record_basics.html.
- **ActionCable**: Action Cable seamlessly integrates WebSockets with the rest of your Rails application. It allows for real-time features to be written in Ruby in the same style and form as the rest of your Rails application, while still being performant and scalable. It's a full-stack offering that provides a client-side JavaScript framework and a server-side Ruby framework. You can access your entire domain model written with Active Record or your ORM of choice. Learn all about ActionCable here https://guides.rubyonrails.org/action_cable_overview.html.
- **Meta Programming in Ruby:** Metaprogramming in Ruby is a powerful feature that allows you to write code that manipulates or generates other code at runtime. It's like writing code that can modify or create new code on the fly! Here is a great introduction to metaprogramming in Ruby https://www.shakacode.com/blog/metaprogramming-in-ruby.

To further enhance your skills, complement your knowledge of Ruby on Rails with an understanding of system architecture and design principles. Exploring these foundational concepts will make you proficient in crafting robust, scalable, and maintainable software systems, elevating your skills from mere coding to expert software design.

Some Useful Resources

We've compiled a list of resources to assist you in learning and staying updated on all the latest trends in the realm of Ruby on Rails.

Ruby and Rails Communities and Conferences

Engaging with communities is vital as it provides a platform to connect with fellow developers, share knowledge, seek advice, and stay updated with the latest developments in Ruby on Rails. Here are some of the communities we recommend:

- **RailsWorld:** Launched for the 20th anniversary of the Rails framework, Rails World is an annual two-day, two-track community conference featuring technical talks, demos, workshops, networking, and keynotes about the latest features and best practices in Rails development.

  Official Website: https://rubyonrails.org/world.

- **RubyConf Pakistan:** RubyConf Pakistan represents a Community of Ruby on Rails (ROR) Engineers and Enthusiasts from all over the country coming together to share insights, experiences, tutorials, and much more regarding this incredible framework.

  Official Website: https://rubyconf.pk.

- **RailsConf**: RailsConf is one of the largest gatherings of Rails developers, brought together to further discussion and learning about building, managing, and testing Rails applications. With a specific focus on Rails, conference topics can range from new users to administration to advanced techniques.

  Official Website: https://railsconf.org.

Here you can access a list of communities and conferences on the official Ruby language website https://www.ruby-lang.org/en/community/conferences.

Newsletters

There are a ton of newsletters out there managed by community members to help developers around the world stay updated with everything happening in the Ruby on Rails world.

Here is a list of some insightful newsletters handpicked by the author of this book:

- **Ruby on Rails Monthly:** Stay ahead in the world of Ruby on Rails with this exclusive newsletter, personally curated by the author of this book. Get the latest insights, tips, and updates, all in one place - the only Ruby on Rails newsletter you'll ever need to subscribe to.

  Subscribe to Ruby on Rails Monthly here: https://sajjadumar.substack.com.

- **This Week in Rails:** Your weekly inside scoop of interesting commits, pull requests, and more from Rails.

  Subscribe to This Week in Rails here: https://world.hey.com/this.week.in.rails.

- **Short Ruby Newsletter:** Get a weekly summary of Ruby community news and updates, curated from top sources, every Monday morning.

  Subscribe to Short Ruby Newsletter here: https://newsletter.shortruby.com.

- **Ruby Weekly:** A free, once-weekly e-mail round-up of Ruby news and articles.

  Subscribe to Ruby Weekly here: https://rubyweekly.com.

YouTube Channels

There are a wealth of YouTube channels out there, run by passionate community members, dedicated to helping developers worldwide stay up-to-date with the latest developments and trends in the Ruby on Rails ecosystem.

Here is a list of some insightful YouTube channels handpicked by the author of this book:

- **Desi Developer:** Managed by the author of this book, where he shares his experiences and knowledge with the community.

  Subscribe here: https://www.youtube.com/@desi-dev.

- **Go Rails:** Unlock the secrets of Ruby on Rails with GoRails screencasts, your guide to demystifying the framework's complexities. Get a unique, behind-the-scenes look at a professional developer's environment and thought process, as Chris Oliver shares his expertise to help you overcome confusion and become a confident, skilled developer.

  Subscribe here: https://www.youtube.com/@GorailsTV.

Answers to Short Quizzes

This section includes answers to all the **Short Quiz** multiple choice questions given at the end of each chapter.

Chapter 01

1. a) A programming language
2. a) Yukihiro Matsumoto
3. a) Simplicity and productivity
4. a) Class, method, variable
5. c) Separating application logic and user interface
6. a) Handling user input and interacting with models
7. a) Model
8. c) User interacts with the controller, which manipulates the model and updates the view
9. b) Defining the structure and layout of the web page
10. c) Handling incoming requests and serving responses

Chapter 02

1. c) To adapt to changing requirements and deliver value early
2. d) Difficulty in adapting to changing requirements
3. b) To address the limitations of traditional approaches
4. c) Individuals and interactions, Working software, Customer collaboration, Responding to change
5. d) Extreme Programming (XP)
6. b) To monitor project progress and identify bottlenecks
7. c) Lean Software Development
8. d) Extreme Programming (XP)
9. c) To guide teams in implementing Agile practices and principles
10. c) Early delivery of value and frequent customer feedback

Chapter 03

1. c) It is where the main application code, including models, views, and controllers, is placed.
2. b) db
3. d) It stores important configuration files.

4. d) test
5. a) Convention over Configuration
6. c) It lists all the third-party gems and libraries required for the application.
7. b) It stores the version information of all installed gems, ensuring consistency across different environments
8. b) db
9. c) Inside the root directory of the application
10. d) Version Manager (for example, rbenv or RVM)

Chapter 04

1. c) Create, Read, Update, Delete
2. a) Most Valuable Code
3. b) Displaying data to the user
4. d) Delete
5. a) Creating new contacts
6. c) Update
7. a) Populates the database with seed data
8. b) To enhance data integrity
9. c) seeds.rb
10. b) Routes that handle CRUD operations for a resource

Chapter 05

1. c) Cascading Style Sheets
2. a) Classes
3. d) A layout model describing how elements are rendered
4. c) font-size
5. c) A design that adapts to different screen sizes and devices
6. d) React Native
7. c) To speed up web design and development
8. d) Tailwind CSS

9. c) To target styles for specific devices and screen sizes
10. a) Simplified web development and faster design

Chapter 06

1. c) To verify user identity
2. c) Password-based authentication
3. b) Authorization
4. c) Enabling user access to the system
5. b) Multi-factor authentication
6. b) Controlling user access rights
7. a) Role-based authorization
8. c) Managing authorization policies
9. b) Defining user roles and permissions
10. b) Designing responsive and customizable UI components

Chapter 07

1. a) To ensure the reliability of the application.
2. b) RSpec and Minitest.
3. b) RSpec.
4. b) Minitest has a more compact and traditional syntax compared to RSpec.
5. b) Writing tests that fail.
6. b) To define the expected behavior or outcome.
7. c) To verify the behavior of model methods.
8. a) Writing code to pass the tests.
9. b) Improving code structure without altering functionality.
10. b) Evaluating the functionality of the entire system as a whole.

Chapter 08

1. b) Representational State Transfer
2. c) Statelessness, Client-Server, Uniform Interface
3. b) GET

4. c) To structure API endpoints and manage resource actions
5. c) Using the Net::HTTP library or HTTP client gems
6. d) Utilizing JWT or OAuth to issue and verify tokens
7. b) To secure API endpoints and verify the identity of users or clients
8. c) Validating user roles and permissions
9. d) A mechanism where clients include a unique key in their requests for authentication
10. c) By including a unique API key in the request headers

Chapter 09

1. b) Blue-Green Deployment
2. b) Sharding
3. c) Offloading static assets for faster delivery
4. b) Dynamically adjusting server resources based on demand
5. c) Ensuring that changes integrate smoothly with the main codebase
6. c) Using database scaling options like sharding
7. b) Code Optimization
8. b) Handling increased traffic and user demands
9. b) Infrastructure as a Service (IaaS)
10. b) Simplified deployment process and management of application resources

Chapter 10

1. c) To meet the requirements of the Minimum Viable Product (MVP)
2. a) DRY (Don't Repeat Yourself)
3. c) To reduce code repetition and maintainability
4. b) Access Management
5. a) To define database structure and relationships between tables
6. c) rails generate migration
7. c) `has_many`
8. a) Prawn

9. b) To schedule background jobs
10. a) `perform_now`

Chapter 11

1. b) Handling long-running tasks asynchronously
2. d) Firebase
3. a) Reducing database queries
4. b) Translating the application into multiple languages
5. b) Increased complexity and learning curve
6. d) ActionMailer
7. c) Handling file uploads
8. c) Internationalization
9. b) Handling long-running tasks
10. c) To schedule recurring tasks at specific intervals

Index

A

Agile 27
Agile Development 25, 177
Agile Development, benefits
- communication, enhancing 41
- continuous, improving 40
- Faster Time-to-Market 40
- flexibility, adaptability 40
- morale, collaborating 41
- quality, enhancing 41
- risk mitigation 41
- scope, adapting 41
- transparency, visibility 41
- User-Centric, approach 40

Agile Development, challenges
- client involvement, feedback 42
- dependency, managing 42
- documentation 42
- resistance 43
- resources issues, allocating 42
- scope, creep 42
- speed, overemphasis 43
- team collaboration, communicating 42
- technical debt 42
- uncertainty, instability 42

Agile Development, limitations 26
Agile Development, testing benefits
- communication, enhancing 178
- cost-efficiency 177
- customer, satisfying 177
- Early Bug, identifying 177
- flexibility, adaptability 177

Agile Manifesto 28
Agile Manifesto, value
- contract, negotiation 29
- documentation, comprehensive 29
- individuals interactions, process 29
- plan change, responding 29, 30

Agile, methodologies
- Extreme Programming (XP) 38, 39
- Kanban 34, 35
- Lean Software Development 36, 37
- Scrum 32, 33

Agile, principles
- continuous, improving 31
- continuous pace, developing 31
- customer, satisfaction 30
- Face-to-Face, communicating 31
- individuals projects, collaborating 30
- primary progress, working 31
- requirements, changing 30
- simplicity, maximizing 31
- software work, deliver 30
- Stakeholders, collaborating 30
- teams self-organizing 31
- technical excellence 31

API Authentication 219
API Authentication, types
- API Key-Based Authentication 221
- OAuth-Based Authentication 222
- Token-Based Authentication 219

API Key-Based Authentication 221
API Key-Based Authentication, concepts
access, granting 222
API Key, distributing 222
API Key, generating 221
request, inclusion 222
server, verification 222
API Key-Based Authentication, implementing steps
access, granting 230-232
API key, distribution 225
API Key, generating 224, 225
request, inclusion 226, 227
server, verifying 227-229
app directory, functionality
assets 56
channels 56
helpers 57
JavaScript 57
jobs 57
mailers 57
ApplicationRecord 75
ApplicationRecord, components
associations 76
business logic 76
callbacks 76
database, operations 76
database, representation 76
data, validating 76

B

Background Jobs 294
Background Jobs, concepts
Active Job 294, 295
Queuing Systems 295-300
Blue-Green Deployment 237
Blue-Green Deployment, key points
mechanism, switching 237
parallel, environments 237
Rollback, capability 238
Bootstrap
reference link 116
Bulma
reference link 117

C

Caching 300
Caching, technique
action 300
fragment 301
low-level 301
Page 300
Canary Releases 238
Canary Releases, key points
gradual, exposure 238
performance, monitoring 238
risk, mitigation 238
Cascading Style Sheets (CSS)
about 112
background borders, enhancing 114
core concepts 112
layout, positioning 114, 115
Mox Model, layout 113
properties rules 113
text styles, crafting 113
CI/CD, platforms
AWS CodePipeline 249
Azure Pipelines 249
CircleCI 249
GitHub Actions 248
GitLab CI/CD 248
Jenkins 249
Travis CI 248
CI/CD, practices 248-258
config directory, functionality
application.rb 58
boot.rb 58
cable.rb 58
credentials.yml.enc 58
environment.rb 58
environments 58
importmap.rb 58
initializers 58
locales 58
puma.rb 58
storage.yml 58
Continuous Deployment 237
Continuous Deployment (CD) 248

Continuous Deployment, key points
- automation 237
- Immediate Feedback 237
- Rapid Rollouts 237

Continuous Integration (CI) 248

CRUD Operations
- about 72
- Data Relationships 104
- deletions, managing 101-103
- functionality, upgrading 99-101
- functionality, implementing 84-93
- interactions, managing 79
- key-value, analyzing 89
- models data, generating 73, 74
- MVC Architecture, integrating 73
- read functionality, enabling 94-98
- Ruby/Rails Relationships, optimizing 104
- setting up 80-84

CRUD Operations, methods
- create 80
- destroy 81
- edit 81
- new 80
- show 81
- update 81

CRUD Operations, user interaction
- Create (C) 72
- Delete (D) 72
- Read (R) 72
- Update (U) 72

CSS Frameworks
- about 115
- application, setting up 119-123
- elements styles, adding 123-128
- framework, designing 117
- modular design, reusable 129-131
- MVP, developing 117
- TailwindCSS, installing 118

CSS Frameworks, advantages
- consistency 116
- documentation 116
- efficiency 116
- rapit, prototyping 116
- responsive design 116

CSS Frameworks, types
- Bootstrap 116
- Bulma 117
- Foundation 117
- Tailwind CSS 117

D

Database Expansion, aspects
- Employee Search 270
- Pagination 269

Database Expansion, concepts
- department roles 269
- organization 269
- salary slips 269
- user 269
- user profile 269

Database Management 104

Database Management, concepts
- databases schema, evolving 105
- database with seed data, populating 105
- data integrity, ensuring 106, 107

Database Optimization 302

Database Optimization, concepts
- database, configuring 303
- database, replication 303
- database, sharding 302
- data cleanup 302
- efficient, queries 302
- indexes 302

Data Relationships 104

Data Relationships, categories
- many-to-many 104
- one-to-many 104
- one-to-one 104

Deployment 236

Deployment, components
application server 236
database 236
dependencies 237
web server 236
Deployment, strategies
Blue-Green Deployment 237
Canary Releases 238
Continuous Deployment 237

E

else 8
elseif 8

F

File Uploads 312
File Uploads, storage services
file form, creating 313
file upload controller, handling 313
model files, attaching 313
profile image, displaying 314
for 8

G

GitHub Action, terminologies
caching 249
environment, variables 249
Jobs 249
steps 249
Trigger 249

H

Heroku
reference link 238
Hotwire 310
Hotwire, aspects
stimulus 310
strada 310
tubro 310

I

if 8
Integration Testing 189
Internationalization 305
Internationalization/Localization, benefits
compliance, regulations 307
cultural sensitivity 307
market reach, expanding 307
user experience, enhancing 307
Internationalization/Localization, key components
language files 307
locale, managing 307
translation, workflow 307

J

JavaScript Frameworks
about 307
evolution 308
Hotwire 310
Rails, integrating 308
JavaScript Frameworks, benefits
ecosystem, supporting 308
modular, development 308
performance, improving 308
user experience, enhancing 308
JavaScript Frameworks, drawbacks
compatibility, issues 309
complexity, increasing 309
curve, learning 309
performance, overhead 309
SEO, challenges 309

L

Localization 306

M

master.key 245
migration file 74
migration file, key aspects
database schema, changing 74
idempotent 75
Ruby, script 74
timestamps 74
Up/Down, methods 75

Model-View-Controller (MVC) 15
Monitor Optimization 261
Monitor Optimization, importance
- issues, detecting 261
- opportunities, optimizing 261
- proactive problem, resolution 261

MVP 267
MVP, features
- access, managing 267
- department, managing 267
- employee, managing 267
- organization, managing 267
- salary slip, managing 267
- Simple UI 267

O

OAuth Authorization, flow
- access token, issuance 223
- code authorization 223
- resource, access 224
- resource, request 224
- token, request 223
- user authentication 223
- user authorization 223

OAuth-Based Authentication 222
OAuth-Based Authentication, concepts
- authorization server 223
- client 223
- resource owner 222
- resource server 223
- token, access 223

Object-Oriented Programming (OOP) 9
OOP, key concepts
- classes/objects 9
- Encapsulation 11
- Inheritance 12
- Polymorphism 12-14

P

Pagination 269
Performance Optimization 302
Performance Optimization, strategies
- code, optimizing 261
- database, optimizing 262
- infrastructure, optimizing 262
- profile, monitoring 262

PostgreSQL, advantages
- compatibility 141
- extensibility 141
- features, enhancing 141
- reliability 141
- scalability 141
- security 142

Q

Queuing Systems, capabilities
- DelayedJob 296
- Resque 296
- Sidekiq 295
- SolidQueue 296

R

Rails App, deploying 238-241
Rails Application, securing 310, 311
Rails Application, techniques
- Authentication/Authorization 311
- Content Security Policy (CSP) 312
- Cross-Site Scripting (XSS) 312
- CSRF 312
- HTTPS, encrypting 311
- parameter sanitization, validating 311
- secure session, managing 312
- vulnerability, scanning 312

Rails development, testing process
- continuous integration, deploying 178
- feedback, loops 178
- regression, testing 178
- test coverage, comprehensive 178
- Test-Driven Development (TDD) 178

Rails Framework 14
installing 52
principles, guiding 47, 48
project, setting up 53, 54
Ruby, using 48
Rails Framework, components
Controllers 17
Models 16
Views 16
Rails Framework, database utilizing
browser page, accessing 66, 67
first controller, generating 62, 63
first view, creating 64
route, defining 64, 65
server, optimizing 65
Rails Framework, data flow
controller 18
model 19
rendering 21
response 21
router 18
view 20
web browser 18
web server 18
Rails Framework, key directories
app directory 56
config directory 57
db directory 59
public directory 59
test directory 60
vendor directory 60
Rails, skills
conferences meetup, attending 320
continue, learning 320
open-source projects, contributing 319
open-source projects, reading 319
portfolio, building 320
projects, building 319
topic, exploring 319
render.yaml 241-243
Responsive Design 132
Responsive Design, techniques
breakpoints 133
classes, visibility 132
display, utilities 133
flexbox, grid 132
responsive classes 132
responsive, image 133
responsive, typography 132
utilities, spacing 133
RESTful Architecture 208
RESTful Architecture API, building 210, 211
RESTful Architecture API, implementing 211-215
RESTful Architecture, benefits
flexibility 210
interoperability 209
scalability 209
simplicity, analyzing 209
RESTful Architecture, characteristics
encapsulation 217
maintainability 217
readability 217
reusability 217
RESTful Architecture, key components
HATEOAS 209
representation 209
resources 208
statelessness 209
uniform, interface 209
RESTful Architecture Rails API, consuming 216-219
Role-Based Authorization 154
Role-Based Authorization, implementing 155-163
Role-Based Authorization, key components
permissions 155
roles 155
user-role, mapping 155
Roles Management Authorization 270

Roles Management Authorization, methods
- associations 283
- Organization, managing 271-274
- PDE, creating 283-285
- required routes, adding 274-282
- Salary Slip, managing 282

RSpec Unit Test 185
Ruby
- about 2
- history 3, 4
- Object-Oriented Programming (OOP) 9

Ruby Configure, options
- installers 49
- package, managing 49
- source, building 49
- version, managing 49

Ruby I18n 306
Ruby, installing 49
Ruby, key elements
- Comments 6
- data types 7
- methods 8
- structures, controlling 7
- variables 6

Ruby, key features
- block, closures 5
- Dynamic Typing 5
- Garbage, collecting 5
- Metaprogramming 5
- Object-Oriented Programming (OOP) 5
- rich standard, library 6
- simplicity, readability 5
- strong community, supporting 6

Ruby, key points
- Dynamic Language 2
- object-oriented 3
- open source 2
- productive 3

Ruby Version Manager (RVM)
- about 50
- command, verifying 51
- installing 51

S

SalarySlipGenerator 286
SalarySlipsController 285
Scaling Rails Applications 258
Scaling Rails Applications, factors
- business, growth 259
- performance, degradation 258
- sporadic peaks 258
- traffic, increasing 258

Scaling Rails Applications, tips
- auto-scaling 259
- caching, strategies 259
- Content Delivery Networks (CDNs) 259
- database, scaling 259
- horizontal, scaling 259
- monitor, optimizing 259
- vertical, scaling 259

Sending Emails 303
Sending Emails, concepts
- delivery 304
- Email Configuration, setup 303
- Emails, trigger 304
- Email Templates, creating 304
- Mailer Class, defining 304

T

Tailwind CSS 117
Tailwind CSS, layers
- base 119
- components 120
- utilities 120

TDD, advantages
- code quality 196
- design, improving 196
- faster, debugging 196
- regression, testing 196

TDD, fundametal
Green Phase 197
Red Phase 196
Refactor Phase 197
TDD, principles
fail test initially 196
pass tests 196
refactor 196
test first 196
test, often 196
TDD WagePro, implementing 197-204
Test-Driven Development (TDD) 196
Testing Frameworks 180
Testing Frameworks, aspects
Capybara 181
Minitest 181
RSpec 180
Testing Frameworks, utilizing 181
Token-Based Authentication 219
Token-Based Authentication, aspects
Device Token Auth 221
JSON Web Token (JWT) 221
Token-Based Authentication, concepts
access, granting 220
server verification 220
token generation 220
token inclusion 220
token issuance 220
token, refreshing 221
token storage 220
user authentication 220

U

Unit Tests
about 182
controllers, optimizing 185, 186
models, analyzing 182
Unit Tests, cases
book without author 184
book without title 183
title and author 184
title, return 184
Unit Tests, key aspects
automation 182
granularity 182
independence 182
isolation 182
User Acceptance Testing (UAT) 190
user authentication 138
user authentication, aspects
access, granted 139
cookies 139
data, transmission 139
logout 140
persistent, sessions 139
security, measures 140
server-side, validating 139
session, creating 139
user input 139
user authentication, methodologies
Aglie Approach 140
HomeController, analyzing 144-152
new user, ensuring 152-154
Software as a Service (SaaS) 141
WagePro 142, 143
user authentication, methods
Biometric, authentication 139
Multi-Factor Authentication (MFA) 139
Single Sign-On (SSO) 139
username/password 138

W

Web Development, testing types
Acceptance Testing 179
Accessibility Testing 180
Functional Testing 179
Integration Testing 179
Performance Testing 179
Regression Testing 179
security Testing 179
Unit Testing 178
while 8

Made in United States
Orlando, FL
04 November 2026

90204513R00197